# The American Mission and the "Evil Empire"

David Foglesong tells the fascinating story of American efforts to liberate and remake Russia since the 1880s. He analyzes the involvement of journalists, political activists, propagandists, missionaries, diplomats, engineers, and others in this grand crusade, with special attention to the influence of religious beliefs on Americans' sense of duty to emancipate, convert, or reform Russia. He discusses the impact of popular debates about changing Russia on how Americans felt about the United States, showing how the belief that Russia was being remade in America's image reaffirmed faith in America's special virtue and historic mission. He also demonstrates that, since the late nineteenth century, opposition to the spread of American influence in Russia has been characterized as evil. While the main focus is on American thinking and action, the book also discusses the responses of Russian and Soviet governments, Russian Orthodox priests, and ordinary Russians to American propaganda campaigns, missionary work, and popular culture.

David S. Foglesong is Associate Professor of History at Rutgers University, New Brunswick, New Jersey. He is the author of *America's Secret War Against Bolshevism: U.S. Intervention in the Russian Civil War, 1917–1920* (1995).

# The American Mission and the "Evil Empire"

*The Crusade for a "Free Russia" since 1881*

David S. Foglesong

CAMBRIDGE
UNIVERSITY PRESS

CAMBRIDGE UNIVERSITY PRESS
Cambridge, New York, Melbourne, Madrid, Cape Town, Singapore, São Paulo

Cambridge University Press
The Edinburgh Building, Cambridge CB2 8RU, UK

Published in the United States of America by Cambridge University Press, New York

www.cambridge.org
Information on this title: www.cambridge.org/9780521671835

© David S. Foglesong 2007

First published 2007

Printed in the United Kingdom at the University Press, Cambridge

*A catalogue record for this publication is available from the British Library*

*Library of Congress Cataloguing in Publication data*
Foglesong, David S.
The American mission and the "Evil Empire": the crusade for a "Free Russia" /
David S. Foglesong.
     p.   cm.
Includes bibliographical references and index.
ISBN-13: 978-0-521-85590-7 (hardback)
ISBN-13: 978-0-521-67183-5 (hardback)
1. United States – Relations – Soviet Union.   2. United States – Relations – Russia.
3. Messianism, Political – United States – History.   4. Soviet Union – Relations –
United States.   5. Russia – Relations – United States.   6. Soviet Union – Foreign public
opinion, American.   7. Russia – Foreign public opinion, American.   8. United States –
Foreign public opinion, Russian.   9. Soviet Union – Civilization – American influences.
I. Title.
E183.8.S65F64 2007
303.48 ′2730470904 – dc22
2007012359

ISBN  978-0-521-85590-7 hardback
ISBN  978-0-521-67183-5 paperback

# Contents

# Illustrations

# Preface

The first inspiration for this book came in the summer of 1993, when Valery, my host in Moscow, took me on a boating excursion to the river and canal north of the city. Valery and his friend Boris had "privatized" a small sailboat from their economics institute, but they had not quite figured out how to set the sails and they did not bring gasoline for the outboard motor. As a result, we relied on wiggling the rudder periodically for propulsion and drifted slowly along the river and canal. But that was all right because it was a splendid sunny day and we were in no hurry. Drinking vodka flavored at home with berries, we talked about the history of Russia, including the use of convict labor on major construction projects such as canals. Valery believed that his father had worked on the digging of a canal, but he was not sure because his father had been arrested soon after he was born and never returned.

In the late afternoon, Valery and Boris dropped me off at a dock where I could get a ride back to Moscow on a hydrofoil. Not long after they floated away downstream to meet friends and party through the night, the *raketa* ("rocket") arrived. As the hydrofoil raced against the current, spraying water to its sides, I met a fellow American named Chris, who was wearing dark glasses and an orange T-shirt. A Pentecostal missionary from Florida, Chris was scouting the prospect of a hydrofoil excursion for members of his growing congregation. Giving me a lift in his car into downtown Moscow, Chris told me stories of Russians who soon after their conversion suddenly achieved success and wealth in their long frustrated quests for high-profile careers.

That day in Moscow – at a time when many Americans were still acclaiming the "transition" of the former "evil empire" from communism to democracy and a market economy – left me with an intuitive sense that the Russian and American ships actually were not headed toward the same destination. It also spurred a growing interest in investigating the long-term origins of the protean American drives to transform Russia.

Thanks to a grant from the International Research and Exchanges Board and a fellowship from the Hoover Institution, I began research on this project in 1995–6. Ten years later, it is a pleasure finally to be able to thank all those who helped me to understand how Americans have thought about liberating and remaking Russia, especially: Michael Adas, James Critchlow, Alan Cullison, Richard T. Davies, David Engerman, Todd Foglesong, Lloyd Gardner, Ziva Galili, Alexei Guz, Gordon Hahn, Bert Haloviak, Walter Hixson, Dianne Kirby, Dan Linke, Victor Malkov, Greg Mitrovich, Karl Morrison, Bill O'Neill, L. Dale Patterson, Stanley Rabinowitz, Norman Saul, Katie Sibley, Tomas Tolvaisas, Robert Whittaker, Ted Wilson, Vika Zhuravleva, and Valery Zotov. I would also like to express my gratitude to the Gerald R. Ford Foundation and the Rutgers Research Council for research travel grants.

# Introduction

In the afternoon on March 1, 1881, members of the People's Will revolutionary organization, who believed regicide was a necessary step toward freedom for Russia, threw two bombs at Tsar Alexander II, who had that morning approved the establishment of a consultative commission, a possible step toward constitutional government. The first bomb exploded behind the tsar's carriage, killing and wounding Cossacks and passersby but leaving the tsar unscathed. After Alexander stepped out of the carriage, the second bomb detonated at his feet, mangling his legs and causing him to bleed slowly to death.[1]

News of the gory assassination of the tsar flashed by telegraph across the world and burst across the front pages of American newspapers the next day. In the following months, anti-Semitic riots (pogroms) led many Jews to emigrate to the United States with stories of savage beatings by drunken mobs. Together with lurid tales of the abuse of tsarist political prisoners, these developments spurred a rising American fascination with exotic Russia.

This suggested an opportunity to James William Buel, a Missouri journalist who had just finished a popular account of the exploits of outlaws Jesse and Frank James. With the aid of a German guide and an interpreter, Buel dashed across the tsarist empire in the summer of 1882 to gather material, then quickly published *Russian Nihilism and Exile Life in Siberia*, a thick, lavishly illustrated volume that sold briskly in multiple editions. Written more to appeal to a market than to advance a political agenda, Buel's book abundantly reflected the contradictions in American popular views of Russia. In spite of his scorn for Russian "nihilists" (revolutionaries) as "frenzied" and "insane," Buel thought their "bloody power" was needed to "purge the nation and give it a new growth." Although he doubted whether autocratic Russia could be more progressive than her barbarous neighbors, Buel avowed that Russia would "advance by gradual steps and finally become established as a free and fully enlightened government." Finally, while Buel marveled at the beauty of Russian cathedrals and savored the "delicious" music of Russian choirs, he vehemently condemned the Orthodox Church, whose creed's essence was "ignorance and superstition." Since that church was the primary cause of Russia's backwardness, Buel argued, "the first important step toward reforming Russia must be directed to the curtailment of the Church power and influence." Spurred on by such convictions, Buel boldly prophesied: "Civilization is spreading rapidly eastward, it cannot stop or go around Russia, and whether with bayonet or psalm-book the march will be made through every part of the Czar's dominions."[2]

Buel's ambivalent but zealous book thus foreshadowed American thinking about a wide array of efforts to reform Russia in the following century. While US soldiers went to Russia with bayonets only briefly and peripherally during the civil war of 1918–20, numerous other Americans journeyed to Russia with psalm-books and other products of their civilization, including harvesting machines, steel-making technology, jazz, and economic theories. Although many Americans grew alarmed by the danger of revolution in their own country in the late nineteenth and early twentieth century, even conservatives would hail uprisings in Russia that promised, at least for a time, to liberate and modernize that distant land. Despite their doubts about whether the Russian national character was suited for intelligent self-government, Americans would repeatedly proclaim their faith in the eventual emergence of a free Russia.

Journalists like Buel would play leading roles in this drama by stigmatizing Russian governments as "barbarous" or "Asiatic," by publicizing challenges to the regimes, and by assuring Americans of the ultimate triumph of their civilization or values. Many other Americans would be drawn into efforts to remake Russia as missionaries, propagandists, human rights activists, and economic advisers, as well as diplomats and government policy-makers. Even broader groups of Americans would participate vicariously in the crusades by hearing impassioned public lectures and reading vivid magazine articles about the heroic struggles of Russian dissidents and their brutal repression by Russian despots.

As they thought about changing Russia, many Americans were influenced by ideas rooted in the religious traditions of the United States. In particular, Americans exhibited a belief in a duty to spread their creed, a belief that a benighted foreign people yearned for the enlightenment they could bring, a belief in the possibility of inducing a sudden conversion from an old way of life, a belief that religion is central to the virtue or depravity and the progress or backwardness of societies, a belief in a single ultimate destiny for humanity, and a belief that opposition to the dissemination of their gospel is evil.

These ideas shaped recurring patterns in American views of Russia. At several moments, especially in response to the Russian revolutions of 1905, March 1917, and August 1991, many Americans expressed euphoric enthusiasm about the rapid transformation of Russia into a nation resembling the United States, with democratic institutions, religious liberty, and a market economy. Then, when Russia diverged from that expected course, many Americans grew bitterly disillusioned, blamed defects in the Russian national character for the failure or degeneration of the revolutions, and demonized Russian political leaders who frustrated American aspirations.

While some top US government officials showed little or no interest in a crusade for a free Russia, even they could not completely disregard public indignation about events in Russia and demands to put pressure on Russian governments. Moreover, many US leaders were imbued with the dominant political culture, with its marked evangelistic streak. In several crucial phases, key policy-makers (most notably Woodrow Wilson, George F. Kennan, and Ronald Reagan) passionately shared the popular ambition to liberate Russia, and the sharp antipathy to the malignant forces that resisted that mission.

* * * * *

While focusing on the surges in the American drive for a free Russia and the vilification of Russian tyranny allows us to trace such persistent dynamics over a long term, it also enables us to view American-Russian relations in the wider context of an American global mission and the resistance it has encountered around the planet.

James Buel's venture to the tsarist empire came at a turning point in American-Russian relations and in the American "civilizing mission."[3] From the early Puritan proselytizers through the Protestant agents on Indian reservations two centuries later, missionaries and philanthropists had tried to convert "savages" to Christianity and turn communalist tribes into individualist farmers.[4] Although fewer Indians were Christianized and civilized than were dispatched and dispossessed, in the late nineteenth century a more fervent American mission extended beyond the North American continent. After Commodore Matthew Perry pressed Japan to open its doors in the 1850s, American educators and military advisers eagerly worked to turn Japanese students and soldiers into "Yankees of the East."[5] Following the US defeat of Spain in 1898, American officers and missionaries sought to reconstruct and regenerate Cuba and the Philippines.[6] In the second and third decades of the twentieth century, the United States occupied and tried to guide the development of several neighbors, including Mexico, Nicaragua, Haiti, and the Dominican Republic.[7] At mid-century, Americans undertook their most ambitious and successful efforts to reshape foreign countries, in both Western Europe and the Far East.[8] Most recently, American soldiers, diplomats, and economic advisers have been involved in numerous campaigns to rebuild other nations, including Bosnia, Kosovo, Afghanistan, and Iraq.[9]

American-Russian relations have not often been set in the context of this diverse historical experience. Studies of the attempt to transform post-Soviet Russia have treated it as a distinct post-Cold War project, with little awareness of precedents in earlier decades.[10] The term "Cold War" itself has marked off an era of superpower rivalry (roughly 1945–89) as a discrete epoch, and the campaigns for "liberation" in the early part of that period have often been depicted as responses to the specific menace of Stalinist subversion. Moreover, the triumphalist American interpretation of the Cold War as a necessary struggle against an evil empire that culminated in a decisive, final victory of American moral and political principles[11] has perpetuated a millenarian view of the contest with communism rather than promoting critical analysis of that historical project in the light of other American missions.

There are sound reasons for the conventional focus on the peculiarities of American-Soviet relations. The Bolshevik ideology of world revolution was the sole truly global rival to American liberal universalism in the twentieth century. Soviet nuclear weapons posed a unique threat of total annihilation of the United States. And Russian culture has reflected distinctive minglings of extraordinarily diverse influences from across Eurasia.[12]

Despite the special features of American-Soviet relations and the particularity of the Russian case, it is appropriate to view the American-Russian encounter in the longer and wider perspective of the American global mission. In the late nineteenth century, when American political, commercial, and evangelical energies surged overseas, the tsarist empire was one of many lands Americans sought to liberalize, develop, and redeem. Although US troops occupied only small parts of Russia for short periods around the end of the First World War, some Americans imagined military occupation of the Soviet Union during the Cold War and many viewed post-Soviet Russia as a defeated adversary. Like the spiritual and political leaders of many other countries, Orthodox priests and both tsarist and Soviet rulers stubbornly resisted unwanted penetration of their realms by Protestant faiths, propaganda broadcasts, and rock music. On the other hand, American political ideals and popular culture have at times been as attractive to peoples in Russia as to other peoples of the world.[13] The attempts by tsarist, Soviet, and post-Soviet authorities to prevent or at least contain American infiltration can be seen as part of a worldwide confrontation between American drives to open doors and efforts by leaders of other countries to close or guard their frontiers.

Yet Russian leaders have also sought to attract American investment and acquire American technology to spur the development of their country. Contrary to the assertions of some proponents of globalization, Soviet Russia did not simply isolate itself and became an autarkic outlier of the process of economic integration.[14] It is more useful to view Russia's experience as like that of other "backward" countries that have sought modernization without subordination to more advanced nations.[15]

Impressed by the railway construction and rapid industrialization in the tsarist empire at the outset of the twentieth century, historian Henry Adams envisioned that "The last and highest triumph of history would ... be the bringing of Russia into the Atlantic combine."[16] In subsequent decades, visions of remaking and integrating Russia would be inspired by surges in American trade with that enormous empire. During both world wars, booms in American exports sparked euphoric talk about how Russians were very much like Americans, while the more modest growth in commerce during the détente era figured in the hopes of corporate executives and policy-makers to domesticate the Russian bear.

At some moments, the stream of American goods and ideas flowing into Russia has risen to become a flood. Americans have been of different minds about these inundations. Many have hailed the uplifting, energizing, or liberating influence of products, techniques, and values from the United States, such as Singer sewing-machines in the late tsarist era, Ford tractors during the reign of Stalin, or rock-'n'-roll in the post-Stalin decades. Some recent authors have even suggested that such cultural infiltration played a decisive role in the collapse of the Soviet and East European communist regimes.[17] A smaller number of Russophiles have lamented the ways Russian traditions and institutions have been shaken by a too sudden influx, or gradually undermined by what one called "the termites of western influence."[18] Yet few historians have set the American impact on tsarist, Soviet, and post-Soviet Russia in the context of the broader "Americanization" of the world over the last century.[19]

Like other peoples, Russians have been deeply ambivalent about America. On one hand, both political leaders and popular writers have been fascinated by American speed, energy, and efficiency, and have sought to instill those traits in Russia. On the other hand, many Russians have expressed harshly negative views of the American mania for money-making, the vulgarity of American mass culture, and the hypocrisy of American foreign policy. Hence, while Soviet anti-Americanism may have been primarily a product of "official xenophobia," as some have maintained, it was neither peculiar to the Soviet era, nor propagated exclusively by political elites, nor unique to Russia.[20] In moments of disappointment, Americans have sometimes despaired about Russia's allegedly peculiar inability to change. Yet Russians have in reality been like many foreign peoples in selectively assimilating elements of American culture and adapting them to their own societies; they have altered their habits and values in response to American influences, but not necessarily in the ways Americans wished or expected.[21]

At times of discouragement with Russia's reversion to authoritarianism, Americans have often expressed scorn for Russians as "Asiatic" or "dark," with the latter comparison to Africans being especially irksome to Russians.[22] However, many Americans' religious beliefs encouraged them to set aside racially tinged pessimism and have faith in the elevation of Russia, much as they had faith in uplifting countries such as China. In the late nineteenth century, at the same time as Protestant evangelists from America began to do missionary work inside the tsarist empire, liberal activists in the United States launched a publicity campaign on behalf of a "free Russia." During the following decades, Christian missionaries and secular crusaders who were often influenced by their religious upbringings encouraged many Americans to believe in the redemption and liberation of the peoples of Russia. Until the last years of the twentieth century, this Messianic outlook fostered unrealistic expectations that Russians could overthrow supposedly alien regimes, escape their pasts, and transcend their historical condition.

When those hopes for a free Russia were obstructed, Americans often characterized opposing forces in Russia as not merely despotic but diabolical. Much like the Spanish oppression of Cuba, for example, the tsarist oppression of Russia was denounced as "medieval," "cruel," and "bigoted," thereby reinforcing a sense of the contrasting virtues of the modern, humane, and tolerant United States.[23] Although the results of missions to remake foreign countries such as Russia, Cuba, and China were often disappointing or reversed, the popular sense of engagement in such crusades still had strong influence on how Americans felt about themselves, particularly by offering proof of American idealism and reassurance about the special place of the United States in the world.[24]

Despite those similarities, there was something about Russia that made it more persistently fascinating. Since Russia could be seen as both like and unlike America – both Christian and heathen, European and Asiatic, white and dark – gazing at Russia involved the strange fascination of looking into a skewed mirror. The commonalities such as youth, vast territory, and frontier expansion that made Russia seem akin to the United States for much of the nineteenth century served to make Russia especially fitted for the role of "imaginary twin" or "dark double"[25] that it assumed after the 1880s and continued to play through the twentieth century. Soviet communism, as an atheist and universalist ideology, came to seem, more than any other rival creed, the antithesis of the American spirit. Thus, more enduringly than any other country, Russia came to be seen as both an object of the American mission and the opposite of American virtues.

# 1 "Free Russia": origins of the first crusade, 1881–1905

Through most of the nineteenth century, few Americans considered it appropriate or possible to liberate and remake Russia. As Americans pushed westward and Russians pursued their own manifest destiny to the south and east, Americans tended to regard Imperial Russia as a distant, friendly power and an agent rather than an object of the Christian civilizing mission (see figure 1).[1] Despite their republican convictions, US diplomats showed little interest in reforming Russia, which many of them found unfit for self-government.[2] Although a handful of radical abolitionists embraced the cause of Russian revolutionaries,[3] in decades when African Americans were enslaved and then disenfranchised, the notion of extending democracy to an empire where more than 80 percent of the people were illiterate peasants – the so-called "dark people" – struck many Americans as absurd or grotesque. Long after the take-off of industrialization in the United States, Russia's relatively low level of development, small urban population, and poor transportation system made it seem a weak market, with few attractive opportunities for American manufacturers.[4] And at least until the 1890s, conservatives who feared the rise of anarchism and socialism in the United States tended to sympathize more with the tsarist government than with Russian revolutionaries (see figure 2).

Despite those fears, doubts, and objections, a movement for a "free Russia" developed in the United States in the last two decades of the century. In collaboration with Russian revolutionaries, American activists formed organizations that vehemently denounced political oppression and religious persecution in the tsarist empire. Challenging and reversing conventional images, the crusaders argued that the tsarist government was brutally uncivilized and that the Russian people were capable of orderly self-government. By the time of the Russian revolution of 1905, many Americans came to embrace the idea that Russia could and should be remade to resemble the United States.

The traditional explanation of this dramatic shift has held that a growing "realism" about Russia spurred forceful criticism of tsarist

Figure 1. The present crusade – the attitude of the tsar in declaring war against the Turks. Thomas Nast cartoon, *Harper's Weekly*, May 26, 1877. Tsar Alexander II is depicted as a Christian crusader at the time of the Russo-Turkish War.

Figure 2. The Devil tips his hat to immigrants plotting assassination. *The Judge*, February 21, 1885.

"barbarism" by the 1890s. According to this view, mushy notions of a historic Russian-American friendship were dispelled when leaders of the anti-tsarist movement exposed and documented Russian despotism, anti-Semitism, and other wicked violations of human rights.[5]

It is true that after revolutionaries killed Tsar Alexander II in 1881, the Russian government became more oppressive, and in the late nineteenth century Americans received more information about Russia than they had earlier. However, there are several problems with the "realist" explanation. Treating American critics of tsarism as objective observers ignores their imaginative exaggerations of the evils in the Russian empire. Placing primary emphasis on American sympathy for Russian Jews disregards the intensifying anti-Semitism in the United States. And seeing the movement for reform of Russia as an almost exclusively political phenomenon neglects economic, cultural, and religious influences on the activists' views. Since political oppression and pogroms had not provoked many protests from the United States before the 1880s,[6] one must examine why Americans grew increasingly predisposed to vilify the Russian autocracy. It is therefore essential to examine the crusade for a free Russia in relation to the commercial expansion, racial tension, and religious turmoil in the US in this era.

The principal alternative to the "realist" explanation has been the "revisionist" interpretation that economic competition and expansionist friction in the Far East were the primary causes of the shift away from friendly American-Russian relations. By the 1890s, "New Left" historians have argued, key US officials and intellectual advisers feared that Russia was becoming a formidable industrial rival and a powerful threat to American commercial interests. These Russophobes urged US leaders to oppose Russian expansion in Manchuria, and they published articles that whipped up public antipathy toward the tsarist government.[7]

Some prominent critics of tsarism did, indeed, anticipate a clash between Anglo-American and Russian colonization of Asia, and as early as the 1880s they began trying to prepare public opinion for that collision by agitating against Russian "barbarism."[8] However, the overall significance of export competition and expansionist confrontation should not be exaggerated. Through the turn of the century few Americans greatly feared Russia, which was widely regarded as a backward country – decades, generations, or even centuries behind the United States.[9] While hostility to the prolonged Russian occupation of Manchuria was a major factor in the peak of outrage against the tsarist empire from 1903 to 1905, prior to that time, US businessmen and statesmen had applauded Russian railroad construction and territorial administration as an advance of civilization that opened new commercial opportunities for Americans in Asia.[10]

To understand the shift in American attitudes toward Russia, then, one must recognize not only the intensifying rivalry in the Far East, but also the awakening of American interest in the economic development of Russia itself. In the late 1880s and 1890s, as the tsarist government launched a program of rapid industrialization, some American business leaders began to see enormous export opportunities in Russia.[11] This reconsideration of Russia's potential as a market was one of several factors – including increased immigration from the tsarist empire and the campaign against autocratic oppression – that drew more attention to Russia and led Americans to think in new ways about that land. While South Carolina businessman Alexander Hume Ford dreamed about the "regeneration" of Russian agriculture by American machines, missionary Ludwig Conradi declared that Russia was an "immense field" for evangelism, historian Henry Adams envisioned the Americanization of Siberia as a project worthy of America's great energies, and novelist Mark Twain imagined buying Siberia in order to "start a republic."[12]

Underlying such rethinking was a rising sense that backward Russia, rich in resources but hampered by inefficient agriculture, inept government, oppressive police, and medieval religion, badly needed American help. The terrible famine of 1891–2, which prompted Americans to send several ships loaded with flour to save millions of peasants from starvation, highlighted the misgovernment of Russia and made that country seem less of an agricultural rival than an object of charity.[13] While humanitarian sentiments were aroused by such events, American religious passions also increasingly focused on Russia. As politicians lodged indignant protests against the persecution of Russian Jews and Protestants in the 1890s, American missionaries began to penetrate the Russian frontier and promote opportunities for redeeming the superficially Christianized subjects of the tsarist empire.[14] Thus, Americans increasingly felt that Russians needed and deserved religious liberty, political freedom, and the chance to develop their country unencumbered by stifling bureaucracy. Although the commercial, philanthropic, political, and religious drives were not closely or harmoniously synchronized, they can be seen as different dimensions of an emerging American mission to free Russia.

The crusade had significant implications for Americans' views of themselves. So long as the tsarist government seemed to be the main engine driving Russian development, Americans could imagine the two different countries moving along parallel tracks and the traditional friendship could survive heated challenges. As Russia was battered by assassinations, pogroms, famine, war, and revolution, however, the autocratic regime (along with the Orthodox Church) increasingly came to be seen as an obstruction to needed modernization and the opposite of the forward-looking, uplifting American spirit.

In the late nineteenth century, many thoughtful Americans were uneasy about persistent problems that sapped the vitality and belied the idealistic promise of the United States, including declining religious faith, demoralizing materialism, dishonorable treatment of Native Americans, and the disenfranchisement and lynching of African Americans. Discomfort with such troubles inclined journalists, editors, ministers, and other opinion leaders to emphasize problems in Russia that made American imperfections pale in comparison. Thus, as Americans resolved uncertainties and conflicting notions about Russia, that country gradually came to serve as a "dark double" or "imaginary twin" for the United States.[15]

To fully comprehend the transformation of American views of Russia, then, one must supplement earlier interpretations by recognizing the importance of the increasing demonization of the tsarist empire and the simultaneous engagement in missions to emancipate Russia. Treating Russia as both a whipping-boy and a potential beneficiary of American philanthropy fostered in many Americans a heady sense of their country's unique blessings, and reaffirmed their special role in the world.

### Early criticism of American friendship with tsarist Russia, 1881–6

In March 1881, the front pages of American newspapers were filled with stories of the shocking assassination of Tsar Alexander II by bomb-throwing "nihilists." Editorial reaction was divided and ambivalent. Some editors treated the killing as a just response to a violent despotism and a punishment of Alexander II for being against government of the people (as well as marrying his mistress).[16] However, others lauded the tsar as a reformer, praised his emancipation of Russian serfs, and criticized the assassination as a blow to liberty because Alexander II was reportedly on the verge of allowing a parliament (see figure 3).[17] In an especially revealing shift, some of the editors who initially expressed optimism that the assassination would spur Russia toward constitutional government quickly reconsidered, as they contemplated the character of ordinary Russians and the possible menace of radical immigrants in the United States. Thus, a Utah editor at first imagined "the spectre of Liberty smiling grimly" above the smoke from the bomb and proclaimed that the chains of political prisoners in Siberia rattled in joy at the killing of the autocrat. However, on second thought he feared that the "favored few" in Russia who "behold in our Republic a light which is filling the earth" were trying to turn Russia too fast into "a Republic like our own."[18] Although editors were attracted to the flattering idea that America's shining example would inspire distant Russia to adopt self-government, that notion was outweighed by fears that revolution would entail "murder, arson, anarchy." In the end, most editors still associated the tsarist government with the orderly progress of civilization and blamed Russian barbarism primarily on wild nihilists and the brutish Russian people.[19]

Frustrated by the general sympathy with the Russian government (including heartfelt condolences on the tsar's death from Washington to St. Petersburg), the fieriest American critics of tsarism tried to alter public attitudes by demonizing the autocratic system and challenging Americans to be faithful to US ideals. In a June 1881 address at Harvard, for example, famed abolitionist Wendell Phillips argued that "dynamite and the dagger" were justified in a land where a young Russian girl could be "stripped naked and flogged to death in the public square" because she whispered "her pity for a brother knouted and dragged half dead into exile for his opinions." While hailing the valiant rebellion of Russian slaves against their oppressor, Phillips vented anxiety about the decline of American idealism since the freeing of the slaves, and excoriated "the

Figure 3. "The remedy is worse than the evil. Will it not be the *cap* instead of the *crown* that is buried with him?" Thomas Nast cartoon in *Harper's Weekly*, April 2, 1881. In the aftermath of the assassination of Alexander II, nihilism is associated with anarchy and chaos, while the tsar is mourned as the liberator of the serfs and linked to the hope for liberty in Russia.

cant of Americans bewailing Russian Nihilism" as a repudiation of the tradition of Sam Adams and John Brown.[20]

Like Phillips, William Jackson Armstrong, a commercial agent who had served as inspector of US consulates in Russia, passionately defended

Russian revolutionaries and denounced the tsarist regime.[21] Addressing members of Congress and other prominent citizens in Washington, Armstrong repeatedly attacked the popular association of the "Tsar Liberator" with Abraham Lincoln and asserted that to fulfill Lincoln's legacy, Americans should endorse the nihilists' goal of emancipating the Russian people from a murderous despotism.[22] In this seminal lecture, Armstrong indicted the "Asian brutality" of the Russian government, luridly depicted its bestial assaults on "the most noble and cultured women of Russia," likened reactionary Russians to South Carolina slaveowners, portrayed nihilists as martyrs devoted to American principles, and suggested that the "flawless liberty" of the American republic prefigured "the divine regulation of a heavenly state" while tsarism was an earthly realization of Hell.[23]

Although the sensational imagery Phillips and Armstrong utilized would eventually arouse millions of readers,[24] such emotional anti-tsarist appeals did not immediately win numerous converts.[25] Most of Phillips' Harvard audience, for example, disapproved of his views, and ministers across the country reacted against published reports of his speech.[26] Among those initially unmoved was journalist George Kennan, who had been a warm friend of the tsarist government since his first trip to Russia with the American-Russian Telegraph Expedition of 1865.[27] In a scholarly lecture published in 1882, Kennan coolly argued that the Siberian exile system was no worse than prisons in Europe or America, and that abuses of authority in Russia did not prove that the tsarist regime was "brutal and semi-barbarous."[28] Subsequently, in a blistering exchange of letters, Kennan refuted Armstrong's factual distortions, scorned his focus on moral issues, and concluded that Americans, living in a glass house, should not throw stones at their steadfast Russian friends.[29]

Spurred by his clash with Armstrong, Kennan obtained the backing of *Century* magazine for a thorough study of the exile system, made a brief exploratory trip to Russia in 1884, and then returned in 1885 for an extensive, year-long journey. Utilizing his friendly relations with Russian officials, Kennan secured letters of introduction that allowed him to travel from St. Petersburg to Siberia and helped to open prison doors for his inspections. Although Kennan took pains to present himself as a dispassionate, impartial investigator, by the time he reached eastern Siberia he had become an inquisitor of the exile system, avidly seeking evidence of "evils."[30]

Earlier, Kennan had imagined nihilists as "long-haired, wild-eyed" men and bold, hard, eccentric women. However, meeting his first political exiles in Semipalatinsk – men who were "of the blond type of Russian

young manhood," with good-tempered faces and the bearing of culti-
vated gentlemen – impelled him to begin jettisoning his class and racial
prejudices.[31] In further meetings with hundreds of exiles, Kennan continued to find that they were not "'half-educated school-boys, miserable little
Jews, and loose women,'" as tsarist officials claimed, but sophisticated,
Westernized intellectuals much like himself.[32] A crucial turning point
came when Kennan fell gravely ill near the border of Mongolia, began to
identify fully with the sufferings of exiles who became sick in transit, and
then encountered the stout spirit of Ekaterina Breshko-Breshkovskaia,
whose "heroic self-sacrifice" was "a more bracing tonic than medicine."
Seeing the way exiles like Breshkovskaia nobly and courageously bore
their suffering, Kennan commented, "would have put a soul under the
ribs of death"; it gave him "a spiritual uplift" that he had never had
before.[33]

From the beginning, Kennan's religious upbringing had shaped his
impressions of Russia, and his experiences there in turn provoked spiritual crises. Raised in "a family of Puritan descent and training," the young
Kennan had undergone a conversion, "based on unquestioning belief in
the Bible as the inspired word of God," while he prepared to journey
from California to Siberia in 1865.[34] However, in the wilds of the Far
East Kennan saw many things that convinced him "the world was not
made . . . in the way described in Genesis," and pondering the scripture
on long arctic nights led him to abandon "the Old Testament conception of God."[35] A second trip to Russia and the Caucasus in 1870–1
further shook Kennan's spiritual foundations. Back in the United States,
Kennan spent years unhappily contemplating his religious doubts and
painstakingly investigating the tensions between religion and science.[36]
After discarding "the old Calvinistic theology," especially the doctrine
of original sin, and withdrawing from the Presbyterian church, Kennan
sought a new philosophical foundation. While he succeeded in constructing "a working theory of life," it did not satisfy his spiritual yearnings.
Hence, while Kennan emerged from the uncertainties of the 1870s, and
by the 1880s was achieving renown as a lecturer and journalist, inwardly
he craved an intellectually respectable replacement for the righteous spirit
of his youth.[37]

Witnessing the harshness of conditions in Siberia in 1885–6, Kennan
came to the conclusion that there was "no pity, love, justice, or mercy in
all the universe outside the heart of man," and began to devote himself
to a new humanist creed.[38] Stirred to the depths of his soul by exiles like
Breshkovskaia, Kennan vowed to dedicate his life to expiating the sins of
defending the tsarist government and doubting the nobility of the revolutionaries. Thus, in the fullest sense, Kennan underwent a conversion

to the anti-tsarist cause; in Siberia the old "Puritan" fire rekindled as Kennan embraced a new religion.[39]

## Kennan and the crusade for a free Russia, 1887–94

After returning from Russia, Kennan fulfilled his promise to spread the word about the exiles' martyrdom and their revolutionary gospel by launching a crusade against tsarist oppression. From 1887 through the mid-1890s he published dozens of impassioned articles in popular magazines, produced a massively detailed account of *Siberia and the Exile System* (1891), and delivered hundreds of dramatic lectures to large audiences across the US.[40]

In both his published writing and in private letters Kennan turned again and again to religious language to convey his passionate convictions. In 1889, for example, he declared that one of the evils of the tsarist system was that instead of relying upon the personal consciences of citizens, the government constantly sought to regulate and restrain individual conduct. The Russian police were thus "a sort of incompetent bureaucratic substitute for divine Providence" who were even used to compel "indifferent or backsliding Christians to partake of the Holy Communion."[41] By denouncing that coercive paternalism and attacking the persecution of religious dissenters, Kennan sought to mobilize Anglo-Saxon Protestants who regarded rational religion and freedom of conscience as keys to progress, and who scorned authoritarian churches as bastions of stagnation.[42]

While summoning the evangelical spirit of American Protestants, Kennan also aggressively sought to recast American racial views of Russians. When he disputed the "widely prevalent impression in America" that the revolutionary movement involved "something peculiar and mysterious – something which the Occidental mind cannot fully comprehend," he implicitly argued that Russia should not be categorized as an exotic Oriental "other." Explicitly rebutting assumptions that backward Slavs required authoritarian rule, Kennan argued that "The Russians are as fit for free institutions as the Bulgarians are."[43]

Kennan's central arguments that Russians were capable of self-government and that the tsarist system was monstrously cruel were not simply based on the compilation of incontestable evidence, as some have claimed.[44] Instead, he relied heavily on dramatic storytelling and imagination. In *Siberia and the Exile System*, for example, he acknowledged that the conditions in a prison he visited were not horrible at that time, but encouraged readers to imagine the prison at a different season as "a perfect hell of misery."[45] As biographer Frederick Travis has shown,

Kennan exaggerated conditions and invented episodes in order to paint Siberian prisons "in even blacker colors than the shade that some of them so richly deserved."[46] Only a few years earlier Kennan had maintained that the exile system was no worse than Western prisons, but now he rejected such comparisons and insisted upon absolutist moral condemnation of tsarist brutality.[47] Standing on the stages of lecture halls dressed in the uniform and shackles of a Russian exile, Kennan implicitly suggested that the political prisoners were the essential embodiment of Russia, which was fettered by a tyrannical government. Although Kennan denied that his book aimed to present a comprehensive picture of Russian society, both critics and supporters believed his work implied that Russia was "a vast prison" whose inmates longed to be free to emulate America.[48]

One of Kennan's favorite ways of dramatizing this point was by telling a story that in 1876, when Americans celebrated the Centennial of the Declaration of Independence, three hundred political offenders in a St. Petersburg prison surreptitiously sewed small American flags, then on the Fourth of July bravely displayed them through the bars of their cells in order to demonstrate their devotion to the cause of freedom. Such colorful appeals moved Kennan's audiences to give him standing ovations and issue declarations that Americans should help Russians "who seek to follow their example." The Fourth of July anecdote also had a lasting resonance among Kennan's supporters in the movement for a free Russia, who repeatedly cited and reprinted it.[49] Building upon such stories, Kennan repeatedly urged Americans to believe that "the dawn of a brighter day" would bring the empowerment of Russians who looked "at the United States as the realization and embodiment of all their hopes."[50]

Kennan's emphasis on Russian adulation of America was misleading. While there was a wide fascination with America in the decade after the Civil War, most of the populists (*narodniki*) who traveled to the United States in the 1870s returned disillusioned. By the time Kennan launched his crusade, there were few uncritical admirers of capitalist America among Russian intellectuals and revolutionaries, who were increasingly influenced by socialist ideas. The unrealistic image of the revolutionary movement that Kennan and others presented, however, did help to bypass American hostility to socialist radicalism and foster a more enthusiastic reception of Russian revolutionaries.[51]

Although Kennan ordinarily prided himself on thorough scientific investigation and the lawyerly marshalling of factual evidence, to make the case for Russia's readiness to emulate American democracy, he and other crusaders resorted to tales of the frontier. In 1887, the British-American journalist Edmund Noble conjured a vision of an isolated setting on the southern fringe of the Russian empire where, free from contamination by tsarist policemen and Orthodox priests, native germs of democracy, stimulated by a constant battle with nature, developed into an ideal, multi-ethnic community.[52] A decade later, Kennan developed the frontier fantasy more fully and set it in a region that was attracting greater attention from American businessmen and statesmen. In "A Russian Experiment in Self-Government," Kennan told the story of "The Zheltuga Republic," which was formed in 1883 by Russian gold miners in "the great frontier province of Manchuria." To deal with the problems of claim-jumping, robbery, and murder, Kennan recounted, "the better class of Russian miners, impelled by the instinct of association and cooperation which is so marked a characteristic of the Slavonic race," organized cooperative associations and then assembled in "a Slavonic variety of the New England town meeting." Although the frontier republic was soon crushed by Chinese soldiers, Kennan claimed that it offered "noteworthy proof of the capacity of the Russian people for self-government." Furthermore, the fact that the first republic in Asia "was modeled after" America was a highly significant indication of the form Siberian institutions would take if only the people "could escape from the yoke of the Russian despotism."[53]

In linking Russia's fitness for self-government to American associations with the frontier only a few years after Frederick Jackson Turner first presented his frontier thesis, Kennan showed a keen instinct for tapping American popular mythology. While other writers invoked parallels between Russian and American frontier expansion to emphasize a natural sympathy between tsarist Russia and the United States,[54] Kennan turned the frontier legacy against the autocracy and articulated one of the most persistent reasons for believing that a United States of Russia could develop.[55]

## The "dark people" and the spirit of abolitionism

The most important obstacles to American confidence that Russia was fit for democracy were images of illiterate, inebriated Russian peasants, whose "loitering indifference" was compared to that of freed slaves on Southern plantations.[56] The Russophile translator and critic Isabel Hapgood, whose mother had been raised in Kentucky, was especially inclined to make such comparisons. After an extended tour of Russia, for example, she reported that "all the ex-serfs with whom I talked retained a soft spot in their hearts for the comforts and irresponsibility of the good old days of serfdom."[57] With American magazines in the 1890s full of fictional evocations of the paradisaical antebellum South and stereotypes of wretched freedmen,[58] Hapgood could expect readers to catch her implicit point. Yet, lest there be any doubt, Hapgood made the political implication of the racial comparison quite explicit, writing in *The Nation* that "Americans who are conversant with the negro problem of the South will find no difficulty in understanding" that Russian landowners were compelled to take radical steps to curb "the peasants' abuse of electoral rights."[59]

The question of the racial character of the Russian people posed difficult challenges for champions of a "free Russia," many of whom subscribed to prevailing notions of white superiority in a hierarchy of races. Before he committed himself to the cause of the Siberian exiles, Kennan had drawn a parallel between Russia and the South which suggested that foreigners should refrain from officious meddling with the peculiar institutions of other societies.[60] When he covered the Spanish-American War at the end of the century, dark-skinned Cubans repeatedly reminded him of ordinary Russians, whom he ranked above Cubans, but below Anglo-Saxons, in a racial hierarchy.[61]

One way to bypass the conventional classification of uneducated Russians with dark peoples was to invoke the spirit of the abolitionists. Thus, as he launched his campaign against the exile system in 1887, Kennan suggested that the Russian populists' "going to the people" campaign to elevate the peasants in the 1870s was analogous to the way "educated and refined young women from the New England States went south to teach in negro schools" following the Civil War.[62] To crusaders for a free Russia, as to the abolitionists who had rapturously hailed the emancipation of the serfs in 1861, Russia's fitness for freedom and democracy was not an issue for empirical investigation and rational deliberation, but a matter of moral principle and faith.[63] Many members of the Boston-based Society of American Friends of Russian Freedom (SAFRF), which was led by abolitionists and their descendants, approached the question in that spirit. In fact, to many SAFRF seemed like a rebirth of the abolitionist movement. The Russian revolutionary S. M. Stepniak (Kravchinskii), who helped inspire the creation of the organization, commented that the list of founders of SAFRF "was such that at first glance one could mistake it for the members of the Boston Anti-Slavery Society."[64] Similarly, Edmund Noble, secretary of SAFRF and editor of the society's organ, *Free Russia*, observed that "there has always seemed a true and close analogy between the agitation which aimed at the abolition of slavery in the United States and the movement that now seeks to bring the blessing of free institutions to the political serfs of Russia."[65]

The genealogy of SAFRF helps to explain why free Russia activists habitually compared the campaign against tsarist despotism to the crusade against slavery. Indiana attorney William Dudley Foulke, one of the most prominent figures in SAFRF, came from a family of Quakers who had been deeply involved in the anti-slavery movement. In his anti-tsarist polemic *Slav or Saxon* (1887), Foulke argued that Russian radicals who espoused revolution "for the sake of the fifty millions of poor ignorant peasants" were "like John Brown," in that they sought no selfish advantage, "but the liberation of oppressed humanity."[66] In the same vein, Rev. Walter Rauschenbusch, a leader of the Social Gospel movement, informed Kennan that although right-thinking Americans would hesitate to support any other revolutionary activity, he would certainly support publicity campaigns for Russian freedom. "I, at least, would as gladly pass on an underground newspaper in Russia," Rauschenbusch wrote, "as I would have passed on a run-away negro en route to Canada."[67] After the Senate in 1893 ratified an extradition agreement with Russia, indignant friends of Russian freedom demanded the abrogation of the treaty, which they repeatedly compared to the Fugitive Slave Law.[68]

Much as abolitionists had argued that the struggle against slavery weighed the moral virtue of a younger America, activists for a free Russia suggested that the battle against tsarist oppression posed a test of American character. "Americans always sympathize with the oppressed and hate the oppressor when they once *understand* the situation," Kennan assured a Russian friend, and such sympathy proved that Americans were "not a mere nation of money-makers and egoists."[69] The stakes were high. "Unless our nation becomes a missionary of liberty in the world," Walter Rauschenbusch advised Kennan in 1889, "it will lose its own liberty." The next year, while ignoring the disenfranchisement of blacks in the South, Rauschenbusch urged the circulation of a petition on behalf of the people of Russia and exulted that "Our institutions are the admiration and the inspirational beaconlight of noblemen from the Straits of Gibraltar to the bleak huts of Siberian exiles."[70]

As African Americans were disenfranchised, segregated more systematically from whites, and lynched throughout the South in the 1890s, enlisting in a mission to emancipate the people of far-off Russia may have eased the consciences of Northerners about abandoning the descendants of slaves.[71] Crusading for a free Russia paradoxically served members of SAFRF as a badge of freedom from the stain of race prejudice while simultaneously marking the racial superiority of Anglo-Americans. The high "racial altitude" of Anglo-Saxons allowed them to make "the best and most sympathetic estimate of the Russian people," Noble expostulated; "and it is, naturally, Anglo-Saxons who have done most to help Russians in their upward movement towards better forms of social and political life."[72] As such comments suggested, in defining the racial status of

Russians – whether Asiatic or Western, inferior Slavs or fellow Aryans – Americans were implicitly defining their own place and role in the world.

In the early 1890s comparison of problems in the United States to troubles in Russia became so common as to seem almost a reflex. Thus, when the *Washington Post* interviewed railroad president Chauncey Depew about a trip to the South, he commented that "Unless Kennan's stories of Siberian horrors are absolutely true there can be no scenes in a civilized country so terrible as in the Southern convict camps."[73] Some Americans compared the exile system to the mistreatment of blacks, and used the parallels to criticize a self-righteous crusading spirit. A Boston meeting to protest tsarist tyranny in 1890, for example, was challenged by critics who asked whether there was a Siberia in America and pointed to abuses in the South.[74] On the other hand, campaigners against tsarist oppression employed contrasts of Russia to the United States to mobilize missionary impulses, demonstrate the virtue of America, and suggest that Americans should "be thankful" that "we don't live in Russia."[75] Even cartoonists who expressed skepticism about whether the Siberian exile system was worse than the American Indian reservation system, or whether pogroms were worse than anti-Chinese riots, showed how Russia was coming to be a sort of "imaginary twin" of the United States.[76]

Launching a mission to free Russia required a repositioning of that empire in the American cosmology. Kennan and his supporters had to overcome repeated reminders by opponents that tsarist Russia had long been a friend of the United States and was an ally of the North during the critical years of the Civil War.[77] To displace Russia from the position of historic friend, Kennan, Noble, and others argued that intolerant autocratic Russia actually had nothing in common with liberal democratic America, contrasted American light to Russian darkness, and excluded barbarous tsarist Russia from the company of civilized governments.[78] That argument had a substantial impact on American thinking, leading many newspaper editors to recast discussions of the United States and Russia in terms of "civilization" versus "barbarism." Thus, citing "stories that come from Siberia," the Philadelphia *Ledger* suggested that "civilized nations should refuse to have anything to do with Russia until she abandoned barbarous practices. . . ." Kennan had "lifted the veil" from the "savagery" of Russia, commented the New York *Evening Post*, and "every country higher in civilization than Dahomey ought to turn the cold shoulder to her. . . ."[79] A cartoon in *Life* magazine in 1890 encapsulated this redefinition of Russia as a dark blot upon the globe rather than a part of the civilized world (figure 4).

NOT A BEAUTY SPOT.

*Civilization:*  WHAT A DREADFUL BLOT!  I CAN'T MAKE ANY IMPRESSION UPON IT'!
*The World:*  OH, THAT'S RUSSIA!

Figure 4.  Russia is envisioned as a blot upon, rather than an agent of, civilization. *Life*, May 8, 1890.

By classifying Russia as a dark land that could be enlightened, Americans placed Russians in the same category as blacks, Indians, Filipinos, and other potential beneficiaries of American humanitarianism. One Boston newspaper, for example, observed that Kennan was like African explorer Henry Morton Stanley: both promoted civilization in barbarous regions, though they labored "for humanity in widely separated fields."[80] Edmund Noble, similarly, suggested a parallel between the crusade for a free Russia and earlier efforts to educate freed slaves and civilize Native Americans. Attacking the idea that Russians were "by nature incapable of development," Noble cried that such a pessimistic view would have kept philanthropists from "instructing our colored people" and working "to elevate the red man."[81] Although William Dudley Foulke maintained that "The Anglo-Saxon form of government is still a long way off from the Russian people," since "it would take some time" to lift them out of "ignorance and habits of unquestioned obedience," he hoped to free Russia, much as he later hoped "that we will stay in the Philippines and give the inhabitants there as much liberty as they can digest."[82] Whether such peoples wanted to be lifted out of barbarism was irrelevant: the consciences and duties of the agents of civilization were ultimately more important.[83] The crusaders' ambiguous categorization of Russia as both "dark" and the object of an American civilizing mission, then, was driven less by realistic analysis of Russian conditions than by a leap of faith in the educability of the Russian people and by a desire to demonstrate America's high idealism.

### Religion and the reformation of Russia

For most of the nineteenth century, few Americans considered the tsarist empire a priority or even a possible mission field. Together, the Russian Orthodox Church and the tsar's armies seemed to be spearheading the spread of Christianity by subjugating the heathen peoples of Central Asia and defeating haughty Muslim rulers.[84] Occasionally, writers decried defects in the Russian Church, such as the lack of "moral preaching" and the use of archaic language that was "not intelligible to the common people."[85] However, such criticisms were not common. Whatever its imperfections, the Orthodox Church seemed a necessary force for orderly progress in a vast, distant empire with a preponderance of illiterate peasants.[86]

This changed in the last decades of the century. As early as 1879, a Catholic critic charged that the Russian Church, with its drunken and debauched clergy, was only a "mock Christianity." Since religion was crucial to both morality and progress, Russia's "greatest need" was "the replacement of shallow superstition by true religion," which was then clamoring "for admittance at the portals of the empire."[87] Over the following years, Catholic and Protestant writers repeatedly concurred that Orthodoxy was a corrupt, lifeless, exclusive creed that retarded the spiritual development of the Russian people, though they disagreed over whether Russians should be rescued through "reunion" with Rome or regenerated by a Protestant gospel. These were not merely abstract or academic discussions: in the late nineteenth century, evangelists from the United States sought to enter the Russian empire to do missionary work, and some were jailed for violating a ban on proselytism among members of the Orthodox Church.[88]

In the same decades, crusaders for a free Russia embarked on a secular mission that often had a spiritual underpinning. George Kennan's personal religious ordeal epitomized the northern Protestant experience of disillusion and revitalization that formed part of the background of the first campaign to liberate Russia. After scientific findings concerning evolution challenged their religious faith, sophisticated Protestants like Kennan who found the old orthodoxy intellectually untenable and the new revivalism emotionally distasteful, frequently felt compelled to rethink their religion. Relocating God from omniscient, omnipotent Father to mere prime mover of the universe resolved some intellectual problems but often left a spiritual void. Like Kennan, many liberal Protestants found a surrogate religion in a new humanitarianism devoted to lifting the whole of humanity up to the level of the advanced Anglo-Saxon race. This new theology facilitated a shift from a traditional focus on the exceptional nature of the American continental empire to the embrace of a universalist crusade – a global mission of Americanization often spearheaded by preachers of a social gospel.[89]

While many Protestant reformers sought to uplift China, the Philippines, and other countries in Asia, a smaller number undertook the emancipation of Russia. Like the Protestant and Catholic critics of Orthodoxy, Kennan repeatedly condemned the Russian Church for inculcating reverent submission to the tsar, obstructing the enlightenment of peasants, barbarously punishing missionaries, exiling dissenters, and inciting xenophobic, reactionary nationalists.[90] In much the same spirit, *Free Russia* regularly featured indictments of religious persecution in Russia and criticized the law against conversion of the Orthodox.[91] In order to lift the Russian people out of their ignorance, poverty and superstition, it was essential to convert them to Protestantism, editor Edmund Noble explained: "The great pillar of autocracy in Russia to-day is the Orthodox Church, and to the autocratic party religious freedom is 'Nihilism' in the domain of faith. You have only to bring rationalism into the belief of the Russian peasant, and his superstition in favor of despotism will go by the board."[92]

Such attacks contributed to a more general revulsion, with many politicians and journalists denouncing Russian religious bigotry. In 1892 the Democratic and Republican party platforms both protested religious persecution in Russia.[93] Editors blasted the "atrocious intolerance" of the Orthodox Church, faulted tsarist anti-Semitism for provoking unwelcome emigration to the United States, and interpreted the persecution of Jews as part of a "Russian retrogradation into Slavonic barbarism."[94] Like Noble and Kennan, many Americans considered religion crucial to the development of civilizations, and as the new century approached, a growing number of them believed that a religious reformation would be essential to the social and political liberation of Russia.[95]

## Globalization and the modernization of Russia

At the same time, optimism mounted about opportunities to contribute to the economic development of Russia. In part because both countries' exports centered on agricultural products, American-Russian trade had been limited, but in the late 1880s American travelers began to report more enthusiastically about the growth of Russia's commerce and industries.[96] As the American economy sank into depression in the mid-1890s, manufacturers who had saturated their markets in North America and Western Europe began to be keenly interested in selling their sewing-machines, harvesters, and other products in the huge Russian empire.[97]

The expansion of American-Russian economic relations had social and cultural ramifications in both countries. News of the building of the Trans-Siberian Railway, for example, promoted the revision of old images of a frozen wasteland and prompted excited comparisons to the development of the American West.[98] Americans were confident that their products would have beneficent impacts upon Russian life. Singer company managers, for example, believed their sewing-machines would relieve Russian men and women of much tedious labor, and free up time for other ventures. Although American agricultural machines were condemned as inventions of the Devil by some Orthodox priests, the harvesters and threshers began to transform ancient farming practices. The harvesters, Alexander Ford enthused, were doing "missionary work" and contributing to the "awakening" of Russia.[99]

Leaders of the drive for a free Russia both reflected and contributed to the growing interest in the economic development of the tsarist empire. In the 1870s Kennan had tried to interest a US company in bringing the American system of grain elevators to the tsarist empire, and when another US firm obtained such a concession he commented that it would be "the most profitable speculation of this century." On his way to Siberia in 1885, Kennan discovered regions that had "much more commercial importance than is generally supposed." Recounting the journey in *Siberia and the Exile System*, Kennan repeatedly juxtaposed American trading opportunity and tsarist inhumanity. For example, at the Siberian frontier, counting hundreds of wagons loaded with commercial products impressed Kennan with the fact that "Siberia is not a land of desolation," while seeing the spot where hundreds of thousands of exiles had said farewell to their friends and homes moved him to reflect that "No other boundary post in the world has witnessed so much human suffering." Thus, Kennan implicitly suggested how humanitarianism and self-interest could mingle in a drive to liberate and develop Russia.[100]

Formerly, the great tsarist empire had been considered beyond the reach of the American civilizing mission, but that was changing. Heightened immigration to the United States created opportunities for the evangelization of Russia, particularly when immigrant converts returned to their native villages. The revolution in transportation and communications technology, especially the invention of the steamship and telegraph, also facilitated missionary work.[101] Journalist James Buel captured the developing outlook when he proclaimed in 1883 that "Civilization is spreading rapidly eastward, it cannot stop or go around Russia. . . ."[102] A decade later *Free Russia* hailed the way that American ideas and institutions were "moulding the world anew, and even making inroads upon the iron fabric of despotism in Russia."[103]

### Successes and failure of the first crusade for Russian freedom

Kennan and his associates succeeded in stirring widespread outrage against tsarist brutality and in arousing the sympathies of many Americans for Siberian exiles. While in early 1888 Kennan had complained bitterly about how "indifferent" Americans were to "the fighters for freedom in Russia," a year later he claimed that his magazine articles had "revolutionized public opinion," causing Russian revolutionaries no longer to be regarded "as half-crazy fanatics and assassins."[104] Although that assessment was premature and somewhat overstated, Kennan and other activists did exert a profound influence.[105] As newspaper editors observed in the early 1890s, Russia was "one of the chief objects now before the public gaze" and "for most people in the United States the gospel according to Kennan has become the truth about Russia."[106] Together, Kennan, Noble, and other activists promoted a reclassification of the tsarist government as barbarous rather than civilized, fostered a gratifying sense of the superiority of American institutions, popularized an image of Russian revolutionaries as patriotic liberals rather than violent anarchists, and laid a foundation for later faith in Russia's democratization.[107]

Yet Kennan and his collaborators were unable to keep the movement for a free Russia from faltering in the mid-1890s. The Society of American Friends of Russian Freedom had fewer than 200 members. Although they were heartened by the "remarkable uprising of the national conscience" against an extradition agreement in 1893, SAFRF and its allies failed to force abrogation of the treaty. The American edition of *Free Russia* was distributed to over 300 newspapers which often reprinted its articles, but it never had more than 900 paid subscribers, faced constant financial difficulties, and was forced to cease publication in July 1894. Even at the peak of his activity, Kennan aroused more humanitarian sympathy than political commitment, and it proved impossible to sustain an altruistic feeling for distant Russians in an era when Americans were discovering other peoples in need of liberation from cruel despotic rule.[108]

In the late 1880s and early 1890s Russian diplomats were irritated by the rise of American philanthropic societies dedicated to interfering in Russian internal affairs, and tsarist security officials worried about the wide scope of Kennan's agitation. However, by 1893 Russian envoys believed their counter-propaganda was proving successful. From then until at least 1901 they believed Russia generally had the sympathy of both the US government and the American people.[109]

When Alexander III died in late 1894, the traditional Russophilia seemed to be resurgent: many editorials invoked the historic friendship between the two countries; the tsar was eulogized as an upright ruler who loved his "barbaric" people and sought to lead them up "to a higher state of civilization"; the repression of "malcontents" was condoned by editors alarmed by socialism and Populism in the US; and a Turkish massacre of Armenians revived the old sense of Russia as a Christian power in contrast to "the unspeakable Turk."[110] While the translator and writer Isabel Hapgood had been told in the early 1890s that she had to "abuse Russia" if she wanted to be popular in America, she and other Russophiles believed that the tendency toward one-sided indictments of Russia abated in the latter half of the decade.[111] Although a rash of British and Anglophile attacks on Russian aggression in Asia broke out in some northeastern periodicals around the time of the Spanish-American War,[112] the prevailing trend in American attitudes toward Russia was reflected in a spate of publications that rebutted Kennan's indictment of the exile system, depicted Siberia as a new frontier rather than a prison colony, stressed the backwardness of the peasantry, lauded the benevolent paternalism of the autocracy, and hoped for gradual development rather than radical reform.[113]

### Revival of the free Russia movement and demonization of tsarist misrule

Thus, despite the emergence of a movement for the reform of Russia, many nineteenth-century American images of the country persisted into the early 1900s. However, as Russia was convulsed by pogroms, war, and revolution from 1903 to 1905, different streams in American thinking converged in opposition to the tsarist regime.

The year 1903 was a turning point for both the American-Russian relationship and race relations in the United States. From Georgia to Texas, bands of "whitecappers" drove blacks off their farms. In Delaware and Indiana, lynchings escalated into race riots.[114] Throughout the North, many wanted to put sectional tensions in the past and leave "the race question" in the hands of white Southerners, though they were troubled by incidents that cast doubt on the South's intentions and provoked foreign criticism.[115]

That spring, news of the pogrom at Kishinev, where hundreds of Jews were killed and wounded, sparked protest meetings throughout the United States, including small Southern towns. Although President Theodore Roosevelt was not converted by his friend George Kennan from a geopolitical strategist into a human rights crusader, he was sufficiently impressed by the political potency of the outpouring of indignation that he agreed to forward a petition to the Russian government. Sensitive to the possible parallel to racial violence in America, rabbis, newspaper editors, and other opinion leaders argued that Russian pogroms were worse than lynching in the United States (which was then causing the deaths of at least a hundred African Americans annually).[116]

Condemnations of the pogrom served to deflect concern about American racial problems (see figure 5). One striking reflection of this dynamic appeared in *The Outlook*, where George Kennan indicted the Russian government for failing to suppress anti-Semitic agitation and denied that pogroms were analogous to lynchings. At the same time, editor Lyman Abbott culminated a year-long campaign against reconstructing the South by endorsing segregation, condoning disenfranchisement, and insisting that the South was "not missionary ground." Amid heated denunciations of his repudiation of the abolitionist legacy, Abbott (one of the founders of the Friends of Russian Freedom) hailed American protests against the Kishinev pogrom as evidence that American sympathy for the oppressed everywhere was unimpaired – a view shared by former President Grover Cleveland and other speakers at mass meetings.[117]

In the same year, Secretary of State John Hay, President Roosevelt, and many others grew increasingly livid about Russia's failure to

EUROPE:—"Shocking, isn't it?"
UNCLE SAM:—"Quite."—*Chicago News*

Figure 5. European indignation at the lynching of blacks in the United States is deflected through criticism of European inaction in response to the Kishinev pogrom. *Chicago News* cartoon reprinted in *Public Opinion*, May 28, 1903.

withdraw as promised from Manchuria.[118] Once again, prominent Americans were conscious of a potential resemblance between Russia and the United States – this time between mendacious tsarist expansionism and the surreptitious US role in detaching Panama from Colombia.[119] Thus, William Dudley Foulke, who served as one of Roosevelt's civil service commissioners from 1901 to 1903, teased the President "that for Machiavellian diplomacy he was as bad as a Russian; that people would be calling Panama our Bulgaria" – a similarity Roosevelt self-righteously denied.[120]

Figure 6. *Philadelphia Inquirer*, May 16, 1903. In response to the Kishinev pogrom, a cartoonist associates Russian misrule with Satan, while depicting American aid to the innocent victims as part of the spread of enlightened civilization.

Already in February 1903, after seeing a nightmarish play that featured gruesome scenes of Russian prisons, the translator and critic Isabel Hapgood was disturbed by the way that "Russia is made to stand for a sort of public scapegoat."[121] The increasing demonization of Russia coincided with a rebirth of the crusade for a free Russia. Amid the furor over Kishinev, Alice Stone Blackwell, the daughter of prominent abolitionists, played a leading role in the reorganization of the American Friends of Russian Freedom, which drew in a new generation of activists.[122] In the most striking illustration of how the vilification of the tsarist empire went hand in hand with the extension of the American mission, a front page cartoon in the Philadelphia *Inquirer* depicted Satan as behind "Russian misrule" while portraying Columbia bringing the light of civilization to that dark land (see figure 6).[123] As such highly charged images suggest, Russia had come to be an important foil for the definition of American identity earlier than historians have realized.[124]

While the Kishinev pogrom alone led many to deny Russia's claim to be a civilizing force and a Christian nation,[125] anger about Manchuria and indignation at Russian suppression of the rights of Finns and Armenians also helped to trigger a re-evaluation of the historic friendship with Russia.[126] After the outbreak of the Russo-Japanese War in February 1904, newspaper editors and cartoonists explicitly disassociated the United States from Russia and identified instead with the "Yankees of the East."[127] In the following year, as Russia's military proved no match for modern Japanese forces and the tsar's soldiers shot down peaceful demonstrators in St. Petersburg, American views of Imperial Russia congealed around the images of a "medieval" barbarism and a vast prison that Kennan and others had propagated for two decades.[128]

Deeply affected by the glaring weaknesses of the tsarist regime, Americans increasingly judged, as the editor of *Collier's* recalled, "that this cruel and unteachable survival could be tolerated no longer. . . ."[129] Although some writers continued to praise the tsarist empire and Orthodox Church as instruments of progress,[130] more commonly they were scorned as causes of Russia's miseries and barriers to her modernization.[131] The prevailing view was thus in line with anti-tsarist activists who treated the transformation of Russia as part of the general process of clearing obstructions to global economic integration and liberalization. "It is the same assimilating world power," Edmund Noble exulted after the battle of Tsushima, "that sweeps the Tasmanian out of existence, that menaces the slowly-vanishing Indian, that subjects the Hindu and Filipino, that buffets into shape by some devastating war the people who, needed for world tasks, are not yet modern enough to co-operate in them."[132]

The spreading conviction that Russia needed to be unshackled from atavistic tsarism did not rest on a resolution of doubts about the Russian race. Even as *The Independent* proclaimed, "Free Russia it is, and free Russia it must and will be," the liberal journal worried that Russia, with its "vulgar, grimy people," was "hardly fit" for a republic.[133]

American racial attitudes were not transformed but momentarily transcended, in part through faith in the spiritual rebirth of Russia. Soon after the "Bloody Sunday" massacre in St. Petersburg in early 1905, a Baptist editor declared that just as "the colored people of the South" prayed for freedom until Lincoln emancipated them from slavery, "the people of Russia under the iron heel of despotism need the united prayers of Christians for their deliverance and elevation."[134] A few weeks later, many believed the prayers were being answered. The tsar's Easter 1905 edict on religious toleration, which some compared to the emancipation of the serfs in 1861,[135] was widely interpreted as opening the door for American

Figure 7. Columbus *Evening Dispatch*, November 1, 1905. After Nicholas II signed the October Manifesto, which many editors interpreted as meaning the end of the autocracy, a cartoonist depicted the light of liberty from the United States breaking through the dark clouds that had hovered oppressively over the simple people of Russia.

missions to redeem Russia. Then, in October, when Nicholas II reluctantly signed a reform manifesto that promised freedom of conscience, freedom of speech, and respect for a parliament, Americans hailed a further weakening of the exclusive and oppressive Orthodox Church.[136]

A cartoonist for the Columbus *Dispatch* captured American enthusiasm about the reforms by picturing the enlightenment of the simple people of benighted Russia by rays of liberty, intelligence, prosperity, and peace from across the ocean (figure 7). An accompanying editorial indicated the source of the light, speculating that prime minister S. Iu Witte, author of the October manifesto, had been inspired by the "object lesson" of "a prosperous, progressive nation" that he had seen when in the United States for the Portsmouth peace conference.[137] In fact,

Witte was disgusted by American food, disdainful of American customs, and astonished by Americans' naïve views of the world. Although Witte only affected a democratic manner to win over American public opinion, many newspapers, from the *Christian Advocate* to the *New York Times*, concurred that his visit to the US had turned him into an agent of the Americanization of Russia.[138]

For a brief moment, newspaper headlines celebrated the miraculous overnight transformation of Russia from an autocracy to a democracy.[139] Then more and more reports arrived about the outbreak of widespread pogroms, which suggested that ordinary Russians were not ready for orderly self-government.[140] The revulsion widened in December, when a general strike in St. Petersburg and an armed revolt in Moscow indicated that the Russian revolution had diverged from the supposed American model of restraint, and instead followed a French-inspired path to terror and socialism.

The unrealistic visions of an imminent remaking of Russia in the image of the United States were founded not simply on ignorance and wishful thinking but also on the deliberate efforts of Russian revolutionaries, American activists, and religious leaders to mold expectations of the political and spiritual emancipation of Russia. Despite the disillusionment in late 1905, the dream of a free Russia had become so deeply rooted and so closely tied to Americans' feelings about themselves that they would revive and persist through the twentieth century.

# 2 "The United States of Russia": culmination and frustration, 1905–20

In the aftermath of the Russian revolution of 1905, an Estonian nobleman journeyed to America in search of financial support for the burgeoning Baptist movement in the Russian empire. Telling stories of how he had been converted by Baptist peasant laborers on his estate and stressing the unprecedented opportunities for preaching the Gospel in Russia, Baron Woldemar Üxküll electrified audiences around the United States, won the support of key religious leaders, and secured pledges of significant contributions from wealthy philanthropists. After hearing Üxküll speak, the editors of *The Missionary Review of the World*, a key interdenominational monthly, declared in 1906 that they had "never been more moved" and urged that Üxküll's appeal should stir "the whole Church of God to immediate action."[1] Welcoming Üxküll with similar enthusiasm, Southern Baptist leader James Gambrell announced, "As I look at the map of the world, I believe the two great foreign mission places today are Russia and China. To bring Russia to the New Testament teachings is to secure for the King eternal a reign of grace over one of the greatest countries in the world, and a country that is just now at the beginning of a development great beyond all human calculations."[2]

As such excited responses to Üxküll's tour suggest, disillusionment with the degeneration and failure of the revolution of 1905 did not deter many Americans from continuing to dream about and work for a reformation of Russia. Following the tsarist government's 1905 proclamation of religious toleration, several American Protestant denominations eagerly took advantage of the opening to increase their support for missionary ventures that, despite their relatively small size, seemed enormous in significance for the future.[3] At the same time, a new cohort of American anti-tsarist activists emerged from among idealistic workers in settlement houses for immigrants from Russia. Although those "gentlemen socialists" scorned the condescending notion of uplifting Russians, and ostensibly repudiated the expectation that a liberated Russia would follow an American capitalist model, many of them were inspired by a quasi-religious zeal and their writing perpetuated Messianic themes introduced by earlier crusaders for a free Russia. Together with the older activists, Christian missionaries, and Jewish-American critics of Russian anti-Semitism, the gentlemen socialists shaped the rapturous American responses to the revolution that finally toppled the autocracy in March 1917.

It has long been recognized that a missionary mindset distorted American reactions to the Chinese revolution in the middle of the twentieth century, particularly by leading many to believe China's destiny was to be Americanized, to resent the communist victory as an unnatural betrayal, and to view the communist government as "not Chinese."[4] Yet, in part because of the neglect of the role of religion in American-Russian relations, it has not been widely understood that a similar mentality influenced American responses to the revolutions of 1917.[5] In the absence of a full critical perspective on the spiritually infused Messianic outlook, Americans have tended to replicate it. Even some otherwise keenly insightful writers have maintained that the United States missed a "gargantuan" opportunity to save "the new Russian democracy," which was then "irretrievably lost to Bolshevism."[6]

The widespread belief in 1917 that the Russian people had set out to follow the American democratic path had profound consequences: it fed the conviction that the Bolsheviks who seized power in November were alien usurpers who would soon be overthrown; it fostered the unrealistic expectation in 1918 that sending small military expeditions to Russia would lead true Russians to rally around anti-Bolshevik forces; and it underpinned the refusal to recognize the Soviet government for sixteen long years. Moreover, the image of Bolsheviks as fiendishly anti-American that became pervasive in the Red Scare of 1919–20 was central to a redefinition of American national identity in opposition to a new, evil enemy.

### American Christian missions to Russia from 1905 to the Great War

When the tsarist government moved between 1903 and 1905 to permit greater religious freedom, the steps aroused intense enthusiasm among leaders of many American religious groups. With the legalization of defections from the Orthodox Church in 1905, that faith appeared to be losing its stranglehold upon millions of Russians, and the gates to a vast empire seemed to be swinging open. The Presbyterian editor of *The Missionary Review of the World* commented that the edict of toleration in April 1905 seemed "great with possibilities for the progress of civilization and Christian truth in Russia."[7] Amid the revolutionary turmoil of 1905 a prominent Catholic educator and priest in Washington predicted that "the makers of the New Russia" would ignore the "dormant," discredited Orthodox Church and borrow government principles and educational ideas from abroad, especially from "Roman Catholic models and institutions."[8] The increased religious liberty thus encouraged a widespread sense that Russia would be more open to Western political and cultural, as well as spiritual, influences. In addition, it spurred three denominations, especially, to expand their missionary efforts: Seventh-day Adventists, Baptists, and Methodists.

Thanks to the tsar's decrees, Adventists finally felt it safe to openly extend their efforts beyond German colonies and to better organize "the native Russian work."[9] Pastor J. T. Boettcher, who agreed in 1907 to go to Russia and became the first president of a new Adventist union there, reported enthusiastically about the opportunities for evangelism.[10] Despite sometimes violent opposition from supporters of the Orthodox Church, Adventist membership jumped from just over 2,000 in 1905 to nearly 5,000 in 1912.[11] Adventist missionaries who worked in Russia passed resolutions of thanks to the tsar for the degree of freedom he granted in 1905 and they emphasized to police officials that their meetings "were in no way political."[12] However, Adventists who did not have to worry about the Russian police could be harshly critical of the autocracy. In 1906, for example, one Adventist writer in the United States prophesied that God would deal severely with "a cruel and despotic power."[13]

Methodist leaders were as quick as Adventists to enlarge their work in the tsarist empire. The bishop who directed Methodist missions in Europe arranged an additional allocation of funds for Russia and encouraged Dr. George A. Simons (1874–1952) to take charge of that formerly languishing field. Simons, who briefly worked as a bank clerk before following his father into the ministry, hesitated to go to turbulent Russia. However, upon arriving in St. Petersburg in 1907 he was exhilarated by "the wonderful opportunity our Church has in this great territory."[14] Within a year Simons confidently concluded that "the Greek Orthodox Church has lost her grip upon the people." Like many other Americans, Simons believed that religious development had far-reaching social and political implications: it indicated that "the old Russia is practically a thing of the past." With large numbers of Russians drifting away from the "pagan" Orthodox Church into "agnosticism and licentiousness," Simons urged, "Now is the time to go to them with a gospel of life, light, liberty and truth."[15]

Simons continued to glow with enthusiasm in the following years. In 1911, for example, he boasted that "our growth and development have been remarkable" and demanded more aggressive investment by the Methodist missionary board.[16] The Methodist missionary supervisor, a veteran of work in the Philippines that had proved more difficult than initially expected, wisely preferred to proceed more slowly and to "build up a church there that will be native in the truest sense, adjusted to the life and giving ability of our Russian converts."[17] However, Simons led at least one member of the Methodist board to agree with him that "Methodism has the secret of Russia's recovery of moral health."[18]

While Methodist evangelism centered on Finnish, Baltic, and German-speaking people in the northwestern corner of the tsarist empire, Baptists drew more converts from ethnic Russians who left the Orthodox Church.[19] As the Baptist Foreign Secretary observed in 1907, it was the new opportunity for work among "the native Russian people" created by their "emancipation from religious bondage" that aroused special interest in the United States.[20] Southern Baptist leader James Gambrell conveyed his excitement in an article for *The Baptist Standard*, explaining that Baptists in the tsarist empire were "at the beginning of a new Russia, when the gospel, as leaven goes through meal, is to renovate and lift the whole land up to a higher level." This suggested that Russia would walk in the footsteps of Americans: the story of Baptists teaching their people how to read the Bible was like "the early days of America over again."[21]

In contrast to the archaic and hierarchical Orthodox practices, Baptists in both Russia and America saw themselves as modern and believed that their voluntary associations offered a model for a more democratic society. As a Baptist report in 1906 explained, in the Russian empire as in the rest of Europe, Baptist churches "disseminated ideals which are the essentials of free institutions."[22] Threatened by the inroads of Baptists on their flocks, Orthodox priests often responded by accusing Baptist ministers and laymen of revolutionary activity and instigating their arrest.[23] Such persecution elicited warm sympathy for Baptists from liberal political opponents of the autocracy who regarded Protestant sectarianism as a part of historical progress.[24] Thus, the flourishing Baptist movement in Russia, which was widely publicized in the American religious press,[25] had significant political implications.

American excitement about missionary work in Russia stemmed, then, not only from the rapid rate of growth of Protestant churches, the enormous size of the total population, and the weaknesses of the Orthodox Church,[26] but also from the sense that foreign-supported evangelism would help Russians to free themselves from the bonds of their ancient institutions. In contrast to the Estonian Baron Üxküll, who described many Russian Baptists as "worse than the American negroes" in intelligence, education, and understanding, Americans who were interested in missionary work in the tsarist empire tended to envision Russians as white,[27] and to believe that they could be made fit for self-government. Thus, even a Baptist editor in Boston who had doubted that the 1905 edict of toleration would lead to genuine religious freedom and who commented gloomily on the autocrat's retraction of democratic concessions in 1906, proclaimed his faith that Russians could follow the American or at least the English trajectory: "For Russia, sooner or later, there will be a Runnymede and a Magna Charta, if not a Bunker Hill and Yorktown."[28]

### The gentlemen socialists and the idea of a free Russia

During the same decade that American enthusiasm about evangelizing tsarist Russia peaked, a group of privileged young men outwardly rejected the prevailing ethos of a civilizing mission. The wealthy socialist William English Walling colorfully coined a motto for the youthful cohort in 1902 when he welcomed Princeton graduate Ernest Poole to the University Settlement on the Lower East Side of New York. Referring to the immigrants from eastern Europe at the settlement house, Walling proclaimed: "They've got a lot to teach us boys, so for the love of Jesus Christ don't let us be uplifters here!" Instead of preaching about how to live to the poor immigrants who thronged the tenements and settlement houses of major cities, Walling, Poole, and their colleagues believed they should listen, learn about the immigrants' struggles, and come to understand their views.[29]

Stimulated by their experiences among the eastern European immigrants, several of the settlement house workers – most notably, Walling, Poole, and Arthur Bullard – felt called to the Russian empire by the revolution of 1905. With commissions from American popular magazines and journals of opinion, they investigated conditions throughout European Russia and wrote numerous articles exposing Cossack brutality, indicting tsarist oppression, and lionizing heroic revolutionaries. In their writing, as in their settlement house activity, the gentlemen socialists rejected moralistic efforts to remold other peoples.

Ernest Poole subtly conveyed this perspective in 1905 by telling a story about a young peasant woman who ultimately rebuffs well-meaning efforts "to *uplift*" her by a professor and his wife, which unfitted her for life in her native village.[30] Walling stated his objections to an American-style remaking of Russians more directly in *Russia's Message* (1908), the most important contemporary study in English of the revolution of 1905. Having become mired in its own industrial and social problems, the United States had lost its position as "the chief inspiration of the other nations," and the torch was passing to a revolutionary Russia, Walling believed. Fearing that Prime Minister P. A. Stolypin's plans to break up the communal system of agriculture would spoil the peasant basis for an egalitarian democracy, Walling sharply criticized the Russian government's desire to "have a few million farmers of the German or American sort." Scorning the idea of Russia imitating the capitalist United States, he predicted that a "regenerated Russia" would be "likely to lead in her solutions rather than to follow."[31]

Like Poole and Walling, Bullard was attracted to Russian Socialist Revolutionaries (SRs) more than to other Russian political groups. Influenced by SRs he met and admired, Bullard argued that "Russia is neither an advanced Asiatic Despotism nor a retarded Western Empire," but a unique Slavic civilization which was not predestined to "run in the same rut as that of Western Europe."[32] While the constitutional monarchist faction within the intelligentsia "dreamed of a republic like France or the United States, which would have the police strength to preserve 'the order' they needed for exploitation," the SRs hoped to bypass the evils of capitalism and create a socialist democracy rooted in Russian traditions. This inclined Bullard to focus more on how a Russian "peasant democracy" could regenerate the spirit of democracy in the West than on how Western ideas could transform Russia.[33]

While such ideas marked a departure from the first American crusade for a free Russia in the 1890s, Poole, Walling and Bullard were all inspired by George Kennan's earlier journalistic campaign against tsarist despotism. As Poole remembered, the settlement house workers "had read George Kennan's accounts of the tragic heroic lives of the early revolutionists."[34] Accepting and praising the "relentless accuracy" of Kennan's exposés "of the horrors of the political prisons in Siberia," the three socialist writers followed Kennan's example in articles about valiant revolutionaries and Siberian exile.[35] Kennan's influence was particularly apparent in *Russia's Message*. Like *Siberia and the Exile System* (1891), Walling's book was a massive (450-page) indictment of the "monstrous" crimes of the tsarist government, and like Kennan Walling portrayed Russia as an enormous prison, with the despotic regime treating peasants as inmates of their villages.[36]

As the years went by Kennan became an increasingly ardent foe of the tsarist government, to the point that during the Russo-Japanese war he led a propaganda campaign among Russian prisoners of war in Japan that sought to turn them into revolutionaries.[37] Like Kennan, the settlement house socialists went beyond writing about the revolutionary struggle to actively supporting it. In Russia they all employed revolutionaries as guides and interpreters. Poole participated in clandestine meetings to plan gun smuggling. Bullard joined insurrectionists behind their barricades in Moscow and helped repair their rifles. Walling and his radical wife Anna Strunsky were arrested on suspicion of revolutionary activity.[38] Back in America, the trio wrote stories to encourage aid to the revolutionary cause, assisted fund-raising tours by Russian radicals, and agitated against foreign loans to the tsarist government.[39]

During this period, many settlement house activists joined the revitalized Friends of Russian Freedom (FRF), which listed George Kennan as Vice-President. Arthur Bullard served as treasurer and a member of the executive committee of FRF. James Bronson Reynolds, the son of a Congregational minister who had been head resident of the University Settlement, was named chairman of the FRF executive committee. Lillian Wald, creator of the Henry Street Settlement in New York, joined Reynolds on the executive committee. Jane Addams, founder of Chicago's Hull House, served on the national committee.[40]

Although the gentlemen socialists diverged from Kennan by sympathizing with moderate socialists rather than bourgeois liberals, they shared with Kennan the assumption that a revolutionary transformation would make Russia more closely resemble the United States. Poole was not inclined to make such assertions bluntly, but his widely read short story-like articles on the revolution of 1905 conveyed the notion indirectly. Although the medieval autocracy and Church were for the moment damming progress, Poole wrote, "an economic revolution like the one now under way in America" had begun in Russian cities, where activists had also started Sunday schools "somewhat like our American night-schools." Noting that Russian workers were "most eager to hear about the labor movement in America," and quoting a peasant saying "It must be fine to live in America," Poole repeatedly hinted at the likely direction of the impending changes.[41]

Along the same line, Bullard reported that the leading socialists and nationalists in the Baltic provinces were striving "to establish a government based on the will of the people." That goal could be achieved not only in the highly educated Baltic region, Bullard believed, but throughout the Russian empire, because peasants were accustomed to self-government in their commune, which was "much more democratic in its working than even a Massachusetts town meeting." Much as Kennan ten years earlier had upheld the "Zheltuga Republic" in Manchuria as proof of Russia's readiness for democracy, Bullard pointed to the story of an isolated village in Siberia, where fugitives from prison camps had lived a clean democratic life, as a clear indication of "what Russia will be like when the governmental exploiters are driven out and the peasant can organize things to suit himself."[42]

Like Kennan, Bullard, and two Russians who lectured in the United States in 1907,[43] Walling found in the peasant commune, the *mir*, the basis for a democratic Russia. Peasant villages, he maintained, were "little immemorial republics . . . ruled by a pure spirit of democracy."[44] At the same time as he acclaimed peasant political culture and institutions, however, Walling declared that what gave Russians such stirring potential was that they were "unhampered by inherent traditions." Since the peasant's undeveloped nature was "unfixed and unspoiled," he would "come to his majority in the twentieth century more freed from tradition than our own pioneers in the nineteenth." While depicting Russians as blank slates, Walling also rebutted stereotypes of "dark" peasants and explicitly defined Russians as members of "the white race."[45] Hence, there were exciting possibilities for foreign inscription. One of the outstanding traits of Russians, Walling glowed, was "their ready assimilation of the world's best thoughts," and the educated class was capitalizing on that by teaching the uncorrupted peasants "foreign history, literature, economics, and politics." This combination of peasant democracy, freedom from tradition, and receptiveness to foreign ideas, Walling suggested, would enable Russians to build a "United States of Russia."[46]

To understand how the gentlemen socialists could reject the application of an American capitalist model to Russia yet popularize different visions of the Americanization of the tsarist empire, we must see them as products of their religious upbringings, not merely as secular liberal advocates of modernization. Although many historians have observed that Protestant educations and secularized religious aspirations widely influenced the activity of Progressive reformers and publicists,[47] it is still striking how strongly Christian values and beliefs shaped the three socialists' attitudes toward and descriptions of Russia.

Though raised in a family of "'dyed in the blue Presbyterians'" who were devoutly committed to charity, Ernest Poole felt his religion slip away at college. Dreading tedious sermons and disdaining dogmatic creeds, after graduating from Princeton he "kept free from churches." While he had loved singing Moody and Sankey hymns as a youth, he had never fully shared his mother's calm, humane nineteenth-century faith. But when she died in late 1904, the shock caused settlement house life in New York to lose its grip on him. "[D]esperately I wanted something new to work for," Poole remembered. "I found it in Russia."[48]

After reaching Russia in early 1905, Poole made the alleged irrationality, superstition, dead formalism, and corruption of the Orthodox Church a recurring focus of articles for American magazines. In much the same vein as Kennan earlier, Poole blamed the Russian Church for the abject submissiveness, poverty, and ignorance of many of the people. While characterizing priests as opponents of all reform and as vampires who sucked the blood of the peasants, Poole suggested that hope for the future lay in schools and the inculcation of a spirit of self-help. "'God! It's always God – God,'" shouts a peasant in one of Poole's reports. "That won't do, I tell you. We must help ourselves."[49]

If Poole's vivid stories exuded a classical liberal anti-clericalism, Bullard reflected a distinct religious tradition – one that extended from a Puritan ancestor through Bullard's father, a Presbyterian minister.[50] Bullard apparently broke with his family's Presbyterianism when he joined the University Settlement and embraced the cause of social revolution as a more effective way to fulfill the "deep revolutionary message in the words of Jesus."[51] Yet in seeking a more practical route to the Millennium, Bullard adapted the Christian tradition more than he repudiated it. While recognizing that Darwin and other scientists had "driven out the old Gods," Bullard lamented the consequences: he decried the way the "so-called 'scientific' explanation of life" had "robbed mankind of all faith and produced a generation of cynics and skeptics." Believing that "man cannot live without faith," Bullard found a new religion among Russian revolutionaries. "The educated men of Russia," Bullard wrote, "are not cynics and scoffers as in Western countries; they are men of fervent faith and devotion." Implicitly he likened Russian revolutionaries to missionaries: "they have pierced the veil of darkness which the Tsar spread over his people and they have carried into the peasant villages and crowded factory tenements the light of great ideals." While undergoing "a Reformation," Russia was giving the world "a new faith – a higher inspiration for our endeavours."[52]

Although Walling's father was a physician rather than a minister, he shared with Bullard a craving for a new "social faith" and a view of revolutionary socialists as spiritual descendants of the early Christians.[53] Walling blamed organized religion in general for keeping the masses in ignorance,[54] but he was especially harsh on the Russian Orthodox Church. In an article in 1907, Walling claimed that "the priest does not seriously enter into the peasant's life," asserted that the peasant was actually "liberal and even independent in his religious views," and suggested that peasants were ripe for spiritual as well as political conversion. "Along with a revolution as profound as the French," he explained, "is going on a popular religious reformation comparable only to the peasants' movements of Luther's time."[55]

Walling expanded on these themes in *Russia's Message*. After describing how even clergy were becoming revolutionaries, Walling endorsed one famous priest's denunciation of the Orthodox Church for failing to bring Russian state and society in line with Christian ethics. Confident that communistic sects like the Dukhobors were going to grow rapidly as soon as full religious freedom was won from the government, Walling predicted that such groups would provide "spiritual reinforcement" to political revolutionaries. "Among the Russian Baptists," he prophesied, dissent was "already taking the form of a religious warfare against the Government as determined and invincible as the religious wars of the English Puritans and Levellers against the king and his church." Thus, in a variety of ways, Walling and other gentlemen socialists suggested that religious developments would be vital to swinging Russia onto the historical road already marched by Protestants in the West.[56]

### The crusade against Russian anti-Semitism

Among the most striking dynamics in the settlement house circles of the early twentieth century were romances between radical young Jewish-American women and privileged Anglo-Saxon Protestant men, who thereby appeared to renounce allegiance to their caste and announce their devotion to altruistic ideals. In 1906, for example, Walling married Anna Strunsky, a passionate socialist who had earlier entranced novelist Jack London. Bullard had a brief romance that same year with Anna's sister, Rose, though she seems to have decided he was not radical enough for her. Earlier, the marriage of "millionaire socialist" Graham Phelps Stokes to Rose Pastor, a poor reporter for the *Jewish Daily News*, had made a sensational story in newspapers.[57]

While such romantic attachments between elite Anglo-American men and Jewish women were in vogue, until 1911 relatively few Americans embraced the cause of reforming Russian treatment of Jews. In contrast to the Kishinev pogrom of 1903, which many had angrily blamed on connivance by tsarist officials, the more widespread anti-Semitic riots in late 1905 seemed to stem from the barbarism of ordinary Russians and that cooled some of the fervor to remake Russia.[58] During the following years, riots against blacks in Atlanta (1906) and Springfield, Illinois (1908) highlighted how the United States had its own problems with racial violence. For example, the editor of *The Nation* declared that the outbreak of racial violence in Atlanta was "as savage as any slaughter of Jews in Russia."[59]

However, indignation at Russian treatment of Jews continued to simmer. It boiled over again in 1911 as a result of a campaign against Russian diplomats' refusal to accept the passports of American Jews.[60] Jewish organizations and their sympathizers demanded that the United States repudiate its commercial treaty with Russia to protest the tsarist government's discriminatory and insulting practices. Since Americans were themselves guilty of discrimination and prejudice, especially against Asian immigrants on the Pacific coast, some journalists were conscious of an element of hypocrisy in the allegations against Russia. Nonetheless, they asserted that the American "pot" had the right to call the Russian "kettle" black.[61]

Deflection of discomfort with American blemishes was more than incidental to the 1911 crusade. Mass meetings across the United States gave Americans an opportunity to demonstrate that despite their occupation with material prosperity, they were still faithful to idealistic principles such as religious toleration. As New Jersey Governor Woodrow Wilson declaimed, putting concern for the rights of Jews above American commerce with Russia would show that "America is not a mere body of traders."[62] While reaffirming their own virtue, American journalists and politicians frequently scorned the oppressive Russian government as hopelessly retrograde and incorrigibly inhumane.[63] In newspaper editorials, the "darkness" of Russia's "superstitious bigotry" was implicitly contrasted with the light of America's supposed tolerance and its religious liberty.[64]

For several months in 1911, the frenzied criticism of Russia continued. Members of Congress vowed to "break down the walls of the Czar," pledged to teach Russia a lesson in civilization, and complained that Russia was refusing to admit Catholic priests and Protestant missionaries, as well as American Jews.[65] Editors decried Russian "religious control of government and of citizens" as "absolutely repugnant" to American doctrines.[66]

At the end of 1911, Jewish activists and their Gentile supporters finally succeeded in compelling the Taft administration to abrogate the commercial treaty with Russia. However, they were not able to sustain their influence on US government policy and American public opinion. The stubborn and scornful reactions of Russian officials led many American politicians to have second thoughts about the wisdom of abrogating the trade treaty, which reduced American exports to Russia without prompting the tsarist government to alter its position on the passport question.[67] US diplomats and businessmen who were eager to expand trade with Russia repeatedly complained about the annoying, counterproductive criticism of Russia from Jewish leaders.[68] And after the outbreak of war in Europe, friction developed between Jewish-American groups and Anglo-Americans who wanted to believe that a new Russia was emerging as an honorable partner in the war of the "civilized powers" against German barbarism. The ardent Russophile Charles Johnston, for example, regretted that "we in America are prone to see the vast nation [Russia] of 180,000,000 through the hostile eyes of 5,000,000 aliens." Since the

United States deprived millions of blacks and Chinese immigrants of their rights, Johnston urged, "let us not be priggish and Pharisaical about the difficulties of others."[69]

## Backlash: religious repression in Russia, 1911–16

The aggressive criticism of tsarist anti-Semitism did not push the Russian government to halt religious persecution. On the contrary, it seems to have aggravated the already increasing harassment of Protestants as well as Jews. In 1913, for example, a British Baptist leader observed that "it was most unfortunate" for the President of the World Baptist Alliance to be "associated with a meeting to protest against Russian treatment of Jews"; that had made it more difficult for Russian statesmen to sanction the work of the Russian Evangelization Society.[70] Even before the 1911 campaign, Adventist leaders began complaining about stricter censorship and new regulations against proselytizing. In 1912 the situation worsened, as the tsarist government ordered the Adventists to close their publishing house in Riga and refused to grant land in Siberia to "sectarians."[71] As Methodist missionary George Simons explained in early 1914, the preceding years brought "a strong political reaction and religious repression, under which practically all Free Church bodies have had to suffer more or less."[72] Following the outbreak of the First World War, the government cracked down more severely. Police officials investigated, arrested, and jailed many preachers, particularly in denominations that had close ties to German colonists and seminaries in Germany, such as the Adventists and Baptists.[73] The aggressive Baptist leader William Fetler was banished from Russia. Many other preachers were suspected of being spies and exiled to distant provinces. Even Simons, who continued to enjoy "a certain amount of liberty" in Petrograd that he attributed "to a quiet, tactful mode of activity and our having American connections," felt it "best to 'lie low' and bide our time."[74]

Underlying this clash between Russian religious "sectarians" and their foreign supporters, on the one hand, and Orthodox priests and Russian policemen, on the other, was a fundamental conflict between two worldviews. American evangelists, whose favorite metaphor for missionary opportunity was the "open door," ideally envisioned the entire Earth opening to their beneficent, uplifting influence (see figure 8). In contrast, Orthodox priests typically conceived of their congregations as needing to be shielded from alien influences who would lead them astray. One especially vivid reflection of this concept depicted the Orthodox faithful as sheep in a corral, menaced by wolves who would lunge through holes in the fences (see figure 9). While the confrontation between these two

Figure 8. "Open Doors to All the World." *The Advent Review and Sabbath Herald*, June 25, 1914.

orientations was particularly sharp in the last decade of tsarist rule, it was also emblematic of the much wider encounter between the American quest for an open world and the isolationist or protectionist policies of Russian political and religious authorities.

Figure 9. "The flock of Christ and the devouring wolves." From a Russian Orthodox church pamphlet, "Stoite v vere!" (Stay in the faith!), first published in 1911. Baptists, Adventists, Tolstoyans, Catholics, and other devilish agents try to steal or lure sheep from the Orthodox corral.

## Images of a new Russia during World War I

Although the intensification of Russian religious persecution disturbed many church leaders in the United States, the start of the First World War triggered a new surge of enthusiasm about an imminent transformation of Russia among American journalists. Upon receiving news of the outbreak of war in August 1914, the *Chicago Tribune* immediately predicted that "Eastern Europe of the kings will be remade" and trumpeted: "The republic marches east in Europe."[75] Along the same line, *The Nation* forecast that the specter of "Slavic terrorism" would soon disappear because the war would cause a revolution in Russia.[76] By November, other American periodicals were glowing about "the conversion of Nicholas II to progressive political ideas" or the "conversion to liberalism" of conservatives in the Duma.[77] As the war raged on, many writers would acclaim the "democracy of human feeling" in Russia or invoke the *mir* to explain how peasants had actually been preparing for centuries for a leap to democracy.[78]

George Kennan contributed to this new wave of enthusiasm by republishing his story of the "Zheltuga Republic" which, he insisted, furnished "striking proof" that Russians were capable of organizing a government that would not be "discreditable to an Anglo-Saxon community." Refuting suspicions that Russians passively submitted to barbarous injustice, Kennan informed the editor and readers of *The Outlook*: "They tolerate it only in the sense that a Negro slave in South Carolina might have been said to tolerate the sale of his wife and children to a planter in Louisiana." While conceding that Russians had "a blood-taint of submission inherited from ancestors who were serfs," Kennan stressed that "the Russians are among the most gifted of the Aryan peoples" and predicted that once they were free from the forces that had warped their characters, they would become a great self-governing people.[79] This racial categorization of Russians enabled Kennan to reaffirm a teleological vision of historical evolution. "The Russian common people are behind the Anglo-Saxon common people in development, in culture, and in prosperity," Kennan explained in 1915, "but they are making progress, and are advancing along the same path that we ourselves have followed."[80]

Americans' wartime hopes for a new Russia were also influenced by their economic ambitions and spiritual aspirations. When war broke out in 1914, Americans were quick to sense opportunities to expand their commerce with Russia, especially by displacing Germany.[81] Journalists who traveled to Russia during the war exhorted Americans to seize what one called "the greatest opportunity for American trade that commercial history has ever offered us."[82] As Russian Ambassador Iu. P. Bakhmetev was pleased to report, representatives of the most important American firms came to the Russian Embassy in Washington and then spread enthusiastic stories about inexhaustible Russian resources and rich potential markets.[83]

To journalists like Stanley Washburn and Richard Washburn Child, the economic development of Russia was part of a broader "awakening" – the dominant metaphor for what was happening in the tsarist empire during the war.[84] Even before August 1914, some American editors praised the Russian bureaucracy for having "awakened" to the evil of alcoholism. After the fighting started and the emperor prohibited the sale of vodka, his decree was immediately hailed as a "big miracle" and compared to the reforms of Peter the Great or Alexander II. Such reactions had unmistakable religious overtones. Impressed by the vodka ban, as well as the way Russia's peasant soldiers were holding their own against Germany, one writer declared that "Russia is awakening" and that "Russia is not heathen by any means." Noting that a Russian temperance proponent had been influenced by a visit to the US twenty years earlier, translator Isabel Hapgood claimed Americans had "supplied the scriptural mustard seed" for prohibition in Russia.[85] While some Russian temperance reformers did indeed urge adoption of American methods, others insisted that Russia look to its own abstainers (Old Believers and Muslims) for inspiration, and the transformation of "the alcoholic empire" was not nearly as sweeping as Americans imagined.[86] Thus, American reactions to the wartime vodka ban were part of a historic pattern of overestimating the scope of Russian changes and exaggerating American influence upon them.

Russian diplomats noted the overdrawn and moralistic nature of American attitudes. As one envoy commented after touring the Midwest in early 1916, unreflective and impressionable Americans, who earlier had been under the influence of stories about cruel pogroms and the horrors of Siberia, were now ready to believe in the spiritual and economic might of Russia. In a similar vein, Ambassador Bakhmeteff observed that in American eyes Russia was cleansed of its evil vices overnight.[87]

More widely than before, Americans deemed it inevitable that the purified new Russia would be refashioned in the likeness of the United States. Confident that Russia needed "American vision" and the products of its "civilization," Richard Washburn Child forecast that business would "be able to force liberalism on Russia."[88] Abandoning his previous emphasis on how Russia was blazing a different path, William English Walling now anticipated "the modernization of Russia" through the establishment "of industrial capitalism and the semi-democratic political institutions that accompany it – as we see them in Great Britain, France, and America."[89] Although the editor of *National Geographic* continued to emphasize traditional Russophile themes, he also praised the Russian government for "following the example of our own country in trying to take the gospel of good farming to the peasantry."[90] Even the Russophile Isabel Hapgood, who had long opposed the radical alteration of Russia's distinct culture, now distanced herself from Slavophile critics of westernization and welcomed the anticipated adoption of the Gregorian calendar, which she asserted Americans had hastened.[91]

The notion that Russia's natural destiny was to follow America's path of development was most often conveyed by homology and historical analogy. Underneath their differences, Russia and the United States shared fundamental similarities, explained one Harvard educator: both occupied great plains regions; each had a history of agricultural pioneering; the Volga river steamers were like those on the Mississippi, and so on.[92] "In many ways Russia, today, presents an enlarged picture of the United States at the close of the Civil War," declared banker Samuel McRoberts.

Siberia, he asserted, was like the American West: a vast public domain awaiting development of her rich resources.[93] Invocation of the supposed common frontier experience became the predominant way of setting aside current differences in political systems and suggesting that Russia was innately "liberty-loving and democratic."[94]

These seductive analogies fostered unrealistic expectations. McRoberts' comparison of Russia in 1916 to the United States in 1865, for example, led directly to his prediction that "an era of individualism and materialism" was about "to be inaugurated in Russia."[95] Child acknowledged that Russians he interviewed suspected America's money-mad civilization was a blight. Yet he encouraged readers to disregard anti-American sentiment by asserting that Russia would be dependent on foreign capital in her period of young growth just as the US had been, and by insisting that the economic forces of global integration were "irresistible."[96]

### Deliverance: American responses to the revolution of March 1917

During the first two years of the Great War, Russia's alliance with the Entente and increased purchases of American products spurred a revival of Russophilia, with its mythology about a historic American-Russian friendship and its approval of the tsarist government's efforts to develop the country.[97] However, toward the end of 1916, Americans expressed mounting frustration with the Russian monarchy, which they believed had fallen into the hands of pro-German reactionaries, mismanaged the war against Germany, delayed negotiation of a new commercial treaty, and cracked down on foreign missionaries.[98]

Consequently, when the faltering autocracy finally collapsed in early 1917, Americans rapturously welcomed the revolution, believing that it would invigorate Russia's fighting spirit and throw open doors to American political, economic, and religious influence.[99] Lillian Wald and other members of the Friends of Russian Freedom rejoiced over the deliverance of the Russian people, which they thought George Kennan had done much to secure. Kennan expressed a similar sense of triumph, wiring one of his liberal friends in Petrograd: "Exiles free" and "Victory at last." In a major article prominently featured in *The Outlook*, Kennan declared that "the struggle for freedom in Russia . . . has ended at last in the complete triumph of democracy." Discounting the possibility of "any serious internal dissension," Kennan predicted that the change of government would soon bring about "a complete regeneration of the people."[100]

"Welcome, Russia!"

Figure 10. "Welcome Russia." *Life*, May 10, 1917.

Such exhilaration extended far beyond the circles of anti-tsarist activists. The US Ambassador in Russia, a bluff, whisky-drinking former governor of Missouri, assured Washington that the revolution was the "practical realization" of the American principle of "consent by the governed." *Life* magazine conveyed the same idea with a drawing that linked the revolution of 1917 to the American revolution of 1776 and depicted the humble Russian people worshiping America's radiant liberty (see figure 10). In the same spirit, in an address to Congress on April 2, President Woodrow Wilson hailed the way the allegedly non-Russian autocracy had been shaken off by the Russian people, who were "always in fact democratic at heart."[101]

Although Wilson did not record the bases for this remarkable view, it is possible to identify several likely influences. First, as the son of a Presbyterian minister, Wilson had an unquestioning faith "in a Divine Providence," and his conviction that God directed the course of history allowed him to believe that erring human societies could be transfigured.[102] Second, as a liberal universalist Wilson had long been inclined to fit Russia within his vision of humanity's movement toward self-government and freedom. Third, George Kennan's indictment of tsarist absolutism in the early 1890s strongly affected Wilson's closest adviser, who helped Wilson prepare to write his speech to Congress: Edward M. House recalled that Kennan's crusade made such a deep and lasting impression that "every one in the liberty-loving countries of the world welcomed the overthrow of a system that exuded injustice and cruelty in its most objectionable forms." Fourth, Wilson's glowing praise of the "naïve majesty" of the Russian people in his address to Congress resembled and may have been influenced by the description of the unspoiled character of Russian peasants in *Russia's Message* by William English Walling, to whom Wilson offered a position on a high-profile mission to Russia that spring. Finally, Wilson's enthusiasm about the "democratic" nature of Russians was probably stoked by his friend Charles Crane, who believed that Russian local self-government was an inspiring form of "practical democracy" and who encouraged Wilson to have a mystical faith in Russia's future. Beyond the question of these specific influences, though, what is most important is that Wilson and many other Americans envisioned the revolution as a moment of transcendence, when Russia broke free from centuries of oppressive historical experience that were now irrelevant to her bright future.[103]

Inside Russia, evangelists joyfully celebrated the overthrow of the tsarist government. From Saratov, where he had been exiled and under virtual house arrest, an Adventist pastor proclaimed that "the Great God of Heaven and Earth has at last visited in great mercy this people to deliver them from the bondage which held them for so long a time."[104] From Petrograd, George Simons declared to Methodists in America that "the most thrilling thing" he had witnessed in his ten-year sojourn in Russia was "the truly miraculous resurrection of this great Slavic nation, almost two hundred million strong, rising in power and majesty from the gloomy tomb of despotic tyranny and mediaeval [sic] terrorism into the joyous light and life of freedom and democracy."[105]

Religious leaders in the United States, including some who had been hesitant before the revolution, now showed much greater eagerness to fund missionary work in Russia. As a Methodist mission director explained, he sought "to develop a stronger program" because he believed "that Russia is opening wonderfully to the message of the Gospel."[106] Several steps by the Russian provisional government, including a law guaranteeing freedom of conscience and the transfer of elementary schools from the Orthodox Church to the Ministry of Education, sustained such optimism. En route to Europe in May 1917, Sherwood Eddy of the Young Men's Christian Association glowingly predicted that the YMCA would "have an opportunity in the period of reconstruction in Russia that is incalculable."[107] The editor of *The Missionary Review of the World* expressed similar excitement about "the thousand-fold enlarged

Gospel possibilities in Russia" after its simultaneous "political and religious emancipation."[108]

## The Bolshevik challenge and American answers

While such evangelical enthusiasm persisted, the initial American euphoria about a new Russian government and a revitalized Russian army soon evaporated. After bread riots, strikes, and soldiers' rebellions in Petrograd broke the autocracy's hold on the empire, two centers of authority emerged: a provisional government composed of conservative and liberal politicians from the tsarist parliament; and a soviet (or council) of workers' and soldiers' deputies, led by socialist intellectuals. The provisional government grew increasingly unpopular as it sought to continue the war against the Central Powers, failed to cope with economic disruptions, and postponed settlement of disputes between peasants and aristocrats over control of land. Although the moderate socialist leaders of the soviet expressed more sympathy with the demands of war-weary soldiers, militant workers, and land-hungry peasants, they hesitated to take power or even to oppose the provisional government. Radical socialists, especially Bolsheviks led by V. I. Lenin, skillfully exploited this situation by promising to bring peace, secure bread for the cities, and authorize peasants to seize land.

Since the United States had entered the war against Germany in April but was not ready to send large American armies to Europe, the Wilson administration was determined to keep Russian forces fighting on the eastern front, even though that jeopardized the stabilization of a relatively free Russia. Within the constraints of that policy, political leaders, diplomats, and propagandists sought to buttress the provisional government and counter the rising radicalism, particularly by offering moral support in high-minded statements, providing loans for the purchase of war matériel, and organizing pro-war publicity campaigns.

One of the primary tactics in the propaganda effort was to play on Russian admiration of America as an advanced industrial society and an idealistic democracy, different from the grasping imperialist powers.[109] Thanks in part to letters from immigrants who boasted about their success in America and in part to cheap popular fiction stories set in a fabulously wealthy United States, positive images of America were indeed widespread in Russia in early 1917.[110] However, it was a mistake to think that Russians' diffuse and fantastic admiration of America would inspire them to fight more valiantly against Germany after years of horrendous losses. It was also a mistake to think that a propaganda campaign stressing America's awesome productivity and Wilson's lofty principles could keep the Bolsheviks from surging to power on a wave of class hatred and anti-war sentiment.

Ironically, one of the most important problems for the publicity campaigns was the sharply contrasting view of the United States conveyed by Russians who returned from America with bitter tales of racial discrimination and capitalist exploitation. Arthur Bullard, who joined the Committee on Public Information (CPI) and spearheaded much of its work in revolutionary Russia, reported that soon after the overthrow of the tsarist government "the exodus of Russian Jewish revolutionists from the East Side began. . . . And they've been busy hating America at the top of their voices ever since." Ernest Poole, who also worked for the CPI, similarly observed the anti-Americanism of "the Bolshevik exiles, returning to Russia from New York." Raymond Robins, a leader of an American Red Cross mission to Russia who likewise engaged in a pro-war propaganda campaign, concurred that "the returning American Russians have been making great trouble" and added: "the hardest nut we have to crack here is the industrial injustice and exploitation of our Free America."[111]

Missionaries shared with the propagandists the assumption that Americans had special opportunities to exert influence in Russia – not only because they represented a prosperous modern country but also because they espoused a progressive Protestantism. As economic and political conditions in Russia deteriorated in the fall of 1917, George Simons informed the leading Methodist newspaper that a Protestant ethic was the cure for Russia's ills. "Only vital, practical Christianity, sane evangelism and Christian education with Anglo-American ideals and spirit," he declared, "can purge Russia's benighted millions of semi-pagan superstitions, evil practices, mariolatry, saint and ikon worship."[112] Even after Bolsheviks seized power in Petrograd in November 1917, missionaries encouraged faith in an American solution for Russia's problems. Thus, urging Pentecostals to go to Russia, evangelist Andrew Urshan asserted in 1918 that "over one hundred and eighty million souls in Russia are eagerly looking toward America for political, commercial and religious help."[113]

President Wilson was not so sure of that. For several months after the Bolsheviks took control and withdrew from the war against Germany, Wilson hesitated to authorize military intervention in Russia, in part because of uncertainty about how Russians would respond to the presence of foreign troops. In June and July 1918, though, as he decided to dispatch military expeditions to northern Russia and eastern Siberia, Wilson received assurances from several sources – including the head of Siberian cooperative societies, an American Red Cross official, and former leaders of the provisional government – that patriotic Russians would rally around the US forces and throw off the yoke of Bolshevism. Wilson alluded to such evidence that the Russian people desired the limited military expeditions when he typed an explanation of his decision to send troops that would "steady any efforts at self-government or self-defence in which the Russians themselves may be willing to accept assistance."[114]

After making that difficult decision, Wilson received further assurances that he had done the right thing. John Mott, the head of the YMCA and an unofficial adviser to Wilson on Russian affairs, told the president that he had been "Providentially guided" in his policy toward Russia, and praised his sympathy with the aspirations of a "'dark people' groping after larger light and liberty." George Kennan, whom Secretary of State Robert Lansing trusted as America's foremost expert on Russia, predicted, in a letter Lansing showed Wilson, that the military expedition to Siberia would inspire popular uprisings that "might bring about the overthrow of the Bolsheviki everywhere."[115]

Such assurances were misleading. The expeditions of roughly 5,000 men to northern Russia and 8,000 men to eastern Siberia were too small to inspire confidence that the Bolshevik menace would be crushed for good. The presence of arrogant British commanders in northern Russia and alien Japanese troops in eastern Siberia antagonized many Russians. So many of Russia's bravest young men had been killed, maimed, or radicalized by the war against the Central Powers, that few remained to rally around the Stars and Stripes. In Siberia some Russians did at first welcome Americans. As one CPI agent who arrived in September 1918 remembered, local government officials glowed with a "dream of constructing a United States of Russia cast in the mold of the United States of America." Yet even such friendly figures were alienated by the passivity of the American expeditionary force, whose role was limited to patrolling the railways and guarding Vladivostok. In addition, the moderate socialists who were the most popular political representatives in Siberia were undermined and antagonized by US diplomats' support for authoritarian officers who seized control of Siberia in the fall of 1918.[116] For those and other reasons, the expeditions failed to help Russians liberate themselves from Soviet rule and turned into major embarrassments for the Wilson administration.[117]

The expeditionary forces were not the only ways in which Americans sought to help non-Bolshevik Russians. Indeed, before he approved the military expeditions, Wilson had intended to make a humanitarian relief mission, led by John Mott, the main thrust of US policy in Siberia.

Yet when Mott declined the position plans for economic aid were set back. Although American railroad experts made heroic efforts to unsnarl the railways, the economic assistance provided by the War Trade Board never amounted to much.[118] The YMCA, the American Red Cross, and the American Relief Administration did distribute food, clothing, and medicine to Russian civilians and to soldiers in anti-Bolshevik armies, not only in Siberia but also in northern Russia, the Baltic states, and southern Russia. Yet those efforts only partially alleviated the human suffering in a protracted civil war.

Some progressive activists urged the United States to do much more. Arthur Bullard, who headed the Committee on Public Information's work in Siberia when it was controlled by anti-Bolshevik forces, dreamed of building "100,000 little red school houses" all across the country and urged a major international effort for "the regeneration of Russia." John Spargo, another veteran of the settlement house and socialist movements, called for Americans to take responsibility for "the economic reconstruction of Russia." Writing in the fall of 1919, when major offensives by White armies made it seem "that the overthrow of the Bolshevist government was a matter of a few days at most," Spargo argued that Americans had a moral duty "to save Russia."[119]

Such appeals were in vain. Wilson and his advisors were preoccupied first with defeating Germany, then with negotiating a peace treaty. Facing an "isolationist" backlash against its international crusade as well as criticism of the small military expeditions to Russia, the Wilson administration could not contemplate sending more troops. It did secretly approve the shipment of millions of dollars worth of military supplies to anti-Bolshevik forces, but it could not provide what the authoritarian White leaders most sorely lacked: the support and confidence of the majority of the Russian people.[120]

### From dream to nightmare: the demonization of Bolshevik Russia

While Reds and Whites battled in Russia, Americans battered the specter of Bolshevism, which came to signify, more than tsarism ever had, the evil antithesis of Americanism. Some of those who had done the most to raise hopes for the creation of a free, democratic Russia now took the lead in stoking hatred of Bolshevism. Soon after returning from Russia, in February 1919, Methodist missionary George Simons was called to testify before a Senate committee investigating Bolshevik revolutionary propaganda that received sensational coverage in newspapers. Recounting his experiences and observations in red Petrograd, Simons repeatedly characterized the Bolshevik spirit as not merely "cruel" but "hellish," "diabolical," and "anti-Christ." In September 1919, after an American diplomat who had served in Moscow urged him to publicly condemn "the evil fatuity of Bolshevism," President Wilson repeatedly decried that ideological "poison." The Bolshevik revolution represented not merely a rival political movement; it constituted "the negation of everything that is American."[121]

William English Walling attacked the Bolsheviks even more aggressively and relentlessly. Although Walling's Episcopalianism may have lapsed, his anti-Bolshevism was fervent. In 1918, after the Bolsheviks signed a peace treaty with Germany, Walling pronounced an anathema upon "the Lenine sect." Over the next two years, that curse remained a favorite part of his rhetorical arsenal. Especially in *Sovietism* (1920), Walling repeatedly assailed Bolshevism in religious terms: he pilloried the "Bolshevist high-priests" and condemned them as militant atheists. More interestingly, Walling charged that the Bolsheviks were "anti-religious fanatics as violent in their beliefs as any of the superstitious religious fanatics of past centuries" and indignantly complained that they were "hiding from the Russian peasant that there are in the world any religious people, . . . except the grossly superstitious with which they are familiar." Thus, in Walling's eyes, the Bolsheviks appear to have replaced "superstitious" Orthodox priests as rivals for molding the pliable character of the Russian people.[122]

While religious language figured prominently in anti-Bolshevik crusaders' vituperation, it also glowed in the admiration of the Soviet revolutionary project by Americans who saw it as parallel, not opposite, to their own social creed. For example, Lillian Wald, leader of the Henry Street settlement and member of the executive committee of the Friends of Russian Freedom, viewed the Russian Revolution as "a spiritual force," believed Bolshevism represented a quest to improve the conditions of life for the masses, and was eager to see her ideas about nursing reforms adopted in Soviet Russia.[123] Raymond Robins' thinking illustrates the point even more powerfully. A veteran of the Chicago settlement movement and an electrifying evangelist, Robins first became prominent in the crusade for a free Russia in 1908, when he organized the successful defense of a revolutionary whom the tsarist government sought to extradite. In 1918, after participating in a futile propaganda campaign to keep the Bolsheviks from coming to power, Robins became convinced that the Soviet government represented the Russians' best hope for the building of a better life. The United States missed a great opportunity to contribute to that construction, he felt: if it had accepted Lenin's proposals for trade, which Robins brought back to America, it "could have furnished the economic brain of Russia." At the frenzied height of the Red Scare, Robins' social Christian vision moved him to be one of the most vigorous opponents of further military intervention and the most tireless advocate of diplomatic recognition of Soviet Russia. As his biographer concludes, "Robins was a missionary . . . in the cause of the social gospel and social justice in Russia as well as in the United States."[124] The clash between anti-Bolsheviks like Walling and Soviet sympathizers like Wald and Robins, then, is best seen not as a conflict between righteous anti-communists and naïve proponents of the Sovietization of America, but as a divergence between two different wings of an American missionary drive.

If religion was one of the major fault lines that divided former colleagues in the movement for a free Russia, the second deep fissure had to do with ethnicity. The marriage bonds between Anglo-American gentlemen and radical Jewish women formed around the time of the revolution of 1905 were shaken severely by the Bolshevik revolution. While William English Walling became a scourge of Bolshevism, Anna Strunsky Walling continued to associate the revolution with "liberty for the common man" or "class freedom," despite being disturbed by Bolshevik brutality. While Graham Phelps Stokes left the Socialist Party in 1917 and then attacked "Bolshevist propaganda" in America, Rose Pastor Stokes asked to be readmitted to the Socialist Party soon after the Bolshevik revolution and went on to be one of the top leaders of the new Communist Party. For Jewish radicals and likeminded Protestants such as Raymond Robins, in spite of the Bolsheviks' ruthlessness, Soviet Russia still reflected "liberation" of the country from the savagery of tsarist anti-Semitism.[125]

In contrast, many foes of the Soviet regime connected it to a malignant Jewish conspiracy. George Simons testified to highly receptive Senators that "more than half of the agitators in the so-called Bolshevik movement were Yiddish" and that the movement could not have succeeded without the support it got from the East Side of New York. To the Senators and many other Americans, the idea of Jewish radicals from America fomenting the revolution in Russia was part of what made Bolshevism seem so "monstrous."[126] Like Simons, Washington officials such as the private secretary to Secretary of State Robert Lansing and military intelligence officers credited the thesis of the fraudulent "Protocols of the Elders of Zion" that the Bolshevik seizure of power was part of a Jewish plot for world domination.[127]

While many thus viewed Soviet leaders as "Hebrews" or "apostate Jews," others regarded them as agents of Imperial Germany, paid to demoralize Russia's armed forces and overthrow the provisional government. Within days after the Bolshevik seizure of power, President Wilson publicly implied that they were tools of Germany. A year later he authorized the Committee on Public Information to publish a collection of purchased documents (later shown to be forgeries) that purported to prove the existence of a German-Bolshevik conspiracy. George Kennan fostered this theory by calling the Bolsheviks "a *camarilla* of usurpers, looters, and German agents." The idea gained further circulation at the Senate hearings in early 1919, when Simons recalled being told in Petrograd, "This is not a Russian Government: this is a German and Hebrew Government."[128]

Much as President Wilson had asserted in April 1917 that the Romanov autocracy "was not in fact Russian in origin, character, or purpose," many Americans now held that the Bolshevik dictatorship was not authentically Russian. This permitted them to continue to have faith – as Kennan, Walling, and others had encouraged them to believe – that Russia's true destiny was to be a democracy like the United States.[129]

## 3 Doors opened and closed: opportunities and obstructions in early Soviet Russia, 1921–40

In the spring of 1927, Paul Peterson, an elder of the Christ Covenant-Glad Tidings Assembly in Chicago, returned from a tour of Europe and delivered a long address on "Mighty Movings of the Spirit in Russia, Poland, and Latvia," which was published in full in the lead Pentecostal newspaper. After the revolution of 1917, Peterson recalled, many Russians "had turned away from God," but then they had been afflicted with a famine so severe that numerous families resorted to cannibalism. "Due to the judgments of God in the land," Russians began to call upon Him again. Now, Peterson exclaimed, "there has come a mighty revival, and it is possibly the greatest spiritual awakening in the history of the Christian church," with millions converted.

In the following years, Peterson and other Pentecostal leaders repeatedly exhorted their denomination to seize "the greatest missionary opportunity of our time" by funding the evangelization of Russia. Even after Bolsheviks launched a vicious persecution of Protestant churches in the late 1920s, the Pentecostal crusade persisted. "Despite the efforts of our adversaries to close the door," Peterson declared in 1931, "it still remains open and millions of white people are waiting for the message of life." As late as 1939, Pentecostal evangelists worked feverishly, "while the door is open," among Russians in eastern Poland. After Soviet troops occupied that area, Pentecostal missionaries hoped their converts would be able to spread Bibles and "proclaim the gospel" inside the expanded borders of the Soviet Union, though they conceded that the door was now "closed."[1]

As the story of Pentecostal evangelism begins to suggest, the Red victory in the Russian civil war did not halt the American missionary drive. For several American religious denominations – especially Adventists, Baptists, and Pentecostals – the 1920s were a period of extraordinary opportunity in Soviet Russia, when Bolshevik toleration of Protestant "sects" allowed them to grow rapidly. Beyond funding Christian evangelism, Americans were involved in a variety of efforts to uplift Russia during the next two decades. When the horrible famine of the early 1920s led the Soviet government to invite the American Relief Administration to distribute food in their country, ARA leaders saw a chance to encourage Russians to emancipate themselves from Bolshevik despotism. In the late 1920s and early 1930s, the Soviet government invited foreign (particularly American) companies and engineers to assist a crash program of industrialization. While many of the engineers simply welcomed gainful employment during the depression in the United States, some saw their work as an idealistic contribution to the modernization of Russia. Although the Kremlin curtailed its recruitment of such foreign assistance by 1933, in that year it opened diplomatic relations with Washington, and the first US diplomats to enter the Soviet Union quickly sought to expand American cultural influence in the country.

In light of all that American involvement in the Soviet Union, the decades between the two world wars must be seen as a part of, not a long pause in, the American drive to remake Russia. Contrary to the conventional view that after the Bolsheviks seized power they immediately isolated Russia from the world,[2] Soviet leaders actively sought foreign (and especially American) participation in the education of the Russian people and the modernization of the Russian economy. Bolshevik leader V. I. Lenin's formula that socialism would result from the combination of "Soviet power + Prussian railway order + American technology and organization of trusts + American public education" was only one of many expressions of Bolshevik desires to utilize American machines and solder an American mentality onto a Russian revolutionary spirit.[3] While vehement anticommunists sought to keep America's doors closed to Soviet propaganda, diplomacy, and trade, many other Americans eagerly entered the doors Bolsheviks opened. To understand the complex ways Americans thought about such opportunities, we must look not only at the ideas of liberal intellectuals (who have been the object of much scholarly attention),[4] but also at the views of religious leaders, journalists, and engineers.

Central to the thinking of many Americans about early Soviet Russia were religious beliefs and sentiments. Like the Christian missionaries, Americans who went to Russia to distribute famine relief often felt impelled by a sense of religious duty.[5] Both sympathizers and opponents of the Soviet experiment commonly viewed Bolshevism as being like a religion, with a fervent faith, a missionary zeal to spread their creed, scripture (the writings of Marx and Lenin), martyrs, saints, and sacred relics (particularly the body of Lenin, embalmed and entombed after his death in 1924). Admirers of Soviet Russia, especially left-leaning Protestants, frequently regarded Bolshevism as effective Christianity: it seemed to embody the sacrificial spirit and egalitarian ethics that they believed their own churches had lost or been unable to implement in the United States.[6] On the other hand, foes of Bolshevism frequently identified godlessness as the essential feature that marked the Soviet Union as the demonic opposite of the United States.[7] This sentiment was most graphically conveyed in a 1923 political cartoon, that showed the light of heaven shining down upon benighted Russia while a Bolshevik tried to paint over the light with blood. (See figure 11.)

Russia thus continued to be a screen on which Americans projected their hopes and fears. "Russia is all things to all men," observed *The Literary Digest* in 1923. "Either it is a land where even hope is stagnant or a new Canaan for the weary and opprest [sic]." Enthusiasts upheld Soviet policies as remedies for American maladies. For example, novelist Theodore Dreiser extolled the way Bolsheviks freed minds from religious dogma that he associated with the suffocating Catholic Church in America, while economist George Soule applauded Moscow's purposeful planning in contrast to Washington's planless drift. On the other hand, detractors maligned Soviet coercive collectivism as the opposite of American individualism.[8]

As they debated about the Soviet Union, Americans often shadowboxed their domestic opponents. Thus, fundamentalist Christians repeatedly invoked the specter of atheist Russia as an omen of the "wickedness and lawlessness" to which liberal modernism was leading America.[9] In return, avowed modernists implicitly rebuked "fundamentalists" in America when they derided the "obscurantist" Orthodox Church and Protestant "sectarians" in Russia who clung "to a literal interpretation of the Bible and an outworn cosmology."[10]

Paradoxically, in a period when Russians were denied political liberty by a dictatorship that grew increasingly violent and autocratic, many Americans hailed different forms of freedom in the Soviet Union. Liberal Protestants set aside the Bolshevik campaign against the Orthodox Church and (at least in the 1920s) acclaimed "the establishment of religious freedom under the Soviets." Many American Jews who had emigrated from the tsarist empire tended to see early Soviet Russia as a land freed from anti-Semitic discrimination. African American radicals often depicted the Soviet Union as a haven from racist oppression. Champions of progress celebrated the Soviet mechanization of agriculture, with Ford tractors hailed as the liberator of the farmer. Supporters of women's rights cheered the enfranchisement and supposed emancipation of Soviet women. Perhaps most important and most classically American, liberals applauded the way the Bolsheviks seemed to have freed Russia from

A LIGHT THAT WILL NEVER FAIL!
—Cargill in the Kansas City *Journal-Post*.

Figure 11. "A Light That Will Never Fail!" Cartoon by Cargill in the Kansas City *Journal Post*. Reprinted in *The Literary Digest*, April 14, 1923.

its past by breaking the ancient ideological bonds, destroying the carriers of old ideas, and adopting a progressive, American-style educational system.[11]

This did not mean that most Americans who traveled to Soviet Russia were passive "pilgrims" who revered all they saw.[12] Contrary to that caricature, key sympathizers with the Soviet experiment reproached its dilatory bureaucracy, chastised its atheism, and sought to redeem it from such errors. Thus, Americans from the modernist left as well as the fundamentalist right embarked on missions to Soviet Russia that carried far-reaching implications for dynamics in the United States.

### Relief missions

In the summer of 1921, a terrible famine began to ravage Soviet Russia. As a result of Bolshevik grain requisitioning during the civil war and protracted drought in the spring of 1921, peasants in the hardest-hit region along the Volga River were reduced to eating grass, leaves, bark, and even human flesh. Unable to cope with the crisis, the Soviet government allowed the famous writer Maxim Gorky to call for aid, and then itself reluctantly appealed to foreign countries for help.[13]

Among the first to respond were Quakers. The American Friends Service Committee, which had distributed food and clothing in Russia earlier, rushed to resume its relief work. However, by far the most extensive aid was provided by the American Relief Administration, a nominally private organization headed by Secretary of Commerce Herbert Hoover. Under an agreement with the Soviet government signed in August 1921, the ARA sent almost 300 relief workers into Soviet Russia, employed 120,000 Russians as assistants, and saved the lives of millions.[14]

In addition to being moved by genuine humanitarian sentiment, influential Americans hoped that the distribution of famine relief would lead to the freeing of Russia from Bolshevism. As early as July 25, 1921, anticommunist activist John Spargo suggested to Secretary of State Charles Evans Hughes that "the crisis presents an opportunity which, if rightly used, may lead to the liquidation of the Bolshevist regime and the beginning of restoration." Since the communist regime had been unable to deal with the calamity, Spargo, Hoover, and others believed that effective aid from the United States would discredit the Soviet system and demonstrate the superiority of the American way. Once American food enabled Russians to regain their physical strength, it was vaguely hoped, they would recover the moral courage to throw off their incompetent oppressors. More concretely, Spargo and Russian exiles proposed that funnelling food through a non-Bolshevik civilian famine relief committee in Russia might empower such a committee to supplant the Soviet government.[15]

Intensely suspicious of possible ulterior motives and subversive intrigues, Soviet leaders ordered the dissolution of the All-Russian Famine Relief Committee as soon as ARA officers entered the country, and then insisted on close surveillance of ARA representatives. In part because of such measures (including the arrest or exile of non-Bolshevik members of the Famine Relief Committee), there was no chance for American visions of the freeing of Russia to be realized. As Colonel William Haskell, director of the ARA operation, reported from Moscow in the fall of 1921, the Soviet government had such a "strangle hold on Russia" that "no opposition dares raise its head."[16]

Nevertheless, the ARA mission had deep and broad impacts on both Soviet and American attitudes. While the distribution of food did not galvanize the emergence of non-governmental organizations, the ARA's employment of thousands of educated Russians did keep alive many members of the intelligentsia and bourgeoisie who embodied pre-revolutionary culture. Although some Russians initially suspected that Americans came to grab control of precious natural resources and others criticized the coldness or arrogance they saw in ARA officers, the dominant popular response was admiration for the relief workers' generosity, energy, and efficiency. Consequently, the ARA's presence in Soviet Russia powerfully reinforced the pre-existing image of "golden America" as a land of magical abundance. It also led to a broader use of the word *Amerikanizm* to refer to a fast-paced, hard-working ethos. Those attitudes did not entail a simple division between popular pro-American sentiment and government-propagated xenophobia. Top Soviet leaders actually enthusiastically embraced the ARA workers as models of businesslike effectiveness, and Bolshevik newspapers repeatedly upheld the vigorous Americans as examples to be emulated by a new type of Russian, an "American Russian."[17]

On their part, American relief workers often saw themselves as agents of social and cultural transformation. While some disparaged Russians as hopelessly passive, listless, and fatalistic – in short, "Oriental" – many others zealously talked about "bringing order out of chaos" and spreading their idea of civilization. As Bertrand Patenaude observes in his excellent and exhaustive study, the ARA men tended to be "crusaders of the Protestant ethic" and "missionaries of a kind."[18]

The idea of the ARA as comparable to religious missions certainly figured prominently in reports to America. At the outset of ARA operations in the fall of 1921, Colonel Haskell warned that "millions of Christian people in Russia face certain death" unless massive assistance arrived soon, and he urged that "as a Christian nation" America had to make a greater effort to avert that tragedy. Two years later, as the ARA ended its work, Haskell informed Hoover that "the Russian common people" regarded the ARA as "a miracle of God which came to them in their darkest hour under the stars and stripes." ARA officers who served under

Haskell widely propagated the notion that Russians worshiped them and the United States. As one ARA man told the Associated Press in 1922, "America is a holy name in Russia and Americans are regarded as super-beings." While few Americans may have desperately needed reassurance about the superiority of their way of life in the booming 1920s, many doubtless found it gratifying to read such accounts that reaffirmed the image of America as a philanthropic nation and a beacon to less fortunate peoples.[19]

### Religious missions

In the first decade of Soviet rule, communist hostility to religion focused above all on the Orthodox Church. The Soviet regime revoked the privileged legal status the church had enjoyed under the autocracy, seized church lands and valuables, imprisoned and killed many leading clergymen, took over church-run schools, and launched an intense propaganda campaign led by the League of the Militant Godless.[20]

Many Americans condoned or justified the persecution of the Orthodox Church. Much like the first crusaders for a "free Russia" in the late nineteenth century, secular and religious liberals depicted the Orthodox Church as a morally corrupt and politically reactionary obstruction that had to be eliminated. After touring the Soviet Union in 1929, for example, Oswald Garrison Villard, editor of *The Nation*, praised the Soviet state for having struck "from the peasants the shackles the orthodox Russian church placed upon their spirits and their entire mental development." It was better, Villard elaborated, "that the churches should all be closed than that they should be continued as the handmaidens of ignorance, as teachers of degradation, of superstition, of fetish- and image-worship." Although Villard had an idiosyncratic and dogmatic interpretation of Christ's ethical teachings, his cold-eyed condemnation of the Orthodox Church was typical. Like Villard, a correspondent for the avowedly ecumenical *Christian Century* downplayed the Soviet campaign against religion, reporting that in Moscow "young people wear atheistic badges, but it is only in protest against the pagan church of the past."[21]

Since the Orthodox Church had sided with the Whites in the Russian civil war, the YMCA evangelist Sherwood Eddy and others suggested that the Bolshevik repression of the Orthodox clergy was a justified form of self-defense. Since Orthodox priests had not provided moral teaching for the Russian people and had not encouraged direct, individual relationships with God, both radical and fundamentalist Protestants argued, Orthodoxy was not "true Christianity." Indeed, Soviet hostility to the Orthodox Church seemed to serve a divine purpose; by loosening the church's grip on the Russian people, it created great opportunities for Protestant evangelism. Communist anti-religious propaganda posed "no danger for real spiritual religion, but rather is an indirect ally to it," declared a radical Methodist. "God is doing a gracious work in eliminating the 'wood, hay and stubble' of religious formalism," a Pentecostal paper explained in 1928.[22]

Thus, not for the last time, many Americans stood not for a general principle (in this case, religious freedom), but for a specific outcome (the conversion of Russians to Protestantism or the development of a "higher," "purer" religion). The persecution of the Orthodox Church could be justified both in the name of hastening the second coming of Christ, and in the interest of building a Kingdom of God on Earth. With their eyes set on the future, Christian evangelists and liberal humanitarians shed few tears for an atavistic creed destined for the dustbin of history.

Protestant groups inside Soviet Russia benefited both tangibly and intangibly from the Bolshevik attacks on the Orthodox Church. After the state seized Orthodox buildings, Protestant "sectarians" arranged to rent them. When Bolsheviks forced open the coffins of Orthodox saints, many evangelical Christians applauded the move against "superstition." In this context, there was a tacit alliance between Protestants and Bolsheviks through most of the 1920s. Key Soviet officials looked favorably upon the energy and sobriety of the Protestants. In turn, many Baptists and Evangelical Christians (the two largest groups of "sectarians") presented themselves as partners in the building of socialism.[23]

Protestant leaders in both the Soviet Union and the United States sometimes wildly exaggerated the growth of their denominations. In 1927, for example, one Pentecostal evangelist reported estimates that in the "marvelous revival" since the Bolshevik seizure of power, "thirteen millions of Russians have been saved." (That would have been almost a tenth of the population of the Soviet Union then.) Despite such fantastic claims, it is clear that the Baptists, Evangelical Christians, Pentecostals, Adventists, and others grew rapidly in the 1920s. The membership of most of the denominations seems to have doubled or tripled. Pentecostal churches, which first began to be formed in Russia during the First World War, counted 25,000 members by 1929. Adventist membership grew from about 6,000 in 1920 to 14,000 in 1929. Baptists rose to 200,000 adherents by 1929.[24]

American efforts to support and lead the development of Protestant religious groups in Soviet Russia in the 1920s were often spearheaded by immigrants to the United States who returned to their native lands. In 1921, for example, J. E. Voronaeff (I. E. Voronaev) sailed with his family from New York to Odessa, where he assumed leadership of the

Assemblies of God. Similarly, G. H. Schmidt, the descendant of German colonists in the tsarist empire, returned from Los Angeles to lead Pentecostal evangelism in Poland and western Russia.[25] Although the number of such missionaries was not large – probably fewer than a dozen – their efforts were prominently publicized by popular magazines as well as denominational papers. The most dramatic and controversial of all these efforts centered on a radical Methodist, Dr. Julius F. Hecker.

Born in St. Petersburg in 1881, Hecker became involved in the Russian revolutionary movement and then emigrated to America. After converting to Methodism in New York, he studied theology at the Drew and Union seminaries. He then went on to earn a Ph.D. in political science at Columbia, writing a dissertation that reflected his continuing sympathy with opponents of the Russian autocracy. In the 1910s Hecker's work reflected his deep commitment to "the social Gospel": he served as a pastor to Russian immigrants in a New York church, headed the Russian section of the East Side Parish Settlement from 1910 to 1916, and worked with the Prisoners of War service of the YMCA in Europe from 1916 to 1917. As revolutions shook Russia, Hecker's radical views made him a target for Red-hunters in America: his belief that capitalism conflicted with Christianity prompted YMCA leaders to ask him to resign from that organization, and his opposition to US intervention in Soviet Russia spurred the Justice Department to blacklist him "as Bolshevik."[26]

Although Hecker left America under a cloud of suspicion, that did not deter key Methodist leaders from embracing him as a subtle evangelist inside Soviet Russia. Frank North, the secretary of the Methodist missionary board who had helped to craft the "social creed" of Methodism years earlier, respected Hecker's dedication, was deeply interested in his possible role in Russia, and provided a monthly subsidy to his family after their departure from the United States. Bishop John L. Nuelsen, who supervised Methodist work in eastern Europe from Zurich, had concluded in 1917 that "no other country will present after the war such a tremendous opportunity as Russia," and he viewed Hecker as uniquely qualified for work there. In 1921 Nuelsen and North commissioned Hecker to enter Soviet Russia, distribute famine relief, and report on conditions in the country.[27]

Much as leaders of the American Relief Administration initially hoped that the distribution of food would serve as an entering wedge for wider political influence and commercial opportunities, Hecker advised North that humanitarian aid and educational work would facilitate the entry of more Methodist representatives into Russia, where they would then "be quite free to put across the whole program." As Hecker's wife, Elizabeth, excitedly explained in 1922, Soviet leaders in charge of education warmly welcomed Hecker to Moscow and enlisted him to organize a nationwide program of correspondence courses. Since Hecker had gained the "complete confidence" of figures such as Lenin's wife, Nadezhda Krupskaia, and Commissar of Education Anatolii Lunacharskii, he would "be able later to open the doors for all those who wish to come and work in Russia unselfishly in the spirit of the Master." In the same vein, Hecker informed Nuelsen in 1923 that if Methodists helped to organize industrial and agricultural settlements for the numerous homeless children in Russia, the settlements "would lend themselves as a base for an extensive evangelization campaign."[28]

While Hecker and other left-leaning Protestants strongly sympathized with what they believed to be the idealistic goals of Bolshevik leaders, they sought not merely to support but also to guide the Soviet government. The global evangelist Sherwood Eddy, who led numerous tours of the Soviet Union in the 1920s and 1930s, sharply criticized the "coarse" anti-religious policies in conversations and debates with leading Communists, hoping "to open a little wider the door of tolerance and religious liberty." The controversial Methodist activist Harry F. Ward, who declared in 1919 that "the aim of the Bolsheviki" to create a state "controlled by producers" was "manifestly a Scriptural aim," also argued that the task of Western sympathizers was to "help them toward the light." Hecker, who had been a student of Ward's, maintained that despite their antipathy to the Orthodox Church, Soviet Communists felt "strongly their kinship with the religious message of the prophets and of Jesus." Citing the Bolsheviks' "spirit of service and their self sacrifice," Hecker argued that "much good could be accomplished by any one who would develop and direct the potential religious forces of the communist movement." Through "an offensive of love," Mrs. Hecker exclaimed in 1922, even the stony Bolsheviks could be led "to turn from their ways." A year later Hecker explained his mission even more emphatically: "My hope and dominant desire," he wrote to North, "is by the preaching of the Gospel to elevate, enoble, Christianize Communism."[29]

Hecker pursued that goal in several ways. First, his correspondence courses, which reached more than 15,000 people (mostly teachers) by late 1923, helped to complete the education of many Russians, which had been interrupted by war and civil war. Although none of the extension courses was on a religious subject, Hecker's influence gave the program "a Christian basis," as Bishop Nuelsen proudly reported. Second, at the invitation of Soviet leaders, Hecker became a professor at a graduate school of pedagogy in Moscow, where he lectured to future teachers and school superintendents on American educational theories and practices, which then keenly interested many Russians.[30] Third and most important, Hecker developed close relations with leaders of the pro-Soviet "renovationist" faction of the Orthodox Church (known as "the Living Church"), who asked him to use the correspondence school method to disseminate knowledge among their clergy and laity. This gave him an extraordinary opportunity for "the evangelization of the Russian Church": by the summer of 1923 he was suggesting topics for sermons and distributing outlines for sermons in thousands of copies.[31]

Using his intimate ties to the Living Church and warm relations with Soviet officials, Hecker facilitated visits to Russia by Methodist leaders, including Nuelsen and Bishop Edgar Blake, who was based in Paris. Conversations with Living Church leaders in the spring of 1923 convinced the Methodist visitors that there were thousands of Russian priests who "sincerely and eagerly search for light and call to us: Come over and help us," as Nuelsen reported to the Methodist Board of Foreign Missions. In the spirit of the moment, Blake impetuously pledged $50,000 for the education of Russian clergy. Troubled by the impression of siding with a faction of the Orthodox Church, the Methodist governing board repudiated Blake's pledge. Beyond the denomination, rumors spread that the Methodists had been duped into thinking that the Living Church leaders "wanted to reorganize Russian Christianity on a Methodist basis." In the aftermath of the Soviet execution of the Vicar-General of the Roman Catholic Church in Russia, the idea of collaborating with the pro-Soviet Living Church provoked wide indignation, and Blake was denounced for his alleged "blessing of Communism."[32]

Undeterred, Blake and Nuelsen appealed for funds on their own. In a brochure, Blake declared that "It is within our power, if we will, to shape in a large measure the evangelistic and social ideals of the Russian Church, and to determine in a large degree the lines of its future development." And in a circular letter the bishops proclaimed that "God has opened a providential door . . . through which . . . Methodism may help to save Russia and the Russian people."[33] Thus, it should be underlined, the bishops articulated in their Christian idiom two of the cardinal assumptions that underpinned the wider American Messianic approach to Russia.

Blake and Nuelsen succeeded in raising about $30,000, which allowed the Living Church to open or reopen two seminaries, but their achievement came at the cost of a searing embarrassment to the Methodist Church. In early 1924, North was compelled to end the subsidy to Hecker, because his "rather violent opposition to the organized social order" and his "close identification" with the Soviet regime created "marked difficulties" with the church's financial supporters and board.

For several years Nuelsen then covered Hecker's expenses in distributing lessons on preaching to clergy in Russia (including Baptist, Evangelical, and Adventist pastors, as well as Orthodox priests). During that period, Hecker's relations with Soviet officials began to deteriorate: he stopped working for the Commissariat of Education and he depicted his religious efforts more sharply as a struggle to "combat atheism."[34]

While the Soviet regime had indulged or at least tolerated the small number of Protestants in the early 1920s, it turned sharply against the "sectarians" in the late 1920s. The Soviet anti-religious drive had failed to transform popular beliefs. Although many Orthodox priests had been killed or exiled, believers continued to worship, especially in rural areas, and atheist agitation often intensified the fervor of the faithful. In that context, Bolsheviks came to view the flourishing Protestant churches as dangerous rivals, especially in the competition for the allegiance of young Russians. With financial support from abroad, Protestant denominations could build schools and offer social services that the Soviet government could not match. Since the Protestants had also "done away with the more silly ritualistic practices" of the Orthodox Church, one young communist explained, they were "our most dangerous enemies." In 1929, the Soviet government promulgated a new law to curtail Protestant activity, restricting ministers to preaching at their home churches, barring the dispatch of missionaries to other regions, and forbidding the creation of mutual-aid funds by religious organizations. While the Soviet regime had begun arresting, jailing, and exiling "sectarians" in 1927, at the end of the decade it broadened the persecution. By March 1930, for example, Voronaeff and the other Pentecostal leaders in Russia were all imprisoned, with several ministers sent to the dreaded Solovetsky Island in the White Sea.[35]

The expansion of Soviet religious persecution provoked widespread condemnation in America that was more intense and enduring than the denunciations of anti-Christian "evil" had been in 1923. "Red Russia's reported crucifixion of all faiths and mockery of God has at last set the whole world ablaze with indignation," observed *The Literary Digest*. In a pendular dynamic, the euphoria over opportunities earlier in the decade seems to have heightened the bitterness of denunciations of the new Soviet barriers to religious observance. Many Protestants joined Catholics and Jews in appeals on behalf of persecuted Russians. Representative Hamilton Fish, Jr., of New York proposed a resolution declaring that Soviet actions were "repugnant to the ideals of civilized nations." The interdenominational American Committee on Religious Rights petitioned the President and Senate to refuse to recognize the Soviet government until it halted its persecution of religion. Even liberals like Villard who approved the mustering out of "a corrupt medieval state church" vigorously censured the Bolshevik strike at Protestant sects.[36]

The demonization of Soviet Russia as anti-Christian was not universal; leftist Protestants continued to portray Soviet communism as moving toward fulfillment of the social gospel or the development of a higher religion. As Bolsheviks attacked Protestant "sectarians" in the late 1920s and 1930s, Hecker privately lamented the "many adverse things" that were happening, yet in his public writing and speaking he emphasized the positive. In *Religion Under the Soviets* (1927), he argued that "the Soviet regime is most favorable for true religious expression" and predicted that Soviet economic development would yield "an enormous surplus" of "spiritual energies." In *Religion and Communism* (1933), Hecker again averred that "the coming Communist classless society should be the most favourable environment for the development of a spiritual culture." Hecker also influenced Western views through his prominent friends. When Protestant leaders such as Sherwood Eddy and Harry F. Ward came to the Soviet Union, Hecker served them as translator, host, and guide. They then cited him as an authority and concurred with his views in their own publications. The title page of Ward's book, *In Place of Profit* (1933) graphically conveyed this leftist Protestant perspective with an image of rays of light streaming down from the heavens to illuminate the Soviet people (see figure 12).[37]

However, arguably of greater long-term significance was the way American apocalyptic or premillennial Christians who earlier viewed the Bolshevik seizure of power as part of God's plan for the evangelization of the world now depicted the revolution as a satanic conspiracy. Red Russia's attack upon God was inspired by Satan, Pentecostals repeatedly declared in the 1930s. Citing Ezekiel 38 and 39, Pentecostals and other fundamentalist Christians now firmly identified Russia as the locus of evil in their apocalyptic visions of the future Armageddon – a worldview that would rise in importance as conservative evangelicals flourished and mainstream liberal Protestants faded in the following five decades.[38]

### Developmental missions

In the 1920s and early 1930s, thousands of Americans went to the Soviet Union to contribute to the advancement of agriculture and the development of industries. Many technical experts regarded their work primarily as much needed employment, especially after the onset of the Great Depression in America. However, hundreds of other Americans idealistically viewed their labor as part of the mission of building the first socialist society. Some of these radicals made positive impacts and

Figure 12. Title page of *In Place of Profit: Social Incentives in the Soviet Union*, by Harry F. Ward. Drawing by Lynd Ward. New York, 1933. Reprinted with the permission of Scribner, an imprint of Simon & Schuster Adult Publishing Group, from *in place of profit* by Harry F. Ward. Copyright 1933 by Harry F. Ward; copyright renewed 1961 by Harry F. Ward. All rights reserved.

retained their idealism. Yet many faced hostility from Russian workers, met protracted resistance from Soviet bureaucrats, and experienced bitter failure. Thus, the story of American aid to Soviet economic development can be seen as part of the broader experience of missionary enthusiasm and disillusionment.[39]

Between 1920 and 1924, several hundred Americans, many of whom had emigrated from Russia before the revolutions of 1917, purchased tools, gathered supplies, and moved to Russia to establish farm communes with names that reflected their socialist commitments, such as "Red Banner" and "Proletarian Life." Despite Lenin's personal endorsement of the idea of establishing American agricultural communes in southern Russia as models for the surrounding areas, nearly all the communes failed because of the loss or theft of their equipment, the unsuitability of the land they were given, exorbitant taxation, and other problems.[40]

More widely publicized than the farm communes was an "industrial colony" formed by about 500 Americans in western Siberia. Early in 1922, the radical journal *The Liberator* published an appeal for "American pioneers" to "build up the industries of Siberia in a free environment" and "show the world what free workingmen can do when their genius is unhampered by the profit system." Responding to that call and to an earlier letter from Lenin asking for help from American workers, several hundred leftists set out for the coal mines of the Kuzbas region in 1922 and 1923. Beyond the physical hardships of the rough conditions and a cold winter, the American volunteers faced resistance from aristocratic Russian engineers and tsarist-era managers who viewed the foreigners as threats to their prestige and established practices. Even more disruptive were the clashes between the colony's leaders, who were determined to impose Bolshevik discipline, and members of the Industrial Workers of the World (IWW), who resented such subordination that violated their principles of industrial democracy. As Frank Kennell, a former Unitarian minister from San Francisco, observed, "The IWWs feel that they must either choose to accept wage slavery in a state capitalist enterprise, controlled from above, or to go home." While many of the IWWs did go home, the Americans who stayed succeeded in dramatically boosting the productivity of the coal mines. Despite the friction between the more romantic volunteers and the demands of Bolshevik-style modernization, the industrial colony left a legacy of warm feeling toward Americans among the people of the Kuzbas region long after the colony was absorbed into the Soviet system (according to Marxist writers who sought to appeal to American sentiment in the 1970s and 1980s).[41]

One even more successful project became legendary. In 1927, Hugh L. Cooper, who had supervised construction of three major dams in America, was appointed chief consultant for the building of one of the world's largest dams and hydroelectric plants on the Dnepr River in Ukraine. In public speeches about his experiences, Cooper stressed that he did not believe in communism or socialism, but highlighted the possibilities for cooperation between Americans and Soviets in industrial uplift. Sounding somewhat like a Christian missionary describing the plight of the heathen, Cooper observed that 93 percent of the world's people were "groping in economic darkness with no safe beacon to lead them to light." Well-off Americans thus had a duty to assist the less fortunate. That was feasible in the Soviet Union because Soviet leaders were "strong men" who had "studied intensely how to improve the living conditions of the downtrodden people." In contrast to the "selfish autocracy" that had subjected Russia to "nearly one thousand years of economic slavery," communist leaders showed "a zeal and unselfishness that challenges one's admiration." Moreover, the educable Russian people, "thirsty for knowledge," were "looking particularly to America now for guidance in building a new Russia." Americans could respond to that call, Cooper assured his audience, "without departing from or sacrificing any of our ideals."[42]

Contrary to the notion that anti-Americanism in early Soviet Russia was primarily the product of Kremlin propaganda, engineers often felt that top Bolshevik leaders were their key allies against stonewalling bureaucrats, theory-obsessed engineers, and lazy workers. "[W]e were not liked very well" by the German-trained technicians "we had to break in," Hugh Cooper reported, "but fortunately for us, we had the support of the men at the top," who believed in American experts and wanted to "parallel" American development.[43]

The most striking illustration of this theme can be seen in the experiences of California construction engineer Zara Witkin. Born in 1900 to Jewish parents who had emigrated from Russia, Witkin was electrified by the Bolshevik revolution, which seemed to promise a "more beautiful, more comradely" life for mankind. Excited by the prospect of contributing to the rational remolding of a great nation, Witkin did consulting work for Amtorg, the Soviet commercial agency in America, in the 1920s. Then, at the end of 1929, he was enchanted by the Soviet film, "Her Way," which depicted Russia's struggle "up from darkness, fear and misery, towards self-realization and light." Anticipating "spiritual" rewards from heeding the "great call" of the Soviet Union to "the socially minded technical brotherhood of the world," and obsessed by a desire to meet the actress who played the heroine in the film, Witkin journeyed to Moscow in early 1932.[44]

While waiting to begin work for the Soviet construction industry, Witkin made an inspection tour of southern regions, where he was appalled by the indolence, indifference, and irresponsibility of workers, as well as the confusion and carelessness he blamed on managers. Even before his official employment commenced, Witkin suggested faster, cheaper building techniques, proposed more efficient routing of Moscow tram lines, and devised a system to reduce the amount of time people spent away from work while waiting in queues for scarce goods. Although many of his proposals were declined or only partially adopted, Witkin continued his crusade in the construction industry. Beyond his specific technical recommendations, Witkin planned to form a society of civil engineers to apply professional pressure to apathetic officials, and he sought through numerous personal confrontations to reform Soviet bureaucratic culture. This campaign won the support of some high-ranking leaders and crusading journalists, who encouraged Witkin to believe that the secret police (the GPU) were allies of foreign engineers and that appealing to Joseph Stalin (General Secretary of the Communist Party) was the way to overcome bureaucratic resistance. In his belligerent manner, Witkin boasted to a friend in June 1932, "I will blast my way to Stalin, if necessary, to get my projects accomplished."[45]

For months thereafter, Witkin thought that Stalin had ordered action in response to his appeals. By early 1934, however, Witkin deduced that "the attention of Stalin had been diverted" from his projects and that the bureaucracy had evaded or outlasted his crusade. Bitter that his work had gone "largely unrealized," Witkin left the country in February 1934 and later sharply criticized not only the "unshakable bureaucracy," but also the "brutal and stupid governmental policies" and the "official terrorism" of the GPU.[46]

While publishers declined Witkin's melodramatic memoir, his friend, the journalist Eugene Lyons, told the story of how the idealistic young American had been "profoundly hurt" by his "futile" efforts in the Soviet Union. In his own memoir of disillusionment, *Assignment in Utopia* (1937), Lyons recounted how Witkin "had come to Russia to give himself unreservedly to the task of Soviet construction," but had met suspicion and obstruction from officials whose minds had been poisoned by "a perverted materialism." Thus, through Lyons' widely read book, Witkin's story contributed to rising American awareness of the ways Soviet doors were closing in the late 1930s, when the Soviet Union was racked by an escalating xenophobic hysteria.[47]

## Diplomatic missions

In contrast to American engineers and religious leaders, Republican Presidents and Secretaries of State showed little interest in developments in Soviet Russia between 1920 and 1933. Following the precedent set by the Wilson administration, they rejected diplomatic relations with the Bolshevik renegade until it halted its world revolutionary propaganda, compensated Americans whose assets had been nationalized, and accepted responsibility for the debt of the provisional government of 1917. Only then, President Calvin Coolidge declared, would America be able to come "to the economic and moral rescue of Russia." With the US economy thriving, Republican leaders felt little pressure to relax restrictions on trade with Russia or to ease their demand that Soviet markets be made safe for capitalists. Moreover, maintaining the non-recognition policy had the gratifying effect of affirming the righteous honor of the United States, in contrast to the less scrupulous Europeans who signed trade agreements with the Bolsheviks and sent ambassadors to Moscow in the early 1920s.[48]

While Republican leaders were thus content to wait for a free Russia to emerge at some point in the future, Democrat Franklin D. Roosevelt made it clear soon after he became President in 1933 that he intended to recognize the USSR and press for changes in some of its policies. Although FDR probably viewed recognition of Moscow primarily as a gesture that might deter further Japanese aggression in Asia, he also appears to have hoped that he could induce Soviet leaders to moderate their regime. Acutely aware that establishing diplomatic relations with Soviet Russia could provoke accusations that they were tacitly condoning Bolshevik persecution of religion, Roosevelt and Secretary of State Cordell Hull made the issue of religious freedom a high priority when Soviet Foreign Commissar Maxim Litvinov came to Washington for negotiations in November 1933. In addition to insisting that the Kremlin guarantee Americans the right to worship freely in the Soviet Union, FDR personally appealed to Litvinov as if he were a prodigal son, predicting that when he was on his deathbed he would want "to make his peace with God." Both Litvinov and Soviet leaders in Moscow resisted the US demands as interference in Soviet internal affairs, but after several days of negotiations they relented. Even then, FDR kept hammering away, directing Litvinov to "tell Stalin that the antireligious policy is wrong. God will punish you Russians if you go on persecuting the church." The agreement Roosevelt and Litvinov signed did not include a provision suggested by presidential adviser William Christian Bullitt that "Freedom of conscience be guaranteed in Russia for all Russian citizens," as well as foreigners. Nonetheless, as another presidential counselor observed, FDR appears to have believed that "recognition would be helpful to religious Russians in various ways any imagination can conceive."[49]

Roosevelt's expectation that the pledge on religious freedom for Americans in Russia would assuage opposition to recognition proved well-founded. Even the Catholic press, which had objected vehemently to relations with godless communists, praised the president's championing of the importance of spirituality in what one paper called a "thrilling diplomatic duel" with the emissary of materialist Russia.[50]

Neither Roosevelt nor Bullitt, who went to Moscow as US Ambassador, aggressively pursued the issue of religious freedom in the next few years. Although Bullitt's uncle, an archdeacon, denounced recognition of the "pariah" Soviet Union, Bullitt's own Episcopalian convictions were not so fervent at that time. In correspondence and conversation with FDR and others, Bullitt habitually made religious references, but often in a jocular vein.[51]

However, in his own way, Bullitt did untertake a mission to Moscow. When top Soviet leaders lavished personal attention on him in December 1933, the euphoric Bullitt concluded that Americans could "have a really immense influence" in the Soviet Union. In pursuit of that influence, Bullitt imported polo ponies and equipment to teach Red cavalry commanders how to play that upper class sport, launched the more democratic game of baseball in Russia, and dreamed of building a replica of Thomas Jefferson's Monticello mansion on a prized hill in Moscow. More generally, Bullitt urged his Russian-speaking diplomatic assistants to develop close ties with the Russian people in what one of them, Charles ("Chip") Bohlen, called a "people-to-people campaign."[52]

To Bohlen, George F. Kennan and other American diplomats who served under Bullitt, the doors to Soviet Russia seemed to be open during their first year in Moscow. That was a time when the USSR not only established diplomatic relations with the United States but also entered the League of Nations; hence, it seemed to Bohlen that "the isolation of the Soviet Union was ending." Until the popular Soviet leader Sergei Kirov was murdered in December 1934, Kennan remembered, "the Russian state had been developing along lines which, while hardly democratic, at least presaged a certain decentralization of authority and a more liberal approach to the outside world." Top generals, who hoped to throw off control by the "Byzantine" Bolshevik party, "enjoyed association with foreigners and travel abroad, Kennan continued, while "their wives were interested in Paris fashions." Such people, Kennan concluded, "were hoping to lean on the outside world, and to learn from it."[53]

With the assassination of Kirov, however, the doors began to close. The "rise of a new gang of young and ruthless party careerists" led, Kennan observed, to bloody purges (especially of older, more cosmopolitan Bolsheviks) and to a climate of fear so intense that few dared have contact with foreigners. Back in Washington in 1938, Kennan still maintained that "the Russian people are eager for cultural contacts with foreign countries, particularly with the United States." But the Soviet regime, like earlier Russian governments, felt that it could not "risk extensive foreign influence upon the popular mind for any length of time." Preferring "to keep their people in darkness rather than risk illumination by contact with foreign culture and foreign ideas," the Kremlin pulled down a curtain of terror between the Russian people and representatives of the outside world.[54]

These experiences and observations in the mid-1930s exerted deep and lasting influence on the American diplomats. In an extreme pendular swing, the volatile Bullitt's illusions about exerting immense influence on Russia would turn after 1935 to the bitterest enmity toward the "Asiatic despotism" of the Bolsheviks. Even more important, Kennan's conviction that Russians needed to learn from Americans such things as "our sense of personal independence" and his desire to breach the barriers erected by the Stalinist state would underpin his approach in the next decade, when he would rise to become a prime architect of US policy toward the Soviet Union.[55]

## Soviet xenophobia and American demonology

Sympathetic interest in the Soviet experiment persisted in the late 1930s, especially among liberal and radical Protestants. Joseph Davies, a wealthy lawyer whom FDR dispatched to Moscow in 1936 to replace Bullitt, was one of those who continued to highlight a parallel between Christian ethics and Soviet communist aspirations "to better the conditions of life of common men." The faith instilled by Davies' mother, a Congregational preacher, inclined him to accept the idea "that all believers in Christ and Christ's teachings are theoretical communists, to the degree that they are 'for' the brotherhood of men." As Davies reported in 1937, he was impressed not only by the "economic progress" in Russia, which was "quite remarkable," but also by the audacious Soviet effort to "bring society to a selfless motive in human conduct."[56]

Further to the left than Davies, ex-Congregational minister Albert Rhys Williams extolled the way communism allowed man to move beyond guilt and sin and realize his full potential.[57] More influential than either Davies or Williams was Sherwood Eddy, whom Soviet officials had long regarded as "sympathetic" and "helpful." Although Eddy grew increasingly concerned about the "evils of the Soviet system" (bureaucracy, lack of liberty, "ruthless violence," and "dogmatic atheism"), he continued to put more emphasis on the "advances" it was making. In several widely read books and numerous articles and lectures, he repeatedly opposed the demonization of the Soviet Union as so unmitigatedly evil that Anglo-Saxon countries had nothing to learn from it. In 1931, for example, Eddy attacked "hysterical" denunciations of Soviet communism that served to silence concerns about evils in capitalist America. Even after his annual tour in 1937, when he found that "Moscow was fast closed to foreign visitors, with fear and suspicion," Eddy's teleological vision of historical progress inclined him to highlight improvements in the lives of the masses.[58]

However, the Stalinist terror not only appalled sympathizers in the United States but also physically eliminated many of the dwindling band of Americans who remained in the Soviet Union. For example, Lovett Fort-Whiteman, the militant founder of the American Negro Labor Congress who had sought to educate leaders of the Communist International about racism since the early 1920s, was exiled for "anti-Soviet agitation" in 1937 and died in the gulag (a system of convict labor camps) two years later. In April 1938, even the staunchly pro-Soviet Julius Hecker was arrested, accused of being a spy for the US, and shot.[59]

While many Americans had abhorred Soviet Russia as beyond the pale of civilized countries throughout the interwar years, they were now opposed by fewer and fewer friends of Soviet communism. For much of the 1930s, Christian socialists such as Reinhold Niebuhr had argued that Soviet communism was not as bad as fascism, but when the Soviet Union signed a non-aggression pact with Nazi Germany in August 1939, it became extremely difficult to dispute the widespread identification of "Red fascism" and "brown Bolshevism" as twin totalitarianisms. Even the pro-Soviet liberal Oswald Garrison Villard, who had been "deeply impressed by the extraordinary progress" in Russia in 1929 and had then refrained from expressing his waning faith in the communist experiment in the subsequent years, was so disgusted by Stalin's "perfidy" in 1939 that he denounced the Soviet dictatorship as "just as crooked, treacherous, and criminal" as the Nazis'.[60]

As Americans watched war erupt in Europe, both those who felt the United States should stay out of the fray and those who believed it would have to intervene condemned godless communism and affirmed belief in God as central to American national identity. At a "Mass Meeting for America" in Madison Square Garden around Thanksgiving, 1939, Martin Dies, the isolationist Texas congressman who headed the House Un-American Activities Committee, blamed "naziism," fascism, and communism all on Marxist materialism, the polar opposite of Christian spirituality. As he summoned Americans to "a crusade" against domestic subversives, Dies also called upon them to "reaffirm our allegiance to the God of our fathers." A few weeks later, columnist Dorothy Thompson observed in a nationally broadcast address that communism had owed "a very large part of its emotional appeal to the fact that it has incorporated some of the ideals of its enemy: Christianity." Yet in the wake of the Nazi-Soviet pact, the ideal of communism was dead and the West had an opportunity to "re-vivify" its principles. The daughter of a Methodist minister, Thompson argued that as part of a broader renewal of confidence in Western civilization, Americans "must stop being afraid to say that we are Christians."[61]

President Roosevelt issued the most important rebuke to Soviet communism combined with an affirmation of American religious faith. "In the early days of communism," FDR recalled in February 1940, he recognized that Soviet leaders were bringing education, better health, and opportunity "to millions who had been kept in ignorance and serfdom" under the tsarist regime. Although he had "heartily deprecated the banishment of religion" by the Bolsheviks, he remained confident "that some day Russia would return to religion" since "mankind has always believed in God, in spite of many abortive attempts to exile God." However, angered by the Soviet invasion of Finland, Roosevelt declared that his hope that Russia would "become a peace-loving, popular government with free ballot" was either shattered or in storage. Americans had to face the fact, he concluded, that the Soviet Union was run by "a dictatorship as absolute as any other dictatorship in the world."[62]

### The American mission and the fascination of early Soviet Russia

Whether as diabolical despotism or as vanguard of social progress, Russia fascinated Americans in the 1920s and 1930s. "As soon as one mentions Russia, people are interested," Pentecostal leader Paul Peterson noted in 1927. "Russia is today the best known of all foreign countries to the average citizen," New York Times correspondent Anne O'Hare McCormick observed in 1931. That same year, evangelist Sherwood Eddy declared at the outset of his widely read book, *The Challenge of Russia*, "For good or evil, Russia matters profoundly."[63]

What happened in Russia had tremendous implications for America, either as inspiration or as warning. To Protestant liberals and radicals such as Sherwood Eddy and Harry F. Ward, Soviet communism's appeal to cooperative or altruistic ideals rather than selfish profit motives suggested limitless possibilities for the development of individuals and society.[64] To conservatives, on the other hand, godless, totalitarian communism was an omen of the hellish world toward which liberal modernism was moving.

With Russia continuing to stand as a "mirror for us," as *The Literary Digest* put it in 1931,[65] imagining the conversion or transformation of Russia could serve to affirm the mission, values, and attractions of the United States. In 1935, when many newspaper editors were struck by reports that the Soviet Union was retreating from ascetic, atheistic cultural revolution and rediscovering the importance of traditional family life, the Philadelphia Inquirer wondered whether Russia "eventually will get around to the Golden Rule and the Ten Commandments." The next year, a Finnish-American minister writing in the *Pentecostal Evangel* anticipated that either Bolshevik leaders would themselves, upon hearing the gospel, "put all their ability in the evangelization of their country," or that "a real Biblical revival" would "sweep away Bolshevism."[66]

While journalists and evangelists perpetuated such visions of the redemption of Russia, filmmakers propagated notions about the consumerist seduction of communists that would have enduring appeal. In the fall of 1939, millions of Americans watched the lightheartedly anticommunist movie "Ninotchka," in which a stringently idealistic Soviet trade representative travels to Paris, where she succumbs to the seductive appeal of Western fashion and the sparkle of capitalist culture. This story line, which *Time* magazine found "winning and plausible," was so popular that MGM used variants in two more movies the following year. In "Comrade X," a hard-drinking, wisecracking American reporter in Moscow encounters an ardently communist trolley driver who parrots propaganda about millions of starving unemployed in the United States, but ultimately she flees with him to America and embraces the superiority of a land of baseball, hot dogs, and boogie-woogie.[67]

Thus, while the actual American opportunities to evangelize and modernize Russia were cut off by Stalinist isolationism in the late 1930s, ideas of converting Russians remained alive in the realm of popular fantasies. The dreams would gain new vitality in 1941, after Nazi Germany attacked the Soviet Union, the Kremlin halted its religious persecution, and the United States became an ally of Russia in a new world war.

# 4    Revival: hopes for a new Russia during the Grand Alliance, 1941–45

At Christmas 1943, after Joseph Stalin allowed leaders of the formerly persecuted Russian Orthodox Church to elect a new patriarch, *Time* magazine celebrated by putting the patriarch on its cover, with the portentous caption, "God sits in the corner – but waits." (See figure 13.) Hailing the official restoration of the Church as an almost miraculous breakthrough, *Time* observed that the patriarch had once passed through the United States and noted that he still liked "to practice his fragments of half-remembered American." More to the point, the magazine highlighted the patriarch's "understanding of the church's basic strength (the religious masses) and the Soviet Government's basic weakness (the religious masses)." Although *Time*'s writers recognized that Stalin might be planning to use the Church in the extension of Soviet control over the Balkans, they suggested that the resurrection of the Church would lead to the overthrow of Stalinism. Hitler's invasion of the USSR in 1941, they explained, had turned "Russia from a country in which a majority of defenseless Christians was ruled by an aggressive anti-religious minority into a nation in arms, in which the majority, though intensely patriotic, was no longer defenseless." Hence the conclusion that "even in totalitarian darkness, God sits in the corner – but waits."[1]

The *Time* feature was not an anomaly.[2] Throughout the Second World War, popular magazines and many religious periodicals expressed great enthusiasm about a spiritual revival in Russia that was expected to have profound significance for the postwar world, and to create opportunities for Americans to assist a broader regeneration of Russia. Implicit in much of the excitement was a hope that a religious revival – even with a supposedly corrupt form of Christianity such as Orthodoxy – would lead to a wider reformation of society.

Such hopes for a spiritual rebirth of Russia, neglected in many fine studies of American opinion on the Soviet Union during World War II,[3] are best understood as part of a broader missionary outlook. From a long-range perspective, what was most important about American views of Soviet Russia during the Grand Alliance was not how Americans

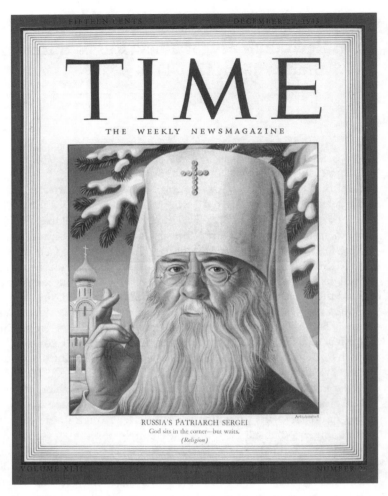

Figure 13. "Russia's Patriarch Sergei. God sits in the corner – but waits." *Time*, December 27, 1943.

were divided between naïve, pro-Soviet New Dealers and tough-minded "realists,"[4] or between realistic cosmopolitans and ignorant provincials,[5] but how Americans in a variety of different ways shared a faith in the possibility of reshaping Russia.

Some Americans, especially centrists and progressives, thought that the Stalinist regime was easing or losing its dictatorial control over the Russian people, and that after the war Russia would therefore be more democratic.[6] Others, particularly liberal and moderate businessmen who were cheered by the dramatic wartime increase in exports to Russia, hoped trade would continue to grow after the war, believed that the Communist system was evolving toward capitalism, and thought that American aid and advice would lead to the liberalization of Russia.[7] Still other Americans, encouraged by the greater Soviet wartime openness to news, films, and music from the US, believed they had a great opportunity to influence Russian cultural development. Like the hopes of American Christians for a Russian religious revival, these expressions of optimism about remaking Russia can be seen as part of an "evangel of Americanism"[8] that was global in scope but had a special fervor in relation to Russia, which had long been a sort of *alter ego* for the United States. The different evangelical drives were key sources of unrealistic expectations that would lead to disillusionment and bitterness after the romance of the Grand Alliance ended.

The wartime beliefs that the Soviet Union was becoming more like the United States have often been attributed to government and media manipulation of a gullible populace or to President Franklin D. Roosevelt's alleged delusion that the USSR was converging with the US.[9] Such interpretations have tended to blame wrong-headed assumptions on naïve leaders and a sentimental public, while lauding the supposedly more realistic recommendations of some tough-minded diplomats. That approach ignores how the "realists" themselves envisioned liberating or liberalizing the Soviet Union.

This chapter develops a broader, multidimensional perspective on how American government officials, religious leaders, journalists, and businessmen imagined the future of Russia in the years when the United States and the Soviet Union were allied against Nazi Germany. It discusses how Americans perceived and sought to influence Russia's religious revival, economic development, political liberalization, and cultural opening. American expectations, hopes, and dreams, it will be argued, were not merely products of peculiar wartime conditions but also reflections of aspirations that affected American-Russian relations for more than a century.

### Spiritual regeneration

When German armies invaded the Soviet Union in June 1941, many Americans expected the blitzkrieg to lead quickly to the overthrow of the Stalinist regime. In contrast to more realistic British observers, US military attachés in Russia, influenced by their scorn for the "Asiatic" backwardness of Russians and by their vehement anticommunism, predicted that the Germans would occupy Moscow in July, and reported that the "great majority" of the Soviet people wanted a change of government. Military experts in Washington agreed that the Red Army was certain to be defeated in a matter of weeks. Numerous columnists expressed the hope or belief that the Soviet state was doomed.[10]

Like secular journalists, many religious writers anticipated the political emancipation of Russia, but they turned more attention to the prospect of a rebirth of Russian Christianity. When liberty came, evangelist Sherwood Eddy predicted, a vital reformed religion would return in power. Similarly, the liberal Catholic magazine *Commonweal* forecast the "fall of Stalin," anticipated "a powerful revival of the Russian national spirit," exulted that "We can reach now deep into the conscience and the hopes of the Russians," and glowed about the "marvelous opportunity for the regeneration of the masses of the Russian people."[11]

Such zealous enthusiasm was not uniform across the political and religious spectrum, of course. On the left, some Christian socialists were still more interested in the way Soviet centralized planning and collectivist idealism could serve as models for the postwar United States. And on the right, dogmatic conservatives (often Catholics) emphasized the eternal, unalterable conflicts between Christianity and Communism, Civilization and Barbarism.[12]

American antipathy to Bolshevik atheism was so strong that editors who favored US intervention in the world war worried that Hitler's supposed holy war against communism would send reinforcements to the camps of isolationism and appeasement.[13] It also created a serious public relations challenge for the Roosevelt administration. In his initial public comment about the German invasion, Under Secretary of State Sumner Welles acknowledged that since the Soviet and Nazi regimes both denied their peoples the freedom to worship God (which was "the great and fundamental right of all peoples"), they were equally intolerable. However, Welles argued, "a realistic America" had to provide aid to Soviet armies in order to counter the more immediate threat from Hitler.[14] That course was vehemently opposed by isolationists in Congress who repeatedly denounced "godless" communism and claimed that an alliance with the "atheistic" Soviet Union could not be reconciled with Roosevelt's rhetorical commitment to the "Four Freedoms." Yet the "America first" anticommunists so starkly and categorically denied the possibility of any religious freedom in the USSR that they gave FDR the opportunity to undercut them with evidence of Soviet toleration of Christianity.[15]

As the administration moved toward providing assistance to the Soviet Union, Catholic clergy who favored such aid stressed to Welles and FDR that in order to overcome protests against the policy, it was essential to keep reiterating that helping the Red Army did not imply any support of communism outside Russia. One Catholic leader further suggested that if guarantees of freedoms could be obtained from the USSR as a condition of US aid, "not only would the dangers of the present position be obviated but its providential character would stand revealed."[16]

Such advice seems to have been favorably received by Roosevelt, whose sense that greater Soviet toleration of religion would significantly influence American opinion had been evident eight years earlier, when he had pressed the Soviet Foreign Minister to concede Americans in Russia the right to worship freely. On September 3 FDR sent a letter to Pope Pius XII expressing the belief that there was "a real possibility that Russia may as a result of the present conflict recognize freedom of religion in Russia." A week later, in a meeting with the Soviet Ambassador to Washington, FDR emphasized that publicity concerning freedom of religion in Russia "might have a very fine educational effect before the next lend-lease bill comes up in Congress."[17] Not content to rely on the Soviet ambassador's promise to attend to the publicity, Roosevelt instructed multimillionaire businessman Averell Harriman to extract from the Kremlin public affirmations of the principle of religious freedom while he was in Moscow to assure Soviet leaders of Western aid. Then, on October 1, FDR seized on news that the Soviet government had agreed to allow Poles in the USSR to worship freely. This, he claimed, indicated that "an entering wedge for the practice of complete freedom of religion is definitely on the way." Blithely pressing further, the president suggested at a press conference that the Soviet constitution guaranteed religious freedom comparable to that in the United States. A few days later the Soviet government, prodded by Harriman, duly corroborated the president's statement.[18]

At first, FDR's gambit appeared to backfire: priests, politicians, and editors heatedly criticized Roosevelt's pronouncement as a cynical attempt to whitewash the anti-religious Soviet regime or at least a dismaying "boner."[19] The *Washington Post* thought the president had "not helped the cause of aid to Russia by his effort to dust off the forgotten Soviet constitution," and suggested that converting Stalin to respect for religious freedom should be a lower priority than speedy military aid.[20] The *Chicago Tribune* derided "Mr. Roosevelt's attempt to picture Red Joe as a Christian gentleman" and published hostile, sarcastic cartoons on the subject (see figure 14).[21] FDR himself was sharply disappointed that Harriman was not able to procure a more stirring Soviet commitment.[22]

However, Roosevelt may have succeeded in shifting attention from past Bolshevik persecution of religion to a possible future revival of Christianity in Russia. While the Catholic magazine *America* initially insisted that

1941.

THE BLACKGUARD AT THE ALTAR

Figure 14. "The Blackguard at the Altar." Cartoon by Parrish. *Chicago Tribune*, October 3, 1941. The bearded, bloodstained Bolshevik uses a false profession of freedom of worship to extract aid and sympathy from the reverent Uncle Sam.

no religious liberty was possible under communism, a week later it published Monsignor Fulton Sheen's prediction that the war would bring the end of communism and that after the war Russia would be "one of the greatest missionary fields in the world."[23] In mid-October *The Christian Century* was still indignant about the president's "shocking" attempt to wash away the Stalinist crimes against religion, but it also contemplated how a revival of Christianity in Russia would pose a threat to the Soviet state, which "rests on an ideological base of atheism."[24] A correspondent for the *Christian Science Monitor* also cast an optimistic eye on the future, writing: "If there is to be a revival of religion in Russia, there has not been a more opportune time since the Revolution, and Russia in travail, crowding its limited churches, awakens the hopes of world Christianity."[25]

Almost as if on cue, in early October *Life* magazine published a photographic essay that graphically showed Bolshevik persecution had failed to eradicate the deep religiosity of the Russian people. In fact, according to *Life*, "Persecution broadened and deepened the spiritual life of the truly pious in Russia," so that "a real faith entered the once-hollow rituals of the splendid and dusty cathedrals." The significance of this persistence and strengthening of Russian Christianity, *Life* explained, was that "it precisely contradicts the fanatical atheism of the Communist State." With interfaith evenhandedness, the magazine both trumpeted the fact that "The Reformation has come to Russia, 400 years late" and cited Monsignor Sheen's beliefs that "Russians are natively pious, that Marxism which came to them from Germany is unnatural to them and that after the war a great wave of piety may sweep All The Russias."[26]

This burst of attention to religion in Russia was strongly influenced by considerations of political expediency. Although Henry Luce, publisher of *Life*, was the son of missionaries and famously hoped to Americanize the world, he was deeply suspicious of Stalinist Russia, and seems to have had little faith in the possibility of redeeming the Soviet Union. The main reason Luce "featured very extensively" Margaret Bourke-White's "remarkable pictures from Russia" was that he thought they were "a real ai[d] in helping America accept wholeheartedly the idea of military assistance to the Soviet Union."[27] Similarly, FDR's pressure for a Soviet statement of support for the principle of religious liberty stemmed primarily from a desire to allay opposition to the extension of lend-lease assistance to the USSR.[28]

However, it would be a mistake to dismiss FDR's campaign as merely a shallow, momentary ploy.[29] As Harriman recalled, the religious issue "was regarded by Roosevelt as a matter of the highest domestic priority." Throughout the war, FDR's envoys pressed Soviet leaders for further statements or concessions on religious freedom and for an easing of tension with the Vatican.[30] While FDR was not intensely religious, he had been raised in the tradition of seeing Christianity as a foundation of western civilization, and in his dreamier moments he may have imagined that greater religious freedom would uplift Soviet Russia, which had been "cut off from civilization" in the interwar years.[31] FDR's emissary to the Vatican may have reflected Roosevelt's aspirations when he prepared to tell the Pope that Russia was being asked "to make religion really free within her borders" and that it was possible that the Russian government might "yield to the influence of an association with Christian allies. . . ."[32]

Regardless of how cynical or dreamy FDR was, his push for publicity about growing religious freedom in the USSR helped to defuse opposition and embolden his Russophile supporters to go on the offensive. After anticommunists failed to bar lend-lease aid to Russia in October 1941, denunciations of Soviet atheism became much less frequent in Congress, where some members directly attacked the labelling of Russia as "godless." By late 1943, Roosevelt's aides and friends in Congress were flatly asserting that Soviet citizens enjoyed full freedom of worship.[33]

Together, the Roosevelt administration and the Luce magazines helped to stir widespread optimism about the spiritual regeneration of Russia. In 1942 a Russian emigré historian assured the readers of *Christianity and Crisis* that although it was impossible to know "exactly what is going on within the present-day Russia," there was undoubtedly "an intense, even fiery religious enthusiasm" burning underground.[34] By 1943 the *Christian Science Monitor* was confident that a very significant revival of the innate religious spirit of the Russian nation was underway, a revival the paper hoped would lead not to the reestablishment of a state church but to "more wholesome" and individualistic religious activity.[35] *The Christian Century*, now more friendly to the battered Orthodox Church than it had been a decade earlier, was pleased that it had returned to "virtually full freedom" and anticipated that "Russian communism may detach itself even more completely from its Marxist atheistic ideology than it already has. . . ."[36] At the height of the Soviet struggle against Nazi Germany even the vehemently anticommunist *Catholic World* exuded enthusiasm, editorializing that the "resistance of the Russian people to the repeated efforts to make atheists of them has been miraculous. Russian religion emerges from the crucible deep and strong and alive."[37]

A few anti-Stalinist intellectuals such as Max Eastman and William Henry Chamberlin still publicly insisted that there was no freedom of religion in the Soviet Union and dismissed Orthodox leaders as stooges. But more typical of mainstream American attitudes was C. L. Sulzberger of the *New York Times*, who reported that "the Kremlin's attitude toward religion has evidently undergone a striking change" and interpreted the re-establishment of the Orthodox Church as one of the most important signs of Russia's movement from "isolationism" to American-style freedoms.[38]

US diplomatic experts on Russia tended to have more cynical views of the Soviet government's permission of the wartime religious revival. Career foreign service officers such as Charles Bohlen and George F. Kennan believed the Stalinist regime planned to use the Orthodox Church to extend its sway over neighboring lands, and they emphasized that religious ceremonies were publicized in order to appease (or deceive)

Western audiences.[39] Harriman, who became Ambassador to Moscow in late 1943, was also skeptical: he presciently expected the Soviet regime to keep religious worship "under careful control like a fire which can be stamped out at any time."[40]

However, Harriman's predecessors attached greater importance to the possibility of a spiritual revival. According to Father Leopold Braun, a Catholic priest in Moscow, Ambassador Laurence Steinhardt realized in 1941 "how great the influence of religion would be if the inner spiritual convictions of worshipers were finally given an opportunity to manifest themselves normally without restraint." Admiral William Standley, Ambassador from 1942 to 1943, similarly recognized the "profound importance to the future of Russia and of the entire world" of the fact that religion was vigorously opposed by the ruling minority but widely practiced by the Russian people.[41] And even more experienced diplomatic observers like Loy Henderson were impressed by how the Kremlin's concessions to the Orthodox Church "caused a sensation among the Russian people," stirring hopes for greater postwar freedoms.[42]

Among the Soviet experts, Kennan especially came to stress the potential significance of the greater religious toleration and the growing spiritual revival. In 1942, when FDR's envoy to the Vatican requested his observations about religion in Russia, Kennan (then posted in Lisbon) confidently declared that the inevitable failure of the Bolshevik effort to replace spiritual faith with materialistic doctrine "is obvious to all of us who have been brought up in a Christian atmosphere," though he expressed doubts about whether "it could be proved to the Soviet leaders that religion need no longer constitute a challenge to their political authority."[43] By 1944, when Kennan returned to Moscow for the first time in seven years, he believed that "the spiritual life of the Russian people" was "the most important" dimension of developments in the Soviet Union. Although the Kremlin was still guarding "the souls of its human charges" like a jealous shepherd, Kennan was inspired by indications that Russians were only superficially sheeplike, that the Bolshevik anti-religious campaigns had failed to dry up the springs of Russian spirituality, and that "the Russian 'soul'" was a bastion of resistance to Soviet totalitarianism.[44]

As the war against Germany ended in the spring of 1945, Kennan grew even more excited by the startling "demonstrations of religious feeling," declared that the Soviet government had "lost moral dominion over the masses of the Russian population," and predicted that if the spiritual sources of human action were "ever to be grasped and activated by outside influence, the danger to the regime would be incalculable."[45] In contrast to Russia experts who scorned the Orthodox hierarchy as minions of the

Stalinist regime, Kennan regarded top church leaders as "highly astute," prudent, and patient. "Of all the people I have ever seen in Russia," Kennan confided to a diplomatic colleague, "I consider them the only group who may some day prove to be politically a match for the people in the Kremlin."[46]

Thus, while Kennan has often been viewed as a "realist," aloof from American moralism, he was squarely within the mainstream of American Christian hopes for a religious reformation of Russia. Kennan's strict Presbyterian upbringing in what he called a "Puritan" home seems to have contributed to his deep interest in the potential regenerative power of Russian religiosity. His vision of a possible future triumph of the Orthodox Church over the Soviet state is especially noteworthy because it foreshadowed a key element in an American drive to liberate Russia from Soviet tyranny in the early Cold War, in which he would play a leading role.[47]

Although American visions of a Russian spiritual revival or even revolution involved much wishful projection, they were not simply fantasies or delusions. During the Great Patriotic War, thousands of churches reopened in both occupied and unoccupied Soviet territory. Across the USSR, numerous baptisms, church marriages, and religious funerals reflected a widespread spiritual revival. In many regions there was an impressive reawakening of religious sentiment, with congregations swelling to include not only grandmothers but also men and women of combat age.[48]

However, Americans who posited a fundamental conflict between religious faith and the Soviet system neglected the Orthodox Church's historical experience of subordination to the tsarist state, and failed to recognize the possibility that a nationalistic religion would support rather than clash with the Soviet government. As Daniel Peris has pointed out, the spritual revival was not necessarily or inherently anti-Soviet: many religious petitioners desired "an organic, inclusive state" and hoped for unity between the church and the Soviet government.[49]

Neither the fusion of Orthodoxy and Stalinism in a nationalistic synthesis nor the Soviet government's determination to control the scope of the revival made the Kremlin's concessions on religious freedom meaningless. Although the Kremlin in 1943 established a special council, headed by a secret police colonel, to control the Orthodox Church, it also tacitly legitimized a potential rival for the allegiance of the Russian people – as *Time* magazine writers and others thought. What many Americans did not understand, though, was how timid the surviving Orthodox leaders were after more than two decades of violent persecution. The idea that it was possible that "the church will eventually get up and control the Kremlin," as a visiting US congressman put it, was therefore quite unrealistic.[50]

### Democratization?

If the role of religion in American wartime views of Russia has been neglected, the idea that Russia was undergoing democratization has received unwarranted attention. The oft-cited pronouncement by World War I ace Eddie Rickenbacker that Russia was likely "to come out of this war the greatest democracy in the world" is actually not a reliable indicator of American attitudes.[51] In fact, the conservative airline president was himself more enthralled by the iron discipline in Soviet factories and the respect for rank in the Red Army than by any loosening of centralized state controls. Like some key American diplomats, Rickenbacker privately thought an army takeover, not a democratic revolution, was the most likely post-war and post-communist scenario.[52] Moreover, the pro-Soviet progressives who talked most often about Russia's evolution toward democracy focused primarily on economic or industrial rather than political democracy.[53]

True, some politicians indulged in rhetoric about the democratization of the USSR. Six weeks after the German invasion, for example, Congressman Adolf J. Sabath buttressed his call for aid to Russia by prophesying that Russians shortly "will have a democratic form of government that will give the great people of Russia the liberty, freedom, and justice that they have sought for centuries."[54] That notion was also fostered by Russian emigrés like Alexander Kerensky, who declared that German cannon were "punching holes in the almighty bureaucratic machine of the dictatorship" and the Russian people were recovering their democratic spirit.[55]

However, on the whole such claims about democratization seem to have been strained and outside the main stream of American thinking. Thus, when historian Arthur Upham Pope sought to make the case for Stalin's Russia going democratic, he had to resort to the fatuous old cliché about the roots of democracy in the peasant commune.[56] What is more striking is how often intellectuals denied or at least deferred Russia's move to democracy. Socialist leader Norman Thomas believed "that the Russian type of totalitarianism will remain a bureaucratic state capitalism, undemocratic, ruthless, and Machiavellian."[57] Ex-socialist and increasingly conservative individualist W. H. Chamberlin thought the war might be sapping the foundations of the totalitarian regime, but insisted that the USSR would not evolve toward democracy under Stalin; Russia might achieve democracy only through a future revolution.[58] *New*

*York Times* correspondent Cyrus Sulzberger, who spent six months in the Soviet Union after the German invasion, made the classic Russophile arguments that it was unfair to judge Russia by western democratic customs and that one should "remember the heritage of centuries of serfdom."[59]

Some critics of FDR's Soviet policy decried what they thought were dangerous illusions that Stalin and the Soviet Union could be converted to democracy. Journalist Eugene Lyons, for example, repeatedly complained that liberals were succumbing to the illusion of Soviet democratization because they believed that was necessary to make post-war cooperation possible.[60] Yet liberals like Secretary of the Interior Harold Ickes and former Ambassador to Moscow Joseph Davies usually did not stress the democratization of Russia; on the contrary, they tended to argue that Americans should not be concerned with the form of government in the USSR. For example, in the blatantly pro-Soviet film "Mission to Moscow," which FDR encouraged and Davies closely supervised, Davies' character tells his American friends that how the Russians "keep their house is really none of our business."[61] When Davies tried to make Soviet Russia seem like the United States, he was more inclined to claim that "there is God in the hearts of those millions of Russian people" who were fighting, and to argue that Soviet socialism, like American Christianity, was an altruistic creed.[62]

In mid-1943, when the Red Army still carried by far the largest burden of the war against Germany, Davies believed that American public opinion recognized the necessity of a global partnership with Russia, "regardless of its religion or its political belief." But a year later, after the western allies finally opened a second front in France, Davies grew increasingly worried about an intensifying "conflict of ideology and religion" between Americans and the USSR. By the end of 1944, he lamented that "much of our public opinion require [sic] that they shall accept our views on politics and religion as a condition of any confidence."[63] If Davies' reading of popular attitudes was correct, it appears that as the US played larger, more direct roles in the defeat of Germany, many Americans became more adamant about the need for political and religious freedom in the Soviet Union. Thus, demands for Russian democratization were not unimportant, but desires for Russian religious liberty were at least as significant.

Even in the middle of the war some prominent figures, notably Henry Luce and the embittered former ambassador to Moscow, William Christian Bullitt, began to call for a crusade for democracy in Europe, but Luce and Bullitt actually had little faith in democratizing the Soviet Union. In 1943, Luce urged the United States to rededicate itself to "the quest of political freedom," but he anticipated that that "mission" would lead to a clash with Russia rather than the acceptance of American principles by Soviet leaders. Bullitt insisted to FDR that there was no evidence to support the thesis that Stalin had changed his political philosophy, which would be "as striking as the conversion of Saul on the road to Damascus." In place of a policy based on such "wishful thinking," Bullitt proposed a course of "realism," involving the use of "the carrot and the club . . . to make Stalin move in the direction in which we want him to move." However, Bullitt and Luce were ultimately much less interested in the coercive democratization of the Soviet Union than the demonization of that Asiatic, atheist dictatorship as a threat to "Christian civilization."[64]

### Conversion to consumerism?

In January 1945, *Fortune* magazine devoted its "America and the Future" department exclusively to relations with Russia. Although the editors believed Americans had "legitimate reasons for mistrusting Russia" and even raised the specter of a future air war with the USSR, they set aside suspicions and downplayed differences between the two nations' political systems. Highlighting the kinship between American and Russian pilots who shared "a passion for machines and gadgetry," the editors even ventured, "Maybe Russia is in many ways not so very different from the US under the New Deal." This positive spin seems to have been influenced strongly by optimism about the prospects for profitable postwar exports to Russia. As *Fortune* explained, the "Russian population, tried by years of war and preparation for war, hungers for a taste of the reasonably good things of life. Not luxuries. Just suits, soap, shoes, frying pans, butter, cigarettes, radios, ice cream, movies, nutmeg, and notions. Here," the magazine concluded, "is one of the world's prime potential markets for both capital and consumption goods."[65]

Such dreams of a vast Russian market were not new. As noted earlier, in the late nineteenth century, some manufacturers had seen enormous opportunities in the tsarist empire, and a dramatic increase in trade during the First World War had inspired American visions of eclipsing European rivals for the postwar Russian market. After the US slid into a deep depression in 1929, many businessmen viewed Soviet purchases as vital to keeping their companies afloat.[66] Hopes rose again between 1941 and 1945, when American exports to the USSR increased from 2% of the US total to as much as 24%. By the spring of 1944, *Business Week* was saying that "Russia is bidding to become this country's best postwar customer" if it could obtain sufficient credits and a number of major corporations were discussing postwar trade with Soviet officials.[67]

This renewed enthusiasm mingled during the Grand Alliance with the notion that Soviet Russia was reverting to capitalism, which was promoted by Joseph Davies, the editors of the *New York Times*, and others.[68] As the two lines of thought merged, key business leaders, influential journalists, and some government officials came to regard exports to Russia not only as a way to avoid a postwar recession and unemployment[69] but also as a noble opportunity to elevate the Russian standard of living, and thereby contribute to a wider liberalization in the Soviet Union. These ideas were fostered above all by men who had met with Stalin, were aware that Soviet leaders were determined to maintain the government monopoly on foreign trade, and knew that the Soviet government intended to focus on development of heavy industry rather than consumer goods. Thus, even supposedly hard-headed businessmen and "realist" diplomats succumbed to unrealistic dreams about influencing the Russian future.

Averell Harriman had been one of the few American businessmen who invested in a major way in Soviet economic development in the 1920s, when he ignored the US policy of discouraging trade with the dangerous Bolsheviks and sank millions of dollars into the modernization of manganese mines in Georgia. Although that experience was not a great success – it ended with the financier asking the Soviet government to renegotiate the contract and then let him out of the deal – Harriman believed he gained expertise on the Soviet system, and he may have felt that he had made a contribution to the development of a country he regarded as "fundamentally uncivilized."[70]

In October 1941, when Harriman returned from his special mission to Moscow, he sought to facilitate approval of the extensive aid that he had just promised Stalin by broadcasting an address over the CBS radio network. The members of the British and American mission discovered, Harriman reported, that "a lot of popular notions about the Russians were wrong." Attempting to dispel stereotypes of Russians as slow, lazy, and incompetent, Harriman asserted: "The Russian has become a first class mechanic in this last generation. The American tractor on the farm has played its part. Factories are equipped with the finest and latest American machinery, well laid out and well organized. There is no better work done anywhere."[71] Thus, while Harriman's immediate purpose was to allay concerns that American equipment sent to Russia would be mishandled and wasted, he built upon the pride in America's past assistance to Soviet modernization, and suggested that US aid would further the Americanization of Russian industry.

It is hard to say how far Harriman himself believed the formerly "clumsy Russian Muzhik" was being Americanized as he "learned to use the machine."[72] Certainly Harriman did not believe that the Soviet

Union was "going capitalistic," as Donald M. Nelson, the chairman of the War Production Board, and other prominent American visitors to Moscow asserted.[73] Ultimately, Harriman's principal interest in Soviet-American economic relations was to use US credits, loans, and lend-lease supplies as instruments to modify Soviet behavior, particularly in Eastern Europe. However, Harriman was not merely a cold, calculating "realist." From the beginning of his tenure as ambassador, he believed that the United States was going to be extensively "involved in the Soviet reconstruction problem," in part because the Russians "preferred American equipment."[74] This meant not only that the postwar Soviet Union would be an important outlet for American surplus production, but also that the US could contribute to the modernization of Soviet industry and infrastructure. For example, in early 1944 Harriman suggested to A. I. Mikoyan, the People's Commissar for Foreign Trade, that "The United States had had extensive experience in mine mechanization and United States experts might assist in the application of American methods."[75] Although Harriman persistently argued that US aid to Soviet reconstruction should "depend upon their behavior in international matters," he was eager to assist because he felt strongly that "the sooner the Soviet Union can develop a decent life for its people the more tolerant they will become."[76] Thus, while Harriman eventually focused more on economic coercion than assistance, for much of the war he seems to have genuinely hoped that the US would contribute significantly to the development and hence also the liberalization of Russia.

The most important popularizer of the notion that Americans could simultaneously trade with and uplift Russia was Eric Johnston, President of the US Chamber of Commerce, who toured the Soviet Union in June 1944. At the Kremlin, the former door to door vacuum-cleaner salesman struggled to break through Stalin's initial reserve and seeming lack of interest. In his inspection of Soviet factories, Johnston said approvingly, he had "seen American machines, American techniques, American assembly lines." However, there was still much to be done, he exhorted the Soviet leader, who was doodling absent-mindedly with a red pencil. "In your terrifically congested cities people stand in long queues waiting in line to buy food. It is a waste of human energy that you can ill afford." Johnston therefore recommended "American technical advice on distribution," which could be provided by "experts from our chain stores." Although Stalin only shifted in his chair and sighed, Johnston went on to sketch a glowing picture of how in peacetime "Russia can turn her ever-increasing capacity to the production of consumer goods."

When Johnston asked whether the USSR would "want to purchase consumer goods or industrial equipment" after the war, Stalin clearly indicated that he would focus on heavy machinery. Yet after Johnston returned to the United States, he promoted optimism about a broad expansion of trade in numerous lectures and in widely read articles. Russians "venerate the United States" because of its industrial prowess, Johnston reported. In the postwar world, he predicted, "Russia is going to turn to the United States for the multitude of things she will need not only to rebuild her war-worn economy but to give her people the higher standard of living she has been promising them for 20 years."[77] Through the end of the war in 1945, Johnston continued to emphasize how keenly Russians wanted "to imitate America" and how much Russia had "to learn from us."[78]

Johnston's misleading stories about the Soviet Union seem to have been influenced by his concerns about conditions in the United States. In *America Unlimited* (1944), written around the time Johnston was being mentioned as a possible candidate for the presidency, he showed that he was concerned above all with two things: (1) overcoming the vestiges of self-doubt, cynicism, and "defeatism" bred by "the black depression of the 1930s"; and (2) warding off Utopian economic experimentation in the postwar era. Invoking Stalin's praise of American production and imagining that "Ivan Petrov may not relish" his collectivist system seem to have been part of Johnston's effort to check "ideologies of despair," spark optimism about "our people's capitalism," and reinvigorate "our faith in the American way of life."[79]

Johnston was not the only prominent figure whose statements and aspirations were at odds with his knowledge of Soviet plans. After hearing Stalin's statements to Johnston, Harriman clearly expected that after the war Soviet leaders would "continue to ask the people to give up consumable goods for capital goods as in the Five Year plans," but he still dreamed of making "the East take consumer goods to raise their standard of living."[80] E. C. Ropes, an experienced specialist on Russia at the Commerce Department, thought it was "not unlikely that the Soviet Government will modify its long-standing policy of importing chiefly producers' goods, and will purchase quantities of American automobiles, refrigerators, vacuum cleaners, and many other products that will add to the comfort and ease of the population."[81] More generally, FDR appears to have thought it vital to keep economic channels open to promote a liberalization of the Soviet Union, and he may have dreamed that elements of capitalism within the USSR would lead to modification of its socialist system.[82]

It was not delusional for Americans to think that Soviet leaders admired advanced American technology, were eager to obtain US financial assistance, and hoped thereby to increase imports from the United States.

From the early days of the Soviet state, Lenin and other Bolshevik leaders had expressed special enthusiasm about trade and investment from America.[83] When the two countries renewed their commercial agreement in August 1941, the official Soviet government newspaper paid tribute to the American role in the economic development of the Soviet Union, and predicted an expansion of Soviet-American trade.[84] At the height of the wartime alliance, Stalin affirmed that "the Soviet people . . . preferred American products . . . because of the high quality of those products," while Foreign Minister V. M. Molotov added that "American technical assistants and American experts enjoyed a very high reputation in the Soviet Union."[85]

However, as George Kennan pointed out in September 1944, the Soviet government planned to focus primarily on development of heavy industry, rather than on a rapid improvement in living standards, and it would accept Western assistance in that program only if it was not required to make concessions on matters deemed vital to Soviet security. It was therefore a mistake to think that the Stalinist regime would allow Russia to become dependent on foreign trade, or permit Western assistance to promote such widespread popular enthusiasm about the West that respect for the Kremlin would be shaken.[86] In other words, it was unrealistic to imagine that Russians who had ridden in Lend-Lease Studebaker trucks or eaten bread made from Lend-Lease wheat would be converted into such worshipers of the United States that it would affect the postwar direction of the Soviet Union.[87] And of course it was even more unrealistic to believe that the USSR was already in the course of reverting to capitalism – a view Soviet officials treated frostily when expounded by American visitors.[88]

American hopes for expanding postwar trade with the Soviet Union were not realized. Influenced by Harriman's arguments that postwar financial assistance should be tightly linked to Soviet international behavior, Washington held off on providing the loans or credits needed to facilitate large Soviet purchases.[89] Exports to the USSR declined to 4% of the US total in 1946 and only 1% in 1947. Fewer and fewer businessmen talked about Russia shifting to capitalism as the Soviet Union embarked on an autarkic course of postwar development.[90]

In early 1944 Henry Luce's foreign affairs adviser Raymond Buell counseled that the question of future peace or war might depend on "whether Russia with its extended boundaries intends to revert to a great hermit state after the war, or whether it will participate upon a basis of equality in the economic and cultural life of the world as a whole." Luce himself argued during the Second World War that America's frontier had to be the whole world and that in order "to make and keep ourselves politically free, we must be the sworn enemy of any economic fact that interferes with that freedom."[91] While Soviet obstruction of the American drive for an open door in eastern Europe was not the primary cause of postwar hostility toward the Soviet Union, the frustration of American hopes to participate actively in Soviet postwar economic development was part of a wider disillusionment that contributed to the deterioration of superpower relations.

### Breaking down "the Chinese Wall of the spirit": propaganda and cultural infiltration

During the Second World War, US representatives in Moscow persistently stressed the importance of disseminating information about America in order to overcome Soviet isolationism and xenophobia, strengthen the US–Soviet alliance, and influence the future of the Soviet Union. In 1943, Admiral Standley proposed an exchange of films and distribution of a monthly magazine about the United States as ways to seize a unique, probably short-lived opportunity to overcome the Soviets' tightly centralized control of information.[92] After replacing Standley, Harriman strongly supported such information programs. "Many of the problems of our relations with Russia," Harriman explained in October 1944, "center around the relative isolation of the Russian public from the general currents of world thought and world feeling." Informational activities would therefore be vital to the development of a "satisfactory structure of collaboration between the Russian people and our own" – a view Harriman repeatedly reiterated in subsequent months.[93] Thus, the US wartime propaganda and cultural infiltration was an important arm of the wider effort to penetrate, open, and guide the Soviet Union.[94]

Underlying the information campaigns was a widely shared belief that the Russian people were fascinated by America and admired the United States. Harriman's daughter Kathleen, who did much of the work of the Office of War Information (OWI) in Moscow, found that there was "a terrific interest in anything American," adding that Russian women especially craved and clamored for fashion magazines.[95] John Melby, Third Secretary of the US Embassy, similarly believed that "Among the mass of the people there is a genuine liking and admiration for America and Americans."[96] The most striking illustration of this popular sentiment was the prolonged demonstration by a large crowd in front of the US Embassy in May 1945, when American officers and diplomats were tossed into the air to celebrate the allied victory over Germany. To George Kennan "the demonstrations were an impressive and somewhat startling testimonial to the admiration in which, despite all restraining efforts of the state propaganda machine, our country is held by a large section of Russian people."[97]

This popular enthusiasm gave the United States a unique opportunity to affect or constrain Soviet policies, according to American diplomats. Unlike other foreign nations, Melby reported, the United States did not need "to create a popular body of sympathy for itself." Instead, it could focus on supporting the existing sympathy and "making a convert here and one there." Over a period of years this "gradual penetration of Soviet consciousness" might "create a strong enough feeling of international-ism among opinion-influencing groups in the Soviet Union to have a considerable weight in causing the small top policy group to take a more tolerant attitude toward foreign groups." (Melby did not clearly reconcile this hopeful view with his recognition that the top Soviet leadership "is through its controls [on information] in a position largely to create that public support which it desires for its predetermined objectives.")[98]

While Melby's optimism was somewhat tentative, Harriman was more confident that "the Soviet government's policy would have to continue to be one of cooperation with us on account of public opinion within the Soviet Union," as he told the British Foreign Minister in May 1944. Everywhere he went in the USSR, Harriman explained to journalists in London, there was "tremendous enthusiasm" over the alliance with the United States, and "Stalin cannot face the Russian people with the admission that this relationship with us is a failure."[99] As the Grand Alliance culminated with the long delayed Anglo-American invasion of Western Europe, Harriman and other American diplomats repeatedly noted rising concern among Soviet officials that Russians were becoming too enthusiastic about the alliance and "too international-minded."[100] However, even as American-Soviet relations frayed because of friction over Poland, Harriman continued to believe that "the Russian peo-ple wish collaboration with the United States most deeply" and that it would "be difficult for a government of Russia to carry through policies which would deny them this relationship." In April 1945, after Roo-sevelt's death gave Harriman a greater opportunity to influence US pol-icy, he made this idea central to his policy recommendations to the State Department.[101]

Harriman's stubborn belief in the possibility of enlisting Russian pro-American sentiment to constrain Soviet foreign policy indicates that he was not as shrewdly "realistic" as he claimed and that he never "really fully understood the nature of the Soviet system," as Charles Bohlen concluded.[102] In contrast to Harriman's perspective, Kennan commented in September 1944 that while "the relationship between [Soviet] public feeling and official policy" was "a jealously guarded secret of state," the feelings of Russian civilians "cannot be said to cause political concern or to have political significance."[103]

However, even Kennan and Bohlen were not immune to the hope that Russian popular feeling could be utilized to affect Soviet foreign policy. In fact, Bohlen may have been a key formative influence on Harriman's view: in November 1943, he advised the newly designated ambassador that "the desire of the Soviet people to lead a relatively normal and secure life" was "a political factor of the first importance." Since the Soviet leaders realized that after the war they would not be able to "ask the Soviet people to go through another decade of privation and struggle" in a hostile world, the Kremlin had decided "to work together with Great Britain and the United States."[104] Hence, the illusion that the Russian people could be made allies of US foreign policy should be seen not merely as a reflection of certain individuals' unsophistication, but as part of a wider and more enduring American outlook.

American representatives were keenly aware of Soviet officials' worries about the impact on Russian popular attitudes of information concerning the outside world. In August 1944, for example, Harriman attributed a decreasing Soviet openness to showing Western films to "the old fear of showing the Soviet people anything from which they could conclude that a system or way of life superior in any respect to the Soviet Union exists anywhere in the world." Five months later the chief of the US military mission in Moscow went further, explaining that one of the main obstacles to military collaboration was the Kremlin's hesitation to "bring to the Soviet Union representatives of other countries, particularly Americans, who enjoy a much higher standard of living than the Russians have ever attained. The Soviet authorities fear," General John Deane continued, "that unrest would be caused among the people, not only by visual evidence of the living refinements which the Americans might bring with them, but also by what the people might be told of the American way of life by American soldiers."[105] The potentially subversive appeal of images of America thus hinged not on understanding of Western democracy, about which Russians seemed ignorant, but on the fabulous luxuries of bourgeois civilization.[106]

During much of 1943 and 1944, Soviet officials generally seemed receptive to American proposals for cultural exchanges and greater publicity about the United States. In early 1943, Vice Commissar of Foreign Affairs S. A. Lozovsky responded enthusiastically to Ambassador Standley's proposal to develop an information exchange program and vowed to try to outdo any effort Americans made.[107] At the end of the year even Foreign Minister Molotov gave a vaguely favorable reply to Harriman's proposals, including wider showing of American films and distribution of a glossy monthly magazine.[108] After being prodded by Harriman, Molotov gave final approval to the magazine in March 1944, and the first issue of *Amerika* then passed the Soviet censor in June, when jubilation over the opening of the second front in France brought Soviet cooperation with US cultural initiatives to a high point.[109] As late as the first of August, Harriman remained upbeat, confident that the long awaited magazine would "be eaten up by the Russians."[110]

However, later in August, Harriman began to be disturbed by a reversion to a policy of "isolationism," which was reflected in the purchase of fewer American films, the showing only of films that portrayed America in an unflattering light, and eventually the firm rejection of pleas to set aside a Moscow theatre to show American and British films.[111] In the summer of 1944, John Melby observed, Soviet contacts "became ill or went out of town," the film exchange was closed down, and the Soviet Information Bureau's interest in American material "became vaguer and vaguer." It appeared, Melby speculated, "that some decision had been taken on a high-policy level that foreign activities in the Soviet Union were becoming too extensive, and that as a result some restriction should be placed which would again have the effect of isolating the Soviet population from foreign influence."[112]

This shift in Soviet policy did not cause American representatives to abandon their efforts to penetrate what Melby called a "barrier of fog." Instead, it seems to have intensified their determination. One of the central challenges facing foreign diplomats in Russia, George Kennan argued in September 1944, was to combat the isolationist and xenophobic influences in the Soviet government by opening up "new avenues of contact and of vision . . . between the Kremlin and the world around it. . . ." Employing a commonly used metaphor, Kennan wrote that even the friendliest relations with Russia would not be sound and dependable "until the Chinese Wall of the spirit has been broken down. . . ."[113] Roughly a year later, the head of the Moscow branch of the Office of War Information, former journalist Joseph Phillips, described the OWI mission in Russia in similar terms. In the face of top Soviet officials' "ideological hostility to propaganda from America," Phillips reported, "The work here has been to break down barriers."[114]

American diplomats seem to have been correct in discerning the beginning of a Soviet campaign to curb Western cultural influence. Although Soviet political cartoons and propaganda posters glorified the Grand Alliance, and the propaganda line to Soviet troops remained strongly pro-American through the defeat of Germany, after the war the press began stressing the darker side of American life, particularly by predicting imminent mass unemployment in the United States.[115] In a lighter vein, an article in the satirical magazine *Krokodil* ridiculed the Russian tendency to think that everything foreign, especially American, was perfect, while nothing Russian could ever be as good.[116]

However, Americans who envisioned using cultural and informational programs to drive a wedge between the supposedly cosmopolitan Russian people and the xenophobic Kremlin sometimes disregarded how the war had forged new and stronger bonds between the Soviet state and people, who were proud of their preponderant role in the defeat of Nazi Germany. This tendency was exhibited not only by Ambassador Harriman, but also by US representatives who had closer and more extensive contact with Russians outside the Kremlin. Kennan recognized that the war had "pulled regime and people together," but he still yearned to help the latter break free from the grasp of the former. General Deane reported that the leaders and the people were "inextricably bound together" and that on the whole, the leaders had "the support, confidence, and acclaim of the people," yet he believed that "beneath the oppression of the present Soviet regime is a people with whom we shall someday be proud to march into a happier future."[117] Frederick Barghoorn, who served as an attaché at the US Embassy in Moscow from 1942 to 1947, emphasized the cleavage between the pro-American Russian people and the anti-American Kremlin in his book, *The Soviet Image of the United States* (1950), which included a chapter titled, "The Russian People: The Kremlin's Achilles' Heel." Thus, the notion of a sharp divergence between Russian popular attitudes and official government lines, which would be central to US propaganda and policy in the early Cold War, was foreshadowed and influenced by US representatives who lived in Russia during the Great Patriotic War.

## Postwar aftermath and Cold War legacies

In June 1945, sixty years after George Kennan had launched an inspection of the Siberian exile system, his namesake, the chargé of the US Embassy in Moscow, set off on a journey to Siberia, hoping to investigate popular attitudes across the vast country. Aboard the Trans-Siberian Express, George F. Kennan once again sensed the keenness of Russian enthusiasm about the United States. When he got out copies of the magazine *Amerika*, they sparked "a lively hour of fraternization," but then "suddenly everybody began to look guiltily over his shoulder and the meeting quietly dispersed." Upon reaching the "socialist city" of Stalinsk, Kennan toured a giant metallurgical plant. Although the chief engineer showed "no interest in America," Kennan spotted on a side table a technical journal published by the Soviet trading organization in New York, and he was told that many of the plant's engineers "had been to the United States recently to study American methods." While American technology thus seemed to be having a significant impact on Soviet industries, Kennan was disturbed by the way credulous Russians accepted xenophobic Soviet government propaganda, and by how quickly they clammed up whenever they felt officials were watching them.

At the end of his journey, then, Kennan drew some pessimistic conclusions about the prospects for reaching and influencing the Russian people. Since they were "a talented, responsive people, capable of absorbing and enriching all forms of human experience," they were an especially suitable outlet for the yearning to help others that was a signal trait of the American character. However, an altruistic mission was blocked: a ruthless, jealous regime stood between the gifted Russian people and the outside world, and that regime had the people "completely in its hand." Kennan blamed that condition in part on the people themselves. "When a people places itself in the hands of a ruthless authoritarian regime," he wrote in despairing judgment, "it places itself beyond the power of others to help." Hence, the frustrated diplomat regretfully decided that it was wisest "to leave the Russian people . . . to work out their own destiny in their own peculiar way."[118]

Like Kennan, other Americans decided that the wartime efforts to guide the Soviet Union had failed, and that Russia was withdrawing into its shell. Russians were easily swayed by Soviet propaganda, Harriman concluded. "The theory . . . that bit by bit Russia will move toward the West" had not been borne out, Raymond Buell advised Henry Luce. Whereas in 1943 headlines in the *New York Times Magazine* proclaimed "Russia Lets Down Old Barriers," two years later the same magazine featured the conclusion that enigmatic Russians were reverting to xenophobic isolationism.[119]

Over the long term, many Americans were embittered by this. In the early 1950s, for example, Michigan congressman Gerald Ford not only made a typical Republican attack on the wartime Democratic administration for having been "beguiled by the false assurances of the godless men in the Kremlin," but also recalled that Americans in general had "erroneously believed that the Soviet rulers had abandoned the precepts and teachings of their false prophets." As late as 1959, the prominent theologian Reinhold Niebuhr attributed much of the asperity in American attitudes toward the Soviet Union to postwar disillusionment: "Clearly we are disappointed partners, who mistook a military marriage of convenience for a marriage between kindred souls. Our emotions are now frantic because our hopes were high."[120]

However, the immediate aftermath of the war did not bring a sudden or final end to the American mission to penetrate and remake Russia. As late as the summer of 1946 the president of the Southern Baptist

Convention returned from a preaching tour of nine Soviet cities, euphorically convinced that Russia was "a virgin field for freedom." While *Time* derided the Baptist leader's naïve enthusiasm about Soviet policies, the magazine allowed that "It was just possible that in adding to their list of religious well-wishers, the hardheaded commissars were inviting the innocence of doves to triumph over the wisdom of serpents" – thereby indicating that the magazine's editors still cherished some of their 1943 hope that "God sits in the corner."[121] A Methodist leader who traveled to Russia at about the same time returned more cautiously optimistic that "the message and spirit of Christ can find a way of penetrating the iron curtain of pride. . . ."[122] As American-Soviet relations worsened in 1947, the belief that the USSR was not responding to overtures for cultural relations did not deter *The Christian Century* from insisting that "The Russian people must . . . know about America."[123]

Despite the postwar friction and reduction of contacts, influential Americans continued to draw inspiration from their wartime experiences and observations. In 1950, for example, the Russian-American intellectual Boris Shub recalled how Red Army soldiers in Germany had embraced American troops with a transcendent enthusiasm. "The Russians who met us in 1945," Shub remembered, "knew that America was a land of freedom, and they hoped with all their hearts that . . . they too would know more of the freedom whose reality was revealed to them in every gesture of their American comrades." Shub cited such encounters to support his prediction that the overwhelming majority of Russians would "respond thunderously to a concrete American offer of alliance for their liberation" from totalitarian tyranny.[124] Like Shub, several other men who would become key ideologists for the propaganda campaigns of the early Cold War developed the belief that a wide gulf separated the peoples of Russia from their Kremlin masters during the Grand Alliance.[125] Thus, the rebirth of hopes for a free Russia between 1941 and 1945 created a foundation for the "psychological warfare" of the late 1940s and early 1950s.

# 5    Visions of "liberation," 1945–53

In October 1951, when Soviet-American tensions reached a feverish high, the editors of *Collier's* magazine devoted an entire issue to an imaginative exploration of "Russia's Defeat and Occupation, 1952–1960." The *Collier's* special issue, which featured contributions from prominent writers and intellectuals such as Robert Sherwood and Arthur Koestler, envisioned American victory in atomic war against the Soviet Union, followed by United Nations occupation of the USSR and the "reconstruction" of Russia (see figure 15). Although the editors warned at the outset that "we should not expect from Russia a carbon copy of American democracy or American economy," a missionary spirit pervaded the hypothetical sketches that followed. Thus, in the lead article Sherwood predicted that by 1960 "the light" would be "shining in Russia, and in all other darkened places of the earth." In a more explicitly religious vein, Ukrainian defector Oksana Kasenkina anticipated "a great spiritual reawakening," with Russians "enjoying glorious freedom of religion" as well as "other precious things of the West." And along a similar line, though on a different plane, journalist Marguerite Higgins imagined how thousands of fashion-starved Moscow women would jam a huge soccer stadium to see exhibitions of Western styles.[1]

American diplomats were appalled by *Collier's* exercise in futurism.[2] In particular, George F. Kennan, who would become the US Ambassador to the Soviet Union a few months later, strongly deplored the *Collier's* fantasies, especially the bad taste of imagining staging "Guys and Dolls" in a victory celebration at the Bolshoi Theatre. Yet Kennan and other diplomats were themselves engaged in thinking about transforming the Soviet Union. Indeed, Kennan believed that the *Collier's* special issue was a response to his demand in the April 1951 number of *Foreign Affairs* that Americans try to picture "the kind of Russia which we would prefer to see" and let that "image of a different and more acceptable Russia" guide American policy.[3]

As Kennan's call and the *Collier's* issue suggest, American fascination with liberating and remaking Russia peaked in the late 1940s and early

Figure 15.  *Collier's*, October 27, 1951. "Preview of the War We Do Not Want. Russia's Defeat and Occupation 1952–1960."

1950s. Between the end of the Grand Alliance and Stalin's death in 1953, a wide array of American intellectuals, journalists, politicians, and government officials passionately urged aggressive propaganda campaigns and vigorous covert action to free Eastern Europe and the Soviet Union from Stalinist domination.[4]

Although historians once held that "liberation" was mainly an empty campaign slogan used by Republican critics of the Truman administration's policy of "containment,"[5] the release of many previously classified documents has made it clear that in the late 1940s and early 1950s, the United States was seriously involved in efforts to undermine the Kremlin's control not only of Eastern Europe but also of the Soviet Union itself.[6] As early as the fall of 1947, American officials began to develop proposals for waging "psychological warfare" against the Soviet Union that encompassed propaganda, financial support of anti-communist emigré organizations, and military assistance to anti-Soviet guerrilla forces.[7] With the adoption of National Security Council (NSC) paper 68 in September 1950, the United States formally committed itself to fostering "fundamental change in the nature of the Soviet system" through programs that would "make the Russian people our allies."[8]

The primary means to that end was expanded and more aggressive propaganda. After the end of the wars against Germany and Japan, Ambassador Harriman urged more vigorous information programs in the Soviet Union. In late 1946 the State Department authorized increased publication of the magazine *Amerika* (from 10,000 to 50,000 copies) for distribution inside the Soviet Union. In February 1947, the Voice of America began broadcasting in Russian to the USSR. As American-Soviet friction worsened, those broadcasts grew more sharply critical of Soviet policies and ideology.[9] In 1950 President Harry Truman approved a major expansion of US propaganda, Congress more than tripled the appropriation for information programs, and Radio Free Europe (RFE) began broadcasts to keep alive the hopes of East European peoples for emancipation from the Soviet empire.[10] In 1951 the Central Intelligence Agency began funding the American Committee for the Liberation of the Peoples of Russia ("Amcomlib"), which sponsored its own radio station. In its first broadcast to the Soviet Union on March 1, 1953, Radio Liberation openly urged "the overthrow of the Soviet regime and the liquidation of Bolshevism."[11]

The surge of American enthusiasm about liberating Russia from Stalinism can not simply be explained as the product of realistic assessments of the instability and vulnerability of Soviet power. Occasionally, hopes for freeing Russia were fueled by reports of popular discontent and unrest in the USSR.[12] However, on the whole, American intelligence estimates and diplomatic dispatches from 1948 to 1953 tended to emphasize the stability of Soviet rule.[13] Historians may dispute whether such estimates exaggerated the strength of the Soviet system.[14] However, the last years of Stalin's reign were a period of relative calm for the USSR. Victory over Germany had boosted nationalist pride and Stalin's authority. A sense of security was bolstered by having a buffer zone of satellite states and (after 1949) nuclear weapons.[15] Shoes were scarce but bread was cheap. Hopes at war's end for free and comfortable lives were not realized, yet in contrast to the turmoil of the preceding decades, conditions seemed orderly and predictable to many Soviet citizens.[16] While VOA programs and *Amerika* magazines may have sown some inward discontent, the Soviet regime contained the threat by jamming the broadcasts, dumping many copies of the magazine, and punishing the slightest irreverence.[17] The urban, educated population – the prime target of US propaganda – was thoroughly indoctrinated, and rewarded for conformity.[18] Hence, there were sound reasons for American diplomats to report that Stalin "was genuinely accepted by a large proportion of the Soviet people" and to indicate that a breakdown of Soviet domination of the Russian people was at best a distant prospect.[19]

To some US officials, the difficulty of actually subverting the hermetic totalitarian state was irrelevant. In their eyes, the psychological warfare campaigns were tough-minded responses to Soviet subversion in Europe and the threat of further communist expansion around the world.[20] For such men, the prime goal was not to free Russia but to keep "the Soviet bear so busy scratching his own fleas that he has little time for molesting others."[21] This approach certainly came to be prevalent: in 1950, for example, one idealistic propaganda adviser was deeply disturbed "by the growing American reliance on power politics" and the "Machiavellian" schemes being devised in Washington.[22]

However, to focus narrowly on how cold-blooded Cold Warriors fought fire with fire is to neglect the ideological appeal and domestic meaning of the idea of liberating Russia. To many Americans – including founders, directors, and advisers of the psychological warfare organizations – "liberation" was a heartfelt "crusade."[23] As they urged their fellow Americans to join or support the crusade, such officials offered historical explanations for believing in the possibility of freeing Russia, articulated visions of the kind of Russia they hoped to see, and vented anxieties about problems in the United States that they hoped could be overcome through dedication to the mission of liberation. Analyzing the historical perspectives, racial views, and spiritual aspirations that underpinned the drive for "liberation" makes it possible to see the psychological warfare of the early Cold War not merely as a by-product of the confrontation with Stalinism, but also as part of a century-long American drive to penetrate, open, and remake Russia.

### Precedents for "liberation"

Many of the leaders of the drive for "liberation" saw the struggle of the early Cold War as the heir of earlier movements for a free Russia. The most important figure in the organization of American psychological warfare in the late 1940s, George Frost Kennan, believed himself destined to carry forward the work of his distant relative, George Kennan, who had inspired and led propaganda campaigns against tsarist despotism. When George F. Kennan had been in his teens, the childless and elderly Kennan in effect adopted him as his spiritual descendant.[24] Now, in the late 1940s, much as the elder Kennan had been a leader of the Friends of Russian Freedom, the younger Kennan spearheaded the formation of the National Committee for Free Europe (NCFE), a nominally private organization dedicated to liberating Eastern Europe from communist tyranny.[25] In 1952, when Kennan became Ambassador to Moscow, he felt especially conscious of his forebear's role. As if preordained to follow in the footsteps of his namesake, whose opposition to the tsarist government triggered his expulsion from Russia in 1901, Kennan imagined that he was engaged in a personal confrontation with the Stalinist leadership, and he provoked the Soviet government to banish him from the USSR. The Kremlin expelled him, Kennan claimed, because he "was coming too close to the exposure of some of their frauds and outrages," and because Russian popular enthusiasm for the United States and for him personally made his very presence in Moscow a threat to the regime.[26]

Kennan was not the only US diplomat who perceived a parallel between the movements against tsarist and Stalinist despotism. In January 1951, Frederick Reinhardt circulated to his State Department colleagues a reprint of an article the elder George Kennan had published in 1887. "The Last Appeal of the Russian Liberals," one of the first of Kennan's widely read indictments of the tsarist autocracy, stressed the "unconquerable spirit of rebellion" and the yearning for freedom among the Russian people. Reinhardt believed Kennan's analysis offered "considerable food for thought at the present time" and he suggested that it might be used in "informational work conducted by the Department."[27]

While the elder Kennan had supported liberal and moderate socialist revolutionaries against tsarism, the drive for liberation in the early Cold War entailed collaboration between Americans and another generation of Russian emigrés, many of them Menshevik opponents of Stalinism.[28] Boris Shub, the American-born son of a prominent Russian Social

Democrat, became manager of the New York Program Section (NYPS) of Radio Liberation. Drawing on his father's ties, Shub recruited some veterans of the struggle against tsarism to work for the station. Under Shub's influence, NYPS writers produced a number of scripts that cited the writings of pre-1917 revolutionaries, or featured songs from the movement against the autocracy.[29]

The most significant conceptual continuity between the two eras was a sharp distinction between the Russian people and their government. The elder Kennan urged as early as 1893 that Americans should sympathize with "the Russia of the people, not the Russia of the Czars." President Wilson greatly amplified that theme when he hailed the Russian people's overthrow of the allegedly non-Russian Romanov autocracy, and when he castigated Bolshevik conspirators for imposing a bloodier autocracy on the supposedly democratic Russian people.[30] The idea that a wide gulf separated the peoples of Russia from their Kremlin masters became a cardinal tenet of American propagandists in the early Cold War, who avowed friendship for ordinary Russians while denouncing the Stalinist regime.[31]

Among the most eloquent advocates of that approach was Boris Shub, who had worked as a political consultant on radio broadcasts from the American sector in Berlin (RIAS) before supervising the writing of scripts for Radio Liberation. In his influential book, *The Choice* (1950), Shub repeatedly stressed the need to distinguish "the Russian people" from "the present ruling clique" and urged the President to announce an "alliance with the Russian people over the heads of their despotic rulers." In line with Shub's guidance, the first broadcast of Radio Liberation in 1953 emphatically declared "that Communism and the Russian people are not one and the same, that the Russian people are secretly inimical to Communism and hate their enslavers."[32]

### Foundations of faith in "liberation"

Since most US intelligence estimates and many reports from diplomats in Moscow did not support the idea of a sharp divide between the Soviet state and the Russian people, what were the foundations for American faith in liberation? One platform was an optimistic or wishful reading of Russian history. In contrast to popular stereotypes of Russians as hopelessly submissive, champions of liberation maintained that the history of Russia revealed an inextinguishable passion for freedom churning beneath the lid of tsarist and Soviet oppression. Thus, when the Marquis de Custine's 1839 portrayal of Russians as slavishly obsequious was republished in 1951, George F. Kennan criticized Custine for missing the "vigorous and hopeful fermentation" that was in progress "under the imposing crust of tsarist authority" and argued that "today, again, there is another Russia there, equally obscure to the casual traveller, but equally important for the future."[33] Similarly, the Russian-American journalist Eugene Lyons, the first president of Amcomlib, challenged the "supposed experts abroad who regard the Soviet people as entirely a passive, bovine mass of beaten and intimidated people," in part by arguing that Russian peasants never fully accepted serfdom and despite their centuries of subjection never became slaves.[34]

Turning to the twentieth century, Lyons and many others cited a series of rebellions and defections as evidence that a fire still burned in Russian hearts: the Kronstadt sailors' revolt in 1921; the Vlasov Army's fighting on the side of Nazi Germany during the Second World War; the post-war Ukrainian partisan resistance to Soviet rule; the hundreds of thousands of prisoners of war who refused to return to the Soviet Union after May 1945; and the numerous Soviet soldiers and diplomats who defected to the West in the late 1940s.[35] This historical perspective was widely disseminated by many sophisticated writers, including Boris Shub and historian William Henry Chamberlin.[36] Among its most knowledgeable exponents was Robert F. Kelley, who had earned degrees in history from Harvard, served as a military attaché in Finland and the Baltic states during the Russian Civil War, headed the Eastern European Division of the State Department in the interwar decades, and helped lead Amcomlib and Radio Liberation from their inception. Reviewing the assumptions at the formation of Amcomlib, Kelley wrote in 1956: "Not only the well-known oppressive conditions of the USSR, but numerous acts of hostility by the Soviet peoples against their own government, beginning with the Kronstadt Rebellion in 1921 and culminating in widespread disaffection during World War II, indicated that these peoples could become one of our greatest allies in the cold war."[37]

That historical perspective was misleading. It disregarded how different the relations of Soviet armed forces to the government were between the desperate time of the Kronstadt revolt and the emergence of the Soviet Union as a superpower. It neglected the way victory in the Great Patriotic War re-legitimized the Stalinist regime and forged a new bond between it and the Russian people.[38] Perhaps most important, memories of how the USSR had been more open to American influence during the war obscured how tightly the Kremlin had closed the doors and consolidated its position after 1945.[39]

A second pillar for American faith in the liberation of Russia was religious belief. Many of the key figures in the formation and guidance of American psychological warfare campaigns against the Soviet Union were impelled by their Christian convictions, and believed that appeals to Russian religiosity could be effective.

Since George F. Kennan publicly admonished Americans to suppress their moral and romantic impulses – most famously, in a widely read critique of the "legalistic-moralistic" current in American diplomacy, published in 1951[40] – it is especially striking to see how deeply his own moral values and religious beliefs affected his outlook on Stalinist Russia. As noted in the previous chapter, while serving in Moscow during the Second World War, Kennan had become keenly interested in the possibility that the popular religious revival and the leaders of the Orthodox Church could challenge the Kremlin's control, though he regretfully concluded that for the moment, at least, Communist rulers had cowed the Russian people. When he left the Soviet Union in 1946 Kennan took some encouragement from his impression that, especially for the younger generation, the communist doctrine "was no longer a live and exciting thing," but a mere "recital" or "ritual" comparable to a lukewarm Episcopalianism. If the false religion of communism had lost its ability to inspire devotion, Kennan felt, the West had a new opportunity to reach out to the Russian people.[41]

He found further inspiration from meditating on Russian history. In early 1948, though busy heading the Policy Planning Staff of the State Department, Kennan had time to deliver a talk in New York on "Old Muscovy." In medieval Russia, Kennan observed, "the Grand Duke was not a complete autocrat," since the Orthodox Church "played a tremendous role in providing the checks and balances necessary to modify the power of the state." The Orthodox Metropolitan, Kennan continued, "was a figure at least equal to, and usually greater than, the Grand Duke himself in popular esteem." Thus, implicitly contrasting Old Muscovy to Stalinist Moscow, Kennan still seems to have contemplated the possibility he highlighted in 1945 that Orthodox leaders eventually would be "a match" for the Kremlin rulers.[42]

Although Kennan thought the ancient Orthodox spiritual traditions present in "sheltered" Muscovy offered hope for the regeneration of both Soviet Russia and the decadent, hypermodern West, paradoxically he also maintained that Russia could be redeemed only through the penetration of Western influences. In 1948 he made this point by arguing that only after Peter the Great moved Russia's capital to St. Petersburg, could "a shaft of light from the civilization of the West finally. . . pierce the iron curtain of the centuries" and foster "liberality or humanism in the exercise of state power." Two years later Kennan told students and faculty at Columbia University that what Americans found moving in Russian history was not the isolated Russia vegetating in "archaic darkness," but "the Russia touched by the stream of western civilization," and striving to borrow from it "in order that there might be light where there had been darkness." In these and other instances, when Kennan used the conventional metaphor of Christian missionaries about "light" and "darkness," he revealed a strong evangelical impulse in his approach to Russia.[43]

In the early 1950s, when Kennan took a leave of absence from the State Department, in part because his ability to influence policy had been reduced, he expressed grave reservations about aggressive American psychological warfare against the Soviet Union. Caring deeply about Russians, he was disturbed by the advocacy of an opportunistic and frenzied approach that lost sight of the underlying goodness of the Russian people and that had no chance of success, since the population was "in the hands of a totalitarian regime" that had a monopoly over weapons and communications. In addition, while he approved of covert American assistance to Russian exiles, he believed that overt incitement by the United States would be counterproductive. Upon being called back to serve as Ambassador to the Kremlin in April 1952, he explained his view at a press conference. A change in the type of regime in Russia, he told reporters, "has got to come through the efforts of the Russian people themselves and if another great country gets in it and tries to bring it about and tries to tell people what to do, it's going to confuse that whole issue and perhaps to the detriment of the very things which we would like to see in Russia." More succinctly, he added, "too zealous an interventionist interest by a foreign country in political matters in another country is the kiss of death to the very things that it wishes to favor."[44]

Yet Kennan still believed there might be a spiritual foundation for a regime change. "As a member of the Christian community," he confided to an Orthodox priest in December 1951, "I can and do entertain the hope that the Christian spirit can be kept alive in Russia and that some day victories may be won there in the realm of the spirit which will compensate for all the suffering and horror of the recent past."[45] The next year, while serving as Ambassador to the Soviet Union, Kennan informed Washington that "even in the relatively sophisticated and politically-minded city of Moscow one-fourth to one-third of the population is estimated, on fairly serious evidence, to have some sort of religious faith." This, he portentously concluded, was "a fact of immense underlying importance"; it contributed to his sense of a "spiritual breach between the rulers and ruled."[46] Thus, religion was a central and persistent element in Kennan's thinking about the possibility of liberating Russia from Stalinism.

While Kennan was moody and sometimes contradictory, DeWitt C. Poole, the first president of the National Committee for Free Europe, drew more consistent direction from his religious convictions. Raised in a severe "Puritan" home, Poole was inclined from the beginning of the Soviet state to see the struggle against Bolshevism as a contest between "amorality" and "eternal moral values." Thirty years later, he unequivocally viewed the Cold War as a "spiritual" battle between Christian civilization and communist barbarism. In this "struggle for the souls of men," Poole declared, Americans were called to fulfill their historic "missionary role," in part through radio broadcasts to Eastern Europe that would "keep up hope among those who are loyal to our Western ideas – those who are chips off that small, hard core of common agreement which we call Western civilization, or Christian civilization." Like Kennan, Poole took encouragement from the wilting of communist ideology: he believed that the hollowness of Marxist "claptrap" exposed "the vulnerability of our enemy's intellectual and spiritual position."[47]

Many other figures in the campaigns for liberation shared the assumptions that communism was a spurious pseudo-religion, and that the West could mobilize latent Russian religiosity against the atheistic Soviet regime. For example, James Burnham, an apostate from communism who became an adviser on psychological warfare to the CIA, believed that the West should exploit the failure of the "communist religion" to deliver its promised earthly paradise, which fostered "unrest and division within the souls of communists." Although Burnham attached great importance to converting communist elites, he also suggested appeals to the broader masses of the USSR.[48] In an essay on psychological warfare, Burnham maintained that "Russian soldiers and officers, loyal to God and to their land and people, and therefore against the blasphemous and inhuman communist regime, have kept continuously alive since 1917 germ cells of opposition. . . . Hundreds of martyrs prove that men of God – priests and rabbis and Moslem *imams* – have never accepted the rule of the Party which openly proclaims itself anti-God and Godless." Burnham consequently hoped that American churches would try to communicate with subjects of the Soviet empire: "Religious broadcasts and religious literature," he enthused, "can surely penetrate the Iron Curtain – and perhaps even religious missionaries reviving the heroic tradition of Christianity."[49]

Although some top diplomats and policymakers scorned proposals for emphasizing religious themes,[50] American-supported propaganda organizations embraced that tactic. Assistant Secretary of State Edward Barrett, who headed the US Information Service (USIS) from 1950 to 1952, believed "powerful religious forces" could "become Communism's greatest foe," and under his leadership, American information programs placed increased emphasis on "the great appeal of godliness versus godlessness."[51] A study of the "working assumptions" of US Information Agency officers conducted in 1953–4 found significant emphasis on American spirituality and the conversion of Russians from communism. Voice of America broadcasts in this period repeatedly attacked Soviet tyranny as hostile to religion and denounced Stalin as a "pseudo-God."[52] Admiral Leslie Stevens, President of Amcomlib from 1952 to 1954, directed that propaganda beamed into the USSR should "encourage reliance on traditional indigenous spiritual concepts."[53] Radio Liberation adviser Boris Shub, who stressed that despite Bolshevik atheism, the Russian people had "never learned to live without God," urged Americans to help Russians "mobilize the great spiritual and moral resources that lie within them."[54] With Shub's encouragement, a profoundly influential Russian Orthodox priest, Father Alexander Schmemann, developed a "Sunday Talk" that would be broadcast weekly for more than thirty years.[55] Another Orthodox priest prepared one hundred talks on religion for the Voice of America from 1951 to 1954 and would go on to write almost two thousand scripts for VOA and Radio Liberty in subsequent years.[56]

For some US officials, appeals to religious sentiments were merely a useful Cold War tactic.[57] However, for founders and leaders of American propaganda organizations like Kennan and Poole, the invocation of religious themes reflected deeply felt convictions. Many of these men had been raised during the "Third Great Awakening" of 1890–1920, when Americans had set out to evangelize the world in their generation.[58]

In addition to being a source of personal motivation and a part of propaganda tactics, religion was a vital element in the way Americans publicly discussed and imagined the liberation of Russia. In 1949, for example, the popular magazine *Saturday Evening Post* featured an article by Walter Bedell Smith, a military man who served as Ambassador to the USSR from 1946 to 1949. Headlined, "God Won't Stay Underground in Russia," the article was accompanied by photographs of devout Russians receiving Easter blessings. In his ambassadorial memoirs published the next year, Smith recalled how seeing Easter services in a Moscow cathedral convinced him "of the depth of religious feeling that still, in spite of Communist opposition, animates the masses of Russia. . . ." Quoting almost verbatim from a paper Kennan wrote in 1945, Smith added that if the religious devotion of the Russian people "were ever to be grasped and activated by outside influence, the threat to the regime might be incalculable."[59]

John Foster Dulles, an ambitious Republican and a longtime leader of the Federal Council of Churches, presented similar ideas in *War or Peace* (1950): since Russians were "a religious people," the constraints that the

"Godless" Soviet state placed upon their church were major sources of the "widespread discontent" within the Soviet Union, which the United States could exploit as it mobilized its own "spiritual power" and applied moral pressure.[60] Three years later Eugene Lyons stressed that "The fanatic faith in Bolshevik tenets . . . has crumbled," that "the Russian core has not been corrupted beyond redemption," and that "within, the light still burns." Since "behind the soot there is still the celebrated Russian soul," there was reason to hope for "the overthrow of the Soviet regime."[61]

The realms of confidential government deliberations, public policy discussions, and popular imagination were not rigidly compartmentalized. The Policy Planning Staff of the State Department, for example, seriously considered ideas for propaganda campaigns presented by popular magazines. At the same time, there were close ties between the film industry and propaganda organizations, with Hollywood moguls Cecil B. DeMille, Spyros Skouras, and Darryl Zanuck all serving on the board of NCFE. In that light, it was not so strange that a Hollywood movie featured the idea that religious messages from the West could inspire revolts against communism. In "Red Planet Mars" (1952), Voice of America broadcasts, including a condemnation of worshipping false gods, inspire Russian peasants to rip portraits of Soviet leaders off their walls, dig up their buried icons, and march on the Kremlin. The movie climaxes with an aged, black-robed Patriarch speaking into a microphone, announcing the rebirth of a Christian Russia – an imaginative fulfillment of the vision *Time* magazine had promoted when it put a patriarch on its cover nine years earlier.[62]

A third basis for thinking the peoples of Russia could be liberated from communism was the belief that images of American material abundance would prove irresistibly attractive. Key advisers of propaganda organizations thought that appealing to Russians' unfulfilled hopes for better lives would be an effective tactic for sowing discontent and inducing defections.

Boris Shub, for example, had been impressed by the avid curiosity about the American standard of living expressed by Russian prisoners of war and displaced persons he interviewed in 1945. He suggested then that POWs and DPs who returned to the USSR would challenge Soviet hegemony by privately spreading their admiration of America. Later, as a programming director for Radio Liberation, he continued to be guided by his conviction that millions of Soviets were dissatisfied with the quality of their lives.[63]

Some top political leaders also felt that images of America's economic miracles could help to convert subjects of the Soviet empire into allies of the free world. Thus, Senator Brien McMahon of Connecticut dreamed of having Soviet workers "see at first hand the automobiles and gardens of the typical American workers in Detroit or Omaha." He also suggested "mailing millions of mail-order catalogues to the Iron Curtain countries" so those impoverished peoples could salivate over "the consumers' wonderland contained within the pages of a Sears-Roebuck or a Montgomery Ward catalogue."[64] President Dwight Eisenhower expressed similar enthusiasm. Convinced that "the economic incentive would have terrific attraction in Russia, if it could be got over to the ordinary people," Eisenhower made a pledge of US aid for economic development a centerpiece of his "Chance for Peace" speech in April 1953.[65]

However, in the late 1940s and early 1950s, some prominent figures had serious reservations about preaching American capitalism to the peoples of the USSR. Although there was a broad consensus that it would be desirable to break down Stalinist autarky and integrate the Soviet bloc in the world economy,[66] key experts warned that it would not be feasible for the USSR to make a rapid transition from socialism to a market economy. Since Russia had "scarcely known private enterprise" over the centuries and since the younger generation of Russians knew only "the state capitalism that the Soviet régime has enforced," Kennan cautioned in 1951, it was futile to look for a Russian economy "resembling the private enterprise system as we know it." Instead, Kennan forecast, "large sections of economic life . . . will almost certainly remain in national hands for a long time to come in Russia, regardless of the identity of the political authority."[67] Robert F. Kelley concurred: after more than thirty years of communist rule, state ownership and operation of heavy industry could not be drastically modified by a post-Soviet regime.[68] Eugene Lyons, who interviewed many of the post-war exiles, observed that few of them "are under the delusion that the Soviet economy can be unscrambled or have any hankering for a private-enterprise society in the American sense." Along the same line, Oleg Anisimov, chairman of a Welfare Committee for Russian Refugees in Germany from 1945 to 1951, concluded that the Soviet people did not want to follow the American model, but favored an economy midway between American liberalism and Soviet centralization.[69]

In retrospect, both the psychological warriors who thought dangling the lure of American abundance would work, and the Russia experts who warned that the Soviet people did not want free market capitalism, appear to have been right. Radio broadcasts that described a land of plenty did induce some defections, and Soviet government efforts at suppression or denial may have whetted Russian appetites.[70] Yet a hunger for an easier and better life – which, after all, was part of the promised radiant future of communism – did not necessarily mean uncritical admiration of the American way of life, as many in the United States assumed, then and later.

### Doubts about the Slavic race vs. faith in the Russian people

One of the major obstacles to faith in a popular rebellion against Stalinist tyranny was a widespread American tendency to view Russians as "Oriental" and incapable of changing their national character. Members of the National Committee for Free Europe (NCFE), who focused primarily on liberating the East European satellites from Soviet domination, were especially prone to hurling the epithet "Asiatic" at Russians. For example, DeWitt Poole, who enjoyed pointing out that Lenin's "high cheek bones and slightly upslant eyes" revealed his "Tartar-Russian" ancestry, regarded Hungary, like Poland, as a historic "bulwark on the frontier of European culture" and a safeguard against "barbarism" pressing in from the East.[71] Lewis Galantiere, a longtime NCFE advisor who wrote general recommendations for Radio Free Europe broadcasts, presented the most extreme "Orientalist" view of eternal Russian "national traits" in the prominent journal *Foreign Affairs* in 1949.[72]

While labelling Russia "Oriental" or "Asiatic" served a special function of boundary delineation and enemy definition for propagandists who were chiefly interested in the liberation of Eastern Europe, those labels were also sometimes applied to Russia by men who focused principally on the Soviet Union. According to Leslie Stevens, who had served as naval attaché in Russia from 1947 to 1949, the Russian people had "half-Asiatic minds."[73] William Henry Chamberlin, a journalist, historian, and prominent advocate of "liberation," emphasized the "Asiatic" character of Russians, for example, in alleging that Soviet troops in eastern Europe behaved like "oriental savages."[74] Even George F. Kennan at times described Russia in such terms. In 1950, for example, Kennan warned that the Soviet regime was the "greatest single enemy of western civilization . . . since Turks were at the walls of Vienna," and from Moscow in 1952 he cautioned the State Department about the need for firm and dignified conduct "in this semi-oriental country."[75]

More often, however, Kennan worked to shore up a fourth pillar of belief in the emancipation of Russia from Stalinism, constructed from a non-rational faith in the Russian people and a racial definition of Russians as white Europeans. Echoing the nineteenth-century poet F. I. Tiutchev, Kennan explained that in order "to believe in Russia and in the ultimate destiny of the Russian people," one "had to depart from rationality" and to heed instead a sentimental "admiration for the humble mass of Russian people," whose fine spirit had somehow remained uncorrupted by the cruel despotisms they had long endured.[76] In conjunction with that view, Kennan typically emphasized that while Stalin was "the great Khan," Russians were not Mongols but Europeans.[77]

Kennan's close associate, R. Gordon Wasson, a vice-president of J. P. Morgan who had married a Russian woman and headed a committee for promoting Slavic studies, even more emphatically refuted the conventional notion "that the Russians are Asiatics." Instead, Wasson argued in 1951, Russians were "Slavs and East Europeans"; although their ancestors had migrated eastward from the Vistula, they still shared "the common heritage" of Indo-European peoples. Wasson believed that fulfillment of America's missionary duty required a correct racial definition of Russians: "It cannot help but please the Kremlin when we cast the Russian people into outer darkness by erroneously lumping them with races as culturally remote from us as the Mongols and Hindus."[78]

Like Kennan and Wasson, Eugene Lyons deplored Western "exaggerations about Russia's Asiatic and Byzantine qualities." The medieval historical experience of subjection to the Mongols, he maintained, should not be "mistaken for attributes of the Russian character." Lyons stood out, though, in the relatively explicit way he challenged another racial stereotype that had persisted from the nineteenth century. As an immigrant from Russia, Lyons may have been more sensitive than native born Americans to insidious comparisons of Russians to African American sharecroppers or servants.[79] Angered by such suggestions, he inveighed against the notion that tsarist Russia "was a dark and savage land of slaves and nihilists," and insisted that the Russian peasants were "far removed from the society of meek slaves which is the premise of most present-day judgment of Russia before and after the revolution."[80]

## Democratic vs. authoritarian visions of Russia's future

For Russian-Americans like Lyons and Shub, it was axiomatic that emancipation from Stalinism would lead to democracy. Drawing on a long mythological tradition among Russian intellectuals, Lyons emphasized Slavic democratic traditions dating back to the Novgorod *veche* (popular assembly) of the Middle Ages, while Shub stressed that Russians had been "fighting for freedom for over a century" – first against tsarism and then against Bolshevism.[81] In line with this view, the first broadcast by Radio Liberation emphatically championed democratic principles, repudiating monarchism as well as Bolshevism. Under Lyons' successor, Howland Sargeant, Amcomlib explicitly espoused the goal of "a democratic order on the territories of the USSR" and formally defined "liberation" as "the establishment of a genuinely representative government responsible to the will of the people."[82]

However, others who founded and advised the psychological warfare organizations expressed grave doubts about the possibility of rapid democratization. Their perspectives on Russian history and culture are of particular interest, in contrast to the liberal universalism espoused by US officials from President Wilson in 1917 through the post-Soviet "transition" of the 1990s.

"While Russia has had her moments of liberalism," Kennan warned policy-makers in 1948, "the concepts of democracy are not familiar to the great mass of the Russian people, and particularly not to those who are temperamentally inclined to the profession of government." Since any basic alteration of the "political psychology" of a country could "flow only from the organic experience of the people in question," Americans could not hope "to impose our concepts of democracy within a short space of time upon any group of Russian leaders."[83] Furthermore, because communist terror had eliminated or exiled whatever "democratic elements" had existed in Russia, democracy would not spring up rapidly from Russian soil. In 1951, Kennan even classified Russia as one of those countries where "no popular representative government which would be recognizable as corresponding to our concepts of democracy will ever exist within our time."[84]

Robert Kelley, who had overseen Kennan's training in Russian language and history in the late 1920s and early 1930s, was equally pessimistic about the prospects for democratizing Russia. At the inception of Amcomlib in 1951, Kelley predicted that a post-Soviet regime would "be patterned along lines deriving from Russian historical development and cultural background and will, therefore, probably . . . ignore some political principles and institutions by which the West sets great store." Although Kelley listed the "introduction of a democratic system" as one of four US goals in a post-Bolshevik Russia, he commented that "the peculiarly authoritative [sic] nature of the Russian mind" would make reduction of police power and protection of individual freedom quite difficult to achieve.[85] In later years Kelley even argued that radio broadcasts to the USSR should not use the term "freedom" – that was "a concept which the Russians simply do not understand."[86]

One reason to doubt that Stalinism would be replaced by democracy was that many recent emigrés from the Soviet Union did not share the democratic idealism of Shub, Lyons, and the older generation of Russian exiles. Thus, James Burnham's confidential forecast that "There would have to be an interim period during which some form of semi-authoritarian rule would be necessary," was based not only on the conditioning of "thirty years of totalitarianism" but also on the nationalist and militarist ideology of one of the leading exile organizations. In addition, some of the Soviet emigrés who worked at the Radio Liberation headquarters in Munich were Vlasovites who had fought on the side of the Nazis during World War II, and whose conversion to democratic principles was suspect.[87]

Given US officials' views of the authoritarian political culture inside the USSR and among Soviet emigrés, it was logical that they hoped to induce a coup by Soviet military officers rather than a popular democratic revolution. In May 1951, for example, an Air Force colonel at the War College prepared a statement of US objectives which specified that "our aim is to substitute a nonpolitical, indigenous, military regime" that would "hold power nominally under United Nations' auspices until such time as political reforms and popular education can permit representative government." Kennan praised the paper as "very constructive" and "realistic," then added: "God help us if we ever fight a war with the objective of making the Russians accept democracy."[88] After Stalin died two years later, other papers prepared by the Psychological Strategy Board and National Security Council similarly envisioned inducing "the Soviet armed forces to overthrow the Soviet regime" and stimulating a "Soviet officer conspiracy."[89] In this respect, the confidential thinking of key policy-makers diverged significantly from the way the drive for "liberation" was presented to the American people.

## The liberation of Russia and the revitalization of America

If Americans involved in the psychological warfare against the USSR differed in their visions of democratic and authoritarian futures for Russia, they split even more sharply over the relationship between the crusade for a free Russia and the revitalization of America. Examining the latter division is vital to understanding the domestic reverberations of "liberation."

Although he had been the most important figure in the launching of the psychological warfare campaigns in the late 1940s, Kennan came to emphasize inner purification and domestic improvement over an expansive mission. Already in January 1950, Kennan argued that the Cold War struggle "will be determined . . . less by what we do to the Russians than by what we do to ourselves." Addressing business leaders in Cincinnati, Kennan elaborated, "The issue of this great contest between our western world and the Russian communists will probably be determined in the last analysis by the degree of tone and vigor which we are able to impart to our American society" and to the relationships among non-communist countries.[90]

By the spring of 1951, Kennan's deepening inclination to focus on cleansing the city upon a hill led him to publicly criticize leaders who sought to preach to Russia. In contrast to those who thought of the Cold War as only "a question of external propaganda," Kennan argued that it was "primarily a question of what we urge upon ourselves." The world, he maintained, was "more ready to recognize and respect spiritual distinction than material opulence." Hence, Americans' "first and main concern" had to be with the spirit of American life and the "state of national character."

Kennan's sage advice that Americans should let Russians "be Russians" and should *not* expect Russia to emulate the United States, did not, however, mean that he had totally repudiated his religious upbringing and the example of his namesake, who had worn the shackles of Siberian exiles in his crusade for a "free Russia" sixty years earlier. "[I]f our taper is a strong one," Kennan proclaimed, "we may be sure that its rays will penetrate to the Russian room and eventually play their part in dissipating the gloom which prevails there. No iron curtain could suppress, even in the innermost depths of Siberia, the news that America had shed the shackles of disunity, confusion, and doubt, had taken a new lease of hope and determination, and was setting about her tasks with enthusiasm and clarity of purpose."[91]

In contrast to Kennan, the ailing DeWitt Poole continued to be fiercely committed to the negative goal of "demolishing that combination of Marx, materialism and Machiavelli which is the enemy." However, Poole shared with Kennan the sense that spiritual renewal and ideological reaffirmation in America were even more important. "[U]ltimate victory" in the Cold War could be achieved, Poole declared at a convocation of psychological warriors in 1952, only by generating "a movement of the spirit, which surge on surge will grow into a great wave of feeling, releasing people from uncertainty and fear, stirring enthusiasm, producing conviction and selfless dedication."[92]

Poole and Kennan thus embodied a yearning that was widely felt in the early Cold War. The authors of NSC 68, for example, expressed the common hope to defeat the "fanatic faith" of Communism in part by mobilizing a superior "spiritual counter-force" and awakening "the latent spiritual energies of free men everywhere." Along the same line, John Foster Dulles felt that one of the main benefits of the rivalry with Soviet communism was that it could spur Americans to shake off their apathy, revive their moral vigor, and restore their "sense of mission in the world."[93]

While the craving for a spiritual revival was widespread, advocates of "liberation" disagreed over whether the desired revitalization should come primarily from domestic housecleaning or from demonization of Soviet tyranny. James Burnham felt that Kennan was too "pale and abstract," that his publicly proclaimed policy of containment failed to meet the "moral and spiritual demand" for a crusading ardor, and that victory over the forces of darkness hinged on willpower rather than noble character. Chastising those who failed to evince a powerful hatred of communism, Burnham declared: "By their emotions shall ye know them." Like a revivalist preacher, Burnham thundered: "Does the United States *choose* to win?" If it answered with a resounding yes, then success would be assured. With doubt vanquished, America would lead a spiritual revival of the West, and Christian civilization would triumph over Red satanism.[94]

For Burnham and other conservative anti-communists, it was essential to avoid becoming preoccupied with overcoming domestic evils such as poverty, slums, and racial discrimination. The idea "that 'the best defense against communism is to improve political and social conditions at home,'" Burnham asserted, had been planted in the non-communist world as part of the Soviet plot to enervate the West.[95] Eugene Lyons developed a similar argument. Instead of concentrating on the defeatist task of self-perfection or wallowing in guilt about Western sins, Americans should make a firm commitment to the annihilation of "Soviet barbarism." Such an unequivocal pledge of liberation would quickly "end the confusions in which the free world has been floundering" and "bring an invigorating clarity to our relations with the Kremlin."[96]

Vilification of the evil empire was essential to such men. In 1953, after Kennan delivered a speech endorsing John Quincy Adams' statement that "America goes not abroad in search of monsters to destroy," he was rebuked by historian William Henry Chamberlin, who insisted on the need for tough methods in the "bar-room brawl" against an "utterly unscrupulous enemy."[97]

As the tension between Kennan's introspective reformism and the crusading anticommunism of Burnham and Lyons suggests, American thinking about liberating Russia was intimately bound up with feelings about the United States. While the two approaches had much in common – as late as June 1951 Kennan said he had "nothing but sympathy for the things which make Eugene Lyons and others feel the way they do" – they ultimately represented two very different ways to revitalize America.[98]

## Waning of the campaign for liberation

By 1952, many US intelligence analysts and diplomats were growing more dubious about the possibility of liberation. National Security Council staff and State Department officials were increasingly conscious of the limits of US psychological warfare and the risks of provoking the now nuclear-armed Kremlin. One CIA assessment in May 1952 bluntly stated that "the liberation of the Russian people is not considered to be a feasible undertaking for the next several years." In Moscow as US Ambassador, the ambivalent Kennan still anticipated a crisis of Soviet rule, but he reluctantly concluded that few Russians could "imagine any other sort of government," that there was "an increasing acceptance of Soviet power," and that there would be "no early revolt in the Soviet Union."[99] Kennan's colleague Charles Bohlen, then Counselor of the State Department, repeatedly criticized schemes for undermining the Soviet regime as futile, counterproductive, and dangerous. The Stalinist leadership, Bohlen argued, was determined to retain power, a hostile international environment actually helped it maintain control, and provocative US actions might prompt the apprehensive regime to lash out.[100]

As Kennan back-pedalled, and Bohlen's views became dominant in the Truman administration, passionate champions of "liberation" began to hope that a new Republican administration would unleash more vigorous action. Psychological warriors urged public commitments to "liberation," and were heartened when John Foster Dulles made such a pledge in his May 1952 call for "A Policy of Boldness." The Republican presidential candidate, General Dwight Eisenhower, had been convinced of the value of psychological warfare during World War II, had served on the board of the National Committee for Free Europe, and had for years urged expansion of the use of psychological warfare, which he viewed as an all-encompassing struggle for the minds and wills of humanity. Eisenhower's election in November, and his appointment of Dulles as Secretary of State, therefore seemed to set the stage for fulfillment of the promise of liberation.[101]

On the night of March 1, 1953, only hours after the first broadcast by Radio Liberation, Joseph Stalin suffered a stroke that led to his death four days later. This was the moment psychological warriors had been anticipating. A crisis of succession, they thought, offered a prime opportunity to destabilize the Soviet regime and mobilize the Russian people as allies of the West. Yet, in spite of the numerous psychological warfare papers that had been drafted and re-drafted in the preceding years, Eisenhower was dismayed to find that there were no specific plans for exploiting the situation. The president's special adviser for psychological operations, C. D. Jackson, urged a message from Eisenhower to the Soviet people to capitalize on the "great emotional shock" of Stalin's death. However, John Foster Dulles and others in Ike's Cabinet decided it would be unseemly to call on the Soviet people to rise up against their rulers in a period of mourning. Moreover, Bohlen and other State Department officials argued, aggressive action and a heightening of pressure would actually help the new Soviet regime to consolidate its authority.[102]

Stalin's successors feared that there would be chaos. Yet the overriding response to Stalin's passing was an outpouring of grief that reflected widespread reverence for the ruler who had directed the industrialization of the country and led it to victory in war. "All Russia wept," poet Yevgenii Yevtushenko remembered. The shock of Stalin's death, Under Secretary of State Walter Bedell Smith concluded, had "produced for the time being unity and coherence in the regime," not panic or instability. Although strikes broke out in the summer of 1953 at some of the concentration camps in the Arctic, and the Soviet regime had to use tanks to crush an uprising in East Berlin, by September US national security officials agreed that the Kremlin had not been impaired by such events and was not likely to be significantly weakened in the near future.[103]

The Eisenhower administration did not publicly repudiate the goal of "liberation," in part because top officials felt a rhetorical commitment to that aspiration was useful in sustaining the morale of the West. Privately, though, Eisenhower began to shift course, away from efforts to destroy the Soviet state and toward negotiations, coexistence, and a relaxation of tensions.[104]

The fizzling of hopes to free the Soviet empire in 1953 did not mean that "liberation" was merely an idle dream or a cynical campaign slogan. The wide gap between the torrent of words (books, articles, speeches, policy papers) and the trickle of action does suggest, though, that the perceived domestic benefits of the crusade were an important attraction all along, and that the campaign had a greater impact on how Americans felt about themselves than on conditions inside the USSR.

## Lessons and legacies

Some Americans involved in the drive for "liberation" drew inspiration from their experiences in the early 1950s that would shape their approaches as policy-makers many years later. For example, Richard Pipes, a young participant in the Soviet Vulnerabilities Project at MIT and Harvard, carried a belief in the possibility of cracking the Soviet system from that political warfare research to his work on the National

Security Council staff three decades later. The president Pipes served in the 1980s, Ronald Reagan, was active in the 1950s in a different way. The handsome actor gave enthusiastic speeches in 1950 on behalf of the Crusade for Freedom, an effort to mobilize popular support for radio broadcasts to Eastern Europe. As head of the Screen Actors Guild, Reagan also participated in a plan to cooperate with the government in making movies a "vital weapon" in the ideological war against communism. Hollywood leaders convinced him that images of the standard of living enjoyed by ordinary Americans could have earthshaking effects behind the Iron Curtain, thereby nurturing a dream Reagan would cherish through the end of his presidency. And in a tribute to a conservative writer who profoundly influenced his anticommunist views, in 1983 Reagan would award a Presidential Medal of Freedom to James Burnham, the most prolific and imaginative advocate of "liberation" in the years when that notion was most in vogue.[105]

However, in the shorter term, many US officials concluded that the campaign for liberation was futile and counterproductive. Logically implicit in the recognition by State Department advisers that tensions with the outside world tended to justify and sustain repression within the Soviet Union, was the idea that an easing of tension – détente – would be more effective than hostile confrontation in loosening the communist grip on the Soviet empire. This reasoning was not fully developed or explicitly articulated in the early Cold War, when policy planners like George F. Kennan were often strongly influenced by emotions, including fear of communist subversion, a romantic faith in the Russian spirit, and a righteous anger at the monstrous tyranny of Joseph Stalin. However, after Stalin's death the Eisenhower administration would begin to develop a new policy to promote a gradual opening of the Soviet system rather than its revolutionary transformation.

# 6    Evolution, not revolution:
The eclipse of "liberation" and the
pursuit of "liberalization," 1954–74

In the spring of 1958, David Lawrence, the seventy-year-old founder and editor of *U.S. News and World Report*, provoked a protracted epistolary exchange with John Bennett, a professor at Union Theological Seminary and an editor of *Christianity and Crisis*, a leading liberal journal of opinion. What set Lawrence off was an editorial by Bennett that urged Americans to "avoid the perpetual official moral diatribe against Communist countries," to "accept the fact that communism is here to stay" in Russia and China, and to relax tensions as the best way to encourage the communist countries to "move in a more humane direction." In his initial response, Lawrence stressed the difficulty of coexistence, since communism had "set out to destroy Christianity." When Bennett coolly replied that it was "going to be easier for Christianity to co-exist with communism than with the missile race," Lawrence grew more agitated and insisted that the missile race "merely accentuates the power of evil." In a characteristically Wilsonian spirit, Lawrence argued that "there can be no safety in the world as long as we have autocratic governments." Hence, the problem for Americans was how to make contact with the people of Russia and "how to get rid of their malevolent rulers." That, Bennett answered, was "a very hazardous thing," and it was needlessly risky because of changes underway that "will make Communism easier to live with." Lawrence then denied that communism itself was changing, and he chastised contemporary clergy who were "willing to overlook sin and evil." In his last response to Lawrence, Bennett calmly explained that theologians in recent years had emphasized "that there is no policy that does not involve choice of a lesser evil." The key challenge, then, was to shift away from a rigid, doctrinaire policy that had "helped to make the communists more intractable" and to find a policy that would "prevent the most devastating evil" (nuclear war).[1]

Although Lawrence was on the offensive in the fight he picked with Bennett, by the late 1950s advocates of uncompromising opposition to communism and aggressive efforts to free the peoples of the Soviet bloc had lost their hold on US policy and popular attitudes. The very shrillness of conservative anticommunists like Lawrence reflected the decline of their influence since the early 1950s, when "liberation" had been the great rallying cry. Despite the implausibility of a successful anticommunist revolution in the wake of the brutal crushing of revolts in East Germany (1953) and Hungary (1956), Lawrence and others clung to the *idea* of "liberation" because it was vital to their definition of American identity and purpose. Emphasizing the menace of communism in general and the threat from the Kremlin in particular were not sufficient; they also needed to summon an idealistic sense of mission, and contrast American spirituality to Marxist materialism in order to roll back its alleged spawn in the United States: the "welfare state."[2]

Such champions of the revolutionary liberation of Russia and Eastern Europe increasingly seemed reckless and irresponsible as the two superpowers expanded their arsenals of nuclear weapons and confronted each other in a series of crises that raised anxiety about the reliability of deterrence. Although liberal Protestants like Bennett had accepted the need for vigorous measures to contain the spread of communism in the late 1940s and early 1950s, many of them argued for a new course a decade later. While adamant anticommunists like Lawrence denied that changes in Russia after Stalin's death altered the essential iniquity of the system, liberals like Bennett argued with growing persuasiveness that the easing of censorship and the greater openness to contacts with the West created opportunities to promote the evolutionary liberalization of the Soviet bloc.[3]

Thus, the private debate between Lawrence and Bennett reflected the contest between two dramatically different approaches to relations with Soviet Russia, each influenced by moral values and religious beliefs. The first approach, which combined moral condemnation of the nefarious Soviet system with the shunning of its rulers and incitement of the Russian people to revolt, continued to have a strong emotional appeal to many Americans, especially East European immigrants and right-wing Republicans. Beyond those groups, however, the demonization of the Soviet empire had decreasing resonance. A growing majority of Americans favored a relaxation of tensions and increase in contact with Soviet leaders, which, exponents of the second approach argued, would open the way for the gradual softening of the oppressive and offensive aspects of Soviet communism.

Viewed from the vantage points of the White House and the Kremlin, the emergence of détente is conventionally seen as a pragmatic groping for accommodation between top political leaders who had largely abandoned hopes to transform their counterparts' societies.[4] Yet when we widen the perspective to include lower level officials, insurgent politicians, religious leaders like Bennett, and journalists like Lawrence, it becomes possible to see this era as the seed-time for two different triumphalist views of the Cold War. Even as their influence on mainstream opinion declined, right-wing political activists were building the organizational base and ideological foundation for a new crusade against Soviet communism that they claim ultimately caused the collapse of the "evil empire." At the same time, Americans involved in penetrating the Soviet Union through educational exchanges, cultural exhibitions, and toned-down propaganda broadcasts believed they were chipping away at the ideological pillars of the Soviet system that would crumble in the late 1980s.[5]

While both triumphalist interpretations involve leaps of faith and are impossible to verify definitively, it is possible to analyze how the Soviet government first opened the door to Western influences and then sought to combat their subversive impact. Following Stalin's death, Soviet leaders sought to break out of their political and economic isolation, but in trying to reduce foreign hostility and increase trade, they allowed tourists, evangelists, musicians, business executives, and US Information Agency guides to enter their country and contact their people in ways that were difficult to control. Although the cumulative effects of these contacts are difficult to assess, the strenuous efforts by the Soviet government to contain them indicate that they feared the Americans' evolutionary approach to changing the Soviet system could have revolutionary consequences.

### The eclipse of "liberation"

From the mid-1950s through the early 1970s, US presidents repeatedly disavowed the idea of liberating Russia from communism. Already in January 1955, at a National Security Council (NSC) discussion of the exploitation of Soviet bloc vulnerabilities, Dwight Eisenhower observed that the US "was not in a position to state that it would promote revolution in the Soviet Union." In 1959, as he prepared to welcome Soviet leader Nikita Khrushchev to Washington, Eisenhower remarked on "how we have changed our view of the Soviet people," from picturing them in 1956 as "sullen and discouraged," to recognizing that "they are able to maintain a high morale." The president thus implicitly repudiated the notion that discontented Russians could be encouraged to overthrow their government.[6]

As a college student on a European tour twenty years earlier, John F. Kennedy seems to have concluded that communism suited Russia as much as democracy suited America. As a Senator in 1958, Kennedy rejected approaching the Cold War as "a moral crusade." As President in 1961, he suggested to Nikita Khrushchev's son-in-law that "we should consider how we can get along, and not attempt to impose our views, one on the other or on anyone else." More bluntly, Kennedy told Khrushchev himself: "you aren't going to make a communist out of me and I don't expect to make a capitalist out of you, so let's get down to business."[7]

Although Lyndon Johnson had endorsed a political offensive for victory over communism in the Senate in 1955, when that idea was still in vogue, as President he defined America's task as "reconciliation with the East" through a policy of "peaceful engagement." At a press conference in 1966, Johnson explained that neither superpower "is going to convert the other" and declared that "the United States has no interest in remaking the Soviet Union in our image."[8]

Richard Nixon's changing views illustrate the evolution of top policy-makers' thinking even more dramatically. In 1955 the famously combat-ive anticommunist Vice-President had been more inclined than Eisen-hower to the use of "revolutionary methods" against the Soviet empire. However, by 1959, when Nixon met with several top Soviet leaders, he repudiated the idea that the Soviet Union was so beset by internal prob-lems that it would collapse, and he privately concluded that "the only long-range answer to the Russian problem is a gradual opening of the door through contacts." When he accepted the Republican nomination for President in 1960, he still endorsed the crowd-pleasing idea of an ideological offensive for victory over the communists, but he cautioned that the President "must never engage in a war of words which might heat up the international climate to the igniting point of nuclear catastro-phe." Twelve years later, upon returning from meeting Soviet leaders in Moscow, Nixon soberly informed Congress that the two nuclear nations had "no alternative but to coexist peacefully," and added optimistically that the superpowers had embarked on a path of cooperation that would transcend the differences between their systems.[9]

To the presidents and almost all of their foreign policy advisers, attempting to free Russia seemed impossible. True, in some moments of enthusiasm in the mid-1950s, Secretary of State John Foster Dulles predicted that the "Iron Curtain" would disappear and the West would win the Cold War by 1960.[10] However, US intelligence assessments and diplomatic reports repeatedly indicated that the Soviet Union would not collapse, and the indoctrinated or docile population would not rebel in the foreseeable future. Charles Bohlen, who sharply differed with Dulles during his tenure as Ambassador to Moscow from 1953 to 1957, judged that even the turmoil in Poland and the revolt in Hungary in 1956 had not threatened the stability of the Soviet regime. While he recognized the existence of restlessness and doubts among students, he emphasized that in the society as a whole there was "a wide degree of acceptance of the

Soviet system as a fact of life," as he told CIA experts in 1957. Along the same line, a National Intelligence Estimate (NIE) concluded three years later that the Soviet political system was "stable" and would not "be openly challenged by the Soviet people," who were "in general hopeful for improvement in the conditions of their life and patriotically moved by the USSR's achievements" – including being ahead of the United States in launching satellites and cosmonauts into space. In addition to citing the strong national pride of the Soviet people, another NIE in 1962 explained that they were "accustomed to authoritarian rule."[11]

Such intelligence reports underestimated the scope of discontent in the Soviet Union, especially among consumers, religious believers, and intellectuals. Despite the USSR's rapid economic growth, there were shortages of food and price increases that sparked several localized protests, including a riotous strike at Novocherkassk that Soviet forces bloodily suppressed in June, 1962. A new Communist drive to close churches and seminaries between 1958 and 1963 provoked popular resistance and resentment. And the relaxation of censorship emboldened intellectuals, some of whom were further radicalized when Khrushchev's successors sought to clamp down on their dissent.[12]

By 1963, US intelligence organizations recognized the emergence of "strong antiregime overtones" in the work of rebellious writers and acknowledged the public dissatisfaction with shortages of consumer goods, but they continued to discount the possibility of serious challenges to the regime's control. American diplomats generally shared that perspective. Llewellyn (Tommy) Thompson, who succeeded Bohlen as Ambassador in Moscow from 1957 to 1962 and served a second "sentence" there from November 1966 to January 1969, was among the most influential advisers on Russia in that era; both Kennedy and Johnson valued his judgment. In dispatches between 1961 and 1968, Thompson reported that "the Soviet people in general supported the system," noted that the people sought "evolution and not revolution," and repeatedly predicted that Communist leaders would "remain securely in power" for a long time.[13]

In addition to seeming futile, efforts to liberate Russia appeared unconscionably dangerous. Even before the Soviet Union developed intercontinental ballistic missiles that could carry nuclear warheads to American targets, State Department and NSC officials repeatedly argued that proposals for aggressive destabilization of the Soviet empire risked provoking war with the nuclear-armed USSR. In reality, Soviet leaders were keenly aware that nuclear war would be catastrophic for their country, and they were unlikely to respond to American propaganda barrages by launching missiles at Munich or sending planes to bomb Washington. Nonetheless, especially in the years when the volatile Nikita Khrushchev bluffingly threatened to rain rockets down on Paris or London, that specter frightened America's European allies and it chilled US enthusiasm for psychological warfare.[14]

In that climate, champions of "liberation" felt increasingly frustrated and marginalized. C. D. Jackson, the manager of Time-Life, Inc. who worked as Eisenhower's propaganda adviser from 1953 to 1954, continued to lobby for psychological offensives in the late 1950s, but most of his proposals were shunted aside. David Sarnoff, the head of the Radio Corporation of America, submitted a detailed program for a political offensive against communism to Eisenhower in April 1955, which the White House released to the press but otherwise neglected. By 1961, feeling that none of his speeches and writings had had much effect on US policy and that the desire for an accommodation with the Soviet Union blocked a crusade, Sarnoff stopped talking publicly about communism. Eugene Lyons, the first head of the American Committee for the Liberation of the Peoples of Russia and a senior editor of *Reader's Digest*, relentlessly dramatized the "ominous rumblings of mutiny" in Russia, where he insisted there was "a continuous civil war between the regime and the people." However, from the late 1950s through the mid-1960s he struggled to overcome the powerful impression made by Soviet Sputnik satellites, the reports by tourists that the people supported the Soviet regime, and the eagerness of businessmen to make deals with communist rulers. Frank Barnett, President of the National Strategy Information Center, a New York-based think tank with ties to military and corporate leaders, tried in 1964 to revive a "Forward Strategy for Freedom," but his efforts to rally anticommunist organizations were at odds with what he called "the mood of 'peaceful coexistence' now tranquilizing many sections of US public opinion."[15]

Following the Cuban missile crisis of October 1962, American-Soviet relations stabilized: Khrushchev stopped rattling his rockets, the two superpowers signed a treaty banning atmospheric tests of nuclear weapons in 1963, and Khrushchev's much less boisterous successors plodded toward the goal of "peaceful coexistence" after ousting him in October 1964. With the calming of American-Soviet relations loosening the hold of the traditional anticommunist worldview,[16] American conservatives had an interest in accentuating instability in the Soviet Union. Thus, in the 1960s and even in the early 1970s, James Burnham and William F. Buckley of the *National Review* called upon Washington to exploit the "illegitimacy" of the Soviet regime and to seize upon "the crisis in Russia" to hasten "the dawn of liberty for the tormented Russian people."[17]

While Buckley and Burnham have received much attention from students of the conservative movement, they did not reach as wide an audience as David Lawrence, who wrote a weekly column distributed to three hundred newspapers as well as editorials for *U.S. News & World Report*, which claimed one million readers in 1958 and two million by 1973. Lawrence, who counted former President Herbert Hoover, John Foster Dulles, and evangelist Billy Graham among his long-time friends, had championed the liberation of Russians from totalitarianism ever since 1939. His persistent faith that Americans could stimulate an inevitable revolt by the Russian people centered on his Wilsonian belief in the efficacy of "moral force" applied through propaganda, his sincere conviction that no country ever deteriorated "to the point where its salvation is beyond human effort," and his enduring hope that Russians would "return to God."[18] Although his 1950 prediction that the Russian people would "change their rulers" in "a year or two" was not borne out, that did not keep him from continuing to forecast a revolution through the next two decades. In the same period, *U.S. News & World Report* repeatedly published articles that highlighted "unrest" or featured scholarly prophecies of revolt. The sheer number of times such prophecies were made may have undermined their credibility. Certainly by the mid-1960s Lawrence's old-fashioned emphasis on morality and religion seemed out of step with the more permissive and secular times. As Barry Goldwater, a Republican Senator from Arizona, commented in an admiring letter in 1965, Lawrence had become "almost a voice in the wilderness."[19]

Goldwater, who spearheaded a grassroots conservative movement to revitalize a traditional faith in American individualism, was himself the most strident advocate of "liberation" in the early 1960s. In the ghost-written manifesto, *The Conscience of a Conservative* (1960), Goldwater went far beyond the standard call for America to encourage "the captive peoples" to "overthrow their captors"; he urged the US to furnish underground leaders with weapons, and even to "be prepared to undertake military operations against vulnerable Communist regimes." Specifically, Goldwater proposed that when a major uprising comparable to the Hungarian revolution of 1956 developed, the US would "move a highly mobile task force equipped with appropriate nuclear weapons to the scene of the revolt," thereby forcing the Kremlin to choose between accepting the liberation of a satellite and "total destruction of the Soviet Union." He did not say directly whether he would employ the same tactic in the USSR itself. Assuming that the Russian people "are basically on our side," Goldwater apparently planned to rely mainly on withdrawal of diplomatic recognition of the Soviet Union as a way to encourage the Russians to free themselves from communist rule (without recognizing that this approach had been tried without success between 1917 and 1933).[20]

Liberal reviewers of Goldwater's book derided the notion of buying "enough atomic bombs to over-awe a recalcitrant Russian Government" and emphasized that "there is no such thing as victory in an all-out war." Yet within two years more than a million Americans purchased copies of *The Conscience of a Conservative*, which powerfully appealed to militant nationalists. Pat Buchanan, a college student in the late 1950s and early 1960s, recalled that after the frustration of watching Hungarians being butchered and the humiliation of being beaten to space by the formerly ridiculous Russians, "America seemed on a downhill slide." To crewcut young Americans like Buchanan who were in search of a cause, Goldwater's "sermon of fire and brimstone" became their "new testament."[21]

Many of the domestic policies championed in *The Conscience of a Conservative* that might have seemed blatant appeals to self-interest acquired an idealistic sheen from being linked to the theme of a crusade for freedom: the freedom of Southern segregationists from federal intervention; the freedom of businessmen from the coercive power of monopolistic labor unions; the freedom of tax payers from the burden of subsidizing others' welfare. Thus, however unrealistic and risky the proposals for liberating the communist empire were, they served a vital rhetorical function.

That the domestic ideological effects were more important than achieving actual results in the Soviet bloc became even clearer when Goldwater published a new best-seller, *Why Not Victory?*, in 1962. Challenged by William Fulbright, Chairman of the Senate Foreign Relations Committee, to explain more specifically how victory could be achieved "in this age of ideological conflict and nuclear weapons," Goldwater spluttered in indignation and alluded vaguely to "psychological warfare" as the answer. Like James Burnham a decade earlier and like other right-wing anticommunists in the early 1960s, Goldwater suggested that winning the Cold War was more a matter of will than of a carefully developed strategy: the key step was simply to declare the aim of victory. Although one of Goldwater's grandfathers had emigrated from Russia in the nineteenth century, that apparently did not lead him to develop much interest in or knowledge of Russian history and culture. In *Why Not Victory?* he simply posited that the United States would not have to occupy Russia and re-educate the Russians in the ways of democracy because the vast majority were not communists. (That was technically correct, since only a minority were members of the Communist Party, but it disregarded how deeply many Russians had been Sovietized through the processes of socialization of two generations.) Reflecting a wishful expectation of magical transformation that would influence other Americans' thinking in later decades, Goldwater anticipated that Russians would, "with proper guidance, take care of their own freedom once they are released from the iron grip of Communist dictatorship."[22]

Many eastern intellectuals scornfully dismissed Goldwater's "dogmatic assertions" and treated such fanatical anticommunist crusaders with "amused contempt." However, George F. Kennan, who returned to the United States in 1963 after serving for two years as Ambassador to Yugoslavia, was seriously disturbed to find "a great and important body of opinion" in favor of a policy that would lead "to the final and irreparable disaster which is in all our minds" (nuclear war). In a lecture subsequently published by the prestigious Council on Foreign Relations, Kennan chastised those who persisted "in viewing Communism as the only serious evil in the world" and refused to recognize how communism was changing. Rebuking "ardent liberationists," Kennan argued that "popular revolt against a ruthless, experienced modern dictatorship" was impossible. Instead of trying to promote the break-up of the Soviet Union, which could lead to a horrific civil war, US policy should focus, Kennan urged, on encouraging "hopeful forces and currents of opinion" in the Communist orbit, and facilitating the "evolution" of the Soviet system through a relaxation of tensions.[23]

Such prominent criticism of Goldwater's ideas did not check his political momentum. By the summer of 1964, Goldwater secured the Republican nomination for President, though he had not persuaded moderate Republicans to endorse his foreign policy vision. Reiterating his idea of a new "crusade" for freedom to the Platform Committee at the Republican convention, he berated members of the committee for not addressing the menace of communism with sufficient ardor. (The platform's foreign policy plank, drafted by Henry Kissinger, an adviser to liberal Republican Nelson Rockefeller, did reaffirm commitment to liberation of the Soviet empire, including the Baltic states and Ukraine, but its condemnation of the Johnson administration's quest for "accommodations with Communism" may have been too carefully qualified for Goldwater.) Then, in his acceptance speech, Goldwater summoned Americans to be "freedom's missionaries in a doubting world" and proclaimed a vision of "the *whole* of Europe reunified and freed."[24]

Goldwater's speech stirred rapturous responses from his supporters at the convention and across the nation. As columnist James Reston observed, the "jumble of high-sounding contradictions was wildly applauded by the delegates" in what was "not a convention but a revival meeting." The ultranationalist *Chicago Tribune* hailed Goldwater's call for "a reassertion of faith in our country."[25]

However, Goldwater's militant anticommunism alarmed many others. Worried that his "simplistic" ideas would edge America toward "a direct military confrontation with its enemies," the *New York Times* editorialized that his approach to nuclear weapons and his "formula for mastering communism" would be "calamitous." Disturbed by how zealously Goldwater urged "greater risks of war," Reston caustically commented: "Like the missionaries of old, Barry seems determined to save our souls if he has to kill us in the process." To moderates and liberals, Messianic anticommunism was less appealing than atomic war was frightening, a fact that Johnson's campaign exploited with commercials that associated Goldwater with the detonation of nuclear bombs.[26]

With Goldwater trailing Johnson in polls, the Republican campaign enlisted the genial actor Ronald Reagan to give a nationally televised speech on behalf of its more stiff-necked candidate. After using folksy anecdotes to show how liberalism was a slippery slope down to totalitarianism, Reagan closed by condemning the Johnson administration's "policy of accommodation" with "the most evil enemy" mankind had ever known. "We are being asked to buy our safety from the threat of 'the bomb' by selling into permanent slavery our fellow human beings enslaved behind the Iron Curtain," he declared. Reagan was even vaguer than Goldwater about the alternative to the Democrats' "immorality," his suggestion that Americans should be prepared to run the risk of atomic crucifixion was not very soothing, and the speech did not save the Republicans from a landslide electoral defeat. Yet conservatives celebrated Reagan's stirring performance, which helped to launch his political career and set a foundation for a future revival of crusading anticommunism.[27]

There were striking differences in the backgrounds and outlooks of the leading exponents of liberation in this era. Yet they shared a yearning for the moral clarity of a world divided into forces of light and forces of darkness, and they all rejected "the theory that Communists . . . can be converted into our friends" (as the *Chicago Tribune* put it). Although Reagan would be more receptive to the idea of redeeming Soviet leaders twenty years later, in the early 1960s he agreed with other conservatives that "appeasement" would not lead the enemy to "give up his evil ways."[28]

With the exception of Lyons (who had lived in Moscow in the early 1930s), few of the hard-liners knew or cared much about actual conditions in Russia. Their interest in a rhetorical crusade for liberty in the Soviet bloc appears to have stemmed primarily from its utility in the campaign against liberalism in the United States. Fearing that the easing of tension between the superpowers opened space for unwelcome changes in the United States, conservatives sought to preserve the greatest possible ideological distance between the two poles. Thus, as it endorsed the Goldwater platform in July 1964, the *Chicago Tribune* attacked liberal Democrats for their "totalitarian" imposition of "all-pervasive government" and for their idea "that the way to defeat communism is to 'accommodate' it and work to the end that American liberty and communist despotism 'converge.'"[29]

## The pursuit of liberalization

Despite the objections of obdurate anticommunists, between the late 1950s and the 1970s, US policy aimed to modify the views of communist leaders and encourage a peaceful liberalization of the Soviet system. Top US decision makers tended to focus on the potential political and economic gains from a relaxation of tensions and expansion of contacts: avoiding dangerous confrontations, curbing the costly arms race, and restraining Soviet adventurism in less developed countries. However, many middle and lower level officials had broader visions of promoting social and cultural change in the USSR through toned-down propaganda broadcasts, cultural exchanges, and expanded economic relations.

As the top commander of Allied forces in Western Europe in World War II, Dwight Eisenhower had been invited to the Soviet victory ceremonies in Moscow in 1945. The bond he formed with his Soviet counterpart, Georgy Zhukov, whom he called "a likeable cuss," encouraged him to feel that meetings with Soviet leaders could be productive. Visiting Soviet collective farms and talking with workers there left Eisenhower with an instinctive feeling that it should be possible to appeal to Russians on the basis of the common concerns of everyday life.[30]

Although Eisenhower hesitated publicly to abandon the slogan of "liberation" before the 1956 presidential election, by 1955 he began to show increasing interest in subtler approaches to the Soviet bloc. In January 1955, for example, as he contemplated relations with Stalin's successors, he commented at an NSC meeting that "What we must try to do is win 'these guys' over." Overriding resistance from Secretary of State Dulles, who believed (at least until 1956) that ostracism and persistent pressure would crack the evil Soviet system, Eisenhower flew to Geneva in July 1955 to meet the new Kremlin leaders. Although the Geneva summit meeting did not resolve any issues, Eisenhower continued to express strong interest in contacts that might help to break the "log jam" in Soviet-American relations. One of his pet ideas was to invite ten thousand Russian students to study in American colleges at US expense. Beyond the "great propaganda value" such an invitation would have, Eisenhower was "quite excited at the possible effect of an American indoctrination of 10,000 young Russian students in any given year."[31]

Advisers eventually convinced Eisenhower that the project was impractical, but contacts expanded in other ways. In July 1959, shortly after Eisenhower invited Khrushchev to visit the United States, Vice President Nixon traveled to Moscow to open the American National Exhibition (which will be discussed below). Talking privately with Khrushchev, Nixon disassociated himself and Eisenhower from the ritualistic congressional resolutions for liberation of the "captive nations." He felt other avenues were more promising. The full publication of his exhibition opening speech by *Pravda*, he reported to Eisenhower, was "of major importance as respects [the] long-term struggle" for the hearts and minds of Russians. And the enthusiastic reactions of crowds he greeted in several Soviet cities, Nixon added, demonstrated "the people's readiness to discount the unending propaganda against the American government and its leaders." CIA Director Allen Dulles reinforced this view, commenting at an NSC meeting that Nixon's "statements would have considerable effect in the USSR."[32]

Upon returning to Washington, Nixon cautioned Eisenhower that Khrushchev, a convinced Communist with "a closed mind," would not be impressed by seeing America. Yet he also suggested taking the Soviet leader to Los Angeles "in order to give Khrushchev a chance to fly over in a helicopter and to see vast numbers of houses" comparable to the model home exhibited in Moscow. Eisenhower was receptive to the more optimistic suggestion. Even if the two leaders did not achieve a breakthrough in negotiations, Eisenhower hoped that witnessing "a free people living and working" might have some effect on Khrushchev. When the communist leader arrived in Washington in September, Eisenhower took him up in a helicopter so that he could see how many Americans owned their own cars and lived in comfortable homes. Khrushchev pretended not to be impressed by such evidence of American prosperity, and warned Eisenhower not to expect to change his beliefs or overturn the Soviet system. Still, Eisenhower continued to wish that the communist ruler somehow might be swayed. When Khrushchev returned to the east coast after his cross-country tour, the President considered taking the atheist with him to church. Then, after going alone, Eisenhower informed Khrushchev that "he had just been in church and that his preacher had preached both for Mr. Khrushchev and himself."[33]

Eisenhower's approach thus differed diametrically from vehement anticommunists, who focused not on the chance for conversion but on the danger of contamination and not on prayer but on execration. Reflecting the strong tendency among Catholic leaders to view communism as an absolute and unchangeable foe, the Archbishop of Boston declared: "Inviting Khrushchev here is like opening our frontiers to the enemy in

a military war. He is dedicated to a godless ideology leading to slavery."
The editors of *National Review* were horrified by the idea that the Kremlin
ruler would profane the hallowed grounds of the White House. Several
Senators formed a Committee for Freedom of All Peoples and called
for a time of national mourning. The International Council of Christian
Churches, headed by fundamentalist red-hunter Carl McIntire, held a
protest rally at the Washington Monument.[34]

While the minority of adamant anticommunists feared Khrushchev's
presence would undermine American resolve to combat communism,
most Americans had a guarded hope that the trip would enhance the
prospect of a peaceful future. Although Khrushchev occasionally erupted
at what he considered insults, on the whole his tour – including a benign
visit to an Iowa farm and jovial banter at a Pittsburgh factory – showed
(as he put it) that he did not "have horns," and thereby undermined
demonic images of the Soviet Union.[35]

Khrushchev's trip to America had comparable effects in Russia. Immediately after Eisenhower extended the invitation, Soviet propagandists
turned the volume of anti-American diatribes way down. When a glowing
Khrushchev returned to the Soviet Union with plans to emulate American practices (such as supermarkets and self-service cafeterias), he gave
Soviet citizens the impression that he had broken through the ice of the
Cold War. In the following months, as the Soviet government prepared
to welcome Eisenhower for a reciprocal visit, the image of the United
States as an enemy faded, and ordinary Russians felt much less inhib-
ited about contacting Americans.[36] Although the thaw ended and Eisenhower's trip was canceled when Soviet forces shot down an American U-2
spy plane in May 1960, the steps taken in the late 1950s did constitute a
breakthrough, and contacts would resume after Eisenhower left the White
House.

Eisenhower's successors, preoccupied with crises in Berlin, Cuba, and
Vietnam, expressed less personal concern with the liberalization of the
Soviet Union, but US envoys to Moscow showed strong interest in promoting change there. Thompson advised the White House and State
Department to tell Soviet officials that the United States did not seek "to
sell them our system," but he believed that the Soviet regime eventually
would be obliged to take account of popular "pressures for liberalization,"
and he thought that Americans could "stimulate the liberal trends." Foy
Kohler, the hard-nosed career diplomat who served in Moscow between
Thompson's two terms, from 1962 to 1966, reported that there was "a
very striking ferment throughout Soviet society." In contrast to his previous stint in the Soviet Union in the late 1940s, Kohler informed the State
Department, "the air of pervading fear is gone" and people were "now free

and willing to talk to Americans." With contacts between Americans and Soviets multiplying, Kohler saw significant opportunities for the United States to pursue its objective of "opening up the closed Soviet society."[37] American diplomats and propagandists especially sought to achieve that objective through moderated radio broadcasts, colorful magazines, cultural exchanges, and expanded economic relations.

### From "crusade" to "communication": propaganda and détente

In the years after the bloody Soviet suppression of the 1956 Hungarian revolt, which had been encouraged by some incendiary Radio Free Europe (RFE) broadcasts, US propaganda guidelines emphasized the cautious promotion of gradual change. In 1957 directors of US broadcasting to the Soviet bloc embraced a policy of promoting "evolution, not revolution." In 1959, over the objections of some activists, Radio Liberation became Radio Liberty (RL), a more passive-sounding name. Thereafter, while a few leading figures remained committed to vigorous anticommunist broadcasting, most top officials felt that aggressive propaganda conflicted with the goals of reducing tensions and influencing the evolution of the Soviet system.[38]

After Khrushchev's visit to America, the director of the US Information Agency (USIA) asked the Voice of America (VOA) to eliminate as much provocative material from its programs as possible. Two years later, USIA officials complained to White House advisers about the problems caused by RFE and RL: their allegedly "inflammatory" broadcasts provoked Soviet jamming that interfered with milder VOA programs, and they provided Soviet officials with a justification for the jamming which USIA administrators sought to end. Under the direction of the famed liberal journalist Edward R. Murrow during the Kennedy years, the USIA maintained that Russian audiences wanted straight news rather than denunciations of communism. Murrow, who had helped to organize American-Soviet educational exchanges as a young man in the 1930s, enthusiastically proposed exchanges of broadcasts to his Soviet counterparts, and contributed to the Kennedy administration's increasing emphasis on the common interests of the superpowers. Kennedy himself rejected efforts to "pile up debating points" against the Soviets in a June 1963 speech at American University, in which he stressed the need for peoples with different social systems to "live together in mutual tolerance."[39]

By the late 1960s, the very existence of RFE and RL came into question. As CIA director Richard Helms observed, President Johnson's enthusiasm for programs in Eastern Europe "was never more than tepid" and in November 1967 he shocked Helms by saying that he would not fund the radio stations any longer. Although Helms saved RFE and RL by mobilizing support for them in Congress, the public revelation of the CIA funding for the ostensibly private radio stations contributed to another threat in the early 1970s, spearheaded by Senator William Fulbright. A Democrat from Arkansas who had founded an educational exchange program that bore his name, Fulbright argued that fostering discontent in the Soviet bloc was futile and counterproductive; the Soviet government was more likely to moderate domestic repression in a climate of détente than in an environment of hostile propaganda and pressure. In line with Fulbright, Senator Claiborne Pell declared that Radio Liberty was a questionable venture since "its basic objective is the removal of an indigenous, stable and apparently permanent regime."[40]

Radio Liberty survived the challenge from Fulbright, thanks in part to support from journalists and scholars who argued that the station was promoting the peaceful liberalization of the Soviet Union which did not conflict with détente. Yet the overall trend in the early 1970s was to further dampen broadcasts to the Soviet Union. In 1973, James Keogh, a speech writer for President Nixon, replaced a militant anticommunist as head of USIA and quickly canceled programs that might offend the Soviet government. "Détente has changed what we do in USIA," Keogh explained. US policy was not to "interfere in the internal affairs of other countries" or try to "provoke revolutions."[41]

In this increasingly difficult bureaucratic and domestic political context, how did leaders of Radio Liberty define and pursue their mission? While some Americans on the RL staff believed that the Russian people hated the Soviet system and could be guided to cause its demise, those ideas were repudiated as early as 1958 by Howland Sargeant, the debonair President of the American Committee for Liberation from 1954 to 1975. In the early 1960s, Sargeant offered some of the clearest statements of RL's role. Given Soviet citizens' fear of another war and their patriotic pride in their country's recent technological achievements, Sargeant explained, Radio Liberty's task was not to attack the Soviet system directly, but to contribute to public moods that "may ultimately develop into real forces for change." More specifically, RL appealed to Soviet citizens' intense interest in travel, jazz, cars, and fashion and thus gave them "a glimpse of exciting alternatives to their own depressing regimented existence." RL especially sought to reach young members of the elite who were "more outspoken in their demands for freedom" and had "a passionate thirst for contact with the West." Since they would be the future leaders of the country, Sargeant elaborated, nurturing their "*identification* with the West" was particularly worthwhile.[42]

Later in the 1960s, Radio Liberty's public relations officials presented rationales for the continued operation of the station in an era of détente. RL served US interests in a negative way, they explained, by limiting the Kremlin's ability to mobilize the Soviet population against America, and by stimulating public pressure against risky adventures in places like Cuba and Vietnam. More positively, according to the information officers, RL promoted the long-term evolution of the Soviet Union toward "stability and normalcy" by (among other things) breaking down barriers that isolated Soviet citizens from the outside world and "reviving awareness of democratic and humanistic currents in Russian political heritage." Countering the argument that "the West should refrain from any action likely to impair the stability of the world's other great nuclear arsenal," RL information director James Critchlow maintained that the radio station's calm, reasoned, educational broadcasts promoted positive changes.[43]

Some of these statements about Radio Liberty's role were questionable. Many of the post-1945 emigrés on the RL staff in Germany were authoritarian nationalists, and some were admirers of Russian forces that had fought on the side of Nazi Germany at the end of the Second World War – a fact that alienated Soviet listeners. As Sargeant acknowledged in 1963, the peoples of the USSR had no experience with freedom of speech, press, and assembly, and outside the Soviet Union there were no prominent personalities respected by many Soviet citizens who could educate them about such freedoms. In addition, it is not self-evident how appealing to young Soviet elites' avid interest in jazz and Western fashions or the wider population's consumerist aspirations promoted "liberty." As anthropologist Alexei Yurchak has shown, listening to Western radio broadcasts and dancing to jazz music were not necessarily subversive acts. Even ardent activists in the Communist youth league decorated their dormitory rooms with ads from American magazines or empty cigarette packets. University students could wear American jeans without endorsing Western materialism as superior to the ideal of socialism.[44]

Nonetheless, the American leaders and advisers of Radio Liberty genuinely felt that they were engaged in a mission of enlightenment. In striking reflections of this conception of their role, they repeatedly invoked a 1965 study by political scientist Ithiel de Sola Pool, who concluded that "most of the things of a positive character that are happening in the Soviet Union today are explainable only in terms of the influence of the West, for which the most important single channel is radio."[45]

That perspective exaggerated the radio's influence and underrated the importance of developments inside the Soviet Union. Until 1960, RL's transmitters were too weak to allow it to reach a large audience in the USSR. Even after more powerful transmitters were built in dictator Francisco Franco's Spain, RFE and RL for years could not match the reach of the VOA or British and German radio stations.[46] Overall, it is doubtful that the Western radio stations did as much to influence the emergence of more open-minded Soviet officials and dissident intellectuals as the great expansion of Soviet higher education, Khrushchev's encouragement of criticism of aspects of the Stalinist system, the easing of repression, and the reduced popular fear of the state.[47]

However, Soviet officials were genuinely alarmed by Western (especially American) propaganda that undermined the official monopoly on information. They repeatedly blamed RL and VOA (as well as other foreign radio stations) for instilling anti-Soviet attitudes and attacking communist leaders while appealing to the Russian people for friendship. The Soviet regime's enormous expenditures on jamming, which was highly effective in urban centers but did not prevent reception of broadcasts outside the cities, certainly marked the depth of the Kremlin's concern.[48]

In addition to jamming American-supported radio broadcasts, the Soviet government surreptitiously curtailed distribution of *Amerika* magazine, a glossy State Department publication aimed especially at the young, educated, urban population. During the last years of Stalin's rule, the Soviet Foreign Ministry simply ordered the press distribution agency to sell only half (or less) of the 50,000 copies the US published. In the Khrushchev era, the Ministry of Defense sought an outright ban on distribution of *Amerika* in numerous cities it considered sensitive, but the basic Soviet strategy was to impose an arbitrary reciprocity by releasing only the equivalent to the number of copies of *USSR* sold privately in the United States, and returning the rest (as many as 21,000 copies) to the US Embassy as "unsaleable." After American diplomats protested vigorously against this ruse in 1957, pointing to how rapidly *Amerika* sold out at the few kiosks where it was available, they believed distribution improved somewhat. Yet US officials continued to doubt that all copies of the magazine were distributed – a backhanded testament to its popularity. Although some Soviet intellectuals complained that *Amerika* was too slick and shallow, Ambassador Kohler believed it was "highly effective": its "striking and attractive visual depiction [of] American life," he explained in 1966, represented a "first wedge in our efforts to open Soviet society to American periodicals."[49]

Similar dynamics developed in exchanges of cultural exhibitions. Eager to gain knowledge of advanced American technology, the Soviet government agreed to allow the USIA to organize numerous exhibits of industrial products, consumer goods, and artwork in the USSR between the late 1950s and the 1970s. Thus, the Soviet drive for modernization superseded fears about the subversive impact of USIA presentations. On the American side, the prime goal was to affect popular attitudes. While Secretary of State Dulles entertained the hope that information about America would stimulate the Russian people to change their government, most officials had more modest ambitions, including countering Soviet propaganda about the United States, challenging communist ideological pretensions, and encouraging more independent thinking. American officials especially wanted to influence "a new elite" of intellectuals, technicians, bureaucrats, and industrial managers, who rarely had opportunities to go abroad but who were believed to be more pragmatic than the older generation.[50]

The first exhibition, in Moscow in 1959, became most famous for the "kitchen debate" between Vice-President Nixon and Khrushchev over whether a futuristic model American home showed the superiority of capitalism. Khrushchev claimed that the "attempt to lure the Soviet people" toward capitalism "completely failed." Yet USIA officials concluded that the American fair in Moscow "enjoyed considerable success in spite of strenuous and concerted Soviet efforts to discredit it." Despite the Communist Party's restriction of ticket sales, KGB surveillance, police intimidation, and an intense propaganda campaign to belittle the exhibition, it allowed almost three million Soviet citizens to communicate directly with young American guides, including well-educated and well-dressed African Americans whose appearance contrasted starkly with Soviet propaganda stereotypes of oppressed and impoverished blacks. Moreover, the USIA concluded, "visions of opulence enjoyed by the average American" conveyed by the exhibition stimulated Soviet consumer demands and government efforts to satisfy them which would reinforce "liberalizing tendencies in the economy."[51]

In the following decade, the USIA organized nine other exhibitions, with themes ranging from plastics to modern art, that traveled between major cities in the USSR. Lyndon Johnson seems to have viewed the exchanges of exhibitions less as a way to change the Soviet Union than as a way to encourage Americans and Russians "to realize that men and women on the other side of the Iron Curtain were much like themselves." Some of Johnson's advisers expected more from the exchanges. After visiting Moscow in the spring of 1964, for example, Donald Wilson, deputy director of USIA, glowed that an exhibition of graphic arts that traveled from Kazakhstan to Leningrad had been "a resounding and runaway success." Although a number of abstract works were incomprehensible to or derided by many of the 1.5 million Russians who saw the show, it still "opened up something totally new to Russian eyes and they were fascinated." Such exhibits were one dimension of "the all-important exchanges program," which, Wilson urged, "must be continued and expanded where possible" in order to contribute to "the liberalization process."[52]

Hard-boiled conservatives like Barry Goldwater scoffed at the idea that sending opera companies or trade exhibits to the Soviet Union could alter the Kremlin rulers' determination to destroy the American system. Yet, like the American advisers to Radio Liberty, US cultural affairs personnel often felt they were involved in an historic mission. For example, Richard Arndt, who worked for the US Information Agency in the 1960s and 1970s, recalled that "we cultural officers were opening thousands of tiny windows into other societies, in some cases piercing thick walls. In the dramatic Soviet case, the light that filtered through these ragged apertures touched off the implosion of an empire . . . ."[53]

While Americans sought to expand the exchanges, Soviet officials tried to reduce them and some seem to have favored stopping the exchanges entirely, in part to protest the escalation of US military involvement in Vietnam. Beyond its concern about appearing to cooperate with an "imperialist" power waging war against a fraternal socialist country, the Kremlin worried about the impact of cultural exchanges inside the USSR. Consequently, on into the 1970s the Communist Party took steps to contain the impact of American exhibitions. In 1973, for example, when the USIA presented an exhibit on "Recreation in Nature in the USA" in the Siberian city of Irkutsk, with boats, motorcycles, and other vehicles, the city's communist leaders "carried out counterpropaganda" by creating a group of 400 propagandists and sending thirty or forty of them to the exhibit each day. While the American guides generally conducted themselves properly, a Soviet official reported, at the end of the exhibition several guides disseminated propaganda about the American way of life in a more politicized way, one tried to distribute forbidden literature, and Jewish guides tried to establish contact with Soviet Jews. The official listed the names of the offenders, apparently in an effort to prevent them from working as guides for future exhibitions.[54]

Such struggles over the cultural exhibitions, like the battles over the distribution of *Amerika* and the conflicts over Voice of America broadcasts, should be seen in the long-term context of American efforts to penetrate Russian society and Russian or Soviet resistance. The "jamming war" was not only an "emblematic Cold War contest" of ideas, as one RFE/RL veteran put it,[55] but a part of a much wider competition for the hearts, minds, and souls of the Russian people that dated back to the late nineteenth century.

## Trade, modernization, and liberalization

While Soviet leaders sought to contain American political and cultural influence in the USSR, they repeatedly expressed keen interest in expanding economic relations with the United States. When he came to America in 1959, for example, Khrushchev met with business leaders in the hope that they could be induced to develop cooperative relations. Although Khrushchev concluded that, in part because of strong anticommunist sentiment among businessmen, conditions were not yet ripe for broadened trade, he and other Soviet officials continued to convey their desire to develop commerce between the two countries. As in the 1920s, Soviet communists viewed the expansion of trade as a step toward political *rapprochement*, yet they also genuinely admired the high quality of American machinery, and they longed to gain access to American financial credit.[56]

American diplomatic experts doubted that the very limited bilateral trade (roughly $50 million worth in 1961) could grow very much because the Soviet Union had little to sell that would interest US importers. However, White House and State Department officials generally favored taking the small steps that could be taken to improve trade because of the political benefits they anticipated. In the late 1950s, the Eisenhower administration had relaxed controls on trade with Eastern Europe (especially Poland), in the hope of increasing US influence in the region. During the 1960s and early 1970s, the Kennedy, Johnson, and Nixon administrations sought to apply a similar logic in relation to the Soviet Union.[57]

Kennedy's decision at the outset of his presidency to lift a ban on the importation of Soviet crabmeat was only a small goodwill gesture to enhance the environment for future negotiations. But by 1963, when Kennedy approved a more significant Soviet purchase of American wheat, his advisers were thinking about the potential for dramatic effects on the Soviet Union. Under Secretary of State George Ball observed that the Soviet need to buy large amounts of wheat could "be portrayed as a failure of Communism," showing the inability of the Soviet system to feed its people. In a similar vein, an assistant director of USIA commented that the wheat purchase would undermine Khrushchev's boasts about overtaking America and "have a psychological impact on the Soviet people as they found themselves even to this extent dependent upon us."[58]

While Lyndon Johnson saw increased trade mainly as a way of smoothing the path to resolution of problems such as the arms race, some of his counselors expected commerce to have deep impacts inside the Soviet Union. A special committee on trade relations that Johnson appointed in 1965 vaguely predicted that through the "intimate engagement" in bargaining and constructive competition, "men and nations will in time be altered." Three years later, in a lengthy assessment of US policy toward the USSR, the political officers of the US Embassy in Moscow concluded that "commerce remains a largely unexploited area where considerable American influence could be brought to bear" in the overall effort to "stimulate liberalizing trends" and develop genuine coexistence. In 1973, President Nixon explained to Republican leaders that trade "would leaven Communist societies" and "you don't change them by isolating ourselves from them."[59] Outside the US government, the heads of some major American banks and corporations also argued that increased trade would promote peace and encourage change inside the Soviet Union.[60]

Whatever contribution expanded commerce might have made to internal liberalization in the Soviet Union, the idea ran into strong and persistent opposition in Congress. Immigrants from Eastern Europe made it clear to their congressional representatives that they vehemently opposed trade deals with the Soviet Union while it continued to dominate their homelands. Many in Congress indignantly objected to removing tariff restrictions on trade with the Soviet Union while Soviet-supplied weapons killed American soldiers in Vietnam. And Jewish groups lobbied effectively in the early 1970s to require dramatic increases in the emigration of Jews from the Soviet Union in return for loans or most favored nation status – conditions that spurred the Kremlin to reject a trade deal after it was finally negotiated in 1974. Thus, the executive branch's pragmatic pursuit of a more flexible strategy for encouraging the liberalization of the Soviet Union was frustrated by more rigid anticommunist sentiment in the legislative branch and in some sectors of American public opinion.[61]

### Religious missions and religious persecution

While the Stalinist regime had tried to prevent ideological infection by cutting off contacts with the West in the late 1940s and early 1950s, Khrushchev and his advisers sought to break out of the USSR's isolation in order to propagate their revived faith and reduce foreign hostility to the Soviet system. As part of this wider pattern of opening doors to the West, the Soviet government pushed the officially sanctioned Orthodox Church and Baptist union to establish links to foreign religious organizations. In 1960, after the KGB-controlled Council for Religious Affairs prodded leaders of the Russian Orthodox Church to be more active internationally, the patriarch accepted the "recommendation" that the Orthodox Church should join the World Council of Churches (WCC). During the following years, the patriarchate contributed to the Soviet pursuit of peaceful coexistence by participating in numerous international conferences. Along a similar line, the All-Union Council of Evangelical Christians-Baptists re-established ties to the Baptist World Alliance and sent representatives to meetings of the National Association of Religious Broadcasters in the hope of deterring political references in broadcasts to the Soviet Union. In addition, beginning in the mid-1950s, the Baptist union and the Orthodox Church invited American Christians to visit and sometimes preach in the Soviet Union.[62]

At the same time as the Soviet state encouraged more contacts with Western religious groups, it launched a new campaign against religion inside the USSR that was especially intense between 1958 and 1963. Although the drive targeted all religious confessions, it particularly damaged the Russian Orthodox Church. In those years, Soviet government pressure led to the closing of two-thirds of the Orthodox monasteries and nunneries, five of the eight theological seminaries, and thousands of churches. Clerics who resisted were retired or arrested.[63]

Although the Kremlin tried to avoid an international outcry through the use of pretexts and covert maneuvers, Orthodox leaders did inform Western peace groups about the persecution, and Western Christians did learn about many church closings. Late in 1963, for example, the Catholic magazine *Commonweal* noted mounting evidence of a renewed Soviet effort to suppress religion, and cited that as one of the reasons that "any full-fledged, wholehearted détente has to wait for the indefinite future."[64]

Yet on the whole, the Soviet strategy of opening managed contacts with the West succeeded in deterring or minimizing sharp criticism of the repression of religion in the USSR. After the Orthodox Church joined the World Council of Churches, criticism of the lack of religious liberty no longer appeared in formal resolutions of the WCC, which feared reprisals against member churches in Eastern Europe. From the late 1950s through the early 1970s, many Protestant leaders in North America felt that it was better to keep silent about the persecution of believers in the USSR. Some Western religious leaders who visited the Soviet Union were impressed by official tours of the churches that remained open, or assessed religious liberty there narrowly in terms of whether they were allowed to preach freely.[65]

Other visitors feared that direct criticism of the restrictions on religion would provoke the Soviet government to bar them from visiting and preaching in the country in the future. Already in 1955, after a Soviet Baptist leader invited him to come to Moscow, evangelist Billy Graham pledged not to mention political matters while in the USSR. When he finally visited Moscow four years later, Graham was deeply moved by the sight of the vast, empty Lenin stadium and his ardent desire to preach

there someday seems to have inclined him to suppress expression of his
anticommunist feelings. To the dismay of more rigid anticommunists,
Graham's statements to journalists about his trip focused not on "slave
camps," which he did not see, but on the "deepening hunger for God
that penetrates even behind the Iron Curtain."[66]

The refraining from criticism by visitors to the Soviet Union and hosts
of Russian clergy at international conferences did not mean that American
religious groups gave up their dream of evangelizing the Russian people.
American Christians and Jews who went to the Soviet Union as tourists
or as participants in educational exchanges often carried Bibles and other
religious literature with them. A more high-tech way to penetrate the Iron
Curtain was to use radio transmitters. In 1957, for example, evangelist
Oral Roberts began sponsoring short-wave broadcasts into the USSR,
though he discontinued them after two years because of Soviet jamming.
Another Pentecostal evangelist was more persistent. From the 1950s into
the 1970s, Paul Demetrus prepared gospel tape recordings "for invading
the closed land of Russia" that were beamed by transmitters powerful
enough to "override most of the Communist efforts at jamming the programs." Thus, private activity by evangelists paralleled the work of the
government-supported Radio Liberty and Voice of America, which continued to broadcast religious messages by Orthodox priests in the West.[67]

From the late 1950s through the 1970s, writers for American religious
periodicals repeatedly declared that religious faith was not dead in the
USSR, that Orthodoxy was deeply ingrained in the Russian people, and
that Protestant churches were packed with worshipers. Although most of
the authors were not as excited or euphoric as some had been in the early
1920s and early 1940s, many expressed hope for a sweeping religious
revival in the future.[68]

While some envisioned that a revival would generate challenges to
Communist rule, the leaders of denominations that were most active
inside the Soviet Union generally disavowed any interest in promoting
political change. For example, Seventh-day Adventist leaders who visited
the Soviet Union went out of their way to emphasize (both in Moscow
and upon their return to the United States) that Adventists did not seek
to challenge the Soviet state. In 1974, an Adventist Vice-President combined that message with an explicit endorsement of coexistence, declaring
firmly that "the Socialist countries are different and are here to stay."[69]

Despite their verbal restraint and explicit disclaimers of concern with
political questions, Christian visitors and broadcasters received hostile
attention from the KGB and atheist activists. In the early 1960s, for
example, Soviet magazines accused Oral Roberts of concealing his "dirty"
political machinations with diversionist tactics, and published derogatory

cartoons of Billy Graham as a money-hungry gangster. Similar charges of ideological sabotage and collusion with the CIA would be featured in propaganda posters through the 1980s.[70] Thus, in their own way, KGB officers and atheist agitators played roles comparable to the tsarist police and Orthodox priests who guarded their flock against infiltration and depredation by alien evangelists decades earlier.

### Coexistence, moral complexity and American national identity

While the increased Western access to post-Stalinist Russia posed problems for guardians of the communist faith, other developments presented challenges to the traditional American view of the Cold War as a Manichaean struggle between good and evil. True, the idea of an irreconcilable global confrontation between Christian America and godless communism continued to anchor right-wing worldviews.[71] Indeed, that notion became more vital than ever to right-wing groups such as the John Birch Society and evangelist Billy James Hargis's Christian Crusade, which flourished in the late 1950s and early 1960s.[72] Yet, as liberal Protestants like John C. Bennett repeatedly pointed out, striking changes in the world discredited conceptions of communism "as a vast undifferentiated blot of evil."[73] When Stalin's heirs denounced his crimes, released most prisoners from concentration camps, and repudiated his doctrine about the inevitability of war between capitalist and socialist countries, it became apparent that the Soviet government was not an unchanging, monolithic entity. After the defiantly independent stances of some East European leaders revealed the splintering of the Soviet bloc, hotheaded Chinese communist attacks on Soviet "revisionism" in the early 1960s and military skirmishes between the two countries at the end of the decade made it obvious that the world communist movement had fractured.

Conservative anticommunists often denied or minimized the importance of these developments. Khrushchev's domestic thaw was superficial and temporary, they argued, and his talk of "peaceful coexistence" merely masked communists' continuing ambition to conquer the United States and enslave the world. The Soviet imperialist leopard "does not change his spots," they insisted. The rhetorical fireworks set off by Chinese and Russian communists were a ruse to hide their continuing nefarious collaboration, they claimed.[74]

Such denials became increasingly dubious to many Americans, including the architects of US policies in the early Cold War. In 1950 Paul Nitze had been the primary author of the NSC-68 paper that divided the world into two spheres of "freedom" and "slavery," but in 1961 he bluntly recognized that "we live in a complex, multi-dimensional world which cannot be viewed in the absolutes of black and white." George F. Kennan's bold advocacy of a demilitarized Europe in the late 1950s placed him outside the mainstream of the foreign policy establishment, but he spoke for many when he argued in 1961 that "we have much more difficult problems with the Chinese than with the Russians," who "have more in common with Western civilization."[75]

Morally debatable US actions in the 1960s made it less convincing to depict global politics as a confrontation between an American sheriff in white hat and a Soviet outlaw in black. On the eve of the CIA-organized invasion at the Bay of Pigs in April 1961, White House aide Arthur Schlesinger warned that "Cuba will become our Hungary." In June of the same year, when a State Department official urged that the US make an issue of Soviet interference in various countries, Secretary Dean Rusk replied that that would be difficult because "our hands are not too clean."[76]

Later in the 1960s, escalating US military operations in Southeast Asia, including the widespread spraying of defoliants and intensive bombing that caused numerous civilian casualties, further weakened the credibility of a self-righteous American nationalism. Saddened by "the apathy of the mass of American intellectuals" about the Kremlin's repression of "the Soviet New Left," a Radio Liberty veteran asked in the liberal Catholic journal *Commonweal*, "Is it because of a feeling that the Soviet government opposes LBJ and napalm . . . and should therefore have its sins remitted . . . ?"[77]

When Warsaw Pact forces extinguished a Czechoslovak experiment with reform communism in the summer of 1968, opponents of the US war in Vietnam, such as Senator Eugene McCarthy, drew parallels between the two military actions. The widespread indignation that erupted in response to the comparisons showed how even after several years of détente, Russia continued to serve as a foil for American identity. Syndicated columnist David Lawrence chastised the "few politically minded critics who immediately cried out that Russia is merely doing what the United States did in Vietnam," insisting that "no parallel" existed. Secretary of State Rusk declared that any attempt to liken the Soviet invasion of Czechoslovakia to the US involvement in Vietnam reflected "moral myopia," since the two cases were as different as "black and white." More aggressively, the Chicago *Tribune* proclaimed that the crushing of the Prague spring proved that "international immorality is a monopoly of communists."[78]

This "pharisaical self-righteousness" appalled the liberal Protestant *Christian Century*. "We desperately need a scapegoat for our own guilt," the editors commented, and the Russians had obliged Americans by perpetrating "an act that parallels our intervention in Vietnam and our invasion of the Dominican Republic" in 1965. What particularly disturbed the *Christian Century* about this scapegoating, was that a revival of "anticommunist hysteria" would mean an evasion of America's own "evils," above all its "patent racism and its blood guilt in Vietnam." Instead of using Russia as a whipping boy, the editors wished, America should focus on its own sins.[79]

The *Christian Century*'s fear of an imminent revival of rampant anticommunism in 1968 was premature, but its insight into the way Americans continued to use the Soviet Union as a scapegoat was acute. As conservative political activist Pat Buchanan remembered, when Americans became more and more deeply mired in Vietnam, "we not only disagreed about how to wage Cold War, but about whether America was a good country serving a moral purpose in the world."[80] When the United States' military involvement in Vietnam ended five years later, the way would be opened for a revival of American righteousness assisted by an intensifying demonization of Soviet communism.

# 7    Recovering the faith:
renewal of the crusade, 1974–80

For almost twenty years, the crusade for a free Russia was in abeyance. Although low-key efforts to promote the gradual liberalization of the Soviet empire continued, the toned-down propaganda campaigns and cultural exchanges rarely garnered much attention from top policy-makers, and they did not capture the public imagination. Then, in the mid-1970s, the idea of liberating the suppressed peoples of the Soviet Union and Eastern Europe once again began to be widely discussed. With rising vehemence, conservative politicians repudiated the live-and-let-live approach to détente, demonized the Soviet empire in Manichaean terms that had been out of fashion for years, and upheld the goal of liberation again. On the other end of the political spectrum, liberal activists inside and outside the government championed the cause of human rights in Russia and Eastern Europe with increasing energy and zeal.

What explains the resurgence of vilification of the Soviet Union and the renewal of the mission to free Russia? It was not simply a response to worsening persecution of dissidents and Jews in the Soviet bloc: the Brezhnev era crackdown on dissent had begun ten years earlier and the rising criticism of Soviet emigration policies in 1974–5 provoked more than it followed tighter restrictions on the exit of Jews. It also was not primarily a reaction to Soviet international adventurism: although Soviet support for communists in Vietnam and Angola angered some politicians in the mid-1970s, the action that triggered much more widespread outrage came near the end of the period, when Soviet forces invaded Afghanistan in December 1979. Nor was the revived crusade a result of a change in US foreign policy. Although President Gerald Ford and Secretary of State Henry Kissinger later claimed to have been genuinely concerned with the liberalization of the Soviet bloc,[1] the records of Ford–Kissinger policy-making abundantly demonstrate that they did not believe it was feasible to alter the Soviet system, and that they stubbornly resisted pressure to make the promotion of human rights a policy priority. After exploiting discontent with the perceived amorality of Kissinger–Ford policies in the

1976 presidential campaign, Jimmy Carter did make human rights in the Soviet bloc a more prominent theme of his presidency. Yet Carter rode a wave he did not create, most of his foreign policy advisers opposed strident criticism of Soviet oppression, and the impetus to champion freedom in the Soviet sphere continued to come more from outside the US government. While the development of transnational links between activists in the west and the east spurred a widening movement, abstract concepts such as "globalization" or "the information age" do not go very far to explain the renewal of the crusade for a free Russia: contacts between American activists and Soviet bloc dissidents relied on much of the same transportation and communications technology that had been used eighty years earlier, especially letter-writing and newspaper or magazine publicity.[2]

To understand the new surge of demonizing the Soviet empire and championing of liberation, it is vital to set these developments in their social and cultural context. As a result of the divisive and futile war in Vietnam, energy shortages, economic stagnation, revelations of presidential misconduct, sensational exposés about the nefarious actions of US intelligence agencies, and challenges to traditional values from a youth culture and a feminist movement, by 1975 the United States was in the midst of a crisis of self-confidence.[3] Many Americans came to doubt that the United States exemplified a special virtue or offered a model for the rest of the world to emulate. Reacting to that climate, Barry Goldwater lamented on the floor of the Senate that "we seem to be losing our faith" in American principles and "our national will to survive in freedom." As Daniel Patrick Moynihan, the US Ambassador to the United Nations in the mid-1970s, recalled, the American electorate craved "some assertion of our strengths, some insistence that the political culture of the democracies was *superior* to that of the despotisms, left and right, all around us."[4] In that context, reaffirmation of traditional American beliefs had wide resonance and vilification of the Soviet Union had powerful political appeal.

That does not mean that all expressions of concern about Soviet repression were empty, demagogic gestures. In the late 1970s, the Carter administration significantly increased funding for radio broadcasts to the Soviet bloc, some members of Congress energetically worked to free political prisoners, and private individuals launched important initiatives for human rights. However, for American society as a whole, the primary meaning of the revived crusade for a free Russia was the way it served to restore faith in the United States as a virtuous nation with a unique historical mission.

## The Solzhenitsyn affair

In the summer of 1975, a bearded prophet rode into Washington and called upon Americans to repent. At the invitation of the AFL-CIO, which had long crusaded against slave labor in the Soviet Union, on June 30 the exiled writer Alexander Solzhenitsyn exhorted 2,500 leading Americans to repudiate one-sided détente with the Soviet regime and return to being allies of the liberation of the Russian people. In a ninety-minute harangue that received prominent coverage in national newspapers, Solzhenitsyn demanded that liberals repent for having forgotten the meaning of "liberty," that businessmen repent for having allied with Soviet communist leaders because of their "burning greed for profit," and that wealthy Americans repent for the complacent materialism that had blinded them to the menace of world communism.

Americans should not hesitate to view the world as divided into spheres of light and darkness, Solzhenitsyn declared: the very notion of "the relativity of good and evil" was a communist invention, the Soviet regime had been a murderous despotism from the beginning, and whatever flaws there might be in the American system paled in comparison to the pervasive repression in the USSR. Since one country after another had been surrendered to communism for the last thirty years, the danger was grave. Yet if Americans overcame their "flabbiness" and regained the nerve to oppose the spread of communism, they would find allies behind the Iron Curtain. "[F]or all ordinary Soviet citizens," the dissident author asserted, "America evokes a mixture of admiration and compassion," and "under the cast-iron shell of Communism . . . a liberation of the human spirit is occurring." All the United States had to do, Solzhenitsyn explained to members of Congress in another address on July 15, was to stop trade and loans to the Kremlin; that would force the Soviet system to relax and allow the liberation movement to triumph.[5]

Solzhenitsyn's jeremiads and their enthusiastic reception in the US capital were peculiar. When George Meany, President of the AFL-CIO, extolled Solzhenitsyn as "the single figure who has raised highest the flame of liberty," he (like many others) disregarded how the Russian writer stood for the kind of reactionary Slavophile authoritarianism that had been the enemy of the first crusade for a free Russia in the late nineteenth century.[6] Indeed, without citing George Kennan by name, Solzhenitsyn rebuked such insufficiently scrupulous Western critics of the tsarist autocracy, which he claimed executed only "an average of seventeen persons a year."[7] While a number of writers, including dissident Russian physicist Andrei Sakharov, had called attention to Solzhenitsyn's nostalgic, xenophobic nationalism, their warnings did not keep prominent Americans from embracing him as a symbol of freedom.[8] Apparently oblivious to how many of his American admirers strongly favored the warming of US relations with the People's Republic of China, Solzhenitsyn shrilly insisted that all the apparent differences in the world communist movement were imaginary, and communism was still a monolithic menace. While Solzhenitsyn claimed to be the voice of voiceless millions of ordinary Russians, in reality few of them yearned for spiritual liberation from communism in an era of relative stability, security, and national pride.[9]

None of this deterred the odd coalition of Solzhenitsyn's sponsors, some of whom were less interested in what they could do to liberate the peoples of the Soviet Union than in what embracing Solzhenitsyn's message could do for the people of the United States. Americans, George Meany declared, "desperately" needed the power of Solzhenitsyn's vision "to teach the new and the forgetful generations in our midst what it means not to be free." Conservative Republican Senator Jesse Helms may not have read Solzhenitsyn's work, but he championed the Russian writer as "a Christian," in part because he saw emphasis on the denial of freedom by godless communists as a way to drive home threats to freedom in America.[10]

When Helms and Senator Strom Thurmond pushed for a meeting between Solzhenitsyn and the President at the White House, Ford and most of his closest aides resisted. Such a meeting would have been contrary to the spirit of Nixon-Kissinger-Ford policy toward the Soviet Union. Within days of Solzhenitsyn's expulsion from the USSR in early 1974, Nixon publicly interpreted it as evidence of the mellowing of the Soviet system, noting at a press conference that earlier Russian dissidents "would have been sent to Siberia or probably worse."[11] Soon thereafter, Robert Goldwin, an intellectual adviser to the Nixon and Ford administrations, drafted a defense of a policy of being "friendly with those who persecute Solzhenitsyn." "Great sufferings follow from the quixotic, self-righteous attempt to eradicate all evil in the world," Goldwin wrote. The United States, he suggested, "must acknowledge [its] own flaws" and refrain from trying "to correct the errors of other sovereign nations."[12]

In earlier decades, Gerald Ford had been more inclined to castigate the evil Soviet empire. As Representative of a Michigan congressional district that included recent immigrants from Eastern Europe, Ford had repeatedly denounced Russian imperialism and championed the cause of the "captive nations" in the 1950s and 1960s. In 1952, for example, he had assailed the "ruthless atheistic" Russians, and in 1954 he had maintained that America had "a strong but often silent ally . . . behind the bars of [Soviet] dictatorship."[13] When the Democratic administration of Lyndon Johnson pursued détente with the Soviet Union, Ford (then Republican Minority Leader in the House of Representatives) deplored the way that "values and ideals which once were treasured are now cast aside in the name of 'liberalization' and 'progress.'" Rejecting the "myth" that trade and aid to the captive nations would lead to the break-up of the Communist monolith, and chastising the Voice of America for being "tongue-tied," Ford called for a renewal of the ideological offensive against the Soviet Union.[14]

However, after Nixon became President in 1969 and especially after Nixon visited Moscow in 1972, Ford, as a loyal Republican, adopted a much more positive view of the relaxation of tensions between the superpowers. Following the June 1973 summit between Nixon and Soviet leader Leonid Brezhnev, Ford even declared that "the word, détente, has a magic ring to it."[15] Convinced by Kissinger of the benefits to be gained, particularly through arms control agreements, Ford firmly committed himself to working together with Soviet leaders when he became President upon Nixon's resignation in August 1974.[16]

One of the issues Ford had to face in the first year of his presidency concerned an agreement, negotiated by the Conference on Security and Cooperation in Europe (CSCE), that accepted the existing borders of European states and stipulated that they could be changed only by peaceful means. Although Ford was mildly concerned that the agreement would appear to confirm permanent Soviet control over Eastern Europe, he recognized "the facts of life" in that region.[17] While he worried that signing the CSCE agreement in Helsinki would "raise hell with our Baltic friends," he calculated that the majority of Americans did not want to go "back to Cold War."[18] Hence, on the eve of Solzhenitsyn's arrival in Washington, Ford remained strongly committed to improving the US-Soviet relationship, and the White House maintained the public line that that was the best way to advance human rights in Eastern Europe.[19]

Out of the public eye, though, Kissinger repeatedly expressed utter disdain for the promotion of human rights. In September 1974, he explained to Ford and Soviet Foreign Minister Andrei Gromyko that he had told European diplomats who were pressing for Soviet concessions on human rights issues that "the Soviet Union won't be overthrown without noticing it, and certainly not because of things like increased circulation of newspapers. . . . "[20] In subsequent meetings with Soviet leaders, Kissinger regretted that many issues in the CSCE negotiations "had become absurd" and treated the "Basket III" human rights provisions as a joke.[21] Kissinger "didn't care" about the CSCE because he did not believe it advanced US national interests. "There is nothing in it for us," he told Ford in April 1975. In addition, he thought it would be futile or even counterproductive to try to reform or overthrow the Soviet system. "I don't think you'll change your system as a result of Basket III," he told Gromyko in their final discussions of the CSCE agreement in May 1975. Bantering with the Soviet Foreign Minister, Kissinger added that "If the Soviet system toppled, . . . I am not sure the successor wouldn't be more of a problem. The government Solzhenitsyn would establish would be more aggressive." Ironically, then, Kissinger may have contributed to the promotion of human rights in the Soviet bloc less by getting tough in the final negotiations, as some have claimed, than by leading Gromyko and Brezhnev to believe that the US would not hold the Soviet Union to the commitments it made at Helsinki.[22]

Given Kissinger's quip to Gromyko about Solzhenitsyn, it is not surprising that a month later the Ford team almost unanimously opposed a meeting with the exiled writer. Solzhenitsyn's political views were "an embarrassment even to his fellow dissidents," declared the Executive Secretary of the State Department. "The Soviet Government would not be pleased by the President's meeting with Solzhenitsyn," observed A. Denis Clift of the National Security Council staff.[23] Sensing that right-wing Republicans were setting some kind of trap for the moderate President, and wanting to avoid antagonizing Soviet leaders a month before seeking an arms control breakthrough at Helsinki, the White House decided against a meeting with Solzhenitsyn, whom Ford called "a goddamn horse's ass."[24]

The spurning of the Russian writer sparked a furor. Although the *Washington Post* thought few Americans shared Solzhenitsyn's obsessive opposition to compromise with "the devil" or his dangerously "fierce commitment to a Russian renaissance," that pro-détente paper underestimated how many Americans embraced Solzhenitsyn's demonization of the Soviet regime and his appeal for the revitalization of the West. As columnist Joseph Kraft sensed, the "worship" of Solzhenitsyn's presence in Washington reflected "a nostalgia for the simple certitudes of the cold war." The snubbing of "one of the moral heroes of the 20th century," pundit George Will acidly commented, showed the absence of moral sensibilities in the US government.[25] To one Republican Representative from Idaho, Ford's unwillingness to meet with Solzhenitsyn, who had bravely spoken for freedom "in the face of the most tyrannical political system in existence," raised doubts about the genuineness of the US commitment to liberty. Disturbed by the bad press and the damage to the administration's relations with the right wing, White House aide Dick Cheney urged reconsideration of a visit with Solzhenitsyn. It was essential to clarify, Cheney argued, that détente did not imply approval of the Soviet way of life, and it did not mean "that we've given up our faith in our fundamental principles concerning individual liberty and democracy."[26]

By mid-July, the White House mail was 478–0 against the snub of Solzhenitsyn. Congressional liaison Max Friedersdorf advised Ford that the Solzhenitsyn issue was not going to go away with conservatives, and it had an adverse impact with liberals, too.[27] Preparing to challenge Ford for the Republican presidential nomination in 1976, California Governor Ronald Reagan seized on the issue. The refusal to see the "profound spokesman for human freedom and morality," Reagan declared in his syndicated column, was a repudiation of American principles. It was also a miscalculation, Reagan claimed: meeting Solzhenitsyn might have prompted the Kremlin to relax "some of the more visible signs of repression."[28] On the same day that the *Wall Street Journal* calculated that not meeting Solzhenitsyn had caused a 10 percent drop in his approval rating, Ford announced in an interview with journalists that the Russian writer had "an open invitation" to come to the White House.[29]

Despite that gesture, Ford had not had a change of heart about Solzhenitsyn[30] and, as Friedersdorf predicted, the issue did not go away. Through the end of 1975, National Security Adviser Brent Scowcroft kept in mind the need to avoid "another Solzhenitsyn affair."[31] The fiasco made such a searing impression on American public consciousness that Scowcroft's successor, Zbigniew Brzezinski, would conclude more than a year later that the Carter administration absolutely had to respond to a letter from Andrei Sakharov, or it would invite adverse comparisons to Ford's refusal to meet with Solzhenitsyn. In fact, as late as 1989, when Scowcroft served again as National Security Adviser, memory of the Solzhenitsyn controversy impelled him to meet with another visiting Russian, Boris Yeltsin.[32] Thus, the Solzhenitsyn incident in the summer of 1975 had enduring significance as a sign that it was politically unacceptable to appear to be indifferent to the cause of freedom in the Soviet empire.

### The irony of Helsinki

Although the uproar over the Solzhenitsyn snub had no impact on Ford-Kissinger policy toward the Soviet bloc, at around the same time momentum began to build inside and outside the government for real (not merely rhetorical) promotion of the liberalization of the Soviet bloc. While Ford had only a vague notion of the provisions of the CSCE agreement that he signed in Helsinki on August 1,[33] some US diplomats recognized at the time that the Helsinki accords offered important opportunities to loosen the grip of Soviet and communist power in Eastern Europe. Ambassador to Moscow Walter Stoessel showed an especially keen appreciation of the opportunities. A career foreign service officer who had focused on Soviet affairs since the 1940s, Stoessel argued in July 1975 that, contrary to the "myth being propagated in the American press" that the CSCE agreements consolidated Soviet control over Eastern Europe, the provisions that allowed for peaceful change of borders and promoted wider East-West contacts had the potential, as Soviets feared, to "unhinge" the political status quo. While he expected Soviet officials to "work hard to blunt the effects of Basket III," Stoessel urged Washington not to be "supine" in the face of such efforts. Instead, the United States should do its utmost to publicize the Helsinki obligations – for example, by devoting a cover of *Amerika* magazine to Brezhnev and Ford signing the CSCE documents – and the State Department should undertake a careful effort "to monitor the record of compliance by CSCE signatories." In striking contrast to Secretary of State Kissinger's *realpolitik*, Stoessel held that "one extremely important long-range purpose in promoting a policy of détente is the hope that by doing so we can help to foster a more humane society in the USSR."[34]

Some members of Congress shared that aspiration, and would soon press the executive branch to follow through on the Helsinki promises. Shortly after Ford returned from Finland to Washington and pledged "to encourage the full implementation of the principles embodied in the C.S.C.E. declarations," a congressional delegation traveled to the Soviet Union. In Leningrad and Moscow, the congressional representatives met with Jews who had been refused the right to emigrate and dissidents who had formed small human rights groups. Representative Millicent Fenwick, an aristocratic woman whose voice reminded many of actress Katherine Hepburn, was so deeply moved by the suffering she saw in the faces of the "refuseniks" that she determined to do something for them when she got back to the United States. In September, Fenwick, a Republican from New Jersey, introduced a bill to create a congressional commission to monitor the fulfillment of the commitments nations had made in the Helsinki Final Act. Although Kissinger and other administration officials stubbornly resisted what they saw as congressional encroachment on executive branch prerogatives in foreign affairs, Fenwick was supported by her fellow New Jersey Republican, Senator Clifford Case, and by the canny Florida congressman Dante Fascell. With important backing from Jewish and East European ethnic organizations (who had earlier denounced the Helsinki accords as a betrayal of their homelands), the Fenwick-Case legislation was approved by Congress in May 1976. A couple of weeks later, in a ceremony that NSC officials ensured was low-key, Ford signed the bill.[35] While the State Department continued to object that the oversight commission "transgressed the separation of powers," the mounting congressional and public interest in the Basket III human rights provisions would lead even Kissinger to suggest that Ford raise with Gromyko the need for actions to pass the CSCE "litmus test."[36]

As the US Helsinki commission began hearing testimony, gathering evidence, and publishing reports, Fenwick's office started to receive letters from around the Soviet bloc that would form the basis for personal appeals from Fenwick to Communist leaders, to allow families to be reunited and to release prisoners of conscience.[37] Thus, Fenwick and her staff began to act parallel to, and sometimes in conjunction with, nongovernmental human rights organizations such as Amnesty International.

## The 1976 election: the politics of promoting freedom

As Ford's signing the Fenwick-Case bill on the eve of the New Jersey Republican primary suggested, the promotion of human rights in the Soviet bloc had come to be fraught with implications for politics in the United States. During both the Republican primary season and the general election campaign, Ford political aides proposed meeting Solzhenitsyn or sending him a letter – evidence of how the issue continued to hurt Ford.[38] In April, conservative activist Frank Barnett pointedly reminded Republican women in Washington, DC, that it had not been the Ford White House which "gave Alexander Solzhenitsyn a forum for freedom in this country."[39] In June, a Ford speech writer bowed to the demands of the campaign with a draft that highlighted how "The United States has stood for something in the world – a dream, a hope, a promise," and vowed that "The world can not be fully safe for us so long as many members of the human race suffer under the heel of authoritarian dictatorship."[40]

Although Ford narrowly survived Ronald Reagan's challenge for the Republican nomination in August, Reagan's supporters succeeded in placing in the party platform a plank on "Morality in Foreign Policy" that praised Solzhenitsyn, and rebuked Ford for signing the Helsinki agreement that allegedly deprived East Europeans of the hope of gaining freedom.[41] As veteran diplomat and politician Averell Harriman told Soviet leader Leonid Brezhnev in September, the campaign Reagan conducted stirred up anti-Soviet emotions that affected not only the Ford campaign but also the campaign of his Democratic opponent, former Georgia governor Jimmy Carter.[42]

If the championing of human rights in the Soviet sphere divided Republicans that year, for Democrats the issue served at least briefly to unite liberals and conservatives.[43] Carter had a deep commitment to human rights, rooted in his religious beliefs and his support for the civil rights movement in the South, yet he also was keenly aware of how much Ford could lose and how much he stood to gain on the issue of Eastern Europe. Casting the 1976 election in general as centering on the need for "faith," Carter suggested that he would be more faithful to American ideals than Ford and Kissinger had been. In debates that fall, when Ford made the blunder of denying that Eastern Europe was under Soviet domination, Carter deftly exploited the issue, in part by pledging that after he was elected, he would invite Solzhenitsyn to the White House.[44]

## The Carter administration, human rights, and American opinion

The momentum from the 1976 campaign and the broader symbolic significance the issue had acquired made it inevitable that the promotion of freedom in the Soviet bloc would be a major theme during the Carter presidency. As Carter recalled in his memoirs, by early 1977 "human rights had become the central theme of our foreign policy in the minds of the press and public. It seemed that a spark had been ignited, and I had no inclination to douse the growing flames." After holding his first press conference on January 21, Secretary of State Cyrus Vance reported to Carter that he was "struck by the degree of interest, even sharpness, on human-rights issues." Noting the increased prominence of the issue of human rights in the communist world, in particular, columnist Joseph Kraft concluded that "human rights is here to stay."[45]

The early public statements by Carter and the State Department seemed boldly idealistic. "Our commitment to human rights must be absolute," Carter declared in his inaugural address. Though he did not specifically mention the Soviet bloc, a few days later the State Department chastised Czechoslovakia and the Soviet Union for the repression of peaceful and legal dissent. Those public pronouncements won wide approval, even from commentators who worried that aggressive crusading might backfire or incite revolts that the United States would not be able to support. Especially after the seeming indifference of the Ford administration, the *Washington Post* commented, "it has got to be deeply satisfying to many Americans to see their government thus openly projecting some of its fundamental values into its foreign policy."[46] A Herblock cartoon in early March captured the sense of America's return to beaming the light of liberty into the darkened Soviet sphere (see figure 16). An editorial in the *Chicago Tribune* reflected the way the Soviet Union was once again serving as a foil for the affirmation of American virtue: in contrast to the claims the Kremlin made about its "evil system," it was America that was making "the true effort to support national liberation."[47]

Figure 16. "Would You Kindly Have Her Crouch Down – That Light Bothers Our Patients." Cartoon by Herblock. *Washington Post*, March 4, 1977. Copyright by The Herb Block Foundation.

Privately, Carter and his top advisers were divided and ambivalent about promoting human rights in the Soviet bloc. While Vance wanted a new State Department human rights coordinator to be outspoken, he did not want the coordinator to have a significant role in shaping policy toward important countries, or to interfere with the negotiation of an arms control agreement with the Soviet Union. While he assured members of

Congress that the State Department would seek full implementation of the Helsinki commitments, he was determined to avoid propaganda ploys and polemics.[48] The Polish-born National Security Adviser, Zbigniew Brzezinski, viewed public advocacy of human rights primarily as a way to buff America's tarnished image and "put the Soviet Union ideologically on the defensive." Yet even the pugnacious Brzezinski was wary of being "dragged into every major civil-rights issue," and having US-Soviet relations suffer as a consequence.[49] Carter himself was averse to strident preaching, and preferred to focus on making the United States a shining example to the world. "[T]he best way to enhance freedom in other lands," he declared in his inaugural address, "is to demonstrate here that our democratic system is worthy of emulation."[50]

In line with Carter's preference, a major review of US policy on human rights in the summer of 1977 concluded that "We must avoid self-righteousness and stridency, remembering that our own record is not unblemished." Drafted under the supervision of Deputy Secretary of State Warren Christopher, the review memorandum maintained that while it would be necessary to speak out on some important cases concerning Soviet dissidents, such critical public statements should be used sparingly and be free of polemics.[51]

For many in the Carter administration, a major lesson of the war in Vietnam was that the United States had limited power "to influence the internal workings of other nations." Guided by that lesson, the authors of the review proclaimed, "we do not seek to change governments [or] remake societies." With regard to the Soviet Union specifically, the review determined that it would not be possible to prompt rapid or major changes in the Soviet system. Instead of pursuing such grandiose goals, Carter officials resolved to work quietly toward more modest objectives, including freer emigration and supporting the growth of "democratic forces which may in time contribute to development of more open societies." State Department officials, including Secretary of State Cyrus Vance and his top adviser on Soviet affairs, political scientist Marshall Shulman, feared that public pressure for more dramatic human rights improvements would be counterproductive; they warned that it would provoke greater repression. This gradualist approach dovetailed with Carter's personal belief that in communist countries, "repression was so complete that it could not easily be observed or rooted out."[52]

Despite these convictions, Carter and some of his aides, especially Brzezinski, were attracted by the domestic benefits of championing human rights in foreign countries. Public advocacy of human rights was one of the most effective ways to "arouse the spirit of our own people," Carter felt. By emphasizing human rights, Brzezinski believed, Americans could overcome a spreading pessimism and "infuse greater historical optimism into our outlook on the world." Moreover, Brzezinski advised Carter in 1977, human rights was an issue that had "great appeal" and "reasserting human rights" could make Carter look "tough."[53]

Thus, despite the official Carter administration dedication to the quiet achievement of small but real gains for human rights in the Soviet bloc, the president and his national security adviser were drawn to a more ostentatious approach similar to that favored by the administration's conservative critics. To Henry M. Jackson (D-WA) and likeminded Cold Warriors, emphasizing human rights violations by Soviet communists was a way to maintain or revive American ideological fervor in the post-Vietnam era, when many in the United States had lost or were losing the stomach for containment policies. Jackson felt no compulsion to denounce the arguably worse abuses by communists in China (a country for which he felt a romantic attachment). It also took some strain to see brutal right-wing regimes in countries like Chile, Argentina, Guatemala, Greece, Turkey, or Korea as "less repressive" than Brezhnev's geriatric system.[54] Yet for Jackson, more than for Carter, flailing the Soviet devil served his domestic political ambitions, especially his persistent desire to capture the presidency.[55]

The most influential crusader against the Soviet empire in the late 1970s was Ronald Reagan, whose taped radio broadcasts were aired on almost three hundred stations around the United States and whose columns were printed in more than 200 newspapers.[56] While rehashing articles from conservative magazines of the 1970s, Reagan simultaneously recycled ideas from the peak of enthusiasm for "liberation" in the early 1950s. Thus, in a May 1977 broadcast, Reagan drew on a report that discontented Soviet workers were clamoring for the right to emigrate, to suggest that "We could have an unexpected ally if citizen Ivan is becoming discontented enough to start talking back. Maybe we should drop a few million typical mail order catalogues on Minsk & Pinsk & Moscow to whet their appetites."[57]

Broadcasts and columns about the Soviet Union had many specific uses for Reagan. By emphasizing shortcomings in Soviet health care, he could try to counter proposals for "socialized medicine" in America.[58] By pointing to how many more hours Russians had to work to buy scarce consumer goods, he could try to allay discontent about rising prices and inflation in the US.[59] Perhaps most important, by stressing the evils of "Godless" communists, he could try to offset the belief of American youth that the US war in Vietnam had been "the epitome of evil."[60]

The picture of the Soviet Union that Reagan painted was not strictly realistic. Citing a memoir published by exiled dissident Vladimir

Bukovsky, for example, Reagan exclaimed that Soviet dissidents were not skulking underground but "speaking out openly," thereby "proving that the 60 years of unceasing propaganda has not made the people a docile mass of willing slaves."[61] Bukovsky's ambivalent memoir actually expressed considerable frustration with the ingrained obedience, passivity, and pliability of the Russian people. It also acknowledged that by 1976 the Kremlin had begun to break the small dissident movement through commitments to brutal psychiatric hospitals, expulsions and emigration.[62] Nevertheless, the image of restless masses of Russians hungering for emancipation suited Reagan's desire to muster "a superiority of the spirit" in America, much as ministers of an earlier generation had conjured images of benighted heathens craving enlightenment by missionaries in order to stoke the fires of Christianity in the United States.[63]

This drive to revitalize the American spirit through a crusade for Russian freedom helps to explain why Solzhenitsyn continued to have a strong symbolic appeal to many conservatives long after he had alienated most liberal intellectuals in the United States. Although conservative Christians disputed some of Solzhenitsyn's views, such as his claim that material abundance interfered with spiritual development, they enthusiastically welcomed two central ideas: that the survival of American civilization required a revival of faith, and that the Soviet Union was the prime locus of evil in the modern world.[64]

## Non-governmental organizations and the human rights crusade

In the late 1970s, non-governmental organizations greatly expanded their work on human rights in the Soviet bloc. From the beginning, the Carter administration showed interest in cooperating with private groups concerned with human rights issues. Carter studied reports by Amnesty International, and he directed his aides to work with that organization (which had been founded in London in 1960). Defining its human rights policy in the summer of 1977, the administration anticipated that it would at times "use symbolic acts to identify the United States Government with representatives of human rights organizations" both to demonstrate concern, and to extend protection to the organizations and victims of abuses.[65] Although neo-conservatives would attack the Carter human rights policy for being tougher on right-wing allies than on communist adversaries, the leaders of non-governmental organizations found that they had a feisty and reliable partner in Carter's Assistant Secretary of State for human rights, former civil rights activist Patricia Derian. While Derian thought the United States had less leverage on communist governments than on authoritarian clients, she was determined to speak up for human rights throughout the world and she did not shrink from detailing Soviet repression.[66]

Perhaps the most important non-governmental activist was Jeri Laber, a daughter of Jewish immigrants from Russia whose study of Soviet literature led her to be interested in dissent as early as the 1950s. After working in the 1960s as a writer and publicist in the New York office of the CIA-funded Institute for the Study of the USSR, Laber joined a New York branch of Amnesty International in 1973. At that time, work for Soviet prisoners "seemed like a hopeless project," but Laber began to develop an effective tactic to publicize communist repression and shame foreign leaders. Like George Kennan eighty years earlier, Laber wrote articles that vividly humanized individual political prisoners with strange East European names. Published in the *New York Times* and *New York Review of Books*, Laber's articles succeeded in drawing attention to the cases of specific prisoners (such as Ukrainian nationalist Valentin Moroz, who would be released in 1979).[67]

For Laber and her fellow activists, the start of the Carter administration was "a heady, intoxicating time" that inspired the "conviction that we could change the world." When Random House publisher Robert Bernstein established the Fund for Free Expression in 1977, Laber spearheaded that group's work. The Fund focused above all on the USSR, Laber recalled, because Soviet leaders feared the power of the printed word more than other dictators, and they jailed or exiled more writers. Working parallel to the USIA, Laber and her associates organized an "America Through American Eyes" exhibit at the Moscow Book Fair in 1979, which sought to illustrate the diversity of American life and its difference from life in the Soviet Union. In the same year, with funding from the Ford Foundation, Laber, Bernstein, and others established Helsinki Watch, a private group to monitor compliance with the Helsinki accords. Seeking to show by example how an open society functioned, Helsinki Watch criticized the United States as well as foreign governments. That approach would generate friction with neo-conservatives and conservative Republicans, who wanted to focus exclusively on communist evils and subordinate human rights advocacy to the pursuit of US interests.[68]

### The Carter administration and radio broadcasting to the Soviet bloc

From the outset, the Carter administration took steps to expand and protect radio broadcasts to the Soviet bloc. Ignoring Leonid Brezhnev's denunciation of American interference in Soviet internal affairs, in March

1977 President Carter asked Congress for a large increase in funds to boost transmitting capacity. National Security Adviser Brzezinski warded off German demands for the relocation of Radio Free Europe headquarters away from Munich, telling Chancellor Helmut Schmidt in May that RFE "was an important element of the overall US policy toward the East." Total funding for RFE/RL during the Carter administration rose from around $64 million in 1978 to almost $100 million for 1981. One special initiative of Carter and Brzezinski was to make greater efforts to reach the Muslim peoples in the Soviet Union by increasing VOA and RL broadcasts in seven languages.[69]

Despite such steps, foreign policy advisers to the Ronald Reagan campaign in 1980 saw an opportunity to attack the Carter administration for weakness in "the global war of ideas." Outlining a campaign speech, Kenneth Adelman, a former Defense Department official, asserted that in the Carter years America's penetration of the gloomy regions of despotism had been "all too feeble." Moreover, too many "US information officers overseas exude more shame than pride and fuzz America's virtues rather than exalt them." Instead of being afflicted by guilt, Adelman argued in a *Washington Post* column, the US should launch an offensive that "would paint the East in dark tones for its dreary brutality and the West in light colors for its glowing freedom."[70]

Reagan supporters clearly viewed a propaganda crusade against totalitarianism and for freedom as central to the wider theme of a revitalization of America after the "malaise" of the Carter era. "We must pay more attention to . . . the global propaganda battle," in which the Carter administration had been "tongue-tied," Fred Iklé, chairman of the Republican National Committee's foreign affairs advisory council, declared to the Republican platform committee in 1980. "We . . . have to get rid of the sense of guilt and the spirit of meekness that has been gnawing at our senior policy makers," and recover "an inner sense of righteousness," Iklé urged. To the Reagan team, the image of dissident physicist Andrei Sakharov being sustained in exile by Voice of America broadcasts over his little transistor radio offered an especially stirring reminder of the blessings Americans enjoyed, as well as the revolutionary potential of America's message.[71]

Sakharov had long argued for the convergence of socialism and capitalism, not the simple emulation of the United States. Although he saw the US as a vital and positive force in the world, he noted in his diary in 1980 that "we don't idealize America and see a lot that is bad or foolish in it."[72] Yet Sakharov's story offered Reagan a powerful illustration to accompany his call for Americans to recover from the "VietNam Syndrome" and return to "exporting Americanism." In a speech to the

Veterans of Foreign Wars, Reagan invoked a statement that Sakharov had smuggled "out of the 'Gulag' – the prison which is the Soviet U[nion]," in which the physicist declared: "I consider the United States the historically determined leader of the movement toward a pluralist and free society, vital to mankind." That comment, published in the *New York Times*, enabled Reagan to link America's wish "to see the Russian people living in freedom and dignity" to his wider reminder of America's "pre-ordained destiny to show all mankind that they, too, can be free."[73]

Ironically, then, the Reagan campaign wielded against President Carter some of the same rhetorical weapons Carter had used against Ford and Kissinger. Carter had centered his 1976 campaign on the need for a recovery of faith, and he had begun his administration by assuring Sakharov and others of his commitment to human rights. Yet, after the summer of 1977, in the eyes of Soviet dissidents, Carter retreated from the aggressive criticism of Kremlin repression. While Carter was pleased with the results of quieter diplomacy – including a rise in Jewish emigration and the release of some high profile dissenters – the perception that he had muted his idealistic campaign made him vulnerable to Republican criticism.[74] Especially after Carter's July 15, 1979 speech on a crisis of confidence and excessive worship of consumption in America, Republicans made him a scapegoat for the country's ills. Reagan then seized the opportunity to deny that the United States was in decline and reaffirm how "divine providence" had blessed America with a special place in the world and in history.[75]

### The impact of human rights campaigns on conditions in the Soviet bloc

Soviet dissidents believed that strong and consistent pressure from the West, especially from Washington, could have deterred the Kremlin from cracking down on the human rights movement in the USSR. Sakharov, for example, argued that if the West had responded to an appeal he made in early January of 1977, it might have warded off the new wave of repression. While praising Carter for his sincere commitment to human rights, Sakharov charged that Carter's inconsistent public remarks led the Kremlin to believe he could be manipulated and thus had serious consequences for dissidents.[76]

Although there was some basis for Sakharov's speculation, it is at odds with the available evidence about the reactions of Soviet leaders. Upon Carter's election in November, Soviet leaders worried that he would be influenced by the "rightist trend" evident in the campaign. They decided to reach out to Carter in the hopes of opening "businesslike dialogue," but they also warned the incoming administration against interference in Soviet domestic affairs. When Carter sent a supportive letter to Sakharov in February and the State Department expressed concern about another dissident, Alexander Ginzburg, the Kremlin reacted sharply. The American statements about violations of human rights in the Soviet Union appear to have deeply offended Soviet leaders, who were proud of their government's provision of a higher standard of living, with rights to education, medical care, vacations, and so on. At the urging of the chairman of the KGB, Yuri Andropov, the Politburo directed the Soviet ambassador in Washington to deliver a message to Vance that categorically rejected the right of the United States to raise questions about the Soviet government's treatment of its own citizens.[77]

While the KGB had already been taking steps to curtail American propagandistic activity and curb dissidents, Andropov appears to have persuaded the Politburo that it needed to toughen its position in response to the Carter administration's bolder policy. A report that a US diplomat had said that the Soviet government would not dare to touch Sakharov before the end of the Belgrade Conference on Security and Cooperation in Europe (scheduled to convene in September 1977), may have prodded Andropov to demonstrate his readiness to act against the dissenters. After the Soviet arrest of dissident Anatoly Shcharansky in March, on the eve of a visit by Vance to Moscow, Andropov assured his fellow leaders that their moves were being seen as demonstrations of firmness and decisiveness.[78] Although twenty-eight US senators denounced the arrest of Shcharansky, the Carter administration did not, and that may have led the Kremlin to believe that Carter was backing off, even though he had rejected the Soviet claim that "mistreatment of its citizens is solely its own business" in a speech at the United Nations.[79]

Some Americans dismissed the possibility of a Soviet backlash against the Carter human rights campaign. "Ever since World War II," the *Chicago Tribune* editorialized, "the Russians have become more tractable whenever the West got tough." The Kremlin's reaction to Carter's letter to Sakharov, the paper predicted, would "probably be nothing more than some grumbling words." Syndicated columnist George Will expected Carter's efforts to be effective because the Soviet Union desperately needed trade with the United States in order to modernize; this gave the US "leverage to force some evolution of Soviet society."[80]

While Soviet anger at the Carter human rights campaign did not prevent the eventual negotiation of a new strategic arms limitation treaty by 1979, it does seem to have heightened the Kremlin's determination to repress the dissident movement. Already in March 1977, the *Washington Post* observed that Vance seemed "to have found that, when you

clobber a nation publicly on this issue, you risk arousing its nationalism in a way that . . . rebounds upon human rights."[81] According to
the veteran Soviet ambassador to Washington, Anatoly Dobrynin, Soviet
leaders' strong irritation at Carter prompted them to reject his idea
of exchanging two Soviet spies for Shcharansky in 1978. In addition,
Jewish emigration was sharply reduced in 1980 "mainly because of
Carter's attacks on human rights in the USSR." Thus, Dobrynin concluded, the Carter human rights policy "did more harm than good" to
human rights in the USSR.[82]

Soviet dissidents may have been right that the repression would have
been even harsher without international attention to the Kremlin's
actions. Yet the primary effect of the Carter policy seems to have been
to make the Soviet leadership more intransigent. As Jeri Laber recalled,
the Soviet bloc governments arrested dissenters on the very eve of the
Madrid Conference on Security and Cooperation in Europe in 1980,
thereby "thumbing their noses at the commitments they made when they
signed the Helsinki accords."[83] By the end of Carter's presidency, the
Kremlin had jailed or exiled almost all of the most prominent Soviet dissidents, leaving a handful of elderly women to try to perpetuate the human
rights movement in the USSR. It therefore seems misleading to claim, as
one of Carter's biographers did, that his commitment to human rights
inspired dissidents in the Soviet bloc and thus "dramatically hastened the
ultimate demise of communism."[84]

The monitoring of Soviet bloc violations of the Helsinki human rights
provisions by Congress, the State Department, and non-governmental
organizations ultimately may have contributed to the collapse of communist authority in 1989–91.[85] However, in the short term, the monitors
were unable to compel communist regimes to live up to the accords.

The more immediate significance of the Carter era human rights campaigns, then, was that they raised expectations that were not fulfilled.
While the emphasis on human rights in early 1977 initially seemed to
unify Americans of different political orientations, the crusade proved
increasingly divisive, as liberal internationalists and conservative nationalists fought over where and how to apply American principles.[86] The idea
of freedom in the Soviet bloc that Carter hoped would help Americans to
recover faith in the promise of an evolving liberal democracy, would ultimately be used by his Republican opponents to promote a revitalization
of a more orthodox faith.

# 8    The Reagan mission and the "evil empire," 1981–89

Ronald Reagan had a dream. Anticipating Soviet leader Mikhail Gorbachev's trip to the United States in 1987, Reagan wanted "to take him up in a helicopter and show him how Americans lived." From the air above sun-drenched southern California, Reagan dreamed, "I would have pointed out an ordinary factory and showed him its parking lot filled with workers' cars, then we'd fly over a residential neighborhood and I'd tell him that's where the workers lived – in homes with lawns and backyards, perhaps with a second car or a boat in the driveway." Reagan then planned to turn to Gorbachev and say: "They not only live there, they *own* that property." In case that revelation was not enough to convert the General Secretary of the Communist Party, Reagan "dreamed of landing the helicopter in one of those neighborhoods" and inviting Gorbachev to pick any home he wanted. Together, they would knock at the door and Gorbachev could "ask the people how they live and what they think of our system."[1]

Reagan's dream appears to have arisen from a number of sources. In the late 1940s, Eric Johnston, head of the Motion Picture Association of America, captured Reagan's imagination by recounting how a Polish communist leader was shaken by film footage of American workers' personal automobiles in a factory parking lot. In the early 1950s, Reagan was struck by proposals to send a million Sears Roebuck catalogues into the Soviet bloc – an idea he repeatedly mentioned to aides in the 1980s. Reagan may also have been influenced by memories of how in 1959 Dwight Eisenhower had taken Nikita Khrushchev up in a helicopter over Washington, hoping to wow the communist true believer with all the shiny new cars streaming home to comfortable middle-class houses. Thus, Reagan's dream was not only a personal fantasy, but a distillation of other Americans' visions.[2]

As Reagan's notion of winning over Gorbachev suggests, his famous condemnation of the "evil empire" in 1983 reflected only one half of his approach to the Soviet Union. Especially in his first three years as president, Ronald Reagan repeatedly condemned Soviet leaders' immorality, aggression, and oppression. However, from the beginning of his presidency, he also hoped to convince Soviet leaders to change their outlook, reform their system, and cooperate with him in freeing the world from the threat of nuclear annihilation. Particularly in his second term, Reagan urged Soviet leaders to rejoin the civilized world, realize the benefits of economic integration with the West, and allow the Russian people the freedom to recover their religious faith. Thus, the 1980s marked both a climax of the demonization of the Soviet empire and a culmination of the crusade for a free Russia.

Reagan never fully recognized the tension or contradiction between vilifying the Soviet empire (which tended to provoke hostile, defensive reactions), and appealing to Kremlin leaders to liberalize their system. Instead, for most of his presidency, Reagan vacillated between his conflicting impulses while seeking to placate both militant anticommunist supporters and critics who called for better relations between the superpowers. Hence, contrary to the claims of partisan Republicans and neoconservative ideologues, Reagan did not have a coherent, consistent strategy to cause the collapse of Soviet communism.[3]

Reagan's inconsistency stemmed in part from the division of his advisers into two warring factions, each of which believed it knew what the often taciturn or inarticulate president wanted to do. Hard-line, dogmatic anticommunists in the Pentagon, among White House speechwriters, and for a time on the National Security Council (NSC) viewed the Soviet Union as an irredeemable enemy to be fought, not as a potential partner in negotiations. Moderate pragmatists in the State Department, among the White House political staff, and increasingly at the NSC, believed that Reagan above all wanted to achieve results, including reductions of nuclear weapons, increases in American exports, and re-election in 1984. Neither faction fully understood Reagan's ultimate aspirations. He sought not simply to weaken the Soviet system but to transform it, and not merely to make deals with Soviet leaders but to convert them.

Even more important, Reagan hoped to lead an American recovery from the self-doubt and polarization caused by the Vietnam War, the Watergate scandal, and revelations in the 1970s about clandestine intelligence operations. Denunciations of Soviet wickedness in the early 1980s galvanized the anticommunists who formed Reagan's political base, but alarmed many others who feared that heated rhetoric and an escalating arms race were increasing the danger of nuclear war. After Reagan began emphasizing conciliation more frequently in 1984, he was able to mobilize broader support for his policies. Although diehard anticommunists grew increasingly disgruntled, decreasing tension between the superpowers and rising enthusiasm about promoting change in the Soviet Union ultimately yielded a wider healing of the American spirit than the vehement offensive of the early 1980s.

While the warming of relations between Washington and Moscow in the second half of the decade opened wider spheres for missionaries, peace activists, and other non-governmental groups, Ronald Reagan remained at the center of the story. His rhetoric and decisions lurched uncertainly between belligerence, evangelism, and amelioration, but it is unfair to depict him as a passive ignoramus unable to choose between the competing proposals of zealous and pragmatic officials.[4] Although the genial president hesitated to intervene in the heated debates between rival advisers, his rulings (however cryptically conveyed) were ultimately decisive. It is true that Reagan relied heavily on scripts prepared by NSC staffers or speechwriters,[5] yet he was at key moments the director as well as the lead actor.[6] Hence, before analyzing the course of his administration's policies, it is essential to uncover the roots of Reagan's vision.

### Origins of Reagan's mission

At the age of eleven, Ronald Reagan experienced a religious awakening and was baptized in a Disciples of Christ church in Dixon, Illinois. A denomination that flourished on the westward-moving frontier in the nineteenth century, the Disciples of Christ closely identified their religious convictions with their faith in the destiny of the United States. Many of them believed strongly in an American democratic mission to redeem the world from despotism. Reagan's mother, Nelle, a dedicated member of the church, headed its missionary society in the 1920s and fervently believed in the Christian duty to preach the Gospel throughout the world. Reagan's religious upbringing, including teaching Sunday school and attending a college founded by the Disciples of Christ, instilled ideas that would underpin his approach to the Soviet Union, including faith that God had a plan for him and for the world, a belief in the ultimate triumph of good over evil, and a conviction that America was preordained to carry the torch of freedom in the world.[7]

Although Reagan showed little concern about communism before 1945, as relations with the Soviet Union deteriorated after the Second World War he became increasingly convinced that communism was a false, secular religion that ensnared Americans as well as peoples in Eastern Europe. The writings of former communists, especially Whittaker Chambers, led Reagan to conclude that godlessness was as essential to communism as being Christian was central to being American. At the same time, reading about Chambers' return from communism to

Christianity and assisting the rehabilitation of some Hollywood leftists encouraged Reagan to believe in the possibility of saving even committed communists. A letter that Reagan and others published in the *Hollywood Reporter* in 1951 proclaimed the core message: "You Can Be Free Men Again!"[8]

Reagan's emerging gospel featured a material as well as a spiritual appeal. Influenced by Hollywood leaders, Reagan came to see movies as powerful ways to project irresistible images of American abundance around the world. Thus, films could be vital weapons in the ideological war against communism. Just by showing America's store windows, streets, and parking lots, Reagan told members of Kiwanis International in 1951, movies could counter "propaganda from the other side of the Iron Curtain." Later in the 1950s, as a spokesperson for General Electric, Reagan honed his increasingly conservative message about the superior productivity of American capitalism, provided that it was not fettered by excessive taxation and government regulation.[9]

Long before he became president, then, Reagan developed distinctive traits and themes that would mark his approach to the Soviet Union. He believed that he had a personal calling and that America had a historical mission. He was convinced that communism was evil but that communists could be redeemed. He felt that the prosperous American way of life had enormous potential appeal to the Soviet bloc. And above all he was a dreamer. Raised to believe that he could make dreams come true and undaunted by contrary details, he would hold on to his dreams despite the comments of critics and aides who said they were unrealizable.[10]

### Reagan's first advisers' visions

At the start of Reagan's presidency, few of his advisers shared his belief in the possibility of changing the minds of communist leaders and redeeming the Russian people. Secretary of Defense Caspar Weinberger, whose motto was "not to yield," opposed any serious negotiation with the Kremlin. He preferred to rely on a long-term military build-up that would end only with Soviet capitulation to US demands or with a strengthened America prevailing in a nuclear war. Although Weinberger had glimpsed the impact Pepsi was having on thirsty Russian consumers when he visited the Soviet Union in 1979, he was incapable of imagining a transformation of the communist enemy. Through the end of the 1980s, Weinberger remained convinced that the Soviet system could not be altered in any fundamental way. Even in post-Cold War retrospect, Weinberger insisted that the earth-shaking reforms launched by Soviet leader Mikhail Gorbachev after 1985 were only "a public relations campaign."[11]

Director of Central Intelligence William Casey's vehement anti-communism, rooted in a Manichaean Catholicism, inclined him to share Reagan's suspicion that the Soviet Union was at the root of almost all evil in the world. Casey's obsession with rolling back Soviet geopolitical gains, especially in Central America and Afghanistan, combined with his zealous drive to undermine the faltering Soviet economy, almost completely excluded consideration of the possibility of liberalization of the USSR.[12] According to Herbert Meyer, Vice Chairman of the National Intelligence Council under Casey, Reagan fully agreed with Casey's vision of harsh economic warfare to cause the Soviet state to collapse. Yet Reagan was actually softer than Casey, and that contributed to Casey's contempt for the president as indecisive, passive, and mindless.[13]

The director of Soviet affairs at the National Security Council, historian Richard Pipes, believed that God had saved him from the Holocaust in Poland for the purpose of spreading the message that evil ideas (especially communism) lead to evil consequences. Pipes sought to force the Soviet leadership to abandon communism, but unlike Reagan he did not believe dialogue with the Kremlin would be useful. As he later put it, "one could not negotiate with it its own destruction." In contrast to Reagan's optimistic assumptions, Pipes felt that the brutish, oriental people of Russia could not be freed – they required "a strong hand." The purpose of a confrontational policy, in Pipes' eyes, was "not so much to compel the aggressor to repent and recant as to give expression to moral indignation." Through tough economic sanctions, he hoped to provoke an economic crisis that would make the Soviet system less aggressive and authoritarian rather than totalitarian.[14]

Pipes had few opportunities to influence US policy in 1981, when the National Security Adviser was Richard V. Allen, a former aide to Richard Nixon who monopolized the briefing of Reagan. After Allen was forced to resign in November 1981, Pipes was occasionally able to have more impact, in part because Allen's successor, former California Supreme Court Justice William P. Clark, knew little about foreign affairs and had to rely heavily on the NSC staff. A devout Catholic, Clark shared Reagan's and Pipes' moral revulsion at communism, but was too uninformed about the Soviet Union to initiate steps toward the far-reaching changes Reagan envisioned.[15]

Reagan's first Secretary of State, Alexander Haig, was a career Army officer who had served as head of NATO and chief of staff to Richard Nixon. Haig's emphasis on "reciprocity" in superpower interaction coincided with Reagan's view that détente had been a one-way street in the late 1970s, but Haig's Nixonian "realism" was more geopolitical and short-sighted than Reagan's vision of a moral crusade to transform

American-Soviet relations. Vainglorious and cynical, Haig made the humble and earnest Reagan uneasy. In June 1982, Reagan accepted Haig's resignation, a move that underscored the instability and incoherence of the administration's early foreign policy.[16]

### Early Reagan administration policies: uncoordinated offensives and appeals

Since Reagan's top advisers had different agendas, and Reagan was unable to articulate his divergent aspirations in a comprehensive strategy, the first years of the administration saw uncoordinated offensives and contradictory initiatives. While there was no clear plan to win the Cold War, the administration did simultaneously seek to roll back communism in the Third World, exacerbate Soviet economic difficulties, and challenge communist ideological hegemony in the Soviet bloc.

Casey and the CIA focused above all on supporting anticommunist insurgencies, especially the Nicaraguan *contras* and the Afghan *mujahedin*. In the early 1980s, as in the last year of the Carter administration, the prime objectives of the modest aid to the Islamic rebels in Afghanistan were to make the Soviets pay a high price for their aggression and keep them from using a stable Afghanistan as a springboard for further expansion. Outside the Reagan team, champions of aid to the Afghan "freedom fighters" found additional meaning in the cause. For Charlie Wilson, a hard-drinking Texas congressman who became the most vigorous proponent of bigger appropriations, support for "the muj" was not only a way to do unto the Soviets what they had done unto America in Vietnam but also a path to recovery from his "mid-life crisis" in the late 1970s. Spurred by Wilson, the US dramatically escalated aid to the *mujahedin* between 1984 and 1987. By 1985, fervent anticommunists urged the administration to pursue "victory" over Soviet forces in Afghanistan. Some believed that a defeat in Afghanistan would shake the Kremlin's prestige and weaken its grip on the Soviet Union. Casey, who saw Islam and Catholicism as allies against Soviet atheism, even encouraged some attacks into Soviet territory, though his goal there seems to have been to damage the Soviet Union rather than to bring about the liberation of Uzbekistan or Tajikistan.[17]

While US pressure on the USSR gradually mounted in Afghanistan, there was not such a clear trajectory in US economic policy. Contrary to accounts by some of his conservative admirers, Reagan was too soft-hearted to wage relentless economic warfare against the Soviet Union.[18] At the first meeting of his Cabinet, when the Secretary of Agriculture criticized the embargo on shipments of grain to the Soviet Union that Carter had imposed, Reagan explained: "My whole approach on this is one of mixed emotions. I know it hurts farmers, but [I] don't want to give to [the] Soviets. From now on, I want [a] policy that anytime we give, we get."[19] Thus, on the first major question of policy toward the Soviet Union, Reagan focused not on the possibility of triggering a social crisis through worsening food shortages, but on the need for a balanced, quid pro quo relationship. Pipes, who was not consulted about the lifting of the embargo, has rationalized that grain purchases depleted Soviet hard currency reserves, but for Reagan that was an *ex post facto* justification.[20] At the time, Reagan worried that lifting the embargo might allow the Soviets to spend more on armaments and help to "extend the life of Communism."[21]

Over the following years, Reagan repeatedly backed away from tough measures. In May 1981 he vacillated on how vigorously to obstruct a pipeline that would bring Soviet gas to Western Europe. In December 1981, angered by the Soviet-instigated crackdown on the Solidarity movement in Poland, Reagan approved economic sanctions, yet he refused to break diplomatic relations with the Kremlin and he even urged that a carrot be offered to Brezhnev if he changed his behavior. In late 1982, Reagan wavered again on the pipeline embargoes, which were rescinded in November.[22] And in 1983 he declined to take steps against the Polish Communist regime that would "impose suffering on the Polish people."[23]

Reagan did approve other measures, including a ban on sales of high technology to the Soviet Union and an agreement with European countries to restrict credits to the Kremlin. More important, Casey urged the Saudis to increase their oil production dramatically. When they finally did so in 1985, it sharply reduced the price of oil and hence Soviet export revenue. At Reykjavik in 1986, Gorbachev complained that "all the money the Russians had hoped to spend on grain was in America and Saudi Arabia as a result of lower oil prices." (Either in ignorance or disingenuously, Reagan claimed, "We had no hand in creating the hardships.")[24] Although the administration did not wage relentless economic warfare against the USSR, then, its disjointed steps did painfully aggravate Soviet financial difficulties and heighten Gorbachev's interest in a relaxation of East-West tensions.

While the economic campaign sputtered in the early 1980s, an ideological offensive swept forward on several fronts. With the help of his speechwriters, Reagan delivered many scorching condemnations of Soviet leaders' immoral approach to international relations, and he boldly prophesied the demise of communism.[25] In the same years, the US delegation to a session of the Conference on Security and Cooperation in Europe, held in Madrid, repeatedly excoriated the Soviet persecution of religious believers, Jews who sought to emigrate, and human rights activists. Congressional admirers applauded the way the US delegation thus exposed the Soviets' "brutal suppression of freedom" and demonstrated "to the world the fundamental difference between the Soviet and Western systems of government."[26]

Meanwhile, American-funded propaganda organizations expanded their broadcasting to the Soviet bloc and more aggressively attacked communist hypocrisy and repression. Under the erratic but energetic leadership of Reagan's Hollywood friend Charles Wick, the US Information Agency's budget doubled. It beamed television images into the Soviet bloc – of atrocities in Afghanistan and supermarkets in America – that Communist authorities were unable to jam. Frank Shakespeare, a devout Catholic and ardent anticommunist, was appointed chairman of the Board for International Broadcasting, which oversaw both Radio Free Europe and Radio Liberty. During Shakespeare's tenure, broadcasters were encouraged to make more hard-hitting commentaries. Radio Liberty, in particular, unleashed right-wing Russian emigrés and broadcast many of Solzhenitsyn's writings. Although the transmission of the views of reactionary nationalists struck some propaganda advisers as inconsistent with democratic principles, the offensive spirit fitted Reagan's ideological objectives. In an interview broadcast over RFE-RL in 1985, Reagan declared that the United States intended to "demonstrate that Communism is not the wave of the future" and to "show the captive nations that resisting totalitarianism is possible."[27]

Despite his fiery rhetoric and his commitment to rolling back communism, Reagan wanted to do business with the Soviets and he wanted to encourage them to mend their ways. As Reagan told CBS news in March 1981, he did not believe that calling Soviet leaders liars and cheats made it more difficult to meet with them. On the contrary, Reagan thought of such criticism as part of an effort to convince Soviet leaders that giving up their worldwide aggression and their denial of human rights "might be helpful to them with their own economic problems." The next month, in response to a letter from Leonid Brezhnev, Reagan thought of reminding the Soviet leader of how they had met at Nixon's residence in California in 1973. In addition to recalling how the two had spoken about fulfilling the hopes and dreams of people around the world for peace, Reagan sought to give Brezhnev a mini-civics lesson about how government exists for the convenience of people, "not the other way around." He urged the Communist leader to set aside ideology, and consider how "the average Soviet family" could be better off if the Kremlin ceased its foreign adventurism. Thus, as he recovered from being shot by a deranged young man on March 30, Reagan was moved not only to dedicate the years God had given him to reduce the danger of nuclear war, but also to try to persuade the Soviet leadership to rethink its political and economic philosophy.[28]

Hard-liners scorned Reagan's heartfelt appeal to Brezhnev as "maudlin" or naïve. To Haig and other top officials at the State Department, overtures for a more constructive relationship with the Soviet Union, such as a publicized presidential letter to Brezhnev in September 1981, were part of a "campaign to take the political offensive away from the Soviets." With Haig controlling the drafting of such messages, there was a Nixonian emphasis on the need for Soviet "restraint," rather than earnest pleas for more fundamental change.[29]

Reagan's ambitious idealism found more opportunity for expression after the abrasive Haig resigned in June 1982 and was replaced by George Shultz, the head of Bechtel Corporation who had been Treasury Secretary under Nixon. Shultz provoked disdain from more dogmatic anticommunists like Pipes, who viewed him as a non-ideological, unimaginative problem-solver.[30] Yet Shultz, more than Pipes, Haig, and others, sympathized with Reagan's yearning to promote sweeping changes in the Soviet Union.

The grandson of a Presbyterian missionary who sought to establish a church on the Idaho frontier, Shultz at times displayed comparable zeal. Perhaps influenced by reading Boris Pasternak's novel, *Doctor Zhivago*, or seeing the 1965 Hollywood film based on it, Shultz seems to have had an intuitive sense that under the drab surface of Soviet public life there were vibrant energies that could be unleashed. Shultz had traveled to Moscow as a leader of the US-USSR Commercial Commission in 1973 and had been a member of the US-USSR-Trade Council, but those experiences had not led him to suppress ideological rivalry in the interest of profits. In 1979, for example, Shultz proclaimed freedom the "ideological victor" in the struggle against communism, declared that the "incompetent" Soviet system could not survive, and called for Americans to demonstrate the superiority of free market capitalism. Instead of being a stolid pragmatist, then, Shultz was in tune with Reagan's ideological mission.[31]

### Demonization of the "evil empire" and backlash

As an NSC staffer observed in 1981, one of the Reagan administration's priority objectives was to restore American "self-confidence," in part through the "non-apologetic expression and defense of American values and institutions."[32] A complementary way to revitalize American nationalism was to demonize the Soviet Union. Reagan most famously vilified the Soviet system in an address to the National Association of Evangelicals on March 8, 1983. Although Reagan acknowledged that

"Our nation, too, has a legacy of evil," he suggested that racism was largely a problem of the past, and that the struggle for equal rights was "now a point of pride for all Americans." The token concession of imperfection in America thus cleared the way for a depiction of the world in white and black rather than shades of gray. Since Soviets "preach the supremacy of the state, declare its omnipotence over individual man, and predict its eventual domination of all peoples on the Earth," Reagan declared, "they are the focus of evil in the modern world." America, in contrast, drawing its spiritual strength from free individuals, was the fount of virtue from which the world could be regenerated.[33]

Reagan's condemnation of "the aggressive impulses of an evil empire" thrilled his evangelical hosts, and may have appeased some on the Christian Right who had been disappointed by his failure to appoint more religious conservatives to top posts or to vigorously back anti-abortion measures.[34] However, if the speech was intended to rally broader support for his military buildup and confrontational policies, it failed. While a few prominent conservatives defended Reagan's speech, it was widely criticized for its simplistic theological approach to complex political problems. Reagan's appeal to the evangelicals was attacked not only by liberals like historian Arthur Schlesinger, Jr. (who was disturbed by the "inordinate self-righteousness"), but also by centrists such as *Time* magazine's Hugh Sidey (who was appalled by the pose of a "self-anointed soldier of God"). Leaders of Jewish, Lutheran, and even Southern Baptist organizations criticized Reagan for using the mantle of religion to wrap a political attack on the popular movement to freeze the production of nuclear weapons. Even conservative columnist William Safire, who shared Reagan's "conception of our international enemy," was troubled by the way the president had taken the place of preachers in the pulpit. Reagan's ideological fervor seemed to be not only "out of tune with the sentiments of Americans," as journalist Stanley Karnow commented, but even ridiculous. The *St. Louis Post-Dispatch* compared Reagan's castigation of the Soviet Union to Iranian Ayatollah Khomeini's calling the United States the "Great Satan." Cartoonists mocked Reagan's preaching as frenzied or hysterical.[35] (See figure 17.)

Despite the widespread criticism of the address to evangelicals, Reagan thought "it worked," that it showed "we recognized the Soviets for what they were." Others have argued that the speech succeeded in undermining the legitimacy of the Soviet regime, led Kremlin leaders to recognize that their system was evil, and even pushed them to negotiate with the United States.[36]

The "evil empire" epithet did sting Soviet and Russian leaders. Georgi Arbatov, the senior Soviet expert on the United States, denounced

Figure 17. "Onward Christian Soldiers." Ronald Reagan is depicted as a Christian crusader and juxtaposed to demonstrators for a freeze on the deployment of nuclear weapons, who are led by a priest, a nun, and a bishop. Cartoon by Tony Auth. *The Philadelphia Inquirer*, March 10, 1983. Auth © 1983. Reprinted with permission of Universal Press Syndicate. All rights reserved.

Reagan's "frenzied" and "hypocritical" speech. The aged patriarch of the Russian Orthodox Church assailed Reagan for sowing "seeds of hatred" against Russia, which was not "an evil empire" but a peace-loving country that did the most to defeat "the Fascist hordes" in World War II.[37]

Reagan's rhetoric did not enhance the prospect for dialogue with the Kremlin. *Pravda* immediately declared that the Orlando speech showed Reagan was only capable of thinking in terms of confrontation and anti-Sovietism. Three months later, elderly Politburo member Konstantin Chernenko urged a tightening of ideological controls throughout the Soviet system in response to Reagan's efforts to "poison the minds" of Soviet citizens. Even the younger Mikhail Gorbachev regarded Reagan's infamous phrase as an obstacle, not a spur, to negotiation. While Gorbachev was keenly aware of the abuses committed by Soviet communists – including the arrest and torture of one of his grandfathers in the 1930s – he did not accept the wholesale condemnation of a system he believed had elevated most Russians from primitive to modern conditions. To Gorbachev, Reagan's labelling the Soviet system as "evil" was not a revelation but a sign that it would be difficult to deal with such a political "dinosaur."[38]

## Opening the doors

Around the same time that Reagan publicly lashed the "evil empire," his diplomatic advisers quietly reopened channels of communication with the Soviet government that had been closed or unused. On February 12, 1983, Shultz arranged a meeting between Reagan and Ambassador Anatoly Dobrynin, at which Reagan appealed for the Soviet government to allow the emigration of a group of Pentecostals who had been living in the basement of the US Embassy in Moscow for almost five years. Reagan had long been concerned with the plight of the Pentecostal families: in July 1981 he had pleaded with Brezhnev to release them, to no avail. Now, however, the Soviet response was encouraging. Within weeks, Soviet diplomats offered indirect assurances of a favorable resolution if the matter was handled confidentially. By July 1983, both Pentecostal families left the Soviet Union.[39]

This small humanitarian gesture had great symbolic significance for Reagan. It encouraged him to believe in the possibility of using diplomatic engagement to promote bigger steps toward a more tolerant and humane system in the Soviet Union. As he wrote to Andropov in July, he sought "a more active level of exchange" between the two governments, and he hoped that a summit meeting would allow the two leaders to discuss the variety of "ways in which we can expand east-west contacts."[40] Reagan thus clearly aligned himself with a group of his advisers who urged a relaxation of tension and a reopening of relations.

Jack Matlock, a career diplomat who replaced Pipes as the top Soviet expert at the NSC in 1983, was among the most important members of the administration who believed that "the United States could not, from the outside, bring down the Soviet regime, and that direct attempts to do so would only strengthen it." Like some senior advisers in the late 1950s and 1960s, Matlock thought a subtler strategy was required. Instead of openly demanding the reformation of the Soviet system, Washington should encourage reform through an easing of tension that would give Soviet leaders more "elbow room" and allow Western ideas to pierce the Iron Curtain. As Matlock later recalled, he "was convinced that open borders, the free flow of information, and the establishment of democratic institutions would produce a fundamental change in the Soviet system." A Russophile who had been fascinated by Russian language and literature since the 1940s, Matlock felt that while the Soviet empire was evil, "it was not an empire of evil people." Having studied Russian history and served two tours of duty in Moscow, Matlock knew that isolationism and autarky had deep roots, but he believed they were "not the only roots." Like Reagan, then, but with more knowledge and sophistication, Matlock had faith in the goodness of the peoples of Russia and in the possibility of moving beyond the deadlock of Cold War hostility.[41]

Matlock was able to spearhead the development of a new approach, in part because of support from more highly placed officials. Deputy National Security Adviser "Bud" McFarlane urged the renewal of educational and scientific exchanges that had been cancelled, arguing that US officials had gained insights on fellowships in the USSR and that it was also advantageous to have Russians "exposed to the US."[42] Even stronger backing came from Secretary of State Shultz, who recommended that one of the key US objectives should be "to increase our ideological impact inside the Soviet Union through expanded exchange programs and access of Americans to Soviet society" – an objective formally endorsed in National Security Decision Directive 75 in January 1983.[43]

The US Ambassador in Moscow, Arthur Hartman, concurred with Matlock and Shultz. Although Hartman had not displayed much missionary ardor in the era of détente, when he served under Kissinger as an assistant secretary of state, by the time Reagan made him Ambassador in 1981 he believed that his basic job was "to penetrate a closed society." Influenced by George F. Kennan, Hartman viewed Russians' fear of foreigners as rooted in centuries of historical experience, not merely a product of communist ideology. To overcome the traditional Russian xenophobia and insecurity, Hartman urged a strategy of engagement rather than isolation. In a May 1983 address at Harvard that gave heartburn to hard-liners, Hartman argued that "an approach to the Soviet Union that emphasizes trade and other contacts . . . offers better prospects for a more peaceful world than trying to seal the Soviets off from all dealings with us." To get around Soviet efforts to control all contacts with foreigners, Hartman began inviting American experts on the USSR to the Moscow embassy, where they could exchange ideas more freely with Russian intellectuals and party officials.[44]

Reagan definitely sided with those who wanted to widen American penetration and influence. On April 6, 1983, after members of the National Security Council staff argued that no "approach should be made to the Soviets," Reagan overruled their objections and confided to his diary, "Some of the N.S.C. staff are too hard line." Reagan himself wanted to respond positively to Soviet leaders if they would "show *by deed* they want to get along with the free world." Early in 1984, Reagan met with President Mika Spiljak of Yugoslavia, who had earlier been an ambassador to

Moscow. Spiljak informed Reagan that the Soviets were frightened of the United States, and suggested that "if we opened them up a bit, their leading citizens would get braver about proposing changes in their system." Reagan resolved "to pursue this."[45]

With the president's approval, Matlock explored "steps we might take to bolster our influence among the Russian people." In June 1984, addressing a conference of American organizations that had been active in exchanges with the Soviet Union, Reagan made it clear that "our quarrel is not with the Russian people" and that he wanted to "broaden opportunities for Americans and Soviets to get to know each other better." Such initiatives were not welcomed by the hard-line Soviet officials who were in the saddle after Andropov's death in February 1984: instead, they clamped down further on dissent and ratcheted up anti-American propaganda. Only after the death of Konstantin Chernenko a year later and the waning of the reactionaries' power, would Mikhail Gorbachev approve proposals Matlock developed for a wide array of cultural, educational, and scientific exchanges.[46]

### Domestic politics and overtures to the Soviets

While Reagan's rising interest in loosening the vise-like grip of the Kremlin was genuine, the president and his advisers were also influenced by concerns about the 1984 election. As National Security Adviser Clark acknowledged in May 1983, Reagan shared Shultz's "interest in getting results." Clearly feeling mounting pressure from the White House, Clark recognized the need "to forge a negotiating strategy" so that "a year from now we will have achieved one or two extremely important goals en route to our objectives." By February 1984, Matlock had prepared a checklist of US-Soviet issues to highlight the prospects for reaching agreements during the election year. With polls showing that a plurality of Americans believed the détente of the Nixon – Kissinger era was better than the heightened tension of the Reagan years, the White House had a strong interest in softening the tone of American-Soviet relations.[47]

The centerpiece of the new public approach to the USSR was a speech Reagan delivered on January 16, 1984, after directing aides to soften the language and avoid "kicking them in the teeth." As speechwriter Tony Dolan observed, "for tactical purposes," Reagan did not want to reaffirm "his view of the Soviet Union as an evil empire." Instead, the speech emphasized the possibilities for developing more friendly relations, which Reagan dramatized with a story about an imaginary meeting between Soviet and American couples who find that they have a lot in common. Among the most important points in the speech was an appeal to the Kremlin for more open doors to American influence. "Expanding contacts across borders and permitting a free interchange of information and ideas increases confidence," Reagan explained, while "sealing off one's people from the rest of the world reduces it."[48]

The shift in rhetoric appealed to many Americans. After January 1984, popular approval of Reagan's foreign policy rose. By July, 54 percent of Americans surveyed by the Reagan campaign approved of Reagan's handling of relations with the Soviet Union, an increase the campaign pollster attributed in part to the perception that Reagan was more interested in improving ties and reopening arms control negotiations.[49]

### Dreams of conversion

Although Reagan's more conciliatory tone in 1984 stemmed in part from domestic political calculations, his interest in liberalization of the Soviet Union was deeper than that. From the beginning of his presidency, Reagan had a hunch that "religion may very well turn out to be the Soviets' Achilles' heel." Even as he prepared to denounce the "evil empire" in March 1983, Reagan inserted an old-fashioned missionary appeal: "Let us pray for the salvation of all those who live in that totalitarian darknesss – pray they will discover the joy of knowing God." Reagan's feeling that this might actually happen was fueled by reports from evangelist Billy Graham, among others. Indeed, Reagan's approach paralleled Graham's in many respects.[50]

Graham had dreamed of proclaiming the Gospel in the USSR since 1959. By the early 1980s he was also deeply concerned by the danger of nuclear war. In 1982, despite criticism from those who opposed any compromise with the forces of atheism, Graham accepted an invitation to preach in Moscow, for the first time. Although Ambassador Hartman and the State Department objected that Graham's presence at a church-sponsored peace conference would lend respectability to Soviet anti-nuclear propaganda, Reagan gave his blessing to Graham's trip, writing, "God does work in wondrous ways." In Moscow, Graham privately expressed his concern about prisoners of conscience to a Soviet official but, to the consternation of more rigid anticommunists, refrained from publicly castigating Soviet policies. Although Graham was shaken by criticism of him as naïve or even sympathetic to communism, he felt the Soviet propagandistic exploitation of his visit was outweighed by the unprecedented opportunities to win the peoples of the USSR to Christ. In September 1984 he therefore returned to the Soviet Union, for twelve days of preaching from Leningrad to Novosibirsk. Meeting with top Kremlin officials, Graham emphasized the need to improve the

situation of believers in the Soviet Union in order to clear the way for
better relations with the United States – an appeal he believed influenced
Soviet policy in the following years. After preaching in a Kremlin cathedral on the topic, "You Must Be Born Again," Graham was gratified
when a Metropolitan of the Orthodox Church assured him, "You have a
wide-open door in our country." Those experiences convinced Graham
that there was "a quiet religious revival on throughout the Soviet Union,"
as he informed Reagan in one of many letters to the White House.[51]

Reagan's keen interest in a spiritual awakening in the Soviet Union
was also whetted by scholarly experts who helped him develop more of a
feeling for Russia's people and culture. Suzanne Massie, an art historian
who traveled frequently to the Soviet Union, exerted especially strong
influence on Reagan's imagination. In *Land of the Firebird: The Beauty of
Old Russia* (1980), Massie suggested that "beyond the gray monotony" of
the contemporary Soviet Union there was a vibrant spiritual and cultural
heritage that could arise again, like the firebird of Russian folk tales.[52]
Beginning in late 1983, Massie met with Reagan several times, established
a rapport, and exchanged a number of letters with him.[53]

Drawing on her contacts with cultural figures and church leaders in
the USSR, Massie encouraged Reagan's pre-existing belief in the possibility of a spiritual rebirth of Russia. Meetings with Massie sharpened
Reagan's attention to the prospects for religious renewal. In February
1984, for example, when Reagan watched the televised funeral of Soviet
leader Yuri Andropov, he thought the wife of new leader Konstantin
Chernenko displayed striking piety. Reagan then wrote to Massie: "Like
you, I continue to believe that the hunger for religion may yet be a major
factor in bringing about a change in the present situation."[54]

Soon after Mikhail Gorbachev succeeded Chernenko in March 1985,
Massie spent two months in the Soviet Union and was struck by the "significant change in the atmosphere." Reagan phoned her to talk about
her impressions from the trip, then Massie sent a letter to the White
House to reiterate her points. "Clearly," she reported, "the people long
for a change." It was not merely that people were openly "griping" about
things they had "patiently endured for so long," and it was not simply
that the Russians maintained "a lively affection" for America despite "the
Big Lies" of Soviet propaganda. In Massie's interpretation, what was happening was a "saga of the Russian people's determination to rebuild their
lost past" and rededicate themselves to "ideals of spirituality and beauty."
This message was reinforced when Reagan read *Land of the Firebird* as he
prepared to meet Gorbachev in Geneva in November 1985.[55]

At Geneva, Gorbachev praised God that there had been no war between
the US and the USSR, observed that "God provides information only very

selectively and rarely," and invoked a biblical injunction "to gather stones which have been cast in the past." In response, Reagan himself cited a biblical passage to the effect that "we are all of one blood regardless of where we live on Earth." Given Reagan's religious predisposition and his preparation with Suzanne Massie, it is not surprising that he was captivated by Gorbachev's religious expressions, which led him to wonder whether the General Secretary might be a closet Christian. As Reagan confided to Massie three months later, Gorbachev's invocation of God and the Bible "has stuck in my mind and stays a nagging question that won't go away."[56]

While the spiritual regeneration of Russia fascinated Reagan more than anything else, it overlapped and fused with his sense of the irresistible attraction of American prosperity to Russians who had endured short-ages of consumer goods for decades. The religious and economic dimensions gradually coalesced in a dream or a script that he hoped to act out. Even before he first met Gorbachev in 1985, Reagan yearned to show the Soviet leader the superiority of the American way of life. During the next two years, Reagan repeatedly mentioned to aides and to Gorbachev his desire to demonstrate Americans' satisfaction with their lifestyles. Reagan's elaborate fantasy neared reality in the fall of 1987, when White House arrangers planned a flight for the two leaders over sparkling swimming pools in southern California. However, according to Secretary of State Shultz, Gorbachev ruled out a trip from Washington to the west coast, in part because "he did not want pictures beamed back to his country of the bountiful United States of America."[57]

Beyond the religious and economic dimensions, Reagan also repeat-edly raised with Gorbachev the issue of human rights in the Soviet Union. However, Reagan's proselytizing for the rights of national minorities and political freedoms was less fervent. At Geneva, he prefaced his remarks by saying that "he did not want to interfere in the internal affairs of the Soviet Union," then indicated that Soviet concessions on emigration and the treatment of nationalities were necessary mainly to appease lobbying groups and secure the support of Congress for future steps. At Reyk-javik, similarly, Reagan told Gorbachev that human rights was "a very important issue" because "the degree to which the President could work together with the Soviet side depended on US public opinion." Reagan did explain the American belief "that people should have the right to determine their own form of government," and he encouraged Gor-bachev to allow more than one political party in the Soviet Union. Yet he also "recognized the differences in our two systems," and accepted the idea of living "as friendly competitors."[58]

While Reagan pressed above all for religious freedom, Shultz, a former professor of economics, focused most keenly on educating Soviet leaders about the need to reorient their social and economic system in the "information age." When the relatively young and open-minded Mikhail Gorbachev and Eduard Shevardnadze became General Secretary and Foreign Minister in 1985, Shultz resolved to conduct a "classroom in the Kremlin" on how the Soviet Union had to become a more open society, to avoid falling hopelessly behind the increasingly interdependent capitalist countries. On his diplomatic missions to Moscow, Shultz again and again lectured Gorbachev and Shevardnadze about the need for the USSR to switch to a decentralized, "incentive-based, market-oriented economic system" in order to stimulate the creativity of individuals, spur growth in the crucial sectors of science and technology, and merge with the global economy. Although Shultz was at first uncertain about the effect of his teaching, by the end of 1987 he felt sure that his ideas were having an impact on Soviet leaders' thinking, and at the end of the Reagan era he noted with great satisfaction that Gorbachev had fully embraced his perspective.[59]

## The image of an evil enemy fades in the light of an American mission

By December 1987, when Gorbachev came to Washington to sign an agreement for the removal of short and intermediate range missiles from Europe, the engaging and likeable Soviet leader had made substantial headway in dispelling the image of a diabolical Soviet enemy that he believed was essential to the perpetuation of an arms race. Reagan's acceptance of the genuineness of Gorbachev's commitment to dramatic changes in Soviet foreign and domestic policies infuriated many conservatives. Some were alarmed by the way this threatened the Pentagon budget. As early as February 1986, for example, speechwriter Patrick Buchanan had warned that the softening of Reagan's rhetoric had put the US defense buildup "in deep jeopardy." Others charged that the gullible Reagan was being duped by the wily Gorbachev. Howard Phillips, head of the Conservative Caucus, called the president "a useful idiot for Soviet propaganda." The Arizona *Republic* published a cartoon depicting a soft-headed Reagan at a White House podium, while behind his back a devious aide to Gorbachev snickered that the president was "a sucker." Still others were alarmed by the moral or ideological ramifications of Reagan's shift. Thus, columnist George Will complained that the president had "accelerated the nation's intellectual disarmament" by declaring that the

Cold War was over, that the Soviet system was not inherently wicked, and that Gorbachev had transformed it for the better.[60]

In part to mollify such critics, Reagan and his advisers resolved to make appeals for human rights a prominent feature of his trip to Moscow for another summit meeting in late May and early June, 1988. On leaving Washington, Reagan explicitly argued that the United States could work with the Soviet Union for peace and "still remain true to its mission of expanding liberty throughout the world." Anticipating the celebrations of the millennium of Christianity in Russia scheduled for mid-June, Reagan's aides helped him to make pleas for religious freedom central to his journey. Stopping over in Finland, Reagan called for the Soviet leadership to allow "church bells to ring out again not only in Moscow but throughout the Soviet Union." In private meetings, Reagan encouraged Gorbachev to examine how the US Constitution enshrined religious freedom, and read to him a letter by a Russian soldier who realized that "there is a God" before he died in World War II. Then, at the newly restored Danilov monastery, in a speech drafted by historian James Billington, Reagan expressed the hope that Gorbachev's policy of *perestroika* (restructuring) would be accompanied by "a deeper conversion" and that his policy of *glasnost* (publicity or "giving voice") would "let loose a new chorus of belief."[61]

For many Americans, the most striking moment of Reagan's mission to Moscow came when he was walking with Gorbachev in Red Square. In response to a journalist's question about whether he still considered the Soviet Union "an evil empire," he said: "No. That was another time, another era."[62]

Reagan's remark dismayed ideologues. "[A]bsolution is not Mr. Reagan's to give," fumed A. M. Rosenthal of the *New York Times*. The Kremlin was still "the center of tyranny, terrorism and aggression in the world," columnist William Safire claimed (though he acknowledged that those who thought this were "a dwindling band"). The Soviet Union "continues to be an evil empire," insisted William F. Buckley. Realizing the potency of this sentiment among right-wing Republicans, whose support he needed to succeed Reagan, even Vice President George Bush declared in late June that "the cold war is not over."[63]

By that point, Gorbachev had allowed dissident physicist Andrei Sakharov to return to Moscow from internal exile, freed most Soviet political prisoners, encouraged critical discussion of the Soviet past, agreed to withdraw Soviet troops from Afghanistan, promoted cooperative resolution of conflicts in other regions, and encouraged East European communist regimes to liberalize. Hence, there was something beyond objective description of reality in conservatives' clinging to the notion of an "evil empire." As retired diplomat and historian George F. Kennan sagely observed, "A large segment of the American population has the need to cultivate the idea of American innocence and virtue – which requires an opposite pole of evil."[64]

While more than 50 percent of Americans would continue through 1990 to tell pollsters that the Cold War was not over, the concept of the Soviet system as the polar opposite of American values was weakening. An important factor in this shift was the impression of real movement toward religious freedom in the USSR. Shortly before the Moscow summit, the issue was still being presented in harshly adversarial terms: Congress passed a resolution deploring the Soviet "persecution of religious believers in Ukraine," and one member of Congress summoned evangelicals to "fight for freedom for Christians in the Soviet Union." Yet remarks by Reagan and his advisers, followed by the Millennium celebrations, prompted many to see that they were beating on an opening door. The Soviet commitment since 1917 "to teach atheism has gone down the drain," a high-ranking administration official told a religious correspondent. "Communism is a dying faith," he added, and "in that spiritual desert, there are people really thirsting for a special message."[65]

In this context, the leading evangelical magazine, *Christianity Today*, welcomed Reagan's "dismissal of his 'evil empire' comment," which had been unduly self-righteous. Much as Franklin Roosevelt had calculated half a century before, a columnist for the magazine concluded that "nothing would signal to the grassroots American public more about positive changes in the USSR than increased freedom of religion for all churches and all believers." Moreover, even if vast differences remained between the two political systems, "the free worship of the one true God could establish a bond between the peoples of our countries that in the long run could have the most far-reaching effects."[66]

Although white evangelicals remained more suspicious of the Soviets than any other group of Americans, optimism about expanding opportunities in the Soviet bloc increasingly displaced the traditional antipathy. While some apocalyptic prophets persisted in depicting Gorbachev as Antichrist, such fantastic vilification was increasingly relegated to the fringe of the Christian Right.[67]

America's most famous evangelist, Billy Graham, continued to lead the way in changing attitudes. Once again braving criticism from his more conservative colleagues for making compromises "with a nondemocratic government and a nonevangelical religious body," in 1988 Graham participated in the celebration of a thousand years of Orthodoxy in Kiev and Moscow. As *Christianity Today* commented in a cautious but enthusiastic special report, the "improbable scenario" of "an American clergyman preaching an evangelistic sermon in the Soviet Union amid the gilded trappings of a staid Russian Orthodox cathedral . . . capsulized some of the dramatic changes apparently taking place." Graham did not go as far as Reagan in seeing Gorbachev as a possible closet Christian, but he thought the Soviet reformer in his own secular or Marxist way "reflected a hazy yearning for the Kingdom of God." The growing religious freedom under Gorbachev, with the massive importation of Bibles and even the convening of a school of Protestant evangelism in Moscow by 1991, led Graham to feel that his approach of downplaying differences, encouraging changes, and seizing opportunities, was fully vindicated.[68]

### American impact on Gorbachev and the transformation of the USSR

Although Graham had reason to be satisfied, many other Americans overstated their influence on the reformation of the Soviet Union in the 1980s. One of the most common assumptions was that the USA was the primary model for remaking the USSR. Even at the height of superpower tension in the fall of 1983, historian James Billington promoted this notion by writing that America was Russians' principal "object of fascination," and "the only civilization by which they can measure themselves." While many ordinary Russians were indeed fascinated by aspects of America, particularly its consumer culture, the United States was not the main model for Gorbachev, who viewed the more secular and social democratic Western Europe as the Soviet Union's "basic partner" in fulfilling his vision of "our common European home."[69]

A second form of exaggerating American impact on Soviet changes has been the view that the US was responsible for bringing religious liberty to Russia. One political scientist, for example, asserted that "Reagan's pressure influenced the religious changes Gorbachev made," and claimed that the "first major reforms were set in motion in the spring of 1988, . . . precisely the period surrounding Reagan's full-court press."[70] In reality, while Gorbachev respected Reagan's sincere advice concerning freedom of religion in 1988, his own ideals and objectives had led him to embrace that principle soon after becoming General Secretary. In April 1985, he directed the Communist Party not to permit the "violation of believers' feelings," and by the summer of 1986 he determined that there should be no "infringing on the freedom of conscience." Impelled by his belief in the need to revive a sense of morality after years of rampant corruption and degeneracy, in November 1986 Gorbachev asked leaders of the Orthodox Church to help raise the moral level of the Soviet people and curb alcoholism. The next year, Gorbachev overruled hard-line Communists and supported the Orthodox Church's plan to build a great new cathedral in Moscow. And in 1988, shortly before Reagan traveled to Moscow, Soviet television broadcast the Easter liturgy at the Epiphany Cathedral for the first time.[71]

The most important exaggeration of the US impact has been the belief that the Reagan administration's military buildup, support for anticommunist insurgencies, and confrontational rhetoric caused the Kremlin to retreat and reform. Already in June 1988, Vice President Bush made this claim. Since then, conservative authors have even asserted that US pressures caused the Politburo to select Gorbachev as General Secretary in 1985.[72]

The origins of Soviet retrenchment and restructuring were actually much more complex. Gorbachev's belief that the Soviet Union needed to end its overweening domination of Eastern Europe and liberalize its domestic life dated back to his foreign travel in the 1960s and 1970s, when he had been shocked by the intense resentment of the USSR in Czechoslovakia and struck by the vibrant civil societies of Italy and France. Although the Reagan buildup and deployment of advanced missiles in Europe did put pressure on the Soviet Union to alter its foreign policies, they did not make it inevitable that the Kremlin would opt for conciliation. On the contrary, the heightened tension with the West in the first half of the 1980s undermined the position of Soviet reformers and strengthened the hand of xenophobic, neo-Stalinist hard-liners. Andropov's promotion of Gorbachev and other young officials in 1983 stemmed primarily from his awareness of the need to revive Soviet economic growth after many years of stagnation, not from a desire to propitiate President Reagan.

Upon becoming General Secretary in 1985, Gorbachev did not immediately alter Soviet foreign policy. Only after the Geneva summit, as Gorbachev realized that Reagan was not simply a spokesman for the US military-industrial complex but a sincere human being with a real interest in peace, did he embark on a new course, beginning with the argument that war was not inevitable. Gorbachev's gradual realization that Reagan would not use force to compel the Soviet Union to alter its system helped him to overcome the climate of fear and take the risk of launching a destabilizing restructuring of the Soviet system. In this sense, it was not so much Reagan's missionary drive as his acceptance of the need for the American and Soviet systems to coexist, that facilitated the steps Gorbachev took which led to the unraveling of the Soviet empire.[73]

In the summer of 1991, when thousands of Russians bravely thwarted an attempted coup by authoritarian Communists, American journalists, politicians, and religious leaders hailed a miraculous popular revolution which they predicted would lead rapidly to the consolidation of a liberal democracy, creation of a flourishing market economy, and a widespread revival of Christianity. In the summer of 1998, the infant Russian stock market crashed, the Kremlin defaulted on foreign loans, and an assertive former head of the foreign intelligence service became prime minister, prompting American investors to flee, leading journalists to blame Russians' national character for the failure of their experiment with democracy, and moving Republican politicians to accuse the Democratic administration of having "lost Russia."

Thus, the last decade of the twentieth century witnessed both a culmination of the American mission to extend capitalism, democracy, and Protestantism to Russia, and a reversion toward demonization of unregenerate Russians as superstitious, corrupt, and slavish. The two trends were linked: exaggeration of the spread of American beliefs and values in the early 1990s contributed to excessive pessimism and unwarranted vilification later in the decade.

The problematic assumptions of journalists and policy-makers at the time have been replicated in many scholarly accounts of the turbulent 1990s. These studies can be grouped in two main schools of thought: (1) liberal universalist confidence in the inevitable democratization of the former Soviet Union; and (2) Russophobic pessimism about turning a former totalitarian enemy into a genuine democratic ally.

Influenced by social science theories about modernization and democratization, liberal universalists have maintained that Russia had no choice but to Westernize, that it was impossible for her to pursue some special path in an age of globalization, and that she must conform to the laws of political and economic development.[1] Downplaying or denying the importance of Russia's distinctive culture and historical experience, liberal universalists have suggested that democratization is normal or natural. The Russian government's divergence from that path is therefore to be blamed on sinister machinations by atavistic forces in the Kremlin, and on apathetic leaders in the West who have indulged Russia's regression.[2]

Two central fallacies have undergirded this universalist approach. First is the assumption that in 1991 there was a popular, democratic, pro-market revolution.[3] In fact, only relatively small groups of people in major cities actively opposed the attempted hard-line coup in August 1991, while many of the fence-sitters sympathized with the plotters' goal of preserving the Soviet Union.

Second, liberal universalists have tended to exaggerate the breadth and depth of Russian enthusiasm for America. Although many Russians vaguely hoped at the beginning of the decade that their country could magically become prosperous like the United States, they were soon embittered by skyrocketing prices, outraged by increasingly glaring inequality, disillusioned by how little Western aid reached them, and angered by the eastward expansion of the NATO alliance. Hence, leaders who argued that Russia should not simply follow a Western model but pursue a special Russian path of development were responsive to broad popular sentiment.

In stark contrast to the Messianic universalists, a second group of writers have stressed ingrained resistance to westernization in Russia. Political scientist Samuel Huntington, for example, defined Russia as the core of an Orthodox civilization that was almost impossible to change.[4] In a similar vein, historian Richard Pipes blamed Russia's disappointing progress by the mid-1990s primarily on anti-Western attitudes rooted in an irrational religious heritage.[5] Such authors tended to exaggerate Russia's reversion to Orthodoxy after seventy years of official atheism, to disparage Russians as irredeemably averse to Western values, to disregard how much anti-Western sentiment has been provoked by Western actions, and to discount how much Russia changed in the 1990s.

While Russophobic pessimists stressed essential Russian traits, a third group of authors put much of the blame on American ignorance and arrogance. Citing the drastic decline in average Russians' life expectancy and standard of living in the 1990s, several scholars argued that US "missionary" efforts to guide Russia toward a market economy had been futile or disastrous.[6]

Building upon the insights of such critics, this chapter shows how many Americans, beyond government officials and economic advisers, shared a "missionary" mentality and it sets the dynamics of the 1990s in a longer-term perspective. As in earlier decades, many Americans sought to convert, educate, and otherwise help Russians. For example, Christian evangelists supported publishing houses, political scientists tutored Russian politicians about electoral strategies, Peace Corps volunteers taught English, executives developed business education programs, and lawyers encouraged judicial reform.[7] While these efforts were genuinely well-intentioned, they often failed to achieve the results Americans claimed or expected, some provoked opposition, and many were terminated by the Russian government. Given Russia's historic pattern of throwing open its windows to the West, selectively assimilating foreign influences, and then closing the shutters again, those outcomes should not have been surprising. Yet many Americans reacted with unwarranted alarm and scorn, worrying that if Russia was not remade in the image of the United States it would revert to communism and aggressive imperialism. Thus, the volatile decade of the 1990s was marked by many of the unrealistic hopes and exaggerated fears that had been exhibited in several earlier periods during the preceding century.

### The Bush administration and the demise of the Soviet Union

In the last year of the Reagan administration, a number of breakthroughs created extraordinary opportunities for Americans to influence developments in the Soviet Union. Reagan's speeches in Moscow showed that it was possible to encourage religious and intellectual freedom in a genuine and non-propagandistic manner, without provoking a severe nationalistic or xenophobic backlash. Although Gorbachev displayed some irritation with Reagan's comments about human rights in June 1988, following the Moscow summit Soviet journalists stopped counterattacking American human rights violations and began upholding aspects of the US economy and political system as models for Soviet reforms. The Soviet decision to cease jamming of foreign radio broadcasts enabled Voice of America and Radio Liberty to reach audiences throughout the Soviet Union. The Kremlin's shift from tolerating to promoting a religious revival helped to open doors for American missionaries, while Soviet economic liberalization encouraged ventures by a number of American corporations.[8]

Unfortunately, US leaders did not smoothly continue the positive momentum that Reagan and Gorbachev helped to generate. While Reagan and his diplomatic advisers were guided by their hopes for the best in the Soviet Union, the Bush administration was driven to a great extent by fears – of losing points in propaganda battles, wasting money in economic aid, even facing a reversion to a Stalinist "evil empire." Whereas Reagan, Shultz, and Matlock engaged their Soviet counterparts in sustained discussion of democratic principles and market processes, the Bush team focused too often on personal support for specific Kremlin rulers. As a result, US officials did not make the most of opportunities to influence developments in the last years of the Soviet Union.

In his first four years as leader of the Soviet Union, Mikhail Gorbachev had launched increasingly radical changes in Soviet domestic and foreign policies. As he realized that corrupt and dogmatic bureaucrats were obstacles to revitalizing the economy and society, Gorbachev escalated pressure for change by encouraging public criticism of shortcomings and by promoting political liberalization. In March 1989 these steps culminated in sensational elections, in which a number of old-thinking Communist Party candidates were defeated by reformists and non-communists. On the foreign policy front, as Gorbachev realized that the Soviet Union needed not only to retrench from its overextended global commitments but also to re-enter the world community, he embraced the "new political thinking" developed by academic advisers in the era of détente, which featured concepts such as interdependence and mutual security. Gorbachev demonstrated that this was not merely another propagandistic "peace offensive" by accepting lopsided reductions in Soviet nuclear and conventional forces, promoting the peaceful resolution of conflicts in southwest Africa and southeast Asia, and withdrawing all Soviet troops from Afghanistan by February 1989.[9]

While Reagan had warmly welcomed Gorbachev's dramatic changes, the incoming Bush administration appeared oblivious to them. National Security Adviser Brent Scowcroft, a career military officer who focused on adversaries' capabilities rather than their intentions, completely discounted the Soviet "new thinking" as merely part of a continuing propaganda battle. Scowcroft believed that the Soviet leader's goal was "to compete with the West" more effectively, and that his suave style made him "potentially more dangerous than his predecessors." Even in retrospect, Scowcroft declared: "He was attempting to kill us with kindness." In short, as Scowcroft repeatedly declared throughout 1989, he believed that "the Cold War was not over."[10]

As Vice-President, George Bush had told Gorbachev not to take seriously the hard-line statements he would make in the presidential campaign of 1988, yet when he became President in January 1989, he really believed that the Soviet-American relationship was still a bipolar superpower rivalry. When Gorbachev first came to power, Bush had recognized the interactive nature of American-Soviet relations, saying that how Gorbachev changed his country depended "in part on how we interact with him." Yet in early 1989, Bush espoused the static and essentialist view that Gorbachev was "still a Russian and a Communist." Like Scowcroft, Bush suspected Gorbachev's announcements of arms reductions initiatives were mere "gamesmanship," and he feared that the wily Soviet leader would exploit an early summit meeting to "undermine Western resolve." Instead of engaging Gorbachev in discussion and negotiation, then, Bush took the passive stance of pocketing the concessions Gorbachev had already made and waiting for more. Whereas Reagan had sought to persuade Gorbachev to make the Soviet Union more like the United States, Bush thought more about how to "remind people of the true differences between the Soviet Union and the West."[11]

Secretary of State James Baker, like Bush and Scowcroft, focused initially on the need "to maintain Western cohesion" rather than the opportunity to promote the reform of the Soviet Union. Although some of Baker's aides advised him that Soviet "new thinking" was leading to far-reaching changes, Baker was slow to recognize the implications for US policy. The debate among Sovietologists over whether *perestroika* was merely a "breathing space" or a fundamental transformation seemed to him "mainly academic theology," irrelevant to the immediate challenges of the struggle for world opinion.[12]

Some members of the Bush administration wanted to hold onto old images of the Soviet bloc that were useful in the international competition or domestic politics. Robert Blackwill of the National Security Council staff thought it was a mistake for Reagan "to have said the evil empire was a thing of the past" because that let the Soviets "off the hook." Vice President Dan Quayle, whom Bush selected to appeal to the right wing of the Republican Party, insisted through the end of 1989 that *perestroika* was merely a "form of Leninism", and that the Soviet Union was still a "totalitarian system." For Quayle and other right-wing ideologues, images of a dark Soviet empire were so central to their worldview and so important in defining the contrasting virtues of American freedom that they had difficulty parting with them. Conservative philosopher Allan Bloom, for example, observed that for decades Americans had taken their "orientation from the evil we faced" and worried about the domestic reverberations of the "loss of our negative pole of orientation."[13]

Yet Quayle had little influence on the Bush administration's policy toward the Soviet bloc, which was shaped mainly by the more pragmatic Baker, Scowcroft, and Bush himself. All three had been uncomfortable with Reagan's harsh vilification of the Soviet Union in the early 1980s.[14] What, then, explains the reversion to Cold War thinking and the hesitation to engage the Soviet Union in 1989?

The guarded approach of the Bush foreign policy team stemmed in part from bitter experiences during the Ford administration. Scowcroft, Baker, and Bush had seen disillusionment with détente fuel a right-wing challenge to a sitting president for the Republican nomination and then the defeat of the president by a Democratic challenger who attacked his policy toward the Soviet bloc. Fear of a new round of right-wing criticism contributed to Bush's and Baker's wariness about seeming too eager to negotiate with the Soviet Union.[15]

Yet the Bush team's caution or reserve went deeper than feeling "once burned, twice shy." Whereas Reagan had taken to heart a missionary approach to the Soviet Union, Bush and Baker viewed the USSR with the skeptical self-interest of prudent investors. At least initially, Bush eyed the Soviet Union with the wariness of a businessman who had seen costly oil rigs capsize. In the same vein, Baker's attention was riveted on how "to maximize our diplomatic gains while minimizing risks." Disregarding the need for reciprocity in sustainable relationships, Baker and others criticized Shultz for having paid for concessions that Gorbachev or history would give "for free."[16] By temperament, Bush was also averse to lecturing foreign leaders about human rights or other aspects of their internal affairs.[17] Thus, at the moment when the reforming Soviet Union was most open to American advice and influence, US leaders thought less in terms of how to assist the emergence of a free Russia and more in the terms of a banker coldly evaluating a credit application.

In the spring of 1989, the Bush team's hesitation to meet and negotiate with the Soviet leadership provoked mounting criticism from European leaders, Reagan's friends, and foreign policy experts. Nettled, Bush and his aides first shifted toward more forward-looking rhetoric about moving "beyond containment." Then, as Bush realized that Gorbachev was serious about reducing conventional forces in Europe and crucial to the prospects for liberalization of East European governments, he finally decided to "get engaged" with the dynamic Soviet leader.[18]

While academic experts had cautioned against binding US policy too narrowly to Gorbachev, in July 1989 Bush decided that "this guy *is perestroika*." After Gorbachev accepted anticommunist revolutions in Eastern Europe that fall and met with Bush at Malta in December, US policy centered on personal support for the increasingly embattled Gorbachev.[19]

That did not mean providing substantial financial aid to facilitate Soviet economic reform. Bush worried that aid to an as yet unreformed Soviet system would be wasted, and he feared domestic criticism of what one of his advisers called a "bailout" for the Soviet Union. Although appalled by Gorbachev's ignorance of basic economics, Bush was not inclined to tutor the Soviet leader or "try to fine-tune" the difficult restructuring of the USSR. Exasperated by Gorbachev's increasingly desperate appeals for help, through the summer of 1991 Bush clung to his belief that it would be up to private bankers and investors to provide the loans and capital to restructure and redevelop the Soviet economy.[20]

The Bush administration also exhibited penny-pinching prudence and passivity in its approaches to propaganda and the issue of independence for Soviet republics. From early on, Bush indicated the low priority he attached to promoting American values in the Soviet Union by directing that the U.S.I.A. operate within existing budgetary limitations and encourage more private sector initiatives. By October 1990, with Eastern Europe freed from Soviet control, but the Baltic republics still part of the USSR, the Bush administration decided that "US Government budgetary support for Radio Free Europe and Radio Liberty should eventually be phased out as their mission is completed."[21] While editors at the radios believed they should encourage the dissolution of the Soviet Union, they found that Bush sympathized more with Gorbachev's efforts to hold the union together. The radio stations still played a role in the disintegration of the USSR by furthering the erosion of the Communist Party's monopoly of information. Yet that contribution was made in spite of the Bush administration's overall policy, which Bush expressed most memorably in August, 1991, when he declared in Kiev that "freedom is not the same as independence."[22]

## American responses to the revolution of 1991

In 1990 and the first half of 1991, orthodox communists and leaders of the military-industrial complex fiercely criticized Gorbachev for undermining the Communist Party's power and making one-sided concessions to the West. While Gorbachev appeased those critics by appointing hardliners to top posts, he faced other challenges from independence movements in the Baltic republics and a democratic movement in the Russian republic. Struggling to preserve a reorganized USSR, Gorbachev supervised the drafting of a Union Treaty that was scheduled to be signed by leaders of the republics on August 20, 1991. Believing the treaty would mean the disintegration of the Soviet Union and the loss of their power, leaders of the security organs and military industrial complex declared a state of emergency on August 19 and announced the replacement of Gorbachev by his hard-line Vice President.[23]

President Bush's tepid initial response seemed to many to indicate that he was prepared to accept the "extra-constitutional" events. However, in Moscow, the recently elected President of the Russian Federation, Boris Yeltsin, mobilized resistance with the aid of Radio Liberty broadcasts. After riding a movement of popular protest against the privileged elite to the presidency of Russia (still within the USSR), Yeltsin had distanced himself from idealistic intellectuals and co-opted many members of the ruling class, so he was able to appeal both to ordinary Russians and to key figures in the military and government. Since most of the leaders of the coup did not have the stomach to spill Russian blood, their effort collapsed within two days.[24]

As in 1905 and 1917, many Americans viewed the revolution of 1991 through the prism of their millenarian political culture, and saw a triumph of light over darkness. This inclined them to overestimate the extent of popular involvement in the revolution, to disregard differences between Russian and American popular aspirations, and to neglect the obstacles to the transformation of the Soviet Union.

A number of influential Americans interpreted the attempted coup and its defeat in explicitly religious terms. The editors of the *Chicago Tribune*, for example, commented that it was "the unholy alliance" of the Red Army, the KGB, and "the unregenerate" Communist Party that had staged the coup, which had been foreseen by former Foreign Minister Eduard Shevardnadze, "an apostate from communism."[25] Hailing the victory of "the people" over the plotters, Ronald Reagan proclaimed that "the grand work of human freedom," which was like "the building of a magnificent cathedral," was nearing completion. With the peoples of the Soviet Union "adding their faith and dedication" to the work, he prophesied, the coming decades would see "the worldwide triumph of human freedom under God." In a similar spirit, historian and Librarian of Congress James Billington, who was in Moscow that August, depicted the defeat of the coup as a religious "miracle," with lay Christians and priests playing a significant role. Billington, who described himself as "a visiting Christian privileged to witness the rebirth of another Christian culture," was so inspired by this "transfiguration" that he predicted that "an altogether different Russia would be blooming in both faith and freedom by the beginning of the Third Millennium."[26]

Like Billington, one of the most distinguished scholars of Russian culture in the United States, many less knowledgeable Americans believed that the astonishing events in Russia opened the way to a "mass conversion to Christianity."[27] In the eyes of numerous evangelical Christians, the divinely inspired collapse of communism made the former Soviet Union "perhaps the most open mission field in the world," and they launched ambitious efforts to bring "true Christianity" or "the real Jesus" to that vast, godless land.[28]

Such millenarian euphoria contributed to a widespread exaggeration of popular participation in the events of August 1991. Although thousands of citizens in Moscow and St. Petersburg courageously resisted the *putsch* in August, in Russia as a whole most people sat on the sidelines.[29] An American poll found that Russians "prefer democracy to authoritarianism only by a paper-thin 51% margin." Beyond "the best and brightest" in the big cities, most Russians in smaller towns and villages "endorsed the center, the Communist Party and the status quo."[30]

Yet policy-makers, editors and columnists repeatedly depicted the August events as a broad popular revolt against a small group of Stalinist conspirators. "The people obviously wanted the end of the [Communist] Party" and "had shown their desire for freedom," recalled Secretary of State Baker, though he was warned by Shevardnadze that he should not "judge the country by what was happening in Moscow and St. Petersburg." Confident that "the Moscow Eight" were "altogether lacking popular appeal," the *Washington Post* doubted from the outset that "the Soviet people are going to take the coup lying down." The *St. Louis Post-Dispatch* editorialized that by defying the coup and saving themselves, "the Soviets have shown that they yearn to belong to the West; they have risked their lives to be a democracy." The *Wall Street Journal*'s correspondents in Moscow exclaimed: "For the first time since the overthrow of the Czar in 1917, the Soviet Union has been seized by the collective will of its people."[31]

While some focused above all on the political or religious implications of the August events, others emphasized the economic origins and ramifications. In the preceding years, as McDonald's moved to open its first restaurant in Moscow, American cartoonists had suggested that Russia had accepted the superiority of the capitalist ethos.[32] Building on that notion, a *Chicago Tribune* columnist argued that the coup was defeated and would not easily be reversed because "The people have tasted Big Macs," and such products "symbolized the good life that free enterprise can offer ordinary folks."[33] The idea that the Russian masses were demanding a rapid transition to a capitalist system was most vividly illustrated by a *Chicago Tribune* cartoon that depicted a cleaning woman in a Kremlin office picking up a telephone and insisting that Russia's new leaders "switch to a market economy *right now*!!"[34]

Such notions strongly appealed to Americans who craved confirmation of the bright promise of their own society. "We looked for an entire people to catch the vision of self-directed creation of economic wealth," one columnist explained, because "it would have given us new faith in our own economic traditions" at a time when American capitalism seemed "to have bogged down in a cesspool of greed and caution."[35] In a parallel fashion, evangelicals disgusted by the way American morals had declined to the level of Sodom and Gomorrah could take inspiration from the idea of a mass religious revival in the citadel of godlessness.[36] At the same time, repeated assertions by journalists and politicians that the United States represented a shining example which most Russians eagerly wanted to emulate served to reaffirm that a bright light still radiated from the land of liberty.[37]

Inside the Bush administration, responses to the failed coup were much less exalted. Secretary of Defense Dick Cheney favored encouraging the breakup of the Soviet Union, arguing that "if democracy fails, we're better off if they're small." Baker, fearing civil war ("another Yugoslavia"), argued that Washington should try to "strengthen the center" – meaning backing both Gorbachev and Yeltsin. With Scowcroft ambivalent and Bush vaguely believing that the peoples of the Soviet Union should "define their own future," the White House drifted instead of trying to help Russian leaders to chart a new course. Baker expected Yeltsin to move aggressively on a radical economic reform program, and advised Bush that the US "stake in the success of the democrats" in Russia was "the equivalent of the postwar recovery of Germany and Japan." Yet Bush believed Washington "did not know enough to design any detailed aid programs" and felt the burden was still on Moscow to create a climate for foreign investment.[38] While the Bush administration's ability to provide financial aid was sharply constrained by a large budget deficit, its timidity and its doubts about whether democracy could take root in the former Soviet Union led it to miss an opportunity to influence decisions in Moscow at a time when the door to the West was wide open.[39]

### Yeltsin and the market revolution of 1991–2

Much as in earlier eras Americans had vested their hopes for the transformation of Russia in individual leaders such as Witte, in 1991 they looked to Boris Yeltsin as the bearer of the torch of freedom. In striking contrast to the notion that there had been a popular anticommunist revolution, Yeltsin was often depicted as the man who had single-handedly defeated the coup. For example, borrowing an image from events in China in 1989, cartoonists drew Yeltsin as a lone figure blocking a row of tanks.[40]

Taking the lionization of Yeltsin that far posed serious problems. After receiving a mediocre technical education, Yeltsin had risen through the Soviet system to become a member of the Politburo in the 1980s, and a crude approach to the exercise of power was engrained in him. Not having traveled outside of the USSR, Yeltsin knew little about Western capitalism or democracy. When he did finally visit the United States in September 1989, he was awed by many things, including American housing and farmers' use of computers. Above all, he was astonished by the variety and abundance of goods in a Texas supermarket, which stood in shocking contrast to the empty shelves in Soviet stores. Yeltsin returned to Moscow with the fervor of a convert and a naïve belief that American methods and American plenty could be brought to Russia with almost magical ease.[41] Thus, Yeltsin seemed to fulfill the hopes of American propagandists and leaders from Eisenhower to Reagan for the conversion of a top leader in the Soviet Union, who would put his country on the path to democracy and capitalism.

In the aftermath of the August coup, however, Yeltsin turned his back on the democratic movement that had supported him, and assembled a new coalition that included the "golden youth" from privileged families, directors of industries, and former Soviet officials eager to enrich themselves through currency transactions, commodities trading, and other new opportunities.[42] Many of these figures engaged in a repartition of the country's resources that was based on the strength of their personal connections and the weakness of their moral inhibitions.

Yeltsin's vague vision of a rapid shift to a prosperous market economy was given concrete form by a handful of younger members of the Soviet elite, especially the pudgy economist Yegor Gaidar. The son of a *Pravda* correspondent who had traveled abroad, Gaidar used his privileged access to special library collections to read Western economists from Adam Smith to Milton Friedman. This reading contributed to Gaidar's doctrinaire belief that "the spontaneous economy of natural exchange" would inevitably spring up to replace the ruptured Soviet command economy. To allow the free market mechanism to work its magic, two main steps were needed: freeing prices to rise from their subsidized levels, and privatizing much state-owned property. Anticipating that these steps would be unpopular, Gaidar saw a need to move quickly, while communist hardliners and other potential opponents were in disarray following the defeat of the August coup. Thus, Gaidar believed that "democratic forces" in Russia had to act in an undemocratic way. Invoking authoritarian reformers from the tsarist era, Gaidar held that reforms had to be introduced abruptly from above rather than in a gradual and consensual manner. Thus, Gaidar and the other "Chicago boys" urged a leap toward free market capitalism that might in the short term resemble the era of the "robber barons," but would soon look like the deregulated West of Ronald Reagan and Margaret Thatcher.[43]

At the end of October 1991, Yeltsin unilaterally announced the "changeover to market prices," which would take effect at the beginning of 1992. He then made a woefully optimistic forecast: for six months, "things will be worse for everyone, but then prices will fall, the consumer market will be filled with goods, and by the autumn of 1992 there will be economic stabilization and a gradual improvement in people's lives."[44] Although the Bush administration had steadfastly opposed substantial financial aid to Gorbachev's Soviet Union, Harvard economist Jeffrey Sachs seems to have encouraged Yeltsin and Gaidar to believe that the West would provide significant aid in support of economic reforms, which he and others called "shock therapy." Even if the West did not provide such support, though, Sachs dogmatically maintained that the monetarist program was "the only correct strategy."[45]

As a result of the deregulation of prices, in early 1992 the cost of many staples tripled. Many middle-class Russians whose savings were wiped out by hyperinflation were forced to sell family heirlooms on street corners – a practice that Gaidar callously hailed as a sign of the reviving spirit of private enterprise. The shock therapy policy provoked such strong opposition by communists, nationalists, and even many democrats in the Congress of People's Deputies that Yeltsin threatened in the spring to dissolve the Congress and rule by decree. President Bush's pledge in April of $24 billion in loans, grants, and credits from the International Monetary Fund, World Bank, and G-7 countries may have temporarily buttressed Gaidar's position. Yet by the end of the year, an alarmed Yeltsin abandoned efforts to get Gaidar elevated from acting prime minister to prime minister, and appointed the centrist director of the gas industry instead.[46]

Although President Bush's backing of Gaidar was unsuccessful, key figures in the United States continued to believe that financial aid from the West could keep "reformers" in power in Russia and help them avoid making compromises with the Congress of People's Deputies.[47] Thus, from early in the 1990s American economic advisers and policy-makers were inclined to view aid to post-Soviet Russia more as a way to bypass Russian democracy than to strengthen democratic institutions and processes.

### The Clinton administration and Yeltsin's Russia

In the 1992 presidential campaign, Arkansas governor Bill Clinton repeatedly criticized Bush for being "overly cautious on the issue of aid to Russia" and squandering a historic opportunity to help shape the future of that vast country.[48] Since Clinton and many of his close advisers shared an activist philosophy of government and believed that even Russians could not defy forever the laws of historical development, it might have been expected that they would diverge sharply from the Bush adminis-tration once they took office in early 1993.[49] However, while the Demo-cratic administration's public statements were more grandly idealistic,[50] its policies were not that starkly different from its predecessor's.

Although Clinton talked about helping Yeltsin "big-time" and boasted that he quadrupled Bush's allocation for direct US aid to Russia in 1993, the total package of Western assistance was only slightly larger than the package the Bush administration had put together, and in both cases there was a large gap between what was promised and what was delivered.[51]

While Clinton administration officials paid lip service to the idea of supporting a democratic process rather than specific individuals, in practice they closely identified "reform" and "democracy" with Yeltsin, and their policy was thus as highly personalized as Bush's embrace of Gorbachev.[52] And although the coordinator of policy toward the former Soviet Union, Deputy Secretary of State Strobe Talbott, urged that US policy should be "to nurture the best that might happen" there, in reality Clinton focused above all on averting the disaster of Russia "going bad."[53] Fearing that Russia would "blow up in our faces," thereby sparking a new cold war and jeopardizing his re-election, Clinton thought more about avoiding the worst nightmare scenarios than about how to fulfill the American dream of a free Russia.[54]

Proceeding from the premises that there had been a broad democratic revolution in 1991 comparable to the American revolution of 1776, and that Yeltsin continued to embody the revolution's "progressive" impulse, Clinton and his top advisers lumped together Yeltsin's diverse critics as former Soviet elites and "reactionaries."[55] This perspective ignored how many in Yeltsin's circle were from the Soviet privileged class, and how his opponents included honorable patriots and gradualist reformers. It also conflicted with the rising unpopularity of Yeltsin's economic reforms, which the US sought to promote with promises of more aid. On the eve of an April 1993 referendum on Yeltsin's policies, for example, Clinton "made it plain that a lot of money was coming."[56]

In the summer of 1993, facing charges of corruption in his inner circle and frustrated by opposition from the Congress of People's Deputies, Yeltsin decided to provoke a showdown with the Congress. Informed in advance, the Clinton administration resolved to back Yeltsin to the hilt. When Yeltsin dissolved the parliament in late September and it almost unanimously voted to replace him with Vice-President Aleksandr Rutskoi (a popular nationalist veteran of the war in Afghanistan), Clinton issued a strong statement of his support for Yeltsin. After a Russian tank fired on the parliament building to end the standoff, an unfazed Clinton phoned Yeltsin to reiterate his support, which Yeltsin's aides then stressed to validate their course of action. As a result of the confrontations between forces loyal to Yeltsin and supporters of the parliament (who included violent extremists), almost 200 people were killed and hundreds more were wounded.[57]

Although a few American commentators challenged the idea that the increasingly autocratic Yeltsin was the savior of democracy in Russia,[58] most applauded Yeltsin's action. The *Washington Post* cast the events in Moscow as a battle between "the forces of reform and democracy" on one side, and communists and fascists on the other. Yeltsin was like Lincoln, columnists asserted: he used force to save his country from disunion and proceed to its "reconstruction." The *Christian Science Monitor* acknowledged that "antidemocratic means *are* troubling,"but agreed with Clinton that "Yeltsin is the man to back," since "the word 'democratization' in Russia has little meaning" and "the Russian power game has no use for tolerant liberals."[59] Thus, in the prevailing American view, the ends of modernization, economic reform, and eventual democracy justified departures from democratic processes in a country as rough as Russia.[60] As the prominent historian Martin Malia put it, Yeltsin, like Peter the Great, sought to Westernize Russia, which had "to become European and civilized . . . , even if a political club must sometimes be used to get it there."[61]

In post-Soviet Russia, then, as in late tsarist Russia and in numerous "Third World" countries during the Cold War, many Americans favored an authoritarian style of modernization, with a "strong man" to prevent "chaos" and keep a "backward" country on the preferred course.[62] Yet at the same time leading journalists and politicians wrote and spoke as if this was "the road to democracy." In December 1993, for example, on the eve of a referendum on a new constitution that provided for a super-presidency and a weak parliament, the *New York Times* asserted that "Russia is moving convulsively to a new, more democratic political system."[63]

The *Times* and Clinton administration officials were therefore stunned when Russians voted to put more xenophobic nationalists and communists than liberals in the new parliament.[64] Vladimir Zhirinovsky, the buffoonish leader of the ultranationalist party that captured a quarter of the vote, had vowed to "bring Russia up off its knees," and even blustered about getting Alaska back from the United States. Yet even while acknowledging that this "rebuff" to economic reform and America was "chastening," the *Times* persisted in urging Washington to "keep Russia on the road to reform." The Clinton White House even more resolutely disregarded the expression of rising Russian nationalist and nostalgic sentiment, issuing an upbeat statement that "the Russian people have eliminated the last vestiges of the old Soviet system and replaced them with new and legitimate institutions that will lay a foundation for continued development of a democratic society."[65]

As one veteran columnist observed, the phrases "free-market economy" and "democracy" were being chanted together as a "mantra," ignoring the tensions between them and overlooking Russian popular resentment. While the West should provide more aid to calm "Russia's distemper," the *New York Times* editorialized, it should still "insist it move toward markets." In the same vein, while Deputy Secretary of State

Talbott famously declared that Washington should promote "less shock and more therapy," he and other officials continued to give their Russian counterparts "the spinach treatment," coaxing and coercing them to swallow unpalatable measures.[66]

While many Americans had hoped that supporting Yeltsin's showdown with the Russian parliament would clear the way for the development of democracy and a free market economy, the October confrontation and December election actually set Russia on a course toward autocracy, corrupt profiteering, and war. In response to the election of many anti-Western nationalists to the new parliament, Yeltsin adopted a public pose of defying the West and increasingly ruled by presidential decree, earning the nickname, "Tsar Boris." To win the support of the Minister of Defense for military action against the old parliament, Yeltsin apparently promised him such power and security that he could launch a disastrously incompetent war against the secessionist republic of Chechnya in December 1994 and still retain his profitable post. The brutal war in Chechnya increased the power of hard-liners in the military and security services, divided Russian liberals, and chilled freedom of expression.[67]

Yet the Clinton administration expressed few reservations about Yeltsin's course. "Yeltsin drunk is better than most of the alternatives sober," Clinton maintained. As late as April 1996, Clinton even defended the war in Chechnya by likening it to the American Civil War and comparing Yeltsin to Lincoln. When word reached Washington that Yeltsin, trailing the head of the Communist Party in polls, was considering canceling the 1996 presidential election, Clinton did urge Yeltsin to allow the vote to take place. However, that seems to have stemmed less from attachment to democratic principles than from concern about possible Republican criticism of a suspension of the election and from a belief that the privately pliant Yeltsin was the best available channel for pursuing US interests in Russia.[68]

### Religious missions and Orthodox reaction

While the Clinton administration pursued its shortsighted, politically-driven policy, many Americans were engaged in Russia in more idealistic ways. Philanthropic foundations provided research fellowships for under-paid Russian academics. Feminist groups promoted women's rights. Perhaps most important, several religious denominations greatly expanded their missions and their support for churches in Russia. In the early and mid-1990s, so many American missionaries came to Russia that there were dozens on most flights into the country.[69] The experience of these missionaries in post-Soviet Russia can be seen as emblematic of the wider encounter of Americans and Russians between the early 1990s, when Russian doors opened wide to foreign influences, and the latter part of the decade, when the doors gradually closed.

Especially in the last months of 1991, when Russian store shelves were barren and Russia's post-communist direction was not clearly defined, many Russians showed an extraordinary receptivity to American guidance about religion, as well as about political and economic reform. After accompanying a delegation of evangelical leaders to Moscow, an editor of *Christianity Today* reported that Russian journalists "hung on our words about Christianity as Russian economists hung on words about capitalism, as if we were smuggling in a secret formula from the West that might salvage their land." Even top KGB officers welcomed previously banned evangelists into their Lubyanka headquarters, where they conversed about the need for repentance. Of wider social significance, in 1992 the Russian Ministry of Education even agreed to involve thousands of North American Christians in the reform of school curricula. "Russian education today is open to Christian values," the deputy minister of education declared.[70]

The sheer number of American missionaries made their presence in Russia significant. More than 300 Western church groups had representatives in the former Soviet Union by 1993. In 1996, the Mormon church alone had 300 missionaries in Russia. Two years later, more than 80 US-based Protestant mission agencies were active in the Russian Federation, with more than 1,100 people serving.[71]

For a time, at least, American-supported denominations grew rapidly. Whereas in 1991 there were three evangelical churches in Moscow, by 1997 there were three hundred. One Pentecostal group established in Iaroslavl in 1991 grew to 1,500 members by 1998. The number of Adventists in the former Soviet Union tripled in the course of the 1990s (though that still left Adventists, like other Protestant denominations, a small fraction of the total number of Christians).[72]

The evangelists' work had ramifications far beyond the number of converts won. In addition to preaching the gospel, Americans taught Christian ethics and modeled a Protestant work ethic. (Personal responsibility and energetic action were viewed as Protestant traits by both foreigners and 60 percent of Russians surveyed in 1997.) At the same time, especially in the early 1990s, some spread a gospel of individual success. As one young Pentecostal missionary explained in 1993, Russians he converted suddenly realized dreams by getting jobs as actors or television announcers.[73]

Orthodox clerics viewed the Protestant encouragement of an individualist ethos as a menace. "They are trying to implant the capitalist psychology and set as their primary goal the almighty dollar," warned Metropolitan Ioann of St. Petersburg in 1993. To Metropolitan Kirill of Smolensk and Kaliningrad, the "hordes of missionaries" who dashed into the former Soviet Union were among the spearheads of "an aggressive globalizing monoculture which tries to impose itself everywhere, dominating and assimilating other cultural and national identities."[74]

While many Americans hailed the revival of the Orthodox Church in the late 1980s and even in the early 1990s,[75] negative views of the Orthodox Church were expressed more frequently as the competition for souls intensified. The church leaders, whose predecessors had been lionized in the 1940s and 1950s as potential challengers to the communist rulers, were increasingly depicted as corrupt collaborators with the KGB. Echoing criticisms made a century earlier, American Christians criticized Orthodoxy for hindering direct individual connections to God and for perpetuating an empty ritualism, with laity allegedly ignorant of their faith.[76]

Such criticisms were sometimes expressed in a provincial and scornful way. In May 1995, for example, a blue-collar group from an Assemblies of God church in Louisiana flew to Moscow. Although most of the Pentecostal evangelists did not speak any Russian and could not even pronounce the name of the town that was their destination, they confidently expected to attract the attention of Russian residents by playing music on street corners. Asked about the social and spiritual boundaries of their proselytizing, the pastor who led the group said that they would not attempt to convert members of Baptist denominations, whose Christian faith they respected. However, he felt no inhibitions about proselytizing among Orthodox believers, whose creed was at best a highly diluted form of Christianity. Comparing true Christianity to Coca-Cola, the pastor declared that Orthodoxy had only a drop of the vital syrup that went into "the real thing."[77]

While some Christian missionaries were crudely ethnocentric and offensive on forays into Russia, others (such as Seventh-day Adventists) showed greater cultural sensitivity, attempted to cooperate with Orthodox clergy where possible (for example, in educational campaigns against alcoholism), and committed substantial resources to long-term relationships. Yet even the more sophisticated Adventist missionaries could not avoid a backlash from the Orthodox Church, which they believed inspired hostile articles in newspapers, made it difficult for Adventists to rent public halls, and pressed police officers to expel evangelists from cities.[78]

Aware of negative Protestant views of their church, Orthodox leaders repeatedly expressed sharp hostility to foreign missionaries. Since

Orthodox hierarchs felt that Russia was already a Christian country, they resented the missionary premise that Russia needed to be Christianized. The inevitable tension was exacerbated by an imbalance of financial resources comparable to the disparity in the 1920s. As they struggled to reopen churches and educate a new generation of priests, Orthodox leaders were upset at the lavish spending of American evangelists, who could afford to publish books, distribute magazines, and rent large halls. "Missionaries from abroad came with dollars, buying people with so-called humanitarian aid and promises to send them abroad for study or rest," complained one Orthodox metropolitan. Echoing Soviet-era propaganda, *Izvestiia* reported in 1996 that many residents of one town suspected the CIA provided the funds for an American missionary's work.[79]

Finding it difficult to compete with well-funded foreign missionaries, Orthodox leaders pressed the Russian government to restrict the activity of foreign religious groups in Russia. As early as July, 1993, the Russian parliament voted to bar foreign religious groups from publishing and proselytizing unless they had formal links to indigenous Russian religious groups or obtained official certification. In 1995, the Russian Ministry of Education canceled its agreement with the South Carolina-based CoMission Project, whose training of Russian educators in Christian ethics was seen by Orthodox leaders as a covert way to proselytize Russian children through public schools. Most important, in September 1997 President Boris Yeltsin signed a law that recognized the Orthodox Church as Russia's pre-eminent religious organization, required foreign religious groups to register with the government, and barred them from many public activities unless they had been present in Russia for fifteen years. Under pressure from Washington, Yeltsin had vetoed an earlier version of the law, yet he agreed with Orthodox leaders that it was necessary to "prevent the penetration of radical sects inflicting serious damage to the health and psyche of our citizens." He also could not afford to be seen as caving in to Congress's threat to cut off aid to Russia if the bill became law. Following the adoption of the law, Pentecostals had their registrations suspended, at least one Lutheran congregation that received aid from the US was ordered to be closed, a Baptist missionary was evicted from eastern Russia, and the Jesuits were denied the right to function as an independent organization in Russia.[80]

### Russian nationalist and anti-American backlash

The closing down of opportunities for foreign missionaries was part of a wider backlash against Western cultural penetration of the former Soviet

Union. "Proselytism is not some narrow religious activity," Metropolitan Kirill argued in 1996, but "an invasion by another culture." This invasion, along "the old missionary patterns of colonial times," reflected "not merely a desire to reveal Christ to people . . . but also to refashion their culture in the Western mode." In the same vein, retired general Aleksandr Lebed, who showed strong appeal as a nationalist candidate in the presidential campaign of 1996, attacked both "Western cultural expansion" and "Western preachers." Three years later, another Russian politician demagogically denounced the imposition of a "virtually Protestant model of democracy."[81]

A key element in the rising nationalism and anti-Western sentiment was the decision by Washington and its European allies to expand the North Atlantic Treaty Organization by admitting East European countries that had earlier been part of the Soviet bloc. Already in October 1993 Clinton announced in Prague that NATO expansion was a matter of "when," not "if." Although Yeltsin strongly objected to NATO "enlargement," arguing that it was "too early to bury democracy in Russia," Clinton decided only to delay the process to avoid jeopardizing Yeltsin's re-election in 1996. US policy-makers were fully aware of the possible effects of expansion. Strobe Talbott, the most Russophile of Clinton's advisers, recognized that pessimism about a Russian reversion to imperialism and authoritarianism (a major justification for the eastward extension of NATO) "could be self-fulfilling" by tipping the balance of forces in Russian politics away from democrats and reformers. Madeleine Albright, Ambassador to the United Nations in Clinton's first term and Secretary of State in his second, was ready to risk "recreating our old enemy" in order to "keep faith with Europe's new democracies," including the Czech Republic, her family's homeland.[82]

NATO expansion undermined the already shaky position of pro-Western liberals in Russia, who viewed it as a betrayal. Anatoly Chubais, the architect of the privatization of Russian enterprises, regarded NATO enlargement as a vote of no confidence in Russian reform. Grigory Yavlinskii, head of the Yabloko party, repeatedly charged that NATO expansion showed a lack of faith in Russia becoming a democracy and warned that it would cause a "political earthquake" in his country.[83]

Together with disappointment at the limited financial assistance from the West, disillusionment with capitalism, and bitterness about declining standards of living, indignation at NATO expansion spurred a major shift in the Russian political environment. Whereas a majority of Russians had favored a vague Western model of development in the early 1990s, by the middle of the decade a majority preferred an undefined "specific Russian" path. While many Russians had dreamed that the fabulous "golden America" would reward them for abandoning communism, by 1994 the myth of American munificence had dissipated. Although some American opinion leaders continued to assert that Russians looked to the United States as a model, that ignored the widespread disenchantment. Already in 1993 thirty to forty percent of Russians expressed anti-American sentiment. By 1999, when nationalist filmmaker Nikita Mikhalkov depicted Americans as seducers and despoilers in his overwrought movie, "The Barber of Siberia," between sixty and seventy percent voiced anti-American attitudes.[84]

### Giving up on Russian "democracy"

Hollywood was quick to translate Russian developments into nightmarish fantasies. In "The Saint," released in April 1997, a faltering democratic government, unable to provide heat to keep Russians warm through the winter, teeters on the verge of being overthrown by mutinous armed forces in collusion with a mafia tycoon. Although a miraculous demonstration of the marvel of cold fusion to awed mobs in Red Square saves the day, "The Saint" suggested that the bright promise of the high tech Anglo-American world was not transferable to benighted, irrational Russia. Then, in the summer of 1997, the box office hit "Air Force One" portrayed the Russian President, a personal friend of the US President, as a callous, hard-drinking leader challenged by frenzied ultranationalists who, one columnist commented, sought to revive the "evil empire." Although Americans defeat the vicious zealots, the movie left little ground for optimism about the development of democracy in a country that had descended into a morass of crime, corruption, and prostitution.[85]

Those films were only two of many alarmist depictions of Russia in the mid- and late 1990s. As early as March 1994, Secretary of Defense William Perry declared, "It is possible that Russia will emerge from her turbulence as an authoritarian, militaristic nation, hostile to the West." Disturbed by communist success in the December 1995 parliamentary elections, columnist William Safire warned that "if freedom loses, Cold War III will begin." Fearing communist victory in the 1996 presidential election, Safire moaned, "The lights are going out all over Russia." Political cartoonists captured the widening anxiety with numerous images of an impending reversion to communism, for example, with the awakening of Lenin from his tomb.[86]

Such pessimism was counterbalanced for a time by enthusiasm about opportunities for foreigners in a "gold rush" environment and new economic reforms pushed by younger Russian officials. Attracted by possibilities for rewarding employment, thousands of Americans went east.

Lured by the prospect of quick profits and lulled by a presumption of international backing for Russian market reforms, Wall Street bankers rushed to make bond and stock deals from November 1996 through the middle of 1998.[87] While Russia's parliament showed "little understanding of monetary policy," a *New York Times* correspondent reported, the thirty-five-year-old Prime Minister appointed by Yeltsin had "internalized the principles of the market economy" and sounded "like a conservative American Republican."[88]

By placing their trust in such "reformers" who spoke the language of Westernization, US officials could set aside concern about conditions in the country as a whole, where wages often were not paid, alcoholism was worsening, and life expectancy was declining.[89] Similarly, journalists could overlook resistance from elderly communists to the Western-backed economic program by focusing on "affluent young Muscovites," who drove in Jeep Cherokees to the "mecca" of McDonald's. Thus, optimists set aside unease about Russia's "robber capitalism" by concentrating on how the "new Russians" were becoming more like Americans.[90]

While some remained hopeful about the Americanization and economic development of Russia, by the spring of 1998 many authors were deeply skeptical about the prospects for democracy there. Yeltsin's "credentials as a democrat, long faded," were further tarnished, as one correspondent commented, by his capricious dismissal of his cabinet in March 1998.[91] A few months later, after Yeltsin autocratically imposed a tax package demanded by the I.M.F. but rejected by the Russian parliament, the *New York Times* acknowledged that "governance by decree is undemocratic and ultimately self-defeating."[92]

The Clinton administration was less perturbed by the move. "This is not a moment to kick Yeltsin because some of the Communists in the Duma stood in the way," one official remarked. Then the bubble burst. In August the Russian stock market collapsed, the government defaulted on foreign loans and devalued the ruble, investors fled, and many American expatriates headed home.[93]

Despite the financial collapse, the Clinton administration stuck to its script. In early September, when Clinton traveled to Moscow for a meeting with Yeltsin, he gamely continued to emphasize how far Russia had come on the "road to a vibrant economy and a strong democracy." At the same time, Clinton insisted that there was no other path for Russia to take. In a lecture at Moscow State University that won no applause from the assembled students and business leaders, Clinton sternly spelled out "the rules of the road" and the "imperatives of the global marketplace," especially the need for "equitable treatment of creditors."[94]

In striking contrast, Professor Martin Malia, who had famously championed the notion that there was "no third way" between communism and a market economy a decade earlier, recognized that "Russia's liberal experiment has now collapsed," thereby discrediting the theory "that market democracy has triumphed as a universal ideal."[95] During the following year, harsh judgments of how far Russia had strayed became common. Anticipating the 2000 presidential campaign, Republican leaders fiercely attacked the Clinton administration's alleged indulgence of Russian corruption. Indicting Russia as "the world's most virulent kleptocracy," one Representative suggested in September 1999 that "helping the Russian transition to democracy" should be a lower priority than blocking Russian corruption from corroding American values. A few days later, the Republican majority leader in the House of Representatives declared that Russia had become "a looted and bankrupt zone of nuclearized anarchy." Although some Republican members of Congress still espoused the flattering notion that "the United States offered the quintessential model for Russia's future," during the 2000 campaign they harshly criticized the Clinton administration for exporting the wrong version of the model – big government rather than free enterprise – and as a result putting Russia on the "road to corruption."[96]

Beyond such partisan accusations, a consensus emerged among American journalists that Russia had been lost. "We should butt out of their politics," concluded columnist William Safire. "We have shown we do more harm than good to genuine reform." *Newsweek* writer Fareed Zakaria agreed that "we blew it." American advice proved ineffective or counterproductive, and "the attempt to transform Russia into a liberal democracy is over."[97] Many also wrote off Russia's ability to develop a prosperous economy.[98]

Republican efforts to pin responsibility on the Democratic administration were to some extent deflected by a growing tendency to fault the Russian national character. "Russians bear most of the blame," Zakaria concluded, chiefly because of their congenital corruption. "No one lost Russia but the Russians themselves," with their slavish "Slavic soul" and their scheming thuggery, proclaimed journalist Matthew Brzezinski, nephew of the former National Security Adviser.[99] While Secretary of State Albright denied that Russia had been "lost," she also concluded that it was "beyond our prerogative and our power to determine Russia's future" – a striking contrast to the Clinton administration's initial belief that "we can turn Russia around."[100]

If the American effort to remake post-Soviet Russia was dead by 2000, a sort of epitaph was written in the presidential campaign that fall. In a televised foreign policy debate, Vice President Al Gore maintained that Americans had to "have a sense of mission in the world" and vowed to continue "promoting the values of democracy and human rights and freedom all around the world." Texas Governor George W. Bush responded by holding up Russia as an example of why the United States should not "walk into a country and say, we do it this way, so should you." Then Bush concluded: "The only people who are going to reform Russia are Russians."[101]

The negative judgments about an unreformed or recidivist Russia at the end of the 1990s were as excessive as the euphoria about a miraculous transformation at the beginning of the 1990s. Russians changed in many ways during the decade. Hundreds of thousands converted to Protestant faiths or recovered their families' Orthodox traditions. Millions joined voluntary organizations to protect the environment, enhance medical care, or provide other charitable services.[102] Many others established small businesses. Americans deserved some of the credit for encouraging and supporting the religious renewal, the growing civil society, and the emerging entrepreneurial spirit.

At the same time, Americans deserved some of the blame for negative developments. Personalized backing for the erratic and increasingly autocratic Boris Yeltsin contributed to the discrediting of democracy as *dermokratiia* (shitocracy). Encouraging the hasty privatization of state enterprises abetted the corrupt self-enrichment that many Russians came to call *prikhvatizatsiia* (grabbing). Condoning the reckless invasion and wanton destruction of Chechnya facilitated the resurgence of authoritarian forces in the military and security services. Expanding NATO to the east (in violation of earlier assurances) spurred many Russians to turn away from the West with suspicion and resentment. At bottom, Americans were not as successful as they might have been in promoting a free Russia during the 1990s because they failed to live up to their own ideals; they showed a lack of faith in democratic processes, put short-term expediency above long-term goals, and allowed fears to outrun hopes.

# Epilogue: afterlife of the crusade

In the first years of the twenty-first century, prominent American journalists, intellectuals, politicians, and human rights activists sought to revive a crusade for a free Russia through high-profile indictments of the policies of Yeltsin's successor, Vladimir Putin. Under President Putin, they charged, the Russian government rolled back the freedoms of the 1990s, particularly by extending state control over the mass media, manipulating election campaigns, and stifling political opposition. Such accusations had only a modest impact on the public posture of the Republican administration in Washington, which prioritized cooperation with the Kremlin in the "war on terror" and in efforts to check the proliferation of nuclear weapons. The attacks on Putin also did not stir widespread indignation among the American people, who grew increasingly preoccupied with a war in Iraq that, like the war in Vietnam a generation earlier, raised doubts about America's invincibility and its exceptional virtue. Still, the agitation about Russia's "regression" is of significant interest for the way it perpetuated tendencies to view Russia as an object of the American mission and as a foil for the affirmation of American national identity.

During the presidential campaign of 2000, Republican candidate George W. Bush scornfully criticized the Democratic administration's "nation building" missions in countries such as Somalia and Haiti as costly and futile endeavors. However, after terrorists attacked New York and Washington on September 11, 2001 President Bush adopted an astonishingly Messianic and universalist rhetorical stance. Aided by an evangelical Christian speechwriter, Bush often used explicitly religious language to describe America's "mission" to rid the world of "evil" tyrannies. In November 2003, for example, Bush declared that liberty is "the plan of heaven for humanity" and vowed to stand with the oppressed peoples of countries such as Cuba, North Korea, and Zimbabwe "until the day of liberation and freedom finally arrives."[1]

Bush's rhetoric thus paralleled central themes in the American crusade for a "free Russia" over the previous 120 years. Yet he did not champion

219

a mission to protect freedom in the former Soviet Union from a Russian government that other prominent Americans alleged was reverting to being an authoritarian and imperialist menace. In the 2000 campaign, Bush had scoffed at the Clinton administration for pretending that the corrupt Yeltsin government had made genuine reforms, but in his first term as president Bush and his advisers characterized Russia as "a nation in hopeful transition, a country reaching for a better future based on democracy and the free market." Indeed, in one speech in April 2002, he hailed the astonishing "advance" of values such as peace and freedom in Russia over the previous fifteen years as confirmation "that the demands of human dignity are written in every heart" and "are destined to change lives and nations on every continent." By citing Russia's progress immediately after recalling the post-1945 triumph of American values in Germany and Japan, Bush suggested that the mission of remaking Russia was on the verge of being accomplished and that no new crusade needed to be launched.[2]

While Bush's rhetoric reflected his need to mobilize public and congressional support for costly stabilization and reconstruction missions in Afghanistan and Iraq, his depiction of Russia was not simply a convenient fiction. When Bush met with Vladimir Putin in June 2001, he was moved by Putin's story of how his mother had given him a treasured cross as a symbol of the Orthodox faith. In that meeting, Bush looked into Putin's eyes and "was able to get a sense of his soul." Three months later, immediately after Islamic radicals crashed jets into the World Trade Center and Pentagon, Putin called Bush to offer his support and then provided valuable assistance to the brief war against the Taliban and al Qaeda forces in Afghanistan. That aid led Bush to welcome Russia as "an important partner in the war on terror." When militants from Chechnya who presented themselves as Islamic holy warriors seized hundreds of hostages at a Moscow theater in October 2002, and many of the hostages were killed in the course of the rescue operation, Bush proclaimed a "time of solidarity" with Russia and blamed "the terrorists" for the loss of life. From then through the beginning of his second term, Bush and his top diplomatic advisers repeatedly emphasized that "Russia is our friend." Thus, Bush's view of Putin in some ways resembled American views of Alexander II more than a century earlier as a strong Christian leader who was reforming Russia and fighting a common Islamic enemy.[3]

In contrast, some key political figures viewed Putin's Russia through Cold War lenses as a geopolitical rival in a "zero-sum" competition for influence and access to resources on the periphery of the former Soviet Union. Such figures, including former National Security Adviser Zbigniew Brzezinski, hailed the rolling back of Russian influence in

Georgia, Ukraine, and Central Asia, while warning that the centralization of power under Putin menaced Russia's democratic neighbors.[4] More interesting, though, was how many other Americans viewed Russia in ways that developed before the Cold War and persisted beyond the end of the superpower rivalry.

Influential journalists, human rights activists, and politicians continued to champion the goal of a free Russia. They pushed the Bush administration to halt Putin's steps to curtail Russian freedom, including imposing Kremlin control over television news, making regional governors appointed rather than elected, and persecuting an oil tycoon who dared to challenge the Kremlin's authority.

By the beginning of 2004 (an election year), rising criticism of Russia, especially in Congress and among prospective Democratic presidential candidates, prodded Secretary of State Colin Powell to express concerns about the development of civil society and political values in Russia.[5] Such mild statements did not satisfy many critics. In June 2004, for example, one prominent political scientist challenged Bush's claim to be an heir of Ronald Reagan by arguing that unlike Reagan Bush showed little real concern with promoting democracy in Russia. In September 2004, more than one hundred American and European intellectuals and politicians sent a widely publicized "Open Letter" to European and North American leaders in which they sharply criticized Putin for "breaking away from the core democratic values of the Euro-Atlantic community." At the end of September, in a debate with President Bush, Democratic candidate John Kerry blasted Putin for controlling "all the television stations" and putting "his political opposition in jail."[6]

Kerry's inflated statement alluded to the imprisonment of oil tycoon Mikhail Khodorkovsky, whose arrest in 2003 and trial in 2004 made him a martyr in the eyes of many American critics of the Russian government. Khodorkovsky, whose prosecution was applauded by the overwhelming majority of Russians, was a peculiar symbol of freedom. During the 1990s, he had grown rich through the rigged acquisition of privatized state enterprises, evaded taxes through intricate schemes, robbed foreign investors, and bilked foreign creditors. In addition, he employed a security team that used physical intimidation and perhaps assassination to protect and advance his corporation's interests.[7]

Many American commentators excused Khodorkovsky's means of ascent, however, after he transformed his company into a model of Western-style efficiency and accountability, established an Open Russia charitable foundation, and vowed to use his wealth to build an open democracy in Russia. For example, the director of Russian studies at one Washington think tank condoned Khodorkovsky's tax evasion as "the only strategy that allowed an entrepreneur to pay salaries and invest in his business," then endorsed the idea that "the oligarchs can help to advance the cause of Russian democracy."[8] After Khodorkovsky was convicted and sentenced in 2005, one member of Congress denounced the "kangaroo court" and predicted a "tremendous congressional and public reaction" to the verdict.[9] Although the reaction from Congress was actually less than thunderous, the US Helsinki Commission did invite testimony from one of Khodorkovsky's partners, who had fled to Israel and had been charged with organizing contract killings in Russia. After hearing Leonid Nevzlin testify that "if the Russian people had greater faith in democracy and recognition of their power to demand it, there would be an uprising in the country," a co-chair of the congressional commission declared that the prosecution of Khodorkovsky was "reminiscent of the dissident trials of the Soviet era."[10]

Like the vilification of tsarist Russia a hundred years earlier, much of the criticism of the Kremlin did not stem primarily from close knowledge of actual Russian conditions. Kerry, for example, confused the headquarters of the Russian security service, the Lubyanka, with "Treblinka," a Nazi concentration camp in Poland. The impulse to denounce Putin originated more from a diffuse feeling among American opinion leaders that America had to champion the cause of freedom. As Kerry put it, "we always have to stand up for democracy."[11] The idea of promoting a free Russia did not have the wide resonance it had had in earlier decades, when mass audiences had been thrilled by visions of liberating Russia. Only a quarter of Americans surveyed in 2004 believed that democracy promotion should be a top priority in US foreign policy. Yet key politicians, journalists, and intellectuals seem to have felt that it was vital to affirm America's mission in the world through rhetorical commitment to a free Russia.[12]

As they had for many decades, American observers of Russia often focused on top leaders as agents of transformation. The most striking example of this approach appeared when Alexander Yakovlev, one of the architects of Gorbachev's reforms in the 1980s, died in October 2005. In response, the *Washington Post* proclaimed that "If more Russian politicians, including Mr. Putin," took Yakovlev's moral and political ideals "more deeply to heart, Russia would be a different country."[13] That simplistic view of individual conversion as the key to national reformation ignored the fact that enduring positive change in Russian political culture would hinge less on the convictions of politicians than on social and economic developments, such as the expansion of higher education and the emergence of a sizeable middle class. As the leaders of a Siberian nongovernmental organization observed, a "grassroots" approach to the cultivation of a civil society held more promise than "a top-down approach to democratic development."[14]

At the same time as they demanded the pillorying of Putin and hoped for him to have a change of heart, American critics claimed to champion the interests of the Russian people as a whole. Ever since George Kennan's crusade of the early 1890s, American activists had called for the United States to side with the Russian people rather than the Russian government. The Open Letter of September 2004, sponsored by the neoconservative Project for the New American Century, assumed a similar pose: it proclaimed that the people of Russia deserved the democracy Westerners wished for them, and urged Westerners "to put ourselves unambiguously on the side of democratic forces in Russia." Yet siding with "the tens of thousands of Russian democrats" in practice meant backing a minority of Westernized liberals in major cities rather than the majority of the people who voted for Putin in both the relatively free election of 2000 and the more heavily managed election of 2004.[15] Beyond the Kremlin's own party, United Russia, the most potent political forces in the country were not the tiny, splintered liberal parties but nationalist and ultranationalist groups that exhibited more belligerence and xenophobia than Putin and his advisers did.

When Americans expressed their concern for democracy in Russia in the first years of the twenty-first century, like their predecessors a century earlier they often seemed to envision that Russia would emulate practices and institutions in the United States. When they spoke about the need for "pluralism" or "checks and balances" in the political system, for example, Americans seemed to have in mind the competition of two major parties and the offsetting powers of the executive and legislative branches of government in the United States. In the same vein, when Russia, with the encouragement of US advisers, introduced jury trials in 2001, US officials celebrated the transplantation of what one expert called "a defining characteristic of the US legal system" into "an inhospitable Russian legal culture."[16] It was not necessarily assured that such changes would improve the Russian political and judicial systems: the conflict between the executive and the legislature in the early 1990s had been disastrous, and jury trials created opportunities for wealthy criminals to bribe or intimidate jurors. Yet the actual results of such reforms seemed to be secondary, in the minds of leading Americans, to the ideological gratification of seeing Russia imitate the United States.

President Bush repeatedly repudiated the implicit assumption that democracy in Russia should resemble American democracy. In the spring of 2006, rejecting calls for him to skip a meeting of leaders of industrialized democracies in St. Petersburg, Bush declared: "Nobody is saying to Russia, you must look like the United States of America." At the G-8 summit in July 2006, Bush reiterated, "I don't expect Russia to look like the United States," and noted that Putin had reminded him of how Russia had a different history and different traditions.[17]

Although Bush continued to put his friendly relationship with Putin ahead of democracy promotion, pressure from journalists, politicians, and foreign policy experts mounted to the point that a divided Bush administration altered its public stance. Already in the aftermath of the November 2004 presidential election, the administration launched a policy review that some key figures, including Vice President Dick Cheney, hoped would lead to a more confrontational championing of democracy in Russia and neighboring states.[18] By the end of 2005, Secretary of State Condoleezza Rice, who had emphasized the pursuit of US national interests through a cooperative relationship with the Kremlin, began speaking up more about democracy. For example, she stressed the value of non-governmental organizations (NGOs) that the Kremlin moved to curb, in part from fear that the NGOs could be instruments of their foreign financial supporters.[19] Then, in the spring of 2006, Cheney traveled to Lithuania to denounce the Kremlin for having "unfairly and improperly restricted the rights of her people."[20] Even Bush felt compelled to meet with Russian human rights activists in St. Petersburg in July, to assure them that the US cared "about the form of government in Russia," and to criticize the idea of Putin aides that Russia could have a "sovereign or a special [kind] of democracy."[21] Thus, as in several earlier eras, there was a gap between crusaders for a free Russia and US policy-makers, but the activists eventually succeeded in pressing top officials to shift their public posture.

Despite Putin's persistent popularity, many prominent Americans continued to assume that "democracy" and pro-American sentiment went hand-in-hand. This assumption was most strikingly exhibited in the last months of 2004, when leading American journalists and politicians identified one candidate for president of Ukraine with "democracy" while associating his opponent with criminality and Russian imperialism. The election pitted Viktor Yushchenko, whose wife was an American citizen and former State Department official, against Prime Minister Viktor Yanukovich, whom Putin too ardently embraced. Before the election, Senator John McCain declared his belief that "if offered the choice, most Ukrainians would choose a future tied to the West."[22] In the November run-off election, Yanukovich garnered 49% of the votes to Yushchenko's 46%. Amid charges of electoral fraud in Yanukovich's base in eastern Ukraine, 200,000 protesters rallied in Kiev. Conservative columnist George Will flayed Putin for thwarting the march of freedom, and likened the position of Ukraine thirteen years after it gained its independence from the Soviet Union to the United States thirteen years after it declared its independence from the British empire.[23] Liberal columnist Nicholas Kristof, whose father grew up in southwestern Ukraine, visited the young protesters in Kiev and euphorically reported: "Most Ukrainians love the US and to be an American here – any American – is to be a rock star."[24]

The correlation of pro-American sentiment with "democracy" seemed to be confirmed in December 2004, when Ukrainian Supreme Court judges, five of whom had been tutored on election law in an American Bar Association program, ordered a new election that Yushchenko won by a margin of 8% of the vote.[25] Yet within a year it became evident that many Americans had misjudged the Ukrainian "Orange Revolution" much as they had misinterpreted the Russian revolution of 1991, in part by focusing too much on the actions of young people in the capital and neglecting popular sentiment in many of the provinces. By the fall of 2005, Ukrainian officials who were campaigning to join NATO acknowledged that public support for that step might be as low as 20%.[26] The next year, the Ukrainian parliament rejected a Yushchenko-backed bill to allow foreign troops to enter Ukraine for training exercises, and then Crimean demonstrators blocked preparations for exercises by American soldiers.[27] Even more strikingly, in free and fair elections in March 2006, Yanukovich's party won a strong plurality of the vote. In July, Yanukovich returned to power as Prime Minister.[28] Already in January 2006, a sobered *New York Times* recognized that American views of Yushchenko and the Orange Revolution had been unrealistic: "many in the West saw largely what they wanted to see: a people rising up against corruption, manipulated politics and crude Russian pressures in the name of moving closer to democracy, free markets and the West."[29]

American views of developments in Ukraine were also symptomatic in another way. The treatment of the Orange Revolution as a morality play, with the heroic Yushchenko and his fair-haired ally Yulia Tymoshenko triumphing over the villainous Yanukovich and Putin, reflected a deeply entrenched tendency to cast complex political developments on the territory of the former tsarist and Soviet empires in the stark terms of good and evil.[30] As early as the fall of 1999, when Putin as Yeltsin's prime minister oversaw a second war in Chechnya, American cartoonists began depicting him as a sinister figure in a trench coat (an allusion to his work as an intelligence officer in the 1970s and 1980s). By 2004, cartoonists regularly drew Putin as a medieval tsar, or portrayed him as a fanatical follower of Lenin and Stalin.[31] Prominent political commentators presented similar caricatures. Zbigniew Brzezinski compared Putin to Mussolini.[32] Nicholas Kristof likened Putin to the dictatorial rulers of Chile and Spain: Putin was "a Russified Pinochet or Franco," who was guiding Russia "into fascism."[33] The *Washington Post* called him "an isolated former KGB agent" and a "czar." Like a number of cartoonists, the Post's editors and reporters also blamed Putin for many tragic events in Russia, from the "bloodbath" after Chechen terrorists seized a school in Beslan, to the murder of a liberal Russian journalist who had criticized the war in Chechnya.[34] Such vituperation continued a long tradition that extended back at least as far as the blaming of the Kishinev pogrom of 1903 on Nicholas II.[35]

In the Putin era, as in earlier periods, such vehement vilification stemmed in part from the deflation of inflated hopes for the transformation of Russia. The fullest illustration of this dynamic appeared in *Kremlin Rising* (2005), a widely noted indictment of Putin's "counterrevolution" by Peter Baker and Susan Glasser, Moscow correspondents for the *Washington Post*. Although they went to Russia in 2000, after others had already declared the country "lost," Baker and Glasser still started from the presumption that Russia should be reshaped by its connections to the outside world in order to overcome its "warped" history. In the 1990s, they recalled, "it had been an article of faith" that a new generation of Russian youth, "unencumbered by a Soviet upbringing, would break away decisively from the past." They were therefore disappointed to find that many teenagers, like their parents, inclined to authoritarian collectivism and failed to recognize "the soul-annihilating quality of life in the Soviet Union." In contrast to Khodorkovsky, whom Baker and Glasser upheld as a model of bold self-transformation, high-school students they visited seemed fearfully conformist. While the *Post* correspondents disparaged ordinary Russians' gullible and slavish character, they were most scathing about Putin, who had kept them waiting for hours for interviews and had taken them with him on only one of his trips. Discounting the possibility that Putin might have been influenced by religious beliefs or by his association with democratic reformers in St. Petersburg at the end of the Soviet era, they simply labeled him a "product of the KGB" and "a product of the Cold War, the showdown between democracy and tyranny." From that ideological vantage point, they blamed Putin and his KGB advisers for Russia's reversion from pro-Western democracy to xenophobic authoritarianism.[36]

Such demonization of Putin obscured the complexity of his policies and disregarded the social context in which he operated. As the jailed oligarch Mikhail Khodorkovsky observed, while Putin may not be a liberal or a democrat, "he is more liberal and more democratic than seventy percent of the population."[37] In contrast to more chauvinistic and xenophobic Russian nationalists, during his first term as president Putin rebuked anti-Semites, explicitly defined Russia as "a multi-national and multi-religious society," accepted the establishment of American military bases in Central Asia, and downplayed the expansion of NATO to the Baltic states. (Later, Putin's public statements grew more similar to the rhetoric of the militant nationalists.)[38] In contrast to charges that he was reverting to Stalinist repression and aggression, Putin showed some recognition of the need to avoid repeating the tragic past: he laid a wreath to victims of the Norilsk labor camp in 2002, and four years later he laid a wreath to victims of the Soviet crushing of the Hungarian uprising of 1956, for which he acknowledged Russia bore "moral responsibility."[39]

Although Putin's stifling of the independence of television broadcasters naturally provoked indignation among journalists, it was unrealistic and counterproductive to try to promote freedom in Russia through personalized public attacks on a president who enjoyed approval ratings that hovered around seventy percent.[40] The *Washington Post*'s declaration that if the Bush administration denounced Putin for moving his country in the wrong direction, "Mr. Putin might listen," disregarded that fact that most of the people in Russia approved of Putin's path and greatly preferred it to the policies Americans had promoted in the 1990s.[41] In contrast to the Yeltsin era, during the Putin years most Russians' standard of living improved, they regained a sense of optimism about their future, and they began to recover a feeling of pride about their country. Such trends led many Russians to reject negative American judgments about their country's course. In the spring of 2006, for example, after the Council on Foreign Relations issued a report that criticized "Russia's wrong direction," former leader Mikhail Gorbachev declared that "the West should not be telling Russia that it is headed in the wrong direction."[42]

Instead of prodding Putin to reverse course, Western criticism provoked him to be more outspokenly defiant. In January 2006 Putin declared that the appropriate response to "Sovietologists who do not understand what is happening in our country" was "'To hell with you.'"[43] In July he objected that American talk about spreading democracy resembled the way colonialists had talked a hundred years earlier about how the white man needed "to civilize 'primitive peoples.'"[44] A few days later, when Bush mentioned that a lot of people in America hoped that Russia would follow the example of the free press and free religion that the United States had promoted in parts of the world like Iraq, Putin retorted: "We certainly would not want to have the same kind of democracy as they have in Iraq."[45] Even pro-Western Russians who were troubled by Putin's political manipulations grew increasingly irritated by scolding from the West. They found it especially galling to hear Russia chastised by Americans like Cheney, who with blatant hypocrisy simultaneously embraced authoritarian leaders of other former Soviet republics.[46]

Since condemnations of Putin by American politicians, journalists, and human rights activists did not compel him to alter his policies and instead seem to have made him more obdurate, one must ask what impelled intelligent Americans to continue and even escalate their verbal attacks on the Kremlin. Many of the critics appear to have been influenced by an urge to contrast Russia and the United States in ways that would reinforce a sense of American righteousness and virtue. Even in the aftermath of the terrorist attacks on New York and Washington in 2001, when Putin pursued an alliance with the United States and many Russians expressed strong sympathy with Americans, prominent commentators in the US drew lines between Russia and America. In October 2002, when Chechen rebels seized a Moscow theater and threatened to kill hundreds of Russian hostages, leading American journalists stressed the need to distinguish America's justified war on terrorism from Russia's illegitimate war against Chechnya.[47] An even more dramatic illustration of how Russia continued to be an "imaginary twin" or "dark double" for the United States came in June 2005. Disturbed by how US authorities held Islamic detainees in harsh conditions for indefinite terms, Amnesty International's secretary general described the US prison at Guantanamo Bay as "the gulag of our times." The remark provoked a furor. Editors of the *Washington Post*, especially, were infuriated by "the implication that the United States has somehow become the modern equivalent of Stalin's Soviet Union."[48] The Amnesty International leader's analogy did lack perspective on the vast difference between the Soviet gulag and the American archipelago of prisons in the scope of the abuses. However, the incident still revealed how, long after the Cold War ended, many Americans' sense of the virtue of the United States continued to be connected to differentiation from the Soviet Union and Russia. Political cartoonists captured the sensitivity to such comparisons and contrasts in several images, including one that depicted a dejected Uncle Sam complaining to "Joe" Stalin that "people are likening Guantanamo to one of your gulags – it's giving me a lousy image."[49] This was not merely a hangover from the Cold War, but a reflection of a tendency to use Russia as a foil for American national identity that had emerged more than a century earlier.

Well into the twenty-first century, memories of involvement in a crusade against communist tyranny continued to influence thinking about America's role in the world. US government officials, their neoconservative supporters, and some of their liberal critics recalled that freedom-loving Americans achieved a final victory in an ideological war against an evil empire, and argued that the United States should adapt the principles of that struggle to the fight against a new enemy – Islamic "totalitarianism."[50] That perspective lost sight of how many Americans had sought not merely to defeat a despotic enemy but also to promote a free society – a more difficult challenge. Celebratory invocations of a Cold War victory also disregarded the fact that in the twenty-first century, most Russians did not remember the collapse of the Soviet system as a glorious popular revolution.[51] Nonetheless, a triumphalist recollection of that time in the United States continued to fuel an American drive to remake foreign societies. Such memories thus paralleled the way engagement in the recurring crusades for a free Russia during the previous century had reaffirmed Americans' faith in their global mission.

# Notes

NOTES TO INTRODUCTION

1. W. Bruce Lincoln, *The Great Reforms: Autocracy, Bureaucracy, and the Politics of Change in Imperial Russia* (DeKalb, IL, 1990); Edvard Radzinsky, *Alexander II: The Last Great Tsar* (New York, 2005), 404–22.
2. J. W. Buel, *Border Outlaws* (1881); Buel, *Russian Nihilism and Exile Life in Siberia: A Graphic and Chronological History of Russia's Bloody Nemesis, and a Description of Exile Life in All Its True But Horrifying Phases* (St. Louis, 1883, 1884), 80, 94, 539, 537, 541, 443–56, 539–40. A revised edition in 1899 was titled, *A Nemesis of Misgovernment: Republican, Monarchical, and Empirical Governments.*
3. Michael Adas, *Dominance By Design: Technological Imperatives and America's Civilizing Mission* (Cambridge, MA, 2006).
4. Richard Drinnon, *Facing West: The Metaphysics of Indian Hating and Empire Building* (New York, 1980), James Axtell, *The Invasion Within: The Contest of Cultures in Colonial North America* (New York, 1985); Frederick Hoxie, *A Final Promise: The Campaign to Assimilate the Indians, 1880–1920* (Cambridge, UK, 1989; first edition, 1984).
5. F. G. Notehelfer, *American Samurai: Captain L. L. Janes and Japan* (Princeton, 1985) Joseph M. Henning, *Outposts of Civilization: Race, Religion, and the Formative Years of American-Japanese Relations* (New York, 2000).
6. Stuart Creighton Miller, *"Benevolent Assimilation": The American Conquest of the Philippines, 1899–1903* (New Haven, 1982); Tony Smith, *America's Mission: The United States and the Worldwide Struggle for Democracy in the Twentieth Century* (Princeton, 1994), Chapter 2; Louis A. Pérez, Jr., *On Becoming Cuban: Identity, Nationality and Culture* (Chapel Hill, 1999).
7. See, for example, Hans Schmidt, *The United States Occupation of Haiti, 1915–1934* (New Brunswick, 1971).
8. Howard Schonberger, *Aftermath of War: Americans & the Remaking of Japan, 1945–1952* (Kent, OH, 1989); John W. Dower, *Embracing Defeat: Japan in the Wake of World War II* (New York, 1999); Richard L. Merritt, *Democracy Imposed: U.S. Occupation Policy and the German Public, 1945–1949* (New Haven, 1995); Carolyn Woods Eisenberg, *Drawing the Line: The American Decision to Divide Germany, 1944–1949* (Cambridge, UK, 1996).
9. James Dobbins, et al, *America's Role in Nation-Building: From Germany to Iraq* (Santa Monica, CA, 2003); George Packer, *The Assassins' Gate: America*

*in Iraq* (New York, 2005); Francis Fukuyama, ed., *Nation-Building: Beyond Afghanistan and Iraq* (Baltimore, 2006).

10. Janine R. Wedel, *Collision and Collusion: The Strange Case of Western Aid to Eastern Europe, 1989–1998* (New York: St. Martin's Press, 1998); Stephen F. Cohen, *Failed Crusade: America and the Tragedy of Post-Communist Russia* (New York, 2000); Peter Reddaway and Dmitri Glinski, *The Tragedy of Russia's Reforms: Market Bolshevism Against Democracy* (Washington, 2001); James M. Goldgeier and Michael McFaul, *Power and Purpose: U.S. Policy Toward Russia After the Cold War* (Washington, 2003).

11. "The National Security Strategy of the United States," full text in *New York Times*, September 20, 2002; John Lewis Gaddis, *The Cold War: A New History* (New York, 2005).

12. For a stimulating essay that emphasizes Russia's distinctiveness but sets its historical experience in a comparative perspective, see Marshall Poe, *The Russian Moment in World History* (Princeton, 2003).

13. See especially Alan M. Ball, *Imagining America: Influence and Images in Twentieth-Century Russia* (Lanham, MD, 2003).

14. Philippe Legrain, *Open World: The Truth About Globalization* (Chicago, 2004), 103; Martin Wolf, *Why Globalization Works* (New Haven, 2004), 120; Thomas L. Friedman, *The World is Flat: A Brief History of the Twenty-First Century* (New York, 2005), 181.

15. Concerning the tsarist era, see, for example, Dietrich Geyer, *Russian Imperialism: The Interaction of Domestic and Foreign Policy, 1860–1914* (New Haven, 1987), esp. 187. On the early Soviet period, see, for example, Jon Jacobson, *When the Soviet Union Entered World Politics* (Berkeley, 1994), esp. 254–5, 276.

16. Ernest Samuels, ed., *The Education of Henry Adams* (Boston, 1973; first published 1918), 439.

17. Walter L. Hixson, *Parting the Curtain: Propaganda, Culture, and the Cold War, 1945–1961* (New York, 1997), 223; Reinhold Wagnleitner, *Coca-Colonization and the Cold War: The Cultural Mission of the United States in Austria after the Second World War* (Chapel Hill, 1994), xiv.

18. T. H. von Laue, "Imperial Russia at the Turn of the Century: The Cultural Slope and the Revolution from without," *Comparative Studies in Society and History*, Vol. 3, No. 4 (July 1961), 353–67.

19. Valuable discussions and definitions of "Americanization" include: "Roundtable: Cultural Transfer or Cultural Imperialism? 'Americanization' in the Cold War," *Diplomatic History*, Vol. 24, No. 3 (Summer 2000), 465–528; Gregory Claeys, "Mass Culture and World Culture: On 'Americanisation' and the Politics of Cultural Protectionism," *Diogenes*, Vol. 136 (1986), 70–97; and Rob Kroes, "Americanization: What Are We Talking About?" in Kroes et al, eds., *Cultural Transmissions and Receptions: American Mass Culture in Europe* (1993), 302–18.

20. Frederick C. Barghoorn, *The Soviet Image of the United States: A Study in Distortion* (1950); Jeffrey Brooks, "Official Xenophobia and Popular Cosmopolitanism in Early Soviet Russia," *American Historical Review*, Vol. 97, No. 5 (December 1992), 1431–48; Abbott Gleason, "Republic of Humbug: The Russian Nativist Critique of the United States, 1830–1930," *American*

*Quarterly*, Vol. 44 (March 1992), 1–23; Hans Rogger, "America in the Russian Mind – or Russian Discoveries of America," *Pacific Historical Review*, Vol. 47 (February 1978), 27–51; Jane E. Good, "'I'd Rather Live in Siberia': V. G. Korolenko's Critique of America, 1893," *Historian*, Vol. XLIV, No. 2 (February 1982), 190–206.

21. See, for example, Richard Pells, *Not Like Us: How Europeans have Loved, Hated, and Transformed American Culture Since World War II* (New York, 1997), xv, 243; James L. Watson, ed., *Golden Arches East: McDonald's in East Asia* (Stanford, 1997); Heide Fehrenbach and Uta G. Poiger, ed., *Transactions, Transgressions, Transformations: American Culture in Western Europe and Japan* (New York, 2000), esp. xiv, xxix.

22. David C. Engerman emphasizes the "particularist" views of Russian national character in *Modernization From the Other Shore: American Intellectuals and the Romance of Russian Development* (Cambridge, MA, 2003). For examples of Russian resentment of being treated as black or African, see: the complaint of the Soviet ambassador to Washington, in Memorandum of Conversation by George F. Kennan, April 3, 1952, *Foreign Relations of the United States, 1952–1954*, Vol. VIII (Washington, 1988), 968–9; Eduard Sagalayev, head of TV-6, quoted in David Remnick, *Resurrection: The Struggle for a New Russia* (New York, 1997), 251; and Alexander Solzhenitsyn's remarks, quoted by Celestine Bohlen in the *New York Times*, June 6, 1998; and Vladimir Putin's comments, in "Putin Backs Blair's Agenda for the G8," *Moscow Times*, June 14, 2005; "Putin Warns West to Back Off," *Moscow Times*, December 7, 2004.

23. James W. Cortada, *Two Nations Over Time: Spain and the United States, 1776–1917* (Westport, CT, 1978), esp. 130–43; Philip Wayne Powell, *Tree of Hate: Propaganda and Prejudices Affecting United States Relations with the Hispanic World* (New York, 1971); Kristin L. Hoganson, *Fighting for American Manhood: How Gender Politics Provoked the Spanish-American and Philippine-American Wars* (New Haven, 1998), 49–51; Gerald F. Linderman, *The Mirror of War: American Society and the Spanish-American War* (Ann Arbor, 1974), 123; Louis A. Pérez, *The War of 1898: The United States and Cuba in History and Historiography* (Chapel Hill, 1998), 27, 62; Jules R. Benjamin, *The United States and the Origins of the Cuban Revolution: An Empire of Liberty in an Age of National Liberation* (Princeton, 1990), 32.

24. David Healy, *US Expansionism: The Imperialist Urge in the 1890s* (Madison, 1970), 128–9; Benjamin, *The United States and the Origins of the Cuban Revolution*, 3; Linderman, *The Mirror of War*, 129; Hoganson, *Fighting for American Manhood*, 47, 49, 65–6; T. Christopher Jespersen, *American Images of China, 1931–1949* (Stanford, 1996), xviii.

25. The terms are borrowed from Michael Rogin, "American Political Demonology: A Retrospective," in Rogin, *Ronald Reagan: The Movie* (Berkeley, 1987), 284.

NOTES TO CHAPTER 1

1. "Destiny of Russia," *Southern Literary Messenger*, Vol. XIX (January 1853), 41–9, reprinted in Eugene Anschel, ed., *The American Image of Russia*,

*1775–1917* (New York, 1974), 118–21; Taylor Stults, "Imperial Russia Through American Eyes, 1894–1904: A Study in Public Opinion," Ph.D. dissertation, University of Missouri, Columbia, 1970, 149–54, 203–5, 192–5; Norman Saul, *Distant Friends: the United States and Russia, 1763–1867* (Lawrence, KS, 1991); Saul, *Concord and Conflict*, esp. 97–102 and 117–21.

2. See Max M. Laserson, *The American Impact on Russia, 1784–1917: Diplomatic and Ideological* (New York, 1950), esp. 136–8 and 195; Marc Raeff, "An American View of the Decembrist Revolt," *Journal of Modern History*, Vol. XXV, No. 3 (September 1953), 290–2; James Seay Brown, Jr., "Eugene Schuyler, Observer of Russia: His Years as a Diplomat in Russia, 1867–1875," Ph.D. dissertation, Vanderbilt University, 1971, esp. 83, 213; David Mayers, *The Ambassadors and America's Soviet Policy* (New York, 1995), 19; 25.

3. See, for example, Louis Ruchames, ed., *The Letters of William Lloyd Garrison* (Cambridge, MA, 1975), Vol. IV: 97–187, esp. 98, 125.

4. Fred V. Carstensen, *American Enterprise in Foreign Markets: Studies of Singer and International Harvester Company in Imperial Russia* (Chapel Hill, 1984), 5; 27; Robert Bruce Davies, *Peacefully Working to Conquer the World: Singer Sewing Machines in Foreign Markets, 1854–1920* (New York, 1976), 244–5.

5. Anna M. Babey, *Americans in Russia 1776–1917: A Study of the American Travelers in Russia from the American Revolution to the Russian Revolution* (New York, 1938), 37–65; Thomas A. Bailey, *America Faces Russia: Russian-American Relations From Early Times to Our Day* (Ithaca, 1950), 108–35; 140; 142; Laserson, *American Impact on Russia*, 173; 368; 360; 376–7; 380; M. D. Karpachev and T. V. Logunova, "Amerikanskii Publitsist Dzhordzh Kennan o Revoliutsionnom dvizhenii v Rossii," *Istoriia SSSR*, 1988 (5), 189–99; John Lewis Gaddis, *Russia, the Soviet Union, and the United States: An Interpretive History* (Second Edition, New York, 1990), esp. 28–31; Nicholas Daniloff, "George Kennan and the Challenge of Siberia," *Demokratizatsiya*, Vol. 7, No. 4 (Fall 1999), 601–12.

6. On the feeble and infrequent official expressions of concern about Jews, see Gaddis, *Russia, the Soviet Union, and the United States*, 29, 42; Allan Spetter, "The United States, the Russian Jews and the Russian Famine of 1891–1892," *American Jewish Historical Quarterly*, Vol. LXIV, No. 3 (March 1975), 236–44, and Ronald J. Jensen, "The Politics of Discrimination: America, Russia and the Jewish Question 1869–1872," *American Jewish History*, Vol. LXXV, No. 3 (March 1986), 280–95.

7. William Appleman Williams, *The Roots of the Modern American Empire* (New York, 1969), 162–5, 188; William Appleman Williams, *American-Russian Relations 1781–1947* (New York, 1952), 24–47; Williams, "Brooks Adams and American Expansion," in Thomas J. McCormick and Walter LaFeber, eds., *Behind the Throne: Servants of Power to Imperial Presidents* (Madison, 1993), 21–34; Walter LaFeber, *The American Search for Opportunity, 1865–1913*, Vol. II in *The Cambridge History of American Foreign Relations* (Cambridge, UK, 1993), esp. 33, 111, 121, 137–8, 171–2, and 190–1. Other studies that stress economic competition include Edward H. Zabriskie, *American-Russian Rivalry in the Far East: A Study in Diplomacy and Power Politics* (Philadelphia, 1946), and Shannon Lee Smith, "The Politics of Progress and the American-Russian Relationship, 1867–1917," Ph.D. dissertation, Cornell University, 1994.

8. See especially William Dudley Foulke, *Slav or Saxon: A Study of the Growth and Tendencies of Russian Civilization* (first edition, 1887; second edition, New York, 1899).

9. Henry Cabot Lodge, "Some Impressions of Russia," *Scribner's Magazine,* Vol. XXXI (May 1902), 570–80, esp. 575; W. C. Ford, ed., *Letters of Henry Adams* (Boston, 1930), esp. II: 339–44; Elting E. Morison, ed., *The Letters of Theodore Roosevelt* (Cambridge, MA, 1951), I: 646–7, 656, 769, II: 1053, III: 15, IV: 829; Brooks Adams, *America's Economic Supremacy* (New York, 1900), 200–3, 212–4; Albert J. Beveridge, *The Russian Advance* (New York, 1904), esp. 311–318; Michael H. Hunt, *Frontier Defense and the Open Door: Manchuria in Chinese-American Relations, 1895–1911* (New Haven, 1973), esp. 53, 59, 73–8.

10. See, for example, "Russian Factories in Central Asia," *Bradstreet's,* March 16, 1889, p. 170; Alexander Hume Ford, "America's Agricultural Regeneration of Russia," *Century,* Vol. LXII, No. 4 (August 1901), 501–7; "The United States and Manchuria," *Harper's Weekly* 47 (May 9, 1903), pp. 769–70; *The Letters of Theodore Roosevelt,* II: 1051–2, 1128, III: 105–6, 112; and George S. Queen, *The United States and the Material Advance in Russia, 1881–1906* (New York, 1976), 116–32, 156–74.

11. Davies, *Peacefully Working to Conquer the World,* 255; Carstensen, *American Enterprise in Foreign Markets,*114–5; 119; 128; Stults, "Imperial Russia Through American Eyes, 1894–1904," 169–79; J. M. Crawford, US Consul at St. Petersburg, to William Dudley Foulke, March 12, 1893, Box 3, Foulke Papers, Library of Congress [LC].

12. Ford, "America's Agricultural Regeneration of Russia"; L. R. Conradi to W. C. White, 18 November 1890, E. G. White Estate, Seventh-day Adventist Archive, Silver Spring, MD, cited in Foglesong, "Redeeming Russia?" 355; Henry Adams to Henry Cabot Lodge, August 4, 1891, in *The Letters of Henry Adams* 6 vols. (Cambridge, MA, 1982), Vol. III: 519; Mark Twain, *The American Claimant* (Leipzig, 1892), 177–8. On Adams' persistent fascination with transforming Russia, see Harold Dean Cater, ed., *Henry Adams and His Friends: A Collection of His Unpublished Letters* (Boston, 1947), 475; Ernest Samuels, ed., *The Education of Henry Adams* (Boston, 1973), 409–39. On Twain's views of Russia, see Louis J. Budd, "Twain, Howells, and the Boston Nihilists," *New England Quarterly,* Vol. XXXII, No. 3 (September 1959), 351–71.

13. William E. Bear, "The Russian and Indian Wheat Supply," *Bradstreet's,* February 2, 1889; "Russia's Agricultural Crisis," *Bradstreet's,* March 2, 1889; "The Russian Revolt," *New York World,* February 1, 1892, reprinted in *Public Opinion,* Vol. XII (February 6, 1892); Merle Curti, *American Philanthropy Abroad: A History* (New Brunswick, NJ, 1963), 101–19; Harold F. Smith, "Bread for the Russians: William C. Edgar and the Relief Campaign of 1892," *Minnesota History,* Vol. 42, No. 1 (Spring 1970), 54–62; James Y. Simms, Jr., "Impact of Russian Famine, 1891–1892, Upon the United States," *Mid-America,* Vol. 60, No. 3 (October 1978), 171–84; Shannon Smith, "From Relief to Revolution: American Women and the Russian-American Relationship," *Diplomatic History,* Vol. 19, No. 4 (Fall 1995), 605–6.

14. L. R. Conradi, "A Visit to Russia," in *Historical Sketches of the Foreign Missions of the Seventh-day Adventists* (Basel, 1886), 250–271; Donald Carl Malone, "A Methodist Venture in Bolshevik Russia," *Methodist History*, Vol. XVIII (July 1980), 239–61; Kahlile Mehr, "The 1903 Dedication of Russia for Missionary Work," *Journal of Mormon History*, Vol. 13 (1987), 111–21; Saul, *Concord and Conflict*, 298–300; David S. Foglesong, "Redeeming Russia? American Missionaries and Tsarist Russia, 1886–1917," *Religion, State and Society*, Vol. 25, No. 4 (December 1997), 353–68.

15. Michael Rogin, "American Political Demonology: A Retrospective," in Rogin, *Ronald Reagan: The Movie* (Berkeley, 1987), 284. While Rogin refers to the USSR in the twentieth century, the idea of the "dark double" can also be applied to late Imperial Russia.

16. *Chicago Tribune*, March 14 and 15, 1881; *Columbus Dispatch*, March 14, 1881; Salt Lake *Daily Tribune*, March 15, 1881; Atlanta *Daily Constitution*, March 15, 1881.

17. *New York Tribune*, March 14, 15, and 16, 1881; Springfield *Republican*, March 14, 1881; *Richmond Dispatch*, March 15, 1881; New Orleans *Daily Picayune*, March 15, 1881.

18. Salt Lake *Daily Tribune*, March 15, 16, and 17, 1881.

19. *Columbus Dispatch*, March 14 and 19, 1881; New Orleans *Daily Picayune*, March 15, 1881; *Richmond Dispatch*, March 15, 1881; *New York Tribune*, March 14, 1881; New York *World*, March 15 and 21 editorials and April 11, 1881 book review.

20. "The Scholar in a Republic," June 30, 1881, in Wendell Phillips, *Speeches, Lectures, and Letters* (Boston, 1892), 330–64.

21. Leigh H. Irvine, introduction to William Jackson Armstrong, *Siberia and the Nihilists: Why Kennan Went to Siberia* (Oakland, CA, 1890), 15–17.

22. Armstrong, *Siberia and the Nihilists*, 39–40, 81–6; see also 70 and 76.

23. Armstrong, *Siberia and the Nihilists*, 63, 65, 72, 36, 84, 57–8, 53, 75–6. *Free Russia*, the key organ of the anti-tsarist movement in the 1890s, reprinted (and implicitly endorsed) substantial sections of Armstrong's "spirited lecture" in Vol. IV, No. 9 (April 1894), 4–7.

24. In 1890, for example, the New York *World* wired an urgent request to lecturer George Kennan for a letter detailing how a female school teacher exiled to Siberia "was stripped and publicly flogged," a story that was then featured by other papers. *World* to Kennan, February 11, 1890, Folder 2, Alice Stone Blackwell Papers, Schlesinger Library, Radcliffe College; New York *Evening Post*, March 1, 1890, reprinted in *Public Opinion*, Vol. VIII (March 8, 1890), 512.

25. See, for example, "New Light on Siberia," *The Nation*, March 16, 1882, in which a reviewer scorned "Russophobist stories" and mocked the hypocritical self-righteousness of those who stigmatized tsarist inhumanity while ignoring the use of the lash in Delaware and Virginia.

26. Oscar Sherwin, *Prophet of Liberty: The Life and Times of Wendell Phillips* (New York, 1958), 654; Irving H. Bartlett, *Wendell Phillips: Brahmin Radical* (Boston, 1961), 392.

27. See Travis, *George Kennan and the American-Russian Relationship, 1865–1924*.

28. Travis, *George Kennan*, 46–7; 77; 84; Kennan to C. A. Dana, draft c. July 19, 1881, Box 1, Kennan Papers, NYPL; Kennan, "Siberia – The Exiles' Abode," *Journal of the American Geographical Society of New York*, Vol. XIV (1882), 57–8.

29. Kennan to the editor of the Washington *Chronicle*, reprinted in Armstrong, *Siberia and the Nihilists*, 95–107.

30. See, for example, George Kennan, *Siberia and the Exile System* 2 vols. (London, 1891), II: 4, 6, 14.

31. Kennan, *Siberia and the Exile System*, I: 171–4, 181–7, 234–40.

32. Travis, *George Kennan*, 87–8; 125–32; 50–51; 111; Kennan, *Siberia and the Exile System*, II: 119, 452–4.

33. Kennan, *Siberia and the Exile System*, II: 117–23; Kennan to Alice Stone Blackwell, December 28, 1917, Box 7, Kennan Papers, LC.

34. George Kennan to Kent Kennan, Christmas 1916, Box 10, George Kennan Papers, New York Public Library [NYPL].

35. George Kennan to Kent Kennan, Christmas 1916.

36. See "Objections and Difficulties," undated handwritten notes, c. 1871, Box 56, Kennan Papers, LC.

37. George Kennan to Kent Kennan, Christmas 1916, Box 10, Kennan Papers, NYPL.

38. George Kennan to Emmeline Wald Kennan, January 1, 1899, Box 15, Kennan Papers, LC.

39. Travis, *George Kennan*, 87–8; 125–32; 50–51; 111; GK to Kent Kennan, Christmas 1916, Box 10, Kennan Papers, NYPL; Laserson, *American Impact on Russia*, 379–380; Felix Volkhovsky, "George Kennan in Tomsk," *Free Russia*, Vol. IV, No. 6 (January 1894), 6–8.

40. In 1895 Kennan estimated that he had lectured to between 300,000 and 400,000 people in England and the U.S. in the preceding ten years. Stults, "George Kennan," 280; see also Good, "America and the Russian Revolutionary Movement," 279.

41. Travis, *George Kennan*, 171, 158; Kennan, "The Russian Police," *Century*, Vol. XXXVII, No. 6 (April 1889), 890–3.

42. See, for example, Deborah Pickman Clifford, *Mine Eyes Have Seen the Glory: A Biography of Julia Ward Howe* (Boston, 1979), 262–9. Howe was one of the founders of the Society of American Friends of Russian Freedom.

43. "The Last Appeal of the Russian Liberals," *Century*, XXXV (November 1887), 50–63. Kennan similarly sought to categorize "nihilism" as Western rather than Oriental in *Siberia and the Exile System*, Vol. II: 431.

44. Cf. Laserson, *American Impact on Russia*, 377 and 380; Francesca Wilson, *Muscovy: Russia Through Foreign Eyes, 1553–1900* (London, 1970), 215 and 295.

45. *Siberia and the Exile System*, II: 123–4.

46. Travis, *George Kennan*, 169.

47. See, for example, *Siberia and the Exile System*, Vol. I: 100.

48. Kennan, *Siberia and the Exile System*, I: vi.

49. Kennan to F. V. Volkhovsky, March 17, 1889, Box 6, Kennan Papers, LC; Kennan, "Russian State Prisoners," *Century*, Vol. XXXV (March 1888), 765–6; Kennan, "Russian Despotism," *The Outlook*, Vol. 85, No. 13 (March 30,

1907), 754–5; *Buffalo Express*, June 2, 1891; "Russia and the United States," *Free Russia*, No. 9 (April 1891), p. 7; Boston *Daily Advertiser*, quoted in "Compliments of the Press on Mr. George Kennan's Lectures," October 1, 1892 circular, Box 56, Kennan Papers, LC; "Notes of the Month," and "Two Fourth of July Celebrations," *Free Russia*, Vol. III, No. 12 (July 1893), 1–2 and 5–6.

50. Kennan, "A Voice for the People of Russia," 472; Petoskey, Michigan *Daily Resorter*, July 23, 1895, quoted in Stults, "Imperial Russia through American Eyes," 17, and in Jane E. Good, "America and the Russian Revolutionary Movement, 1888–1905," *Russian Review*, Vol. 41, No. 3 (July 1982), 274.

51. David Hecht, *Russian Radicals Look to America, 1825–1894* (Cambridge, MA, 1947), esp. 152, 213, 219–20; James P. Scanlan, ed., *Historical Letters*, by Peter Lavrov (Berkeley, 1967), esp. 49, 119–21, 266–7; I. K. Mal'kova, "Istoriia i Politika SShA na Stranitsakh Russkikh Demokraticheskikh Zhurnalov 'Delo' I 'Slovo'," *Amerikanskii Ezhegodnik*, 1971, 273–94; Stults, "George Kennan: Russian Specialist of the 1890s"; Good, "America and the Russian Revolutionary Movement, 1888–1905"; Jane E. Good, "'I'd Rather Live in Siberia: V. G. Korolenko's Critique of America, 1893," *The Historian*, Vol. XLIV, No. 2 (February 1982), 190–206; Hans Rogger, "America in the Russian Mind – or Russian Discoveries of America," *Pacific Historical Review*, Vol. XLVII, No. 1 (February 1978), 27–52; Rogger, "America Enters the Twentieth Century: The View from Russia," in *Felder und Vorfelder Russischer Geschichte*, ed. Inge Auerbach, Andreas Hillgruber, and Gottfried Schramm (Freiburg, 1985), 160–77; Abbott Gleason, "Republic of Humbug: The Russian Nativist Critique of the United States, 1830–1930," *American Quarterly*, Vol. 44, No. 1 (March 1992), 1–23; V. Ia. Grosul, "Rossiiskaia Politicheskaia Emigratsiia v SShA v XIX v.," *Novaia i noveishaia istoriia*, 1994 (2), 49–69.

52. Edmund Noble, "Island Democracy in the Caspian," *Atlantic Monthly*, Vol. LX (December 1887), 806–7. Noble earlier supported his optimism about a future Russian democracy by citing frontier history in *The Russian Revolt* (London, 1885), 33.

53. "A Russian Experiment in Self-Government," *Atlantic Monthly*, Vol. 80 (October 1897), 494–507. The Zheltuga Republic is mentioned in Andrew Malozemoff, *Russian Far Eastern Policy 1881–1904* (Berkeley, 1958), 12, 23–4.

54. See, for example, James M. Hubbard, "Russia as a Civilizing Force in Asia," *Atlantic Monthly*, Vol. LXXV (February 1895), 197–205; Archer B. Hulbert, "The Better Side of Russian Rule in Asia," *Independent*, November 1, 1900, 2632–4.

55. During the Cold War, historians sometimes suggested that the Siberian frontier experience showed that Russia could have followed the American model of development if Bolshevism had not intervened. See Donald W. Treadgold, "Russian Expansion in the Light of Turner's Study of the American Frontier," *Agricultural History* 26:4 (October 1952), 147–52; Treadgold, *The Great Siberian Migration: Government and Peasant in Resettlement from Emancipation to the First World War* (Princeton, 1957); and Joseph L. Wieczynski, *The Russian Frontier: The Impact of Borderlands upon the Course of Early Russian History* (Charlottesville, 1976).

56. Buel, *Russian Nihilism and Exile Life in Siberia*, 77, 442–3, 542; Mark Twain, *A Connecticut Yankee in King Arthur's Court* (1889; New York, 1971), esp. 129; "Russia's Abolition of Private Saloons," *Review of Reviews*, reprinted in *Public Opinion*, Vol. XIX (5 September 1895), 301–2.

57. Isabel F. Hapgood, *Russian Rambles* (Boston, 1895), vii, 332, 129, 109.

58. Edward L. Ayers, *The Promise of the New South* (New York, 1992), 32, 348; Logan, *The Betrayal of the Negro*, 248–55.

59. "Stepniak's Last Work," *Nation*, Vol. 62, No. 1596 (Jan. 30, 1896), 104. Hapgood repeatedly opposed universal suffrage in Russia. See *Nation*, September 9, 1897, p. 210; June 8, 1905, p. 450; October 19, 1905, p. 324; January 18, 1906, p. 58.

60. Kennan to C. A. Dana, draft, July 19, 1881, Box 1, Kennan Papers, NYPL.

61. George Kennan, *Campaigning in Cuba* (New York, 1899), 2–3, 20, 27, 103, 176, 177, 193–4.

62. "The Last Appeal of the Russian Liberals," *Century*, XXXV (November 1887), 50–63. Twenty years later Kennan cited Wendell Phillips' 1859 oration on Harper's Ferry to support his argument that the tsarist "pirate ship," like its Southern counterpart, should be "chased off the face of the earth by the civilized powers." "Russian Despotism," *The Outlook*, Vol. 85, No. 13 (March 30, 1907), 753–4.

63. Larry Anthony Rand, "America Views Russian Serf Emancipation 1861," *Mid-America*, Vol. 50, No.1 (January 1968), 43–7. See also Richard Hofstadter's argument that abolitionism "was a religious movement" and lacked a clear conception of "how an illiterate, landless, and habitually dependent people were to become free and self-sufficient." "Wendell Phillips: The Patrician as Agitator," in *The American Political Tradition and the Men Who Made It* (New York, 1948, 1973), 184–5.

64. *Free Russia*, Vol. III, No. 3 (October 1892), 5–6.

65. *Free Russia*, Vol. 14, No. 11 &12 (June/July 1894), 2.

66. Foulke, *A Hoosier Autobiography* (New York, 1922), 2–4, 221; Foulke, *Slav or Saxon* (1887), 141; Aurele J. Violette, "William Dudley Foulke and Russia," *Indiana Magazine of History*, Vol. LXXXII, No. 1 (March 1986), 69–96.

67. Walter Rauschenbusch to Kennan, October 12, 1889, Box 1, Kennan Papers, LC.

68. Foulke letter of June 1887 printed as a pamphlet, Box 3, Foulke Papers, LC; Violette, "William Dudley Foulke and Russia," 80; "A New Fugitive Slave Law," *Free Russia*, Vol. III, No. 11 (June 1893), 9. See also *Free Russia*, Vol. III, No. 8 (March 1893), 5, 10, 11; and Bailey, *America Faces Russia*, 158.

69. Kennan to F. V. Volkhovsky, March 17, 1889, p. 6, Box 6, Kennan Papers, LC.

70. Rauschenbusch to Kennan, October 12, 1889, Box 1, Kennan Papers, LC; Logan, *The Betrayal of the Negro*, 271–2.

71. On the general abandonment, see C. Vann Woodward, *The Strange Career of Jim Crow* (Third edition, New York, 1974), esp. 69–74, and Rayford W. Logan, *The Betrayal of the Negro: From Rutherford B. Hayes to Woodrow Wilson* (New York, 1965; reprint, 1997). On the uneasy backsliding among Bostonian abolitionists and their heirs, see Mark R. Schneider, *Boston Confronts Jim Crow, 1890–1920* (Boston, 1997).

72. "Notes of the Month," *Free Russia*, Vol. III, No. 2 (September 1892), 2–3; Vol. IV, No. 3 (October 1893), 1; Vol. III, No. 8 (March 1893), 3.

73. "Chauncey M. Depew on the Old and New South," *Boston Evening Transcript*, April 8, 1890, p. 6.

74. "The Faneuil Hall Siberia Meeting," *Boston Evening Transcript*, April 5, 1890, p. 5.

75. Stults, "Imperial Russia through American Eyes," 119–21; *Free Russia*, Vol. IV, No. 3 (October 1893), 3; "The Dead Czar," New York *World*, November 2, 1894; "Two Autocrats," New York *World*, November 4, 1894; *Life*, Vol. XVI, No. 398 (August 14, 1890); Vol. XVIII, No. 465 (November 26, 1891).

76. Cartoon by F. T. Richards in *Life*, February 26, 1891, captioned: "Is Russian cruelty worse than American dishonor?"

77. "Russia and the United States," *Free Russia*, No. 9 (April 1891), 7; "Notes of the Month," *Free Russia*, Vol. III, No. 8 (March 1893), 2.

78. *Free Russia*, Vol. III, No. 9 (April 1893), 6, 13, 14, and Vol. III, No. 11 (June 1893), 13; Kennan, "The Russian Extradition Treaty," *The Forum*, May 1893, reprinted in *The Literary Digest*, Vol. 7, No 3 (May 20, 1893), 58–9.

79. Philadelphia *Ledger*, February 17, 1890; New York *Evening Post*, March 1, 1890, reprinted in *Public Opinion*, Vol. VIII (February 22 and March 8, 1890), 468 and 512–3. See also editorials from the *New York Tribune*, Cincinnati *Commercial Gazette*, and Louisville *Courier-Journal*, reprinted in *Public Opinion*, February 22, April 19, June 7, and August 9, 1890.

80. Boston *Evening Transcript*, October 16, 1889, quoted in "Compliments of the Press on Mr. George Kennan's Lectures," October 1, 1892 circular, Box 56, Kennan Papers, LC.

81. "American Notes," *Free Russia*, June 1892, 14–15.

82. *Slav or Saxon* (1887), 38; *Slav or Saxon* (1899), 37; Foulke to John C. Ropes, May 12, 1899, Box 3, Foulke Papers, LC.

83. See Noble, "American Notes," *Free Russia*, June 1892, 14–15; Lyman Abbott, *Reminiscences* (Boston, 1915), 438; Ira V. Brown, *Lyman Abbott: Christian Evolutionist* (Cambridge, MA, 1953), 173, 91.

84. See, for example, "Destiny of Russia," *Southern Literary Messenger*, Vol. XIX (January 1853), 41–9, and *Harper's Weekly*, May 26, 1877.

85. W. P. Garrison, "An English Resident in Russia," *The Nation*, Vol. 3, No. 65 (September 27, 1866), 247–8.

86. See E. Schuyler, "Modern Russia," *The Nation*, Vol. 10 (March 10, 1870), 161–2; Schuyler letter to the editor, *The Nation*, May 5, 1870, p. 287; Isabel F. Hapgood, "The Russian Church: Its Spiritual State and Possibilities," *The Outlook*, Vol. LIII (June 20, 1896), 1142–6; *Nation*, Vol. 62, No. 1612 (May 21, 1896), p. 402; *Nation*, Vol. 71 (Nov. 29, 1900), 432.

87. [Anonymous,] "The Internal Condition of Russia," *ACQR*, Vol. IV (October 1879), 680–693.

88. [J. C. Earle,] "The Russo-Greek Church," *The American Catholic Quarterly Review* (*ACQR*), Vol. XI, No. 43 (July 1886), 507–11; [Anonymous,] "The Russian Empire and the Catholic Church," *ACQR*, Vol. XV, No. 59 (July 1890), 496–508; B. Clinch, "The Russian State Church," *ACQR*, Vol. XX,

No. 79 (July, 1895), 449–59; Address of Rev. George W. Northrup, May 25, 1891, *Seventy-Seventh Annual Report* of the American Baptist Missionary Union (ABMU) (Boston, 1891), 8; Samuel W. Duncan to Joseph Kessler, September 17,1892, Vol. 20 of *Overseas Letters*, Correspondence Files, American Baptist Archives Center (ABAC), Valley Forge, Pennsylvania; *Seventy-Fourth Annual Report* of the ABMU (Boston, 1888), 302; Cyrus Hamlin, "The Dream of Russia," *Atlantic Monthly*, Vol. LVIII (December 1886), 771–82; "Is Russian Progress a Deterrent to Missions?" *Presbyterian* (Philadelphia), reprinted in *Public Opinion*, Vol. XXIV (26 May 1898), 658; Foglesong, "Redeeming Russia? American Missionaries and Tsarist Russia, 1886–1917," *Religion, State and Society*, Vol. 25, No. 4 (December 1997), 353–68.

89. Martin E. Marty, *Righteous Empire: The Protestant Experience in America* (New York, 1970), 188–98; William G. McLoughlin, *Revivals, Awakenings, and Reform: An Essay on Religion and Social Change in America, 1607–1977* (Chicago, 1978), 141–78; William R. Hutchison, *Errand to the World: American Protestant Thought and Foreign Missions* (Chicago, 1987), 43, 86, 103–11.

90. Kennan, "A Voice for the People of Russia," *Century* (July 1893); "Which is the Civilized Power?" *The Outlook*, 29 October 1904, 516–20; "A Sacrilegious Fox Hunt," in *A Russian Comedy of Errors* (New York, 1915), 241–56.

91. *Free Russia*, Vol. III, No. 12 (July 1893), 15–16, Vol. IV, No. 6 (January 1894), 1, 5, 8, and Vol. IV, No. 9 (April 1894), 1–2; Vol. IV, No. 11 (June 1893), 3.

92. *Free Russia*, Vol. III, No. 3 (October 1892), 1–2; Vol. IV, No. 8 (March 1894), 3. For a similar view, see Foulke, *Slav or Saxon* (1887), 36–7; *Slav or Saxon* (1899), 35–6.

93. *Free Russia*, July 1892, 13–14; Kirk H. Porter, compiler, *National Party Platforms* (New York, 1924), 163; 175.

94. "Truth About Russia," *Public Opinion*, Vol. VI (March 2, 1889), 475–6; "Editor's Easy Chair," *Harper's Magazine*, reprinted in *Public Opinion*, Vol. XI (August 1, 1891), 400; New York *Sun* editorial, October 18, 1890, reprinted in *Public Opinion*, Vol. X (October 25, 1890), 55–6; New York *Mail and Express* editorial, April 22, 1892, reprinted in *Public Opinion*, Vol. XIII (April 30, 1892), 84. See also "The Jews in Russia," reprinted from *Free Russia* in *Public Opinion*, Vol. XVI (January 28, 1893), 398.

95. For further discussion, see Foglesong, "Redeeming Russia?"

96. Queen, *The United States and the Material Advance in Russia*, esp. 36–46 and 62–3.

97. Davies, *Peacefully Working to Conquer the World*, 255; Carstensen, *American Enterprise in Foreign Markets*,114–5; 119; 128; Stults, "Imperial Russia Through American Eyes, 1894–1904," 169–79; J. M. Crawford, US Consul at St. Petersburg, to William Dudley Foulke, March 12, 1893, Box 3, Foulke Papers, Library of Congress [LC].

98. Queen, *The United States and the Material Advance in Russia*, esp. 36–46 and 62–3; "Siberia and the Great Siberian Railway," *Bradstreet's*, November 25, 1893, pp. 745–7; Archibald Cary Coolidge, "Across Siberia," *Nation*, September 5, September 19, and October 3, 1895.

99. Davies, *Peacefully Working to Conquer the World*, 280–3; Carstensen, *American Enterprise in Foreign Markets*, 8, 127; Alexander Hume Ford, "America's Agricultural Regeneration of Russia," *Century*, Vol. LXII, No. 4 (August 1901), 503, 505, 507; Queen, 181.

100. Kennan to his sister Jennie, March 25, 1878, Box 56, Kennan Papers, LC; Kennan, *Siberia and the Exile System*, I: 102–3; 14–15; 34–6; 48–54. Kennan further suggested that "American entrepreneurial spirit" would make the mines where prisoners worked safer and more efficient. H. S. Hundley, "George Kennan and the Russian Empire: How America's Conscience Became an Enemy of Tsarism," Kennan Institute Occasional Paper, 2000.

101. Foglesong, "Redeeming Russia?" 357.

102. Buel, *Russian Nihilism and Exile Life in Siberia*, 539.

103. Noble in *Free Russia*, Vol. IV, No. 6 (January 1894), 2; Vol. IV, No. 11 & 12 (June/July 1894), 3; Howells in Vol. III, No. 11 (June 1893), 9. See also *Free Russia*, September 1892, p. 2.

104. Kennan to F. V. Volkhovsky, March 17, 1889, pp. 3–5, Box 6, Kennan Papers, LC.

105. See, for example, Leo Hartman, "A Nihilist's View," *Literary Digest*, Vol. 7, No. 7 (June 17, 1893), p. 193; "Exiled for Protesting," *Chicago Tribune*, March 27, 1890, p. 2.

106. "Russian Traits and Terrors," *Public Opinion*, Vol. XI (September 26, 1891), 618; Milwaukee *Sentinel* editorial, March 13, 1892, reprinted in *Public Opinion*, Vol. XII (March 19, 1892), 598. For additional testaments to Kennan's influence on Americans' great interest in and growing hatred of Russia, see: "Truth About Russia," *Public Opinion*, Vol. VI (March 2, 1889), 475–6; Cincinnati *Commercial Gazette* editorial, May 29, 1890, reprinted in *Public Opinion*, Vol. IX (June 7, 1890), 197; and "Russian Social Life," *Public Opinion*, Vol. X (January 10, 1891), 337.

107. Travis, *George Kennan*, 178–81; Stults, "Imperial Russia through American Eyes," 52–62.

108. *Free Russia*, Vol. III, No. 9 (April 1893), 1; Vol. IV, No. 1 (August 1893), 2; Vol. IV, No. 11 &12 (June/July 1894), 1–3; editorials opposing a treaty between liberty and despotism, reprinted in *Public Opinion*, April 29, May 13, and June 17, 1893; Travis, *George Kennan*, 206–7; 222–3; Kennan to E. E. Lazarev, August 12, 1891, Box 9, Felix Volkhovsky Collection, Hoover Institution Archives. On the multiplicity of foreign causes backed by SAFRF founders, see Arthur Mann, *Yankee Reformers in the Urban Age* (Cambridge, MA, 1954), 215.

109. Struve to Girs, 22 March/3 April 1889 and 13/25 February 1890, Archive of the Foreign Policy of the Russian Empire (AVPRI), Moscow, Fond Kantseliariia MID, op. 470, d. 96, ll. 6–14 and d. 104, ll. 29–32; E. I. Melamed, *Dzhordzh Kennan protiv tsarizma* (Moscow, 1981), 72–3; Kantakuzin to Chichkin, 1/13 February 1893, Fond Kantseliariia MID, op. 470, d. 101, ll. 198–202; Cassini to Lamsdorf, 14/27 February 1901, Fond Kantseliariia MID, op. 470, d. 105, ll. 279–80.

110. *New York Daily Tribune*, November 2, 1894; New York *Herald* comment reprinted in "Darkest Russia," *Chicago Tribune*, November 4, 1894;

*Philadelphia Inquirer*, November 2, 1894 ("barbaric" and "civilization"); Salt Lake *Daily Tribune*, November 3, 1894 ("malcontents"); *New York Daily Tribune*, November 18, 1894 ("unspeakable Turk"). For examples of the fear of socialism, Populism, and anarchy, see *Chicago Tribune*, November 3 and 19, 1894; Salt Lake *Daily Tribune*, November 17, 1894; *Philadelphia Inquirer*, November 2, 1894. One of the fuller Russophile statements was made by former US Minister to Austria-Hungary John A. Kasson, in "America and Russia: Why the Two Countries Have Always Been So Friendly," *Boston Evening Transcript*, November 1, 1894.

111. Hapgood, *Russian Rambles* (Boston, 1895), vi; Nathan Haskell Dole's remarks in *The Bookman*, Vol. 1 (May 1895), 260, and Isabel Hapgood's comments in *The Nation*, Vol. 60, No. 1547 (Feb. 21, 1895), p. 150; Vol. 71, No. 1848 (Nov. 29, 1900), p. 432.

112. David Mills (Canadian Minister of Justice), "Which Shall Dominate – Saxon or Slav?" *North American Review*, Vol. 166, No. 6 (June 1898), 729–39; Lyman Abbott, "The Basis of an Anglo-American Understanding," *North American Review*, Vol. 166, No. 5, 513–21; Brooks Adams, "The Spanish War and the Equilibrium of the World," *Forum* (August 1898), reprinted in *America's Economic Supremacy*, 1–25; LaFeber, *The American Search for Opportunity*, 138 and 172.

113. Stephen Bonsal, "The Convict System in Siberia," *Harper's New Monthly Magazine*, Vol. XCVII (August, 1898), 327–342; "Siberia No Longer a Penal Colony," *Public Opinion*, Vol. XXVII (3 August, 1899), 139; Herbert H. D. Pierce, "The Russian Paternalism," *Atlantic Monthly* (October 1902), excerpted in *Public Opinion*, Vol. XXXIII (23 October 1902), 522; S. M. Williams, "The New California," *Munsey's Magazine*, Vol. XXVI, No. 6 (March 1902), 753–64; George Frederick Wright, *Asiatic Russia* (New York, 1902). See also Stults, "Imperial Russia Through American Eyes," 33–7.

114. James McPherson, *The Abolitionist Legacy* (Princeton, 1975), 367–9.

115. "A Race Problem Incident," *Columbus Dispatch* editorial, May 8, 1903; "Friendly But Futile Advice," *Chicago Tribune* editorial, May 11, 1903; "'Uncle Tom's Cabin,'" New York *World* editorial, April 27, 1903; "'Uncle Tom's Cabin,'" *New York Daily Tribune* editorial, May 21, 1903.

116. "Russia's Indictment," *New York Daily Tribune*, May 18, 1903; Bailey, *America Faces Russia*, 179–182; Philip Ernest Schoenberg, "The American Reaction to the Kishinev Pogrom of 1903," *American Jewish Historical Quarterly*, Vol. LXIII, No. 3 (March 1974), 262–283; Arnold Shankman, "Brothers Across the Sea: Afro-Americans on the Persecution of Russian Jews, 1881–1917," *Jewish Social Studies*, Vol. XXXVII, No. 2 (Spring 1975), 114–121. See also Tyler Dennett, *John Hay: From Poetry to Politics* (1933, reprint, New York, 1963), 398; *Letters of Theodore Roosevelt*, III: 526, IV: 1175; and Smith, "The Politics of Progress and the American-Russian Relationship," 378–9.

117. *The Outlook*, 17 May 1902, 14 March, 2 May, 30 May, 13 June, 25 April (quotation), and 6 June 1903; Abbott, *Reminiscences*, 424; McPherson, *The Abolitionist Legacy*, 334, 373; Report of Cleveland's speech, New York *World*, May 28, 1903; "The Jews in Russia" (editorial) and Clarence Darrow speech

quoted in "Prompt Aid for Jews of Russia," *Chicago Tribune*, May 19, 1903; New York *Evening Post* and Springfield *Republican* editorials quoted in *Literary Digest*, Vol. 26, No. 22 (May 30, 1903).

118. Dennett, *John Hay*, esp. 400–5; Kenton J. Clymer, *John Hay: The Gentleman as Diplomat* (Ann Arbor, 1975), 145–56; *Letters of Theodore Roosevelt*, III: 478, 497, 500–1, 508, 520, 532.

119. See Charles Johnston, "The Manchurian War-Scare," *Harper's Weekly*, May 23, 1903, p. 877; editorials in *Harper's Weekly*, May 16, June 6, and November 21, 1903; Hartford *Times* quoted in *The Literary Digest*, Vol. 26, May 16, 1903, 710–711; Wright, *Asiatic Russia*, 475. See also "Uncle Sam More Guilty Than Russia," New York *World*, May 8, 1903.

120. Foulke, *A Hoosier Autobiography*, 124.

121. Hapgood to Lev Tolstoy, Feb. 19, 1903, N. Velikanova and R. Vittaker (Robert Whittaker), *L. N. Tolstoi i SShA* (Moscow, 2004), 260–3.

122. Alice Stone Blackwell, "American Friends of Russian Freedom," *Free Russia*, April 1, 1904, p. 40.

123. In a similar vein, a front-page cartoon in the *Columbus Evening Dispatch* on May 19, 1903, depicted a shade of Roman emperor Nero reading headlines about the Kishinev massacre in a "Hades Gazette" and saying: "Alas, I Am Indeed, Outdone!"

124. David M. Kennedy, "Culture Wars: The Sources and Uses of Enmity in American History," in Ragnhild Fiebig-von Hase and Ursula Lehmkuhl, eds., *Enemy Images in American History* (Providence, 1997), 339–56; Frank Ninkovich, *The Wilsonian Century: U.S. Foreign Policy Since 1900* (Chicago, 1999), 27, 46.

125. See, for example, "Not a Christian Appeal," Louisville *Courier Journal*, April 10, 1904.

126. Alice Stone Blackwell to Felix Volkhovsky, November 20, 1903, Box 9, Volkhovsky Papers, HIA; "The United States and Russia: A Reexamination of the Traditional Friendship Between Them in the Light of the Past and Present History," *Public Opinion*, Vol. XXXIV (21 May 1903), 680.

127. For example, "Sympathy with Japan," Columbus *Dispatch*, February 13, 1904; New York *World*, February 11 and 14, 1904.

128. On the "medievalism" theme, see the political cartoons in the New York *World*, January 25, February 3, and February 6, 1905; in the Columbus *Dispatch*, February 6, 1905; and in the *Chicago Tribune*, January 24, 1905; see also the editorial, "Cross Currents in Russia," *Chicago Tribune*, January 25, 1905. For a general study of American attitudes, see Arthur W. Thompson and Robert A. Hart, *The Uncertain Crusade: America and the Russian Revolution of 1905* (Amherst, MA, 1970). On Russian diplomats' views of rising press and public animosity in America, see the Cassini-Lamsdorf correspondence, AVPRI, Fond Kantseliariia MID, 1904, Op. 470, d. 129, t. II, ll. 381–3, 402–4, 424–7, and 509.

129. *The Changing Years: Reminiscences of Norman Hapgood* (New York, 1930), 244.

130. For example, G. Frederick Wright, "Russia's Civilizing Work in Asia," *The American Monthly Review of Reviews*, April 1904, 427–32; William Elliot

Griffis, "The Russo-Greek Church and the World's Progress," *The Outlook*, 16 September 1905.

131. See, for example, "What Chiefly Troubles Russia," *Chicago Tribune*, Jan. 26, 1905; Charles Johnston, "Russia's Struggle for Liberty," *Harper's Weekly*, Feb. 11, 1905.

132. Edmund Noble, "American Opinion on the Defeat of the Russian Autocracy," *Free Russia*, July 1, 1905, pp. 87–8.

133. "Free Russia," *The Independent*, November 2, 1905.

134. "Reform in Russia," *The Watchman*, Vol. 87, No. 7, February 16, 1905.

135. See, for example, Ambassador George Meyer to President Roosevelt, 5 May, 1905, in M. A. DeWolfe Howe, *George von Lengerke Meyer: His Life and Public Services* (New York, 1920), 149.

136. Foglesong, "Redeeming Russia?," 356–7; James Creelman, "Full Meaning of the Czar's Surrender," New York *World*, November 1, 1905; "More Promises in Russia," *Chicago Tribune*, November 1, 1905.

137. Columbus *Evening Dispatch*, November 1, 1905.

138. Harcave, ed., *The Memoirs of Count Witte*, 431–442; A. Korelin and S. Stepanov, *S. Iu. Vitte – Finansist, Politik, Diplomat* (Moscow, 1998), 153; Telegramma S. Iu. Vitte v MID o Tseremonii Ofitsial'noi vstrechi delegatsii, 25 July/7August 1905, *Rossiia i SShA: diplomaticheskie otnosheniia 1900–1917*, 93; Thompson and Hart, *The Uncertain Crusade*, 65, 101–2.

139. For example: "The Czar with one stroke of pen gives Russia liberty and kills the autocracy!" Columbus Evening Dispatch, October 30, 1905. See also New York *World*, October 31, 1905, and Philadelphia *Inquirer*, November 1, 1905.

140. Thompson and Hart, *The Uncertain Crusade*, esp. 91, 102, 109.

NOTES TO CHAPTER 2

1. "A Russian Baron in America," *The Missionary Review of the World* [*MRW*] (June 1906), 471.

2. J. B. Gambrell, "Baron and Baroness Uxkull and Their Work in Russia," *The Baptist Standard*, undated clipping (c. March 1907), T. S. Barbour Collection, American Baptist-Samuel Colgate Historical Library (ABSCHL), Rochester, New York. In Russian, Üxküll's name was V. Ia. Ikskul'.

3. Studies of the missions include: Donald Carl Malone, "A Methodist Venture in Bolshevik Russia," *Methodist History*, Vol. 18 (July 1980), 239–61; John Dunstan, "George A. Simons and the Khristianski [sic] Pobornik: A Neglected Source on St. Petersburg Methodism," *Methodist History*, Vol. 19, No. 1 (1980), 21–40; Dana L. Robert, "The Methodist Episcopal Church, South, Mission to Russians in Manchuria, 1920–1927," *Methodist History*, Vol. 26, No. 2 (January 1988), 67–83; Albert Wardin, "Pentecostal Beginnings among Russians in Finland and Northern Russia, 1911–1921," *Fides et Historia*, Vol. XXVI, No. 2 (Summer 1994), 50–61. Mormon leaders who visited Russia in 1903 were more skeptical about the prospects for missions. See Kahlile Mehr, "The 1903 Dedication of Russia for Missionary Work," *Journal of Mormon History*, Vol. 13 (1987), 111–121.

4. See, for example, Paul A. Varg, *Missionaries, Chinese, and Diplomats: The American Protestant Missionary Movement in China, 1890–1952* (Princeton, 1958); Michael Schaller, *The United States and China in the Twentieth Century* (New York, 1990), esp. 4, 127–8; T. Christopher Jespersen, *American Images of China, 1931–1949* (Stanford, 1996); Michael H. Hunt, "East Asia in Henry Luce's 'American Century,'" *Diplomatic History*, Vol. 23, No. 2 (Spring 1999), 321–353, esp. 328.

5. The most important study of the American intellectual encounter with the Russian revolutions, for example, focused on the political thought of liberals and emphasized the Enlightenment roots of liberalism. Christopher Lasch, *The American Liberals and the Russian Revolution* (New York, 1962), xvi; 1–9.

6. Donald E. Davis and Eugene P. Trani, *The First Cold War: The Legacy of Woodrow Wilson in U. S.-Soviet Relations* (Columbia, MO, 2002), 35.

7. "Religious Freedom for Russia!" *The Missionary Review of the World* (June 1905), 469–70; "The Upheaval in Russia," *The Missionary Review of the World* (December 1905), 950–1.

8. Thomas J. Shahan, "Roman Catholicism in Russia (1796–1825)," *American Catholic Quarterly Review*, Vol. XXX (1905), 533–51.

9. Conradi to Daniells, November 17, 1905, RG 21, Secretariat, General Conference Archives, SDA headquarters, Silver Spring, Maryland.

10. Boettcher to Spicer, January 27, 1908, RG 21, SDA archive, Silver Spring, MD.

11. Conradi, "New Developments in Eastern Europe," *Advent Review and Sabbath Herald*, July 4, 1912.

12. L. R. Conradi, "The Meeting at Alexandrodar," *Advent Review and Sabbath Herald*, March 8, 1906; H. F. Schuberth, "Kief and Dobrianka, Russia," *Advent Review and Sabbath Herald*, January 24, 1907, pp. 14–15.

13. K. C. Russell, "Russia's Crisis a Terrible Warning," *Advent Review and Sabbath Herald*, March 20, 1906, p. 20.

14. Dunstan, "George A. Simons and the Khristianski Pobornik," 25–6; Simons to H. K. Carroll, August 5, 1907 and November 10, 1907, Simons file, Missionary Files Series, United Methodist Church Archives, Madison, NJ.

15. Simons to My dear Brother [Dr. Homer C. Stuntz], October 17, 1908, Simons file, Missionary Files Series, United Methodist Church Archives, Madison, NJ.

16. Simons to Stuntz, September 29 and November 7, 1911, Simons file, Missionary Files Series, United Methodist Church Archives, Madison, NJ.

17. Stuntz to Simons, October 23, 1911, Simons file, Missionary Files Series, United Methodist Church Archives, Madison, NJ.

18. G. H. Jones to Simons, January 19, 1914, United Methodist Church Archives, Madison, NJ.

19. Heather J. Coleman, *Russian Baptists and Spiritual Revolution, 1905–1929* (Bloomington, 2005), 80.

20. Thomas S. Barbour to J. B. Gambrell, December 20, 1907, Barbour Collection, ABSCHL. On the special interest in funding missions in Russia see also: Thomas S. Barbour to Friedrich Brauer, August 18, 1908, and George B. Huntington to Friedrich Brauer, August 21, 1908, Official Correspondence,

Board of International Ministries, American Baptist Historical Society, Valley Forge, PA.

21. J. B. Gambrell, "Baron and Baroness Uxkull and Their Work in Russia," *The Baptist Standard*, n.d., c. March 1907.

22. Coleman, *Russian Baptists and Spiritual Revolution,*3, 5, 28; *Ninety-Second Annual Report of the American Baptist Missionary Union* (Boston, 1906), 42.

23. J. Heinrichs, "Account of my Visit to Russia," July 1, 1909, pages 8–10, Barbour Collection, ABSCHL.

24. Coleman, *Russian Baptists and Spiritual Revolution*, 23–4, 102, 119.

25. See, for example, "The Baptist Situation in Russia," *The Missionary Review of the World* (February 1910), 85–6; *American Baptist Foreign Mission Society Report* (1911), 116–7.

26. For illustrations of these points, see David S. Foglesong, "Redeeming Russia? American Missionaries and Tsarist Russia, 1886–1917," *Religion, State and Society*, Vol. 25, No. 4 (1997), 353–68, esp. 355.

27. The Russian-born, British-educated Baptist firebrand William (Wilhelm) Fetler repeatedly characterized Russia as "a nation of white people" in American publications. See The Baptist World Alliance, *Record of Proceedings*, June 19, 1911, 23; "Russia and the Gospel," *The Missionary Review of the World* (October 1912), 740, and *The Missionary Review of the World* (June 1918), 406. See also Andrew D. Urshan, "The Future of Persia and Russia," *The Weekly Evangel*, September 30, 1916, p. 8.

28. "Russia and the United States," *The Watchman*, Vol. 87, No. 19, May 11, 1905; "Religious Toleration In Russia," *The Watchman*, Vol. 87, No. 34, August 24, 1905; "The Russian Elections," *The Watchman*, Vol. 88, April 26, 1906, p. 6.

29. Ernest Poole, *The Bridge: My Own Story* (New York, 1940), 71; recollections of Ernest Poole and Howard Brubaker in Anna Strunsky Walling, ed., *William English Walling: A Symposium* (New York, 1938), 23–4, 35–6. For analyses of Walling's thinking, see Jack Meyer Stuart, "William English Walling: A Study in Politics and Ideas," Ph.D. dissertation, Columbia University, 1968; Keith Cassidy, "The American Left and the Problem of Leadership, 1900–1920," *South Atlantic Quarterly*, Vol. 82, No. 4 (1983), 386–97; and Mark Pittenger, "Science, Culture, and the New Socialist Intellectuals Before World War I," *American Studies*, Vol. 28, No. 1 (1987), 73–91. Regarding Poole's work, see Truman Frederick Keefer, "The Literary Career and Literary Production of Ernest Poole, American Novelist," Ph.D. dissertation, Duke University, 1961; idem, *Ernest Poole* (New York, 1966); and Robert Cuff, "Ernest Poole: Novelist as Propagandist, 1917–1918: A Note," *Canadian Review of American Studies*, Vol. 19 (Summer 1988), 183–94.

30. Ernest Poole, "Dounya," *The Independent*, October 26, 1905, 974–80.

31. William English Walling, *Russia's Message: The True World Import of the Revolution* (New York, 1908), 165, 179, IX, 9. Enthusiastic reviews of *Russia's Message* appeared in *The Nation*, Vol. 87, No. 2249 (August 6, 1908), 120–1; *The Independent*, Vol. 65 (September 10, 1908), 610; *Free Russia*, January 1909, 9–11; and *The Annals of the American Academy of Political and Social Science*, Vol. XXXIII (January 1909), 220–2.

32. Albert Edward [Bullard's pseudonym], "Rise of the Russian Proletariat," *The International Socialist Review*, July 1, 1907, p. 21.

33. Arthur Bullard, "Russia's Revolution," chapter II, pages 7–8 and chapter VIII, page 7, Box 5, Bullard Papers, Mudd Library, Princeton University.

34. Poole, *The Bridge*, 103.

35. Albert Edward [Bullard], "The Russian Revolution," *The International Socialist Review*, September 1907, p. 168; Walling, "How Is It With the Russian Revolution?" *The Outlook*, March 9, 1907, 566; Poole, "Thou Shalt Not Think – In Russia," *The Outlook*, 8 April 1905, 881–2.

36. Walling, *Russia's Message*, xi, 169; 201.

37. Frederick F. Travis, "The Kennan-Russel Anti-Tsarist Propaganda Campaign Among Russian Prisoners of War in Japan," *Russian Review*, Vol. 40, No. 3 (July 1981), 263–77.

38. Poole, *The Bridge*, 153–162; Albert Edwards [Bullard], "An Eye-witness's Story of the Russian Revolution," *Harper's Weekly*, February 24, 1906, 258–61; *William English Walling: A Symposium*, 11.

39. Poole, *The Bridge*, 168, 172–6; Bullard, "The St. Petersburg Massacre and the Russian East Side," *The Independent*, February 2, 1905, 256; Walling, "Will the Peasants Act?" *The Independent*, December 6, 1906, p. 1323; Walling, "An American View," *Free Russia*, April–June 1908, 4–6.

40. Allen F. Davis, *Spearheads for Reform: The Social Settlements and the Progressive Movement, 1890–1914*, 28; Alexis Aladin to George Kennan, June 4, 1907, Kennan Papers, Library of Congress, Box 3, on FRF letterhead, listing the positions of Reynolds, Wald, Addams, and Willoughby Walling.

41. Poole, "St. Petersburg is Quiet!" *The Outlook*, 18 March 1905, pp. 682–5; "'Peasant Cattle': What the Cossacks Think of the Peasants," *Everybody's Magazine*, October 1905, pp. 494–6; "Thou Shalt Not Think – In Russia," *The Outlook*, 8 April 1905, 886; "The Peasant and the War," *The Outlook*, 27 May 1905, p. 220. As one editor observed, Poole's articles "attracted wide attention." Editor's Note, "Peasant Cattle," *Everybody's Magazine*, October 1905, p. 494. See also Keefer, *Ernest Poole*, 33–4.

42. Albert Edwards [Bullard], "Under the White Terror," *Collier's*, April 14, 1906, p. 13, and April 28, 1906, p. 25; "The Russian Revolution," *The International Socialist Review*, Vol. VIII, No. 4 (October 1907), pp. 196–200; Kennan, "A Russian Experiment in Self-Government," *Atlantic Monthly* Vol. 80 (October 1897), 494–507.

43. N. V. Chaikovskii's argument that the peasant commune had instilled habits of sane self-government was publicized in *The Outlook*, February 10, March 17, and April 28, 1906. A. F. Aladin, who appeared alongside Chaikovskii on a lecture tour of America in 1907, was viewed as an authentic, self-educated son of the Russian soil. He therefore seemed to embody the promise that Russian peasants could lift themselves up to be on the level of Americans. See Reginald Frank Christian, *Alexis Aladin: The Tragedy of Exile* (New York, 1999), 66–74.

44. Walling, "The Real Russian People," *Independent*, September 26, 1907, p. 728; *Russia's Message*, 157; also 153 and 161.

45. Walling, *Russia's Message*, 148, 152.

46. *Russia's Message*, 4–5, 148, 152, 162, 163. See also Walling, "The Real Russian People at Church," *The Independent*, Vol. 63, July 4, 1907, 27–8, and Walling, "The Peasant's Revolution," *The Independent*, October 18, 1906, 906–7.

47. See, for example, Robert M. Crunden, *Ministers of Reform: The Progressives' Achievement in American Civilization, 1889–1920* (New York, 1982), and John A. Thompson, *Reformers and war: American progressive publicists and the First World War* (Cambridge, UK, 1987), esp. 12–15, 44–55.

48. Poole, *The Bridge*, 7–8, 27–9, 62–3, 194, 103. On the influence of Poole's Christian upbringing, see Keefer, *Ernest Poole*, 18–19.

49. "St. Petersburg is Quiet!" *The Outlook*, 18 March 1905, 681, 684–5; "Thou Shalt Not Think – In Russia," *The Outlook*, 8 April 1905, 879; "The Story of a Russian Workingman," *The Outlook*, 22 April 1905, 989–990; "Dounya," *The Independent*, October 26, 1905, 977–8; "The Night that Made Me a Revolutionist," *Everybody's Magazine*, November 1905, 637–9; quotation from "The Peasant and the War," *The Outlook*, 27 May 1905, 221.

50. Anonymous obituary, Box 1, Bullard Papers, Mudd Library.

51. Bullard, "The Revolutionist," n.d., Box 2, Bullard Papers.

52. "Russia's Revolution," chapter IX, pages 2–3; chapter X, pages 1–3; chapter VII, pages 7–8; chapter X, page 8; chapter II, pages 6 and 11; chapter III, page 7, Box 5, Bullard Papers, Mudd Library.

53. Walling, *Russia's Message*, 8; 447; Bullard, "The Revolutionist," p. 3; Walling, "Socialism and Liberty," in *William English Walling: A Symposium*, 98.

54. Boylan, *Revolutionary Lives*, 195.

55. "The Real Russian People at Church," *The Independent*, July 4, 1907, 26–32.

56. Walling, *Russia's Message*, 402–412; 8. One reviewer found Walling's chapters on religion "particularly interesting" and valuable. Review by N. I. Stone in *The Annals of the American Academy of Political and Social Science*, Vol. XXXIII (January 1909), 221.

57. Gustavus Myers, "Our Millionaire Socialists," *Cosmopolitan*, October 1906, 596–605; James Boylan, *Revolutionary Lives: Anna Strunsky and William English Walling* (Amherst, MA, 1998), 72, 119. Another marriage involved Miriam Finn and Leroy Scott, who, like Poole, Bullard, and Walling, traveled to and wrote about Russia. See, for example, Leroy Scott, "The Travesty of Christ in Russia," *Everybody's Magazine*, Vol. XVII, No. VI (Christmas 1907), 800–809.

58. Thompson and Hart, *The Uncertain Crusade*, esp. 91, 102, 109.

59. *Nation*, Vol 83, No. 2152 (September 27, 1906). After the Springfield riot, Walling helped to found the NAACP and turned his attention to other domestic reform issues. See Walling, "The Race War in the North," *The Independent*, September 3, 1908, pp. 529–534.

60. New York *Press*, quoted in *Literary Digest*, January 6, 1912, p. 1; *Congressional Record*, Vol. 48: 337–8, 343; *Chicago Tribune* editorials, August 1 and 29, 1914.

61. See San Francisco *Chronicle*, December 8, 9, and 22, 1911; *Chicago Tribune*, December 19, 1911; Boston *Evening Transcript*, December 20, 1911; and especially *The Independent*, November 23, 1911, pp. 1155–6.

62. Wilson address at Carnegie Hall, December 7, 1911, *The Papers of Woodrow Wilson*, Vol. 18: 583–7.

63. Wilson address at Carnegie Hall, December 7, 1911, *The Papers of Woodrow Wilson*, Vol. 18: 583; Cartoon in *New York Times*, December 24, 1911; San Francisco *Chronicle*, December 14, 1911; *The Literary Digest*, January 6, 1912, pp. 1, 2; New York *Evening Post*, quoted in *The Literary Digest*, Dec. 16, 1911, p. 1142; New York *American*, quoted in *The Literary Digest*, Dec. 23, 1911, p. 1184.

64. "A Protest Against Bigotry," *Los Angeles Times*, December 16, 1911.

65. Speeches of December 13, 1911 in *Congressional Record*, Vol. 48, esp. 338, 313, 315, 319, 39, 348.

66. Boston *Transcript*, Dec. 1, 1911; New York *Evening Post*, quoted in *The Literary Digest*, Dec. 16, 1911, p. 1142; New York *American*, quoted in *The Literary Digest*, Dec. 23, 1911, p. 1184.

67. *Rossiia i SShA: diplomaticheskie otnosheniia 1900–1917*, 562–7; Ann Healy, "Tsarist Anti-Semitism and Russian-American Relations," *Slavic Review*, Vol. 42, No. 3 (Fall 1983), 408–25.

68. See, for example, Harper Barnes, *Standing on a Volcano: The Life and Times of David Rowland Francis* (St. Louis, 2001), 187, 202.

69. Charles Johnston, "The New Russia," *Review of Reviews*, Vol. 51 (May 1915), pp. 568–573. See also Stanley Washburn, "America's Chance in Russia," *Harper's Weekly*, February 5, 1916.

70. J. H. Shakespeare to Huntington, February 21, 1913, Official Correspondence, Board of International Ministries, American Baptist Historical Society, Valley Forge, Pennsylvania.

71. Dail to Spicer, December 16, 1910, Dail to Spicer, March 13, 1911, and Conradi to Spicer and Daniells, July 7, 1912, RG 21, SDA archive, Silver Spring, MD; J. T. Boettcher, "Riga (Russia) Publishing Branch Closed," *Advent Review and Sabbath Herald*, July 4, 1912.

72. "Annual Report of the Russia Mission For the Foreign Missions Report of 1913," February 18, 1914, George A. Simons files, United Methodist Church archive, Madison, NJ. For further discussion of the crackdown against Protestant "sects," see Curtiss, *Church and State in Russia*, esp. 330–2.

73. O. E. Reinke to Spicer, October 19, 1914, J. T. Boettcher to Bowen, April 19, 1915, and Dail to Spicer, October 17, 1915, RG 21, SDA archive; *Advent Review and Sabbath Herald*, April 15, 1915 and August 12, 1915.

74. *American Baptist Foreign Mission Society Report* (1915), 197–8; Fetler letter in *The Baptist Times and Freeman*, February 5, 1915; Simons to Dr. S. Earl Taylor, April 18, 1915, and Simons to Frank Mason North, July 5, 1915, Simons file, Missionary Files Series, United Methodist Church Archives, Madison, NJ.

75. "The Twilight of the Kings," *Chicago Tribune*, August 2, 1914.

76. "The Slavic Terror," *The Nation*, Vol. 99 (August 20, 1914), p. 211.

77. "How a New Russia Emerged From the European Crisis," *Current Opinion*, November 1914, pp. 309–10.

78. See, for example, Gilbert H. Grosvenor, "Young Russia: The Land of Unlimited Possibilities," *National Geographic*, Vol. XXVI, No. 5 (November 1914),

453; Richard Washburn Child, *Potential Russia* (New York, 1916), 71, 194; "Jews and Russia," editorial, *Harper's Weekly*, March 25, 1916, p. 292.

79. Kennan to Abbott, May 8 and 9, 1914, Box 7, Kennan Papers, LC; Kennan, "The Russian People: Repression and Oppression," *The Outlook*, 18 July 1914, 647–50; Kennan, "The Russian Muzhik," *The Outlook*, Vol. 109, 24 March 1915, 681n; "The Zheltuga Republic," *A Russian Comedy of Errors* (New York, 1915), Chapter X. See also Kennan to Miller (editor of the *New York Times*), June 2, 1917, Box 7, Kennan Papers, LC.

80. Kennan, "'Public Opinion' in an 'Oriental State,'" *The Outlook*, March 31, 1915, p. 768.

81. James K. Libbey, "The American-Russian Chamber of Commerce," *Diplomatic History*, Vol. 9, No. 3 (Summer 1985), 234–6; Norman Saul, *War and Revolution: The United States and Russia, 1914–1921* (Lawrence, KS, 2001), esp. 5, 14–16.

82. Stanley Washburn, "America's Chance in Russia," *Harper's Weekly*, Vol. LXII, February 5, 1916; Richard Washburn Child, *Potential Russia* (New York, 1916), 179.

83. Bakhmetev to Sturmer, 18/31 July 1916, *Rossiia i SShA: diplomaticheskie otnosheniia 1900–1917*, 631–3.

84. See, for example, Child, *Potential Russia*, 7, 70, 156, 159, 160, 162, 191, 196, 205, 218; "The Reawakening of Russia," *American Review of Reviews*, Vol. 51 (May 1915), 598–9; "An Awakened Russia," *The Literary Digest*, January 6, 1917, p. 14.

85. "Russia Fighting Alcoholism," *The Literary Digest*, March 14, 1914, p. 545; "Banishing An Empire's Vice in One Day," San Francisco *Chronicle*, Nov. 19, 1914; William E. Johnson, *The Liquor Problem in Russia* (Westerville, Ohio, 1915); E. J. De Marsh, "The Russia of Tomorrow," *Harper's Weekly*, January 1, 1916, p. 9; Isabel F. Hapgood, "America's Share in the New Russian Reforms," *New York Times Magazine*, February 21, 1915, 15–16.

86. Patricia Herlihy, *The Alcoholic Empire: Vodka and Politics in Late Imperial Russia* (New York, 2002), 4, 8, 67–8, 147, 57, 107, 125.

87. Report of First Secretary of the Russian Embassy in Washington I. G. Loris-Melikov, "On the Rapprochement of Russia and America," 17/30 March 1916; Bakhmetev to Sturmer, 18/31 July 1916, *Rossiia i SShA: diplomaticheskie otnosheniia 1900–1917*, 620; 632.

88. Child, *Potential Russia*, 184, 219–21, 165.

89. "Nationalism and State Socialism," in *Publications of the American Sociological Society*, Vol. X: *War and Militarism in Their Sociological Aspects* (1915), 88–91; "The Great Illusions," *New Review*, June 1, 1915, 50.

90. Grosvenor, "Young Russia," 506.

91. Hapgood, "America's Share in the New Russian Reforms." For discussion of Hapgood's earlier views, see David Foglesong, "Istoki pervogo amerikanskogo krestovogo podkhoda za 'svobodnuiu Rossiiu,'" *Rossiia XXI*, #5, 2002, 120–5.

92. "Russia: Our Economic Twin," *The Literary Digest*, July 1, 1916, p. 15.

93. Samuel McRoberts, "Russia's Future Needs for Capital," *The Annals* of the American Academy of Political and Social Science, Vol. LXVIII (November, 1916), 210.

94. Elizabeth K. Reynolds, "Russian Art and the Police Force," *Harper's Weekly*, February 12, 1916, p. 158; idem, "America Realizing Russia," *Harper's Weekly*, May 6, 1916, p. 483. On the contrasting implications and interpretations of American and Russian frontier experiences, see Mark Bassin, "Turner, Solov'ev, and the 'Frontier Hypothesis': The Nationalist Signification of Open Spaces," *Journal of Modern History* 65 (September 1993): 473–511.

95. McRoberts, "Russia's Future Needs for Capital," 215.

96. Child, *Potential Russia*, 182–221, 153, 178.

97. Curtis Guild (former US Ambassador to Russia), "Russia and Her Emperor," *Yale Review*, Vol. 4, No. 4 (July 1915), 712–22; De Marsh, "The Russia of Tomorrow," *Harper's Weekly*, January 1, 1916, p. 9.

98. Bailey, *America Faces Russia*, 228–30.

99. Libbey, "The American-Russian Chamber of Commerce," 235; Foglesong, "Redeeming Russia?" 353, 359–60.

100. Lillian Wald to Kennan, March 17, 1917, and Lawrence Abbott to Kennan, April 6, 1917, Box 4, Kennan Papers, LC; Telegram from Kennan to Petrunkevitch, April 4, 1917, Box 7, Kennan Papers, LC; Kennan, "The Victory of the Russian People," *The Outlook*, March 28, 1917, pp. 546–7.

101. Telegram from Francis to Washington, March 18, 1917 and Wilson address to Congress, April 2, 1917, quoted in David S. Foglesong, *America's Secret War Against Bolshevism: U. S. Intervention in the Russian Civil War, 1917–1920* (Chapel Hill, 1995), 49–51. The editor of *The Outlook* prefigured Wilson's shaky historical assertion, declaring that "Prussianism" created the Russian autocracy but that the Russian people never let the Prussianism "touch their mind and soul." "Russia, the Democratic," *The Outlook*, March 28, 1917.

102. Jan Willem Schulte Nordholt, *Woodrow Wilson: A Life for World Peace* (Berkeley, 1991), 40–7; John M. Mulder, *Woodrow Wilson: The Years of Preparation* (Princeton, 1978).

103. Foglesong, *America's Secret War Against Bolshevism*, 28, 50; E. M. House, "Colonel House Finds Soviet's World Policy One of Minority Rule," *Philadelphia Public Ledger*, December 6, 1920, pp. 1, 2; Boylan, *Revolutionary Lives*, 232–3; Norman E. Saul, *War and Revolution: The United States and Russia, 1914–1921* (Lawrence, KS, 2001), 99.

104. Reinke to General Conference, April 3, 1917, RG 21 (Secretariat General Files), SDA archive, Silver Spring, MD. On the parallel Pentecostal enthusiasm, see *The Weekly Evangel*, March 24, 1917, front page.

105. Simons, "Russia's Resurrection," May 1917, Simons file, United Methodist Church Archives, Madison, NJ. Published in *The Christian Advocate*, July 12, 1917.

106. North to Simons, July 11, 1917, Simons file, Missionary Files Series, United Methodist Church Archives, Madison, NJ. North reiterated his enthusiasm in letters to Simons on August 21, 1917, September 28, 1917, and January 8, 1918.

107. G. S. Eddy to Raymond Robins, May 5, 1917, Robins Papers, State Historical Society of Wisconsin, Madison, WI.

108. "Russia on the Threshold of –What?" *The Missionary Review of the World*, Vol. XL (May 1917), 323–5.

109. Foglesong, *America's Secret War Against Bolshevism*, 108–110; Gregg Wolper, "The Origins of Public Diplomacy: Woodrow Wilson, George Creel, and the Committee on Public Information," Ph.D. dissertation, University of Chicago, 1991; James D. Startt, "American Film Propaganda in Revolutionary Russia," *Prologue*, Vol. 30, No. 3 (1998), 166–179.

110. Hans Rogger, "America in the Russian Mind – or Russian Discoveries of America," *Pacific Historical Review*, Vol. 47 (February 1978), 27–51; Jeffrey Brooks, "Official Xenophobia and Popular Cosmopolitanism in Early Soviet Russia," *American Historical Review*, Vo. 97, No. 5 (December 1992), 1431–1448; Alan M. Ball, "The Roots of Golden America in Early Soviet Russia," in William B. Husband, ed., *The Human Tradition in Modern Russia* (Wilmington, DE, 2000), 51–64; Alan M. Ball, *Imagining America: Influence and Images in Twentieth-Century Russia* (Lanham, MD, 2003), esp. 67.

111. Bullard to George Creel, 19 October/1 November 1917, Bullard Papers, Mudd Library, Princeton; Ernest Poole, *"The Dark People": Russia's Crisis* (New York, 1918), 103; Neil V. Salzman, *Reform and Revolution: The Life and Times of Raymond Robins* (Kent, OH, 1991), 180, 199.

112. "From Petrograd," *The Christian Advocate*, November 8, 1917, p. 1166.

113. Urshan, "Russia and Pentecostal People of United States and Canada," *The Christian Evangel*, November 30, 1918. See also "Liberty and License in Russia," *The Missionary Review of the World* (March 1918), 163–4.

114. Foglesong, *America's Secret War Against Bolshevism*, 159–62, 200.

115. Foglesong, *America's Secret War Against Bolshevism*, 163. In the same vein, Simons cabled from Petrograd to ask the Methodist missionary board to "Assure Washington our opinion heart of Russian nation beats warmly for America." Simons to Board of Foreign Missions, New York, August 26, 1918, United Methodist Church archive, Madison, New Jersey.

116. Joshua Rosett, "Kolchak, the Allies and the Siberian People," *New Republic*, July 9, 1919, pp. 323–4.

117. Foglesong, *America's Secret War Against Bolshevism*, 185–7, 220–5, and *passim*.

118. Foglesong, *America's Secret War Against Bolshevism*, 158–9; Frederick C. Giffin, "An American Railroad Man East of the Urals, 1918–1922," *Historian*, Vol. 60, No. 4 (Summer 1998), 813–30; Saul, *War and Revolution*, 342–6. For the contrary view that "sophisticated" US aid to Siberia was "the primary response of American statesmen to events in revolutionary Russia," see Leo J. Bacino, *Reconstructing Russia: U. S. Policy in Revolutionary Russia,1917–1922* (Kent, OH, 1999), 1–3.

119. "Memorandum on the Russian Situation," 28 November 1918, Bullard Papers, Princeton; Arthur Bullard, *The Russian Pendulum* (New York, 1919), 245. John Spargo, *Russia as an American Problem* (New York, 1920), 335, preface, 336.

120. Foglesong, *America's Secret War Against Bolshevism, passim*.

121. Simons testimony, February 12, 1919, *Brewing and Liquor Interests and German and Bolshevik Propaganda. Report and Hearings of the Subcommittee on the Judiciary, United States Senate* (Washington, 1919), 122, 124, 126, 127, 132, 159, 137; Foglesong, *America's Secret War Against Bolshevism*, 40, 45.

122. "The Pro-Bolshevik Propaganda in America," undated (c. summer or fall 1918) article, Box 2, Walling Papers; *Sovietism: The ABC of Russian Bolshevism – According to the Bolshevists* (New York, 1920), 3, 8, 9, 18, 11, 14, 13, 23, 209–14. Walling excoriated Bolshevik heresy with equal vehemence in his private correspondence, such as a letter to John Spargo, June 27, 1919, quoted in Stuart, "William English Walling," 182–3.

123. Lillian D. Wald, *The House on Henry Street* (New York, 1915), 229–47; Wald, *Windows on Henry Street* (Boston, 1934), 5–6, 15, 225, 261–5, 271.

124. Salzman, *Reform and Revolution*, 136–7, 296, 212.

125. Boylan, *Revolutionary Lives*, 245, 248; Anna Strunsky Walling, "Class Freedom in Russia," *Labor Age*, February 1929, p. 29; J. Louis Engdahl, "Rose Pastor Stokes Asks Privilege to Return to Socialist Party Ranks," *The Eye Opener* (Chicago), Vol. 9, No. 26, January 19, 1918, p. 4; Arthur Zipser and Pearl Zipser, *Fire and Grace: The Life of Rose Pastor Stokes* (Athens, GA, 1989); Harriet Sigerman, "Rose Pastor Stokes," *American National Biography Online* (2000); Salzman, *Reform and Revolution*, 353.

126. *Brewing and Liquor Interests and German and Bolshevik Propaganda*, 112–5, 135–6.

127. Foglesong, *America's Secret War Against Bolshevism*, 41.

128. Foglesong, *America's Secret War Against Bolshevism*, 58, 65, 171; Kennan, "Can We Help Russia?" *The Outlook*, 22 May 1918, p. 141; Simons testimony in *Brewing and Liquor Interests and German and Bolshevik Propaganda*, 132.

129. Wilson address on April 2, 1917, quoted in Foglesong, *America's Secret War Against Bolshevism*, 51.

NOTES TO CHAPTER 3

1. "Mighty Movings of the Spirit in Russia, Poland, and Latvia," *Pentecostal Evangel*, May 21 and 28, 1927; Paul B. Peterson, "Russia," *Pentecostal Evangel*, November 26, 1927, p. 8; Paul B. Peterson, "Imprisoned for Preaching Christ in Russia," *Pentecostal Evangel*, August 15, 1931, p. 11; Paul B. Peterson, "The Work of God in Eastern Europe," *Pentecostal Evangel*, March 11, 1939, p. 9; Gustave Kinderman, "The Pentecostal Work in Eastern Europe Today," *Pentecostal Evangel*, January 20, 1940. On the formation of the Russian and Eastern European Mission of the Assemblies of God, see Paul Peterson to Missionary Committee, April 19, 1927, Peterson correspondence, and Paul Peterson, *History of the First Fifty Years (1927–1977) of the Eastern European Mission* (n.d.), Flower Pentecostal Heritage Center Archives, Springfield, MO.

2. See, for example, Philippe Legrain, *Open World: The Truth About Globalization* (Chicago: Ivan Dee, 2004), 103; Martin Wolf, *Why Globalization Works* (New Haven: Yale University Press, 2004), 120; Thomas L. Friedman, *The World is Flat: A Brief History of the Twenty-First Century* (New York: Farrar, Straus and Giroux, 2005), 181.

3. See, for example, Teddy J. Uldricks, "Russia and Europe: Diplomacy, Revolution, and Economic Development in the 1920s," *International History Review*, Vol. 1, No. 1 (January 1979), 55–83; Jon Jacobson, *When the Soviet*

*Union Entered World Politics* (Berkeley, 1994), esp. 253–5, 276; Alan M. Ball, *Imagining America: Influence and Images in Twentieth-Century Russia* (Lanham, MD, 2003), Chapter 1.

4. For example, Frank A. Warren, *Liberals and Communism: The "Red Decade" Revisited* (New York, 1993; first edn., 1966); Richard Pells, *Radical Visions and American Dreams: Culture and Social Thought in the Depression Years* (Urbana, 1998; first edn., 1973); and David C. Engerman, *Modernization From the Other Shore: American Intellectuals and the Romance of Russian Development* (Cambridge, MA, 2003).

5. David McFadden and Claire Gorfinkel, *Constructive Spirit: Quakers in Revolutionary Russia* (Pasadena, 2004), 83, 91; Bertrand M. Patenaude, *The Big Show in Bololand: The American Relief Expedition to Soviet Russia in the Famine of 1921* (Stanford, 2002), 143.

6. See, for example, the memoir and biography of a famous communist daughter of a Congregational minister: Anna Louise Strong, *I Change Worlds: The Remaking of an American* (Seattle, 1979; first ed. 1935); Tracy B. Strong and Helene Keyssar, *Right in Her Soul: The Life of Anna Louise Strong* (New York, 1983).

7. For example, reproaching left-leaning fellow Quakers in 1922, Herbert Hoover declared: "I cannot conceive a greater negation of all that the Quakers stand for than a regime that carries on its banners, 'Religion is the opiate of the people.'" Patenaude, *The Big Show in Bololand*, 141.

8. "The Religious Melee in Russia," *The Literary Digest*, May 26, 1923, p. 32; "The Methodist Split on Russia's New Church," *The Literary Digest*, July 28, 1923, p. 30; Theodore Dreiser, *Dreiser Looks at Russia* (New York, 1928), 11, 172–86; Richard Lingeman, *Theodore Dreiser: An American Journey* (New York, 1993), esp. 432–49; Peter G. Filene, *Americans and the Soviet Experiment, 1917–1933* (Cambridge, MA, 1967), 198; Warren, *Liberals and Communism*, 66.

9. G. Herbert Schmidt, "Bolshevism Battling Christianity," *Pentecostal Evangel*, July 21, 1934, p. 7. For similar warnings, see "The Hidden Anti-christ," *Pentecostal Evangel*, March 8, 1930, p. 9; and "Imprisoned for Preaching Christ in Russia," *Pentecostal Evangel*, August 8, 1931, p. 2; "What is Bolshevism?" *Pentecostal Evangel*, February 15, 1936, p. 2.

10. For example: Albert Rhys Williams, *The Soviets* (New York, 1937), 328–9.

11. "The Religious Melee in Russia," *The Literary Digest*, May 26, 1923, p. 33; John Haynes Holmes, *I Speak for Myself: The Autobiography of John Haynes Holmes* (New York, 1959), 124–8; Filene, *Americans and the Soviet Experiment*, 87, 248; Lewis S. Feuer, "American Travelers to the Soviet Union, 1917–32: The Formation of a Component of New Deal Ideology," *American Quarterly*, Vol. 14 (Summer 1962), 130–3; Kate A. Baldwin, *Beyond the Color Line and the Iron Curtain: Reading Encounters Between Black and Red, 1922–1963* (Durham, NC, 2002); Claude McKay, "Soviet Russia and the Negro," *Crisis*, Vol. 27 (Dec. 1923–Jan. 1924), reprinted in Wayne F. Cooper, ed., *The Passion of Claude McKay* (New York, 1973), 95–106; Dorothy Thompson, *The New Russia* (New York, 1928), 164, 161; Reinhold Niebuhr, "The Land of Extremes," *Christian Century*, October 15, 1930, p. 1242; Floyd

Dell, "The Russian Idea," *Liberator*, Vol. V (January 1922), 26–7, reprinted in Peter G. Filene, ed., *American Views of Soviet Russia, 1917–1965* (Homewood, IL, 1968), 51.

12. Cf. Paul Hollander, *Political Pilgrims: Travels of Western Intellectuals to the Soviet Union, China, and Cuba, 1928–1978* (New York, 1981), Chapter 4.

13. Benjamin M. Weissman, *Herbert Hoover and Famine Relief to Soviet Russia: 1921–1923* (Stanford, 1974), 1–12.

14. McFadden and Gorfinkel, *Constructive Spirit*; Patenaude, *The Big Show in Bololand*, preface, 398.

15. Weissman, *Herbert Hoover and Famine Relief to Soviet Russia*, 15 (Spargo quote), 44, 49, 59, 197, 200; Patenaude, *The Big Show in Bololand*, 42–3; Markku Ruotsila, *John Spargo and American Socialism* (New York, 2006), Chapter 7.

16. Patenaude, *The Big Show in Bololand*, 42, 46, 84, 103–4, 72.

17. Patenaude, *The Big Show in Bololand*, 522, 532, 629, 600–4, 598, 701–9. For varying views on attitudes toward America in early Soviet Russia, see Frederick C. Barghoorn, *The Soviet Image of the United States: A Study in Distortion* (1950); Hans Rogger, "*Amerikanizm* and the Economic Development of Russia," *Comparative Studies in Society and History*, Vol. 23, No. 3 (July 1981), 382–420; Jeffrey Brooks, "Official Xenophobia and Popular Cosmopolitanism in Early Soviet Russia," *American Historical Review*, Vol. 97, No. 5 (December 1992), 1431–1448; Abbott Gleason, "Republic of Humbug: The Russian Nativist Critique of the United States, 1830–1930," *American Quarterly*, Vol. 44 (March 1992), 1–23; Alan M. Ball, *Imagining America: Influence and Images in Twentieth-Century Russia* (Lanham, MD, 2003).

18. Patenaude, *The Big Show in Bololand*, 534–9, 64, 563, 590–1, 594.

19. Weissman, *Herbert Hoover and Famine Relief to Soviet Russia*, 96; Patenaude, *The Big Show in Bololand*, 504–6, 139.

20. Daniel Peris, *Storming the Heavens: The Soviet League of the Militant Godless* (Ithaca, 1998), esp. 25–8; William B. Husband, *"Godless Communists": Atheism and Society in Soviet Russia, 1917–1932* (DeKalb. IL, 2000).

21. Oswald Garrison Villard, "Russia from a Car Window: V. The Soviets and the Human Being," *The Nation*, Vol. CXXIX (December 4, 1929), 654–7, reprinted in Peter G. Filene, ed., *American Views of Soviet Russia, 1917–1965* (Homewood, IL, 1968), 63–4; Oswald Garrison Villard, *Fighting Years: Memoirs of a Liberal Editor* (New York, 1939), 32; Michael Wreszin, *Oswald Garrison Villard: Pacifist at War* (Boomington, 1965), 23–4; John Ray Ewers, "Russia's New Religion," *Christian Century*, October 1, 1930, p. 1196. See also Paul Merkley, *Reinhold Niebuhr: A Political Account* (Montreal, 1975), 90.

22. Sherwood Eddy, *Russia: A Warning and a Challenge* (New York, 1923), 37–8; Eddy, *The Challenge of Russia* (New York, 1931), 156–7, 172; Julius F. Hecker, *Religion Under the Soviets* (New York, 1927), 8, 25, 30, 195; G. Herbert Schmidt, "Bolshevism Battling Against Christianity," *Pentecostal Evangel*, July 21, 1934, p. 6; "The Work in Soviet Russia," *Pentecostal Evangel*, April 7, 1928, p. 8. See also the statement of George S. Counts in *The Literary*

*Digest*, March 8, 1930, p. 19; the statement of the Conference of Younger Churchmen in *The Literary Digest*, March 29, 1930, p. 23; and Albert Rhys Williams, *The Soviets* (New York, 1937), 322–5.

23. Heather J. Coleman, *Russian Baptists and Spiritual Revolution, 1905–1929* (Bloomington, 2005), 177, 160, 156. For reports on how Adventists benefited from Soviet policies, particularly the separation of church from state and school from church, see H. J. Lobsack, "Through Revolution and Famine in Russia," *The Advent Review and Sabbath Herald*, Vol. 99, No. 28, June 15, 1922, pp. 3–7, and E. Kotz, "Good News From Soviet Russia," *The Advent Review and Sabbath Herald*, Vol. 103, No. 56, November 18, 1926, p. 10.

24. Gustave H. Schmidt, "Revival in Russia," *Pentecostal Evangel*, January 15, 1927, p. 11; J. E. Voronaeff, et al, "Report of Assemblies in Russia," *Pentecostal Evangel*, September 8, 1928, pp. 10–11; *Statistical Report of the European Division of the General Conference of Seventh-Day Adventists* (Skodsborg, Denmark, 1920), p. 11; *Seventh-Day Adventist Encyclopedia* (Washington, DC, 1976), p. 1520; Coleman, *Russian Baptists and Spiritual Revolution*, 162–3, 224. One article, "Things as They Are in Soviet Russia," *Pentecostal Evangel*, January 21, 1933, reported an estimate of 75,000 Pentecostal "saints" in Russia. However, the last definite figures showed a membership of 25,000 in July 1929. Paul Peterson to S. H. Frodsham, March 1, 1939, Peterson correspondence, Flower Pentecostal Heritage Center Archives.

25. Voronaeff, et al, "Report of Assemblies in Russia," *Pentecostal Evangel*, September 8, 1928, p. 10; Gustave H. Schmidt, "Judgments of God and Revival Fires in Poland," *Pentecostal Evangel*, March 19, 1927.

26. John L. Nuelsen, "Report on Russia," submitted to the Executive Committee of the Board of Foreign Missions of the Methodist Episcopal Church, September 7, 1923, II:7, and Julius Hecker to Frank Mason North, September 9, 1922 and March 26, 1924, Julius F. Hecker Papers, Missionary Files, United Methodist Church Archives, Madison, New Jersey; Julius F. Hecker, *Russian Sociology: A Contribution to the History of Sociological Thought and Theory* (New York, 1915); Biographical Note in Julius F. Hecker, *Religion Under the Soviets* (New York, 1927), vi; S. T. Kimbrough, "The Living Church Conflict in the Russian Orthodox Church and the Involvement of the Methodist Episcopal Church," *Methodist History*, 40:2 (January 2002), 111. The most valuable source on Hecker's early life is an unpublished biography by his daughter: "Iulii Fyodorovich Gekker (1881 g.–1938 g. (Vesna))." Hecker Family Papers, Kliazma.

27. Doug Rossinow, "The Radicalization of the Social Gospel: Harry F. Ward and the Search for a New Social Order, 1898–1936," *Religion and American Culture*, Vol. 15, No. 1 (2005), 69–70; Nuelsen to North, October 1, 1917 and February 5, 1918, Nuelsen Files, Administrative Files, United Methodist Church Archives, Madison, New Jersey; John L. Nuelsen, "Report on Russia," September 7, 1923, II:8, Hecker Files.

28. Hecker to North, Feb. 6, 1922; Elizabeth J. Hecker to Mr. Bek, June 30, 1922; Julius Hecker to Nuelsen, Nov. 24, 1923, Hecker Files. Lunacharskii certified his approval of Hecker's proposal for the creation of children's homes in a statement on January 12, 1922. Hecker Papers, Kliazma.

29. Eddy, *Russia: A Warning and a Challenge*, 40; Sherwood Eddy, *Eighty Adventurous Years: An Autobiography* (New York, 1955), 138–40; Rossinow, "The Radicalization of the Social Gospel," 79–80; Hecker to North, Feb. 6, 1922; Elizabeth J. Hecker to Mr. Bek, June 30, 1922; Hecker to North, September 24, 1923, Hecker Files.

30. Nuelsen, "Report on Russia," September 7, 1923, II:9–10, Hecker Files; Sheila Fitzpatrick, *The Commissariat of Enlightenment: Soviet Organization of Education and the Arts Under Lunacharsky, October 1917–1921* (Oxford, 1970), xv, 29.

31. Hecker to Nuelsen, January 8, 1923, Hecker Files; Hecker to North, March 24, 1923; Nuelsen, "Report on Russia," September 7, 1923, II:10. On "the Living Church," see Edward E. Roslof, *Red Priests: Renovationism, Russian Orthodoxy, and Revolution, 1905–1946* (Bloomington, 2002).

32. Nuelsen, "Report on Russia," September 7, 1923, II:5–6; III: 4; "All Faiths United by the Red Assault on Religion," *The Literary Digest*, April 21, 1923, p. 35; "The Religious Melee in Russia," *The Literary Digest*, May 26, 1923, pp. 32–3; "The Methodist Split on Russia's New Church," *The Literary Digest*, July 28, 1923, pp. 30–1.

33. Bishop Edgar Blake, "A Plain Statement," n.d., and Zion's Herald Russia Fund appeal, November 1, 1923, Nuelsen Files.

34. Kimbrough, "The Living Church Conflict in the Russian Orthodox Church and the Involvement of the Methodist Episcopal Church," 117; North to Hecker, February 6 and March 5, 1924, Hecker Files; copies of Hecker letters to Nuelsen, n.d., c. 1928, and May 7, 1928, Hecker Files.

35. Husband, *"Godless Communists"*, xv, 50, 63, 85, 146–7, 160; Coleman, *Russian Baptists and Spiritual Revolution*, 157, 200; Eddy, *The Challenge of Russia*, 163; Julius F. Hecker, *Religion and Communism: A Study of Religion and Atheism in Soviet Russia* (London, 1933), 73; William H. Chamberlin, *Soviet Russia* (Boston, 1930), 307–318; Paul Peterson, "A Desperate Situation in Russia," *Pentecostal Evangel*, March 8, 1930, p. 9; Paul B. Peterson to Noel Perkin, June 13, 1929, Peterson correspondence, Flower Pentecostal Heritage Center Archives; Arthur W. Frodsham, "Russia's Defiance of God," *Pentecostal Evangel*, March 15, 1930, p. 6.

36. "Bolshevism's 'Public Challenge to God,'" *The Literary Digest*, April 14, 1923, 7–9; "All Faiths United By the Red Assault on Religion," *The Literary Digest*, April 21, 1923, 33–5; "The Mighty Chorus Against Russia's War on God," *The Literary Digest*, March 8, 1930, pp. 18–9; Villard, "Russia from a Car Window."

37. John Ray Ewers, "Russia's New Religion," *Christian Century*, October 1, 1930, p. 1196; Hecker to John Nevin Sayre, February 26, 1930, Hecker Files; Hecker, *Religion Under the Soviets* (New York, 1927), xv, 190; Hecker, *Religion and Communism* (London, 1933), 273; Hecker to Ralph Dieffendorf, April 15, 1935 (mentioning 1934 trip), Hecker Files; Robert H. Craig, *Religion and Radical Politics: An Alternative Christian Tradition in the United States* (Philadelphia, 1992), 196–7; Eddy, *The Challenge of Russia*, 157n; Harry F. Ward, *In Place of Profit: Social Incentives in the Soviet Union* (New York, 1933), x, 438–458; David Nelson Duke, *In the Trenches with Jesus and Marx: Harry F.*

*Ward and the Struggle for Social Justice* (Tuscaloosa, 2003), 148, 190–1. Max Eastman, radical son of two Congregational ministers, applauded the Bolshevik campaign against religion in the early 1930s. See William L. O'Neill, *The Last Romantic: A Life of Max Eastman* (New York, 1978), 148.

38. "The Hidden Anti-christ," *Pentecostal Evangel*, March 8, 1930, p. 9; Blanche Koon, "Soviet Russia's Attack Upon God," *Pentecostal Evangel*, October 4, 1930, p. 6; J. Edwin Orr, "The Shadow of the Kremlin," *Pentecostal Evangel*, December 7, 1935, p. 6; Thomas M. Chalmers, "Russia and Armageddon," *Pentecostal Evangel*, April 14, 1934, p. 1.

39. On the varied experiences of American technicians, see (in addition to the sources cited below): William Henry Chamberlin, "Missionaries of American Technique in Russia," *Asia*, Vol. 32 (July–August 1932), 422–7, 460; John Scott, *Behind the Urals: An American Worker in Russia's City of Steel* (Bloomington, 1973; first ed., 1942); Stephen Kotkin, *Magnetic Mountain: Stalinism as a Civilization* (Berkeley, 1995), esp. 42–50, 438n; Norman E. Saul, *Friends or Foes? The United States and Russia, 1921–1941* (Lawrence, KS, 2006), Chapter 5.

40. Antony C. Sutton, *Western Technology and Soviet Economic Development, 1917 to 1930* (Stanford, 1968), 48–50, 126–32. Settlements of Soviet Jews in Crimea, supported by the American Jewish Joint Distribution Committee, were more successful. See Jonathan Dekel-Chen, "Philanthropists, Commissars, and American Statesmanship Meet in Soviet Crimea, 1922–37," *Diplomatic History*, Vol. 27, No. 3 (June 2003), 353–76; Dekel-Chen, *Farming the Red Land: Jewish Agricultural Colonization and Local Soviet Power, 1924–1941* (New Haven, 2005).

41. Ruth Epperson Kennell, "Kuzbas: A New Pennsylvania," *The Nation*, Vol. CXVI, No. 3017 (May 2, 1923), 511–2; "The American [sic] at Kuzbas, 1922–24" and Nemmy Sparks, "Lenin and the Americans at Kuzbas," *New World Review*, Vol. 39, No. 4 (1971), 68–86; J. P. Morray, *Project Kuzbas: American Workers in Siberia (1921–1926)* (New York, 1983), quoted at 125.

42. Anne D. Rassweiler, *The Generation of Power: The History of Dneprostroi* (New York, 1988), 61–3; Hugh L. Cooper, "Soviet Russia," Address at Williamstown, Massachusetts, August 1, 1930 (New York, 1930), 1, 2, 3, 5, 6, 8, 9. Cooper again praised the Soviet "uplifting" of living conditions, though with less spiritual language, in an address to the Society of American Military Engineers in Philadelphia, February 25, 1931, published in "Russia," *Engineers and Engineering*, Vol. XLVIII, No. 4 (April 1931), 76–86. On the legendary status of Cooper in the Soviet Union, see, for example, N. S. Khrushchev's mention of him to President Kennedy on June 3, 1961: *Foreign Relations of the United States, 1961–1963, Vol. V, Soviet Union*, Document 84.

43. Cooper, "Russia," *Engineers and Engineering*, Vol. XLVIII, No. 4 (April 1931), 79, 81, 82; Sutton, *Western Technology and Soviet Economic Development*, 48n, 168, 307. See also Strong and Keyssar, *Right in Her Soul*, 94.

44. Michael Gelb, ed., *An American Engineer in Stalin's Russia: The Memoirs of Zara Witkin, 1932–1934* (Berkeley, 1991), 26, 34,

45. *The Memoirs of Zara Witkin*, 53–4, 59, 64, 69, 75, 96, 56, 78, 88–9, 82, 73–5, 292, 77, 83.

46. *The Memoirs of Zara Witkin*, 272, 295, 266, 314–6 (letter from Witkin to Romain Rolland, April 2, 1935).
47. Eugene Lyons, *Assignment in Utopia* (New York, 1937), 618, 529–30.
48. Foster Rhea Dulles, *The Road to Teheran: The Story of Russia and America, 1781–1943* (Princeton, 1944), 174; Dexter Perkins, *Charles Evans Hughes and American Democratic Statesmanship* (Boston, 1956), 126–8; Robert H. Ferrell, ed., *The American Secretaries of State and their Diplomacy*, Vol. XI: *Frank B. Kellogg and Henry L. Stimson* (New York, 1963), 83, 176, 262; Bailey, *America Faces Russia*, 251–2.
49. Orville H. Bullitt, ed., *For the President Personal and Secret: Correspondence Between Franklin D. Roosevelt and William C. Bullitt* (Boston, 1972), 46–8; Beatrice Farnsworth, *William C. Bullitt and the Soviet Union* (Bloomington, 1967), 92–9; John Richman, *The United States and the Soviet Union: The Decision to Recognize* (Raleigh, NC, 1980), 133–161; Michael Cassella-Blackburn, *The Donkey, the Carrot, and the Club: William C. Bullitt and Soviet-American Relations, 1917–1948* (Westport, CT, 2004), 97–102.
50. Richman, *The United States and the Soviet Union*, 155–6, quoting Joseph F. Thorning, "What Russian Recognition Means," *America*, December 2, 1933, p. 200.
51. Bullitt, ed., *For the President Personal and Secret*, 58, 154; Cassella-Blackburn, *The Donkey, the Carrot, and the Club*, 190–2.
52. Bullitt to Roosevelt, January 1, 1934, in Bullitt, ed., *For the President Personal and Secret*, 65; Richman, *The United States and the Soviet Union*, 178; Farnsworth, *William C. Bullitt and the Soviet Union*, 131; Charles E. Bohlen, *Witness to History 1929–1969* (New York, 1973), 20–4.
53. "Fair Day, Adieu!" (unpublished account written in 1938), Box 25, George F. Kennan Papers, Mudd Library, Princeton; Bohlen, *Witness to History*, 29.
54. "Fair Day, Adieu!"; "Some Fundamentals of Russian-American Relations," c. 1938, Box 16; "Russia" (lecture to Foreign Service School, May 20, 1938), Box 16, Kennan Papers, Princeton; Kennan, *Memoirs: 1925–1950* (Boston, 1967), 73–4.
55. Bullitt to FDR, May 20, 1938, in Bullitt, ed., *For the President Personal and Secret*, 263; Kennan, "Russia," May 20, 1938, Box 16, Kennan Papers, Princeton.
56. Joseph E. Davies, *Mission to Moscow* (New York, 1941), xviii, xvi; Elizabeth Kimball MacLean, *Joseph E. Davies: Envoy to the Soviets* (Westport, CT, 1992), 7, 29, 76; Joseph Davies to David Lawrence, Box 29, Lawrence Papers, Mudd Library, Princeton.
57. Williams, *The Soviets*, 334, 325–6.
58. G. N. Sevostianov and J. Haslam, ed., *Sovetsko-Amerikanskie Otnosheniia: Gody Nepriznaniia 1918–1926* (Moscow, 2002), 492–3, 497; I. M. Maisky to F. A. Rotshtein, 14 January 1927, G. N. Sevostianov and J. Haslam, eds., *Sovetsko-Amerikanskie Otnosheniia: Gody Nepriznaniia 1927–1933* (Moscow, 2002), 8–9; Sherwood Eddy, "Russia – Good and Evil," *Christian Century*, September 18, 1935, 1171–2; Eddy, *The Challenge of Russia*, 260, 269–270; Eddy, *Russia Today: What Can We Learn From It?* (New York, 1934); Eddy,

*Europe Today* (New York, 1937), 2, 24–7, 48; Nutt, *The Whole Gospel for the Whole World*, 268.

59. Baldwin, *Beyond the Color Line and the Iron Curtain*, 47, 53, 56, 65–6, 272n44; Duke, *In the Trenches with Jesus and Marx*, 271n33; Alan Cullison, "The Lost Victims," Associated Press report, Nov. 3, 1997.

60. Richard Wightman Fox, *Reinhold Niebuhr: A Biography* (Ithaca, 1996), 170, 190; Les K. Adler and Thomas G. Paterson, "Red Fascism: The Merger of Nazi Germany and Soviet Russia in the American Image of Totalitarianism, 1930s–1950s," *American Historical Review*, Vol. 70 (April 1970), 1046–64; Thomas R. Maddux, "Red Fascism, Brown Bolshevism: The American Image of Totalitarianism in the 1930s," *Historian*, Vol. 40 (November 1977), 85–103; Abbott Gleason, *Totalitarianism: The Inner History of the Cold War* (New York: Oxford University Press, 1995), 38–48; Benjamin L. Alpers, *Dictators, Democracy, and American Public Culture: Envisioning the Totalitarian Enemy, 1920s–1950s* (Chapel Hill, 2003); Oswald Garrison Villard, "Issues and Men," *The Nation*, November 4, 1939, p. 499.

61. Martin Dies, "Insidious Wiles of Foreign Influence," November 29, 1939, *Vital Speeches of the Day*, Vol. 6, No. 5, pp. 152–5; Dorothy Thompson, *Christian Ethics and Western Civilization* (New York, 1940), 5–23; Peter Kurth, *American Cassandra: The Life of Dorothy Thompson* (Boston, 1990).

62. Franklin D. Roosevelt, Address to the American Youth Congress, February 11, 1940, *Vital Speeches of the Day*, Vol. 6, No. 10, pp. 294–7.

63. Paul B. Peterson, "Russia," *Pentecostal Evangel*, November 26, 1927, p. 8; McCormick column of August 16, 1931, in Marion Turner Sheehan, ed., *The World at Home: Selections from the Writings of Anne O'Hare McCormick* (1956; reprint, Freeport, NY, 1970), 79; Eddy, *The Challenge of Russia*, 3.

64. Eddy, *The Challenge of Russia*, 9–10; 254; Ward, *In Place of Profit*, 438–58.

65. "A Russian Mirror for Us," *The Literary Digest*, Nov. 14, 1931, p. 21.

66. "Russia Rediscovers Family Life's Value," *The Literary Digest*, Vol. 120, July 13, 1935, p. 20; N. J. Poysti, "What is Bolshevism?" *Pentecostal Evangel*, March 28, 1936, pp. 8, 9, 11.

67. Charles Brackett, Billy Wilder, and Walter Reisch, screenplay of *Ninotchka* (New York, 1972); "The New Pictures," *Time*, November 6, 1939, pp. 76–7; Alpers, *Dictators, Democracy, and American Public Culture*, 133; "Comrade X" (1940), screenplay by Ben Hecht and Charles Lederer, original story by Walter Reisch.

NOTES TO CHAPTER 4

1. "Break-Through," *Time*, December 27, 1943, pp. 53–8.

2. Other *Time* articles on the "breathtaking" developments in Russian religion, included: "Baptists in Russia," June 15, 1942, p. 40; "Kyrie Eleison," September 13, 1943, p. 45; "Prayers for Stalin," May 8, 1944, p. 42; and "Russian Revival," August 28, 1944, p. 51.

3. Thomas A. Bailey, *America Faces Russia: Russian-American Relations From Early Times to Our Day* (Ithaca, 1950), 289–323; Melvin Small, "How We Learned to Love the Russians: American Media and the Soviet Union During World War II," *Historian*, Vol. 36, No. 3 (May 1974), 455–78; Ralph

B. Levering, *American Opinion and the Russian Alliance, 1939–1945* (Chapel Hill, 1976); William L. O'Neill, *A Better World. The Great Schism: Stalinism and the American Intellectuals* (New York, 1982); Jonathan Evers Boe, *American Business: The Response to the Soviet Union, 1933–1947* (New York, 1987); Eduard Mark, "October or Thermidor? Interpretations of Stalinism and the Perception of Soviet Foreign Policy in the United States, 1927–1947," *American Historical Review*, Vol. 94 (October 1989), 937–62; George Sirgiovanni, *An Undercurrent of Suspicion: Anti-Communism in America During World War II* (New Brunswick, NJ, 1990); Charles Alexander, "'Uncle Joe': Images of Stalin in the Period of the Highest Development of the Anti-Hitler Coalition" (in Russian), *Annual Studies of America/Amerikanskii Ezhegodnik 1989* (Moscow, 1990), 30–42; Frank Costigliola, "'Mixed Up' and 'Contact': Culture and Emotion among the Allies in the Second World War," *International History Review*, Vol. 20, No. 4 (December 1998), 791–805. Gerald Sittser noted the neglect of the role of religion in *A Cautious Patriotism: The American Churches and the Second World War* (Chapel Hill, 1997), ix.

4. Dennis J. Dunn, *Caught Between Roosevelt and Stalin: America's Ambassadors to Moscow* (Lexington, Kentucky, 1998).

5. Levering, *American Opinion and the Russian Alliance*, 141–5.

6. Boe, *American Business*, 216, 340; O'Neill, *A Better World*, 48–71.

7. Levering, *American Opinion and the Russian Alliance*, 156–8; Boe, *American Business*, 188–190, 222–6.

8. Warren Kimball, "This Persistent Evangel of Americanism," Chapter IX of *The Juggler: Franklin Roosevelt as Wartime Statesman* (Princeton, 1991).

9. See, for example, Clayton R. Koppes and Gregory D. Black, "Putting the Russians Through the Wringer," Chapter VII of *Hollywood Goes to War: How Politics, Profits and Propaganda Shaped World War II Movies* (Berkeley, 1990); Dunn, *Caught Between Roosevelt and Stalin*, esp. 5, 111, 129, 135, 138–9, 242, 263–70.

10. Military attachés quoted in Mary E. Glantz, *FDR and the Soviet Union: The President's Battles over Foreign Policy* (Lawrence, KS, 2005), 50–65; "Soviet Defeat is Sure, Say D. C. Army Men," *Washington Post*, June 22, 1941; Levering, *American Opinion and the Russian Alliance*, 46, 56.

11. Sherwood Eddy in *Christianity and Crisis*, July 28, 1941, p. 4; *Commonweal*, August 8, July 25, July 18, August 15, and October 17, 1941, p. 611.

12. See, for example, *Catholic World* editorials "Russia as an Ally?" May 1941, p. 129 and "Covenant with Hell," August 1941, pp. 513–6; "No Alliance with Atheism" cover, January 1943; and articles in November 1941, 140–4; June 1942, 262–4; March 1944, 517; June 1944, 198; April 1946, 3.

13. "Mr. Welles' Realism" (editorial), *Washington Post*, June 24, 1941; "Sucker Bait" (cartoon), *Washington Post*, June 27, 1941. See also Raymond Buell, memo to Henry Luce, June 19, 1941, Box 19, Buell Papers, LC.

14. Welles' press conference statement, in Welles to Steinhardt, June 23, 1941, FRUS, 1941, I: 767.

15. Speeches by Senator Robert Taft, June 25, 1941; Rep. Frederick Smith, June 28, 1941; Rep. Fred Bradley, June 30, 1941; Rep. Hamilton Fish, August 5, 1941; Rep. John Anderson, August 5, 1941; Rep. Robert Jones, August 29, 1941; Rep. Stephen Day, August 1, 1941, and Sen. Pat McCarran,

September 4, 1941, *Congressional Record*, Vol. 87: A3077, 5669, A3207, 6775, A3768, A4181, A3709–10, and 7305.

16. Monsignor Michael J. Ready to Welles, 23 August 1941, and Welles to Roosevelt, August 25, 1941, Box 6, Myron C. Taylor Papers, LC.

17. FRUS, 1941, I: 832, 999n.

18. FRUS, 1941, I: 832, 999–1000n; notes of Harriman conversation with Stalin, September 28, 1941, memorandum of Harriman discussion with A. I. Mikoyan, October 3, 1941, and statement to the foreign press by S. A. Lozovsky, October 4, 1941, all in Box 160, Harriman Papers, LC. See also W. Averell Harriman and Elie Abel, *Special Envoy to Churchill and Stalin, 1941–1946* (New York, 1975), 88, 98. For broader discussions of the role of religion in the selling of the Grand Alliance, see Steven Merritt Miner, *Stalin's Holy War: Religion, Nationalism, and Alliance Politics, 1941–1945* (Chapel Hill, NC, 2003), esp. 216–28; and Dianne Kirby, "Anglican-Orthodox Relations and the Religious Rehabilitation of the Soviet Regime During the Second World War," *Revue d'Histoire Ecclésiastique*, Vol. 96 (2001), 101–22.

19. Rep. Martin Dies to FDR, October 1, 1941, *Congressional Record*, Vol. 87: A4507–8; Father Edmund Walsh and Methodist Bishop Raymond Wade quoted in "God & Lend-Lease," *Time*, October 13, 1941, p. 46; Statement issued by the National Conference of Christians and Jews, reproduced in "Comment," *America*, October 11, 1941, pp. 2–4.

20. *Washington Post*, October 2, 1941; cartoon in *Washington Post*, October 11, 1941. See also Walter Lippmann, "Today and Tomorrow: Russia, America, and Mr. Roosevelt," *Los Angeles Times*, October 7, 1941.

21. "Joe as a Christian Gentleman," *Chicago Tribune*, October 4, 1941. See also "Mr. Roosevelt on Constitutions," October 5, 1941.

22. Harriman and Elie Abel, *Special Envoy*, 104. According to a handwritten note on R. P. Meiklejohn's "Report on Special Mission to the USSR," Box 165, Harriman Papers, "Pres. F.D.R. was not satisfied with Lozovski's statement."

23. "U.S. Raises Question of Religious Freedom in Russia," AP dispatch in *Seattle Post-Intelligencer*, October 4, 1941; "No Freedom in Russia," *America*, October 11, 1941, p. 14; Msgr. Fulton J. Sheen, "Soviet Russia May Be Helped But Russia Must Be Reformed," *America*, October 18, 1941, p. 35.

24. "Are the Four Freedoms a Delusion?" *The Christian Century*, October 15, 1941, p. 1262.

25. "Soviet Russia and Religion: Is War Forcing Policy Change?" *Christian Science Monitor*, October 3, 1941.

26. "Religion in Russia: Red Godlessness Fails to Empty Churches," *Life*, Vol. 11, No. 15, October 13, 1941, 110–21.

27. James L. Baughman, *Henry R. Luce and the Rise of the American News Media* (Boston, 1987), esp. 143–6; Robert E. Herzstein, *Henry R. Luce: A Political Portrait of the Man Who Created the American Century* (New York, 1994), esp. 274–5; Telegrams from Luce to Laurence Steinhardt, October 23? and 26?, 1941, Box 33, Steinhardt Papers, Library of Congress; Luce memo to Policy Committee, November 3, 1943, Box 17, Buell Papers, LC; "The Christianity of the Missionary," September 10, 1946 speech, Box 72, Luce Papers, LC.

28. See, for example, John Lewis Gaddis, *Russia, The Soviet Union, and the United States* (Second edition, New York, 1990), 147, and Lloyd Gardner, *Spheres of Influence: The Great Powers Partition Europe, from Munich to Yalta* (Chicago, 1993), 154.

29. Miner, *Stalin's Holy War*, is contradictory on this issue: compare p. 225 and p. 372n60.

30. Harriman and Abel, *Special Envoy*, 103. In 1943 Hull told Molotov that the question of religion in the Soviet Union continued to be raised by agitators in the United States and was thus one of the difficulties in the way of closer relations. Memorandum of conversation in Moscow, October 23, 1943, Box 175, Harriman Papers, LC. In 1944, FDR's representative to the Pope, Myron Taylor, worked with the Soviet ambassador to London to draft a statement by Stalin proclaiming complete religious freedom. Taylor to Roosevelt, July 17, 1944, FRUS, 1944, IV: 1218. In February 1945 FDR persuaded his friend Edward Flynn to visit Moscow in order to emphasize the importance of the religious issue and to explore the possibility of a rapprochement between the Kremlin and the Vatican. Memorandum of conversation between Flynn and Molotov, February 28, 1945, Box 177, Harriman Papers, LC.

31. Roosevelt to Bullitt, January 7, 1934, in Orville H. Bullitt, ed., *For the President: Personal & Secret. Correspondence Between Franklin D. Roosevelt and William C. Bullitt* (Boston, 1972), 73–4. Divergent views of the depth of FDR's religious beliefs are presented in James MacGregor Burns, *Roosevelt: The Lion and the Fox* (New York, 1956), esp. 237; Geoffrey Ward, *A First-Class Temperament: The Emergence of Franklin Roosevelt* (New York, 1989), 53, 98, 416–7, 587; and Kenneth S. Davis, *FDR: The War President 1940–1943* (New York, 2000), esp. 122, 212.

32. "Informal Memorandum of Myron Taylor for Discussion with His Holiness Pope Pius . . .," September 1942, Box 6, Taylor Papers, LC.

33. Speeches by Sen. Thomas of Utah, November 19, 1942; Rep. Sabath of Illinois, February 8, 1943; Rep. John Rankin of Mississippi, October 4, 1943; Secretary of the Interior Harold Ickes, November 8, 1943, and Rep. John Coffee of Washington, November 14, 1943, *Congressional Record*, 88: A4062; 89: A514, A4108, A4860, A5169.

34. George P. Fedotov, "The Prospects of Christianity in Russia," *Christianity and Crisis*, April 6, 1942, pp. 3–6. For another expression of wishful thinking, see Joseph L. Hromadka, "The Soviet Enigma," *Christianity and Crisis*, January 24, 1944, pp. 2–5.

35. "Religion in Russia," *Christian Science Monitor*, September 7, 1943. Similar optimism about far-reaching evangelization was expressed in "Greater Opportunity for the Russian Church," *Commonweal*, January 7, 1944, p. 292.

36. "Restoration of the Russian Church," *The Christian Century*, September 29, 1943; "A Vatican-Moscow Rapprochement?" *The Christian Century*, August 2, 1944.

37. *Catholic World*, Jan. 1943, p. 393. See also quotation of S. Bolshakoff, June 1942, p. 263.

38. Max Eastman, "To Collaborate Successfully We Must Face the Facts About Russia," *Reader's Digest*, July 1943, inserted by Sen. Gerald Nye in

*Congressional Record*, Vol. 89: A3439; W. H. Chamberlin, "No," in "Can Stalin's Russia Go Democratic?" *American Mercury*, Vol. VIIII, No. 242 (February, 1944), 143; C. L. Sulzberger, "Russia Lets Down Old Barriers," *New York Times Magazine*, November 14, 1943, and "What Russia Is – What Russia Wants," *New York Times Magazine*, January 28, 1945; "Russian Orthodoxy's Offensive," *Newsweek*, December 27, 1943, p. 70. Two other journalists' assessments were more guarded; see Wallace Carroll, *We're In This With Russia* (Boston, 1942), 143–52, and Walter Graebner, *Round Trip to Russia* (1943), 99–104.

39. Durbrow memorandum of October 29, 1943, *Foreign Relations of the United States* [FRUS], 1943, Vol. III (Washington, DC, 1963), 861n; Bohlen memos of May 24 and July 5, 1944, FRUS, 1944, Vol. IV (Washington, DC, 1966), 1214 and 1216; T. Michael Ruddy, *The Cautious Diplomat: Charles E. Bohlen and the Soviet Union, 1929–1969* (Kent, Ohio, 1986), 25; Kennan dispatches of February 3 and 8, 1945, FRUS, 1945, Vol. V (Washington, DC, 1967), 1114–6 and 1119–20. For discussion of the Soviet regime's ulterior motives, see Miner, *Stalin's Holy War*, and Anna Dickinson, "Domestic and Foreign Policy Considerations and the Origins of Post-war Soviet Church-State Relations, 1941–6," in Dianne Kirby, ed., *Religion and the Cold War* (Basingstoke, England, 2003), 23–36.

40. Harriman, "Religion in the USSR," October 4, 1941, Box 160, Harriman Papers; *Special Envoy*, 103.

41. Braun to Myron Taylor, October 5, 1941, Box 6, Taylor Papers, LC; William H. Standley and Arthur A. Ageton, *Admiral Ambassador to Russia* (Chicago, 1955), 183.

42. Loy Henderson dispatch, November 9, 1942, FRUS, 1942, Vol. III (Washington, DC, 1961), 476–7; Kennan dispatch of February 8, 1945, FRUS, 1945, Vol. V, 1119.

43. Kennan to Taylor, October 2, 1942, Box 160, Harriman Papers, LC.

44. "Russia – Seven Years Later," September 1944, reproduced in Kennan, *Memoirs, 1925–1950* (Boston, 1967), 510–511.

45. "Russia's International Position at the Close of the War with Germany," May 1945, reproduced in Kennan, *Memoirs, 1925–1950*, 541–2.

46. Kennan to Secretary of State, February 8, 1945, FRUS, 1945, V: 1118; Kennan to S. Pinkney Tuck (US Ambassador in Cairo), July 14, 1945, Box 181, Harriman Papers, LC.

47. Kennan, *Memoirs*, 5–16. Among the many biographies of Kennan, the most insightful are Walter Hixson, *George F. Kennan: Cold War Iconoclast* (New York, 1989) and Anders Stephanson, *Kennan and the Art of Foreign Policy* (Cambridge, MA, 1989). Neither study analyzed Kennan's views of the role of religion in the Soviet Union during World War II.

48. Graebner, *Round Trip to Russia*, 100–1; W. L. White, *Report on the Russians* (New York, 1945), 96; Wassilij Alexeev and Theofanis G. Stavrou, *The Great Revival: The Russian Church Under German Occupation* (Minneapolis, 1976); Nathaniel Davis, *A Long Walk to Church: A Contemporary History of Russian Christianity* (Boulder, 1995), 16–25; Elena Zubkova, *Russia After the War: Hopes, Illusions, and Disappointments, 1945–1957* (Armonk, NY, 1998)

68–73; Daniel Peris, "'God is Now on Our Side': The Religious Revival on Unoccupied Soviet Territory during World War II," *Kritika*, Vol. 1, No. 1 (Winter 2000), 97–118; Tatiana A. Chumachenko, *Church and State in Soviet Russia: Russian Orthodoxy from World War II to the Khrushchev Years* (Armonk, NY 2002). For a different view of a region in Ukraine, see Amir Weiner, *Making Sense of War: The Second World War and the Fate of the Bolshevik Revolution* (Princeton, 2001), 309–13.

49. Peris, "'God is Now on Our Side,'" 105–7; 116–8.

50. Karl E. Mundt, "Can We Get Along with Russia?" April 8, 1946 address printed in *Vital Speeches of the Day*, Vol. XII (June 15, 1946), 518. Mundt called this only a "dim hope."

51. *Time*, August 30, 1943, p. 26.

52. R. L. Buell memo to Luce et al, reporting on a talk with Rickenbacker, October 8, 1943, Box 23, Buell Papers, LC. For the similar views of Loy Henderson and George Kennan, see Buell memo to Luce, July 3, 1941, Box 19, Buell Papers, and Kennan, "Russia – Seven Years Later," in *Memoirs 1925–1950*, 516.

53. O'Neill, *A Better World*, 60, 48, 50, 61, 69–71. A good example is Harry F. Ward, *The Soviet Spirit* (New York, 1944).

54. Speech by Rep. Sabath, August 5, 1941, *Congressional Record*, Vol. 87: 6772–3.

55. Alexander Kerensky, "Russia is Ripe for Freedom," *American Mercury*, Vol. LVII, No. 236 (August 1943), 158–65.

56. Arthur Upham Pope, "Yes," in "Can Stalin's Russia Go Democratic?" *American Mercury*, Vol. LVIII, No. 242 (February, 1944), 135–42.

57. Norman Thomas letter to the editors, *The Nation*, January 31, 1942, p. 124.

58. William Henry Chamberlin, "No," in "Can Stalin's Russia Go Democratic?" *American Mercury*, Vol. LVIII, No. 242 (February, 1944), 142–8.

59. C. L. Sulzberger, "Report on Russia and the Russians," *New York Times Magazine*, March 29, 1942, p. 35. Others who doubted that Soviet Russia would become an American-style democracy included journalist Larry Lesueur, in *Twelve Months That Changed the World* (New York, 1943), 345, and Brooks Atkinson in "Democracy as Russia Defines It Today," *New York Times Magazine*, November 4, 1945, p. 14.

60. Lyons, "Cooperating with Russia," *American Mercury*, Vol. LVI, No. 233 (May, 1943), 538–9; "The Progress of Stalin Worship," *American Mercury*, Vol. LVI, No. 234 (June, 1943), 697; "The State of the Union," *American Mercury*, Vol. LVIII, No. 245 (May 1944), 571–3. For Max Eastman's similar criticism, see "To Collaborate Successfully We Must Face the Facts About Russia," *Reader's Digest*, July 1943, reprinted in *Congressional Record*, Vol. 89: A3439.

61. Speeches by Ickes, November 8, 1943, and by Rep. John Coffee, November 14, 1943, *Congressional Record*, Vol. 88: A4860, A5169; David Culbert, ed., *Mission to Moscow* (Madison, 1980), 73.

62. Davies comments on Article 135 of the Soviet Constitution in *Life*, March 29, 1943; Stenographic report of Davies address at an Episcopal church in Chicago, February 22, 1942, and Davies address at Indiana University,

May 10, 1942, Box 11, Davies Papers, LC. For further discussion, see Elizabeth Kimball MacLean, *Joseph E. Davies: Envoy to the Soviets* (Westport, CT, 1992), esp. 76. Davies devoted considerable attention to religious issues throughout the Grand Alliance. See, for example, his diary notes and statements for April 4, 1942 (Box 11), June 13, 1944 (Box 14), and September 29, 1944, (Box 15), Davies Papers, LC.

63. Davies to Samuel Rosenman, July 29, 1943, Box 13; "Tragedy and Irony of the Situation," Journal, Oct. 1944, Box 15; and Journal Entry, Dec. 31, 1944, Draft #1, Box 15, Davies Papers, LC.

64. Ohio State University Commencement Address by Luce, June 11, 1943, Box 71, Russell Davenport Papers, LC; Luce memo to managing editors, August 17, 1943, outlining "the Foreign Policy of Free Speech," Box 23, Buell Papers, LC; Bullitt, "The World From Rome," *Life*, September 4, 1944; Bullitt to FDR, January 29, 1943, in O. H. Bullitt,ed., *For the President*, 576–87; Dunn, *Caught Between Roosevelt and Stalin*.

65. *Fortune*, Vol. XXXI, No 1 (January 1945), 145–63, quoted at 145, 147, and 156.

66. Peter Filene, *Americans and the Soviet Experiment, 1917–1933* (Cambridge, MA, 1967), Chapter 8; Joan Hoff Wilson, *Ideology and Economics: US Relations with the Soviet Union, 1918–1933* (Columbia, MO, 1974).

67. Boe, *American Business*, 266–7; *Business Week*, April 15, 1944, reproduced in US Embassy news bulletin, April 22, 1944, Box 172, Harriman Papers, LC; Secretary of State Hull to Harriman, April 22, 1944, FRUS, 1944, IV: 1078–9. For further discussion of the hopes, inside and outside the Roosevelt administration, for a vast market in postwar Russia, see Lloyd C. Gardner, *Economic Aspects of New Deal Diplomacy* (Madison, 1964), 313–4, and Thomas G. Paterson, *Soviet-American Confrontation: Postwar Reconstruction and the Origins of the Cold War* (Baltimore, 1973), 57–8.

68. Davies speeches in Atlanta, May 4, 1942 and Denver, January 26, 1943, Box 11 and Box 12, Davies Papers, LC; *New York Times*, April 2, 1944; Boe, *American Business*, 222, 226.

69. See, for example, the April 27, 1942 memo by John Hazard of the Lend-Lease Administration to the Acting Chief of the Division of Exports and Defense Aid, FRUS,1942, Vol. III: 758–9; Admiral William Standley, "Russia in the Post-War World," *Vital Speeches of the Day*, Vol. 11, January 1, 1945, p. 177.

70. Rudy Abramson, *Spanning the Century: The Life of W. Averell Harriman, 1891–1986* (New York, 1992), 139–63; Harriman and Abel, *Special Envoy*, 49–51; Charles Maechling, Jr., to Yeong-Han Cheong, 12 April 1996, quoted in Yeong-Han Cheong, "No Ground to Stand On: The Diplomatic Biography of W. Averell Harriman," unpublished manuscript.

71. Undated, untitled address, c. October 21, 1941, Box 160, Harriman Papers, LC; Harriman and Abel, *Special Envoy*, 108.

72. Undated, untitled address, c. October 21, 1941, Box 160, Harriman Papers, LC.

73. At a press conference with American correspondents in Moscow on June 20, 1944, Harriman criticized Nelson, who had visited Moscow in October

1943, for the "mistake" of saying that the USSR was "going capitalistic." Box 173, Harriman Papers, LC.

74. Minutes of staff meeting at US Embassy in Moscow, November 9, 1943, Box 170, Harriman Papers, LC.

75. Harriman to State Department, January 9, 1944, and Notes of conversation between Harriman and Mikoyan, January 18, 1944, Box 171, Harriman Papers, LC.

76. Harriman to Secretary of State, January 6, 1945, Box 176, Harriman Papers, LC; Harriman and Abel, *Special Envoy*, 385–6.

77. Eric A. Johnston, "My Talk with Joseph Stalin," *Reader's Digest*, October 1944, pp. 1–10; Johnston obituary, Spokane *Spokesman-Review*, August 23, 1963; notes of conversation between Stalin and Johnston (with Molotov and Harriman also present), June 26, 1944, Box 173, Harriman Papers; Johnston, "A Business View of Russia," *Nation's Business*, October 1944, p. 21. Clippings of numerous editorials citing Johnston's lectures and articles can be found in the Johnston Papers, Eastern Washington State Historical Society, Spokane. For an unusually skeptical reaction see "Johnston's Red Rainbow," *Newsweek*, July 3, 1944, p. 45.

78. Johnston foreword to Hans Heymann, *We Can Do Business With Russia* (Chicago, 1945), viii–ix.

79. Johnston, *America Unlimited* (New York, 1944), 3, 13–6, 113–4, 228–9, 241–2.

80. Harriman remarks at a press conference in Moscow, June 27, 1944, Box 172, Harriman Papers; Eric Johnston notes from conversation with Harriman, n.d., c. June 1944, Box 3, Johnston Papers, Eastern Washington State Historical Society, Spokane.

81. Heymann, *We Can Do Business with Russia*, 119.

82. Kimball, *The Juggler*, esp. 191. After meeting with FDR in November 1944, Harriman recorded that "the President developed the fantastic idea that Stalin might agree to have the city of Lwow . . . governed by an international committee," and that Ukrainian "farmers could come in and sell their produce for rubles." When Harriman said "it was impossible to have a capitalist city in a socialist country" Roosevelt "became annoyed" that his ambassador was "unwilling to dream with him." "Memorandum of Conversations with the President During Trip to Washington, D.C., October 21 – November 19, 1944, Box 175, Harriman Papers, LC.

83. Hans Rogger, "*Amerikanizm* and the Economic Development of Russia," *Comparative Studies in Society and History*, Vol. 23, No. 3 (July 1981), 382–420; Kendall Bailes, "The American Connection: Ideology and the Transfer of American Technology to the Soviet Union, 1917–1941," *Comparative Studies in Society and History*, Vol. 23, No. 3 (July 1981), 421–48.

84. *Izvestiya* editorial, August 7, 1941, paraphrased in Steinhardt dispatch of August 7, 1941, FRUS, 1941, I: 637–8.

85. Memorandum of conversation between Stalin and Donald Nelson, October 16, 1943, FRUS, 1943, Vol. III: 713–4; memorandum of conversation between Harriman and Molotov, December 31, 1943, Box 171 Harriman Papers, LC.

86. "Russia – Seven Years Later," in Kennan, *Memoirs, 1925–1950*, 508, 510.

87. See Standley and Ageton, *Admiral Ambassador to Russia*, 186; "Russian Attitudes as Observed by an American Patient in a Moscow Hospital, March–April 1944," Box 172, Harriman Papers, LC.

88. Memorandum by Ambassador Standley, describing the reactions of Vyshinsky and Lozovsky to a statement by Wendell Willkie in September 1942, FRUS, 1942, III: 646.

89. For examples of Harriman's linkage proposals, see his cables to Washington on January 9, 1944, March 13, 1944, August 25, 1944 (draft not sent), and January 6, 1945, in Boxes 171, 173, and 176, Harriman Papers, LC. On the withholding of postwar aid, see Paterson, *Soviet-American Confrontation*.

90. Boe, *American Business*, 266–7, 215; Paterson, *Soviet-American Confrontation*, 62–5.

91. "Relations with Russia," 2/8/44, p. 158, Box 25, Buell Papers; Luce, "The American Century," reproduced in *Diplomatic History*, Vol. 23, No. 2 (Spring 1999), 159–71; Luce address on June 11, 1943, Box 71, Russell W. Davenport Papers, LC.

92. Standley to Secretary of State, March 31 and September 14, 1943, FRUS, 1943, III: 643–6; 691–4.

93. Harriman to Secretary of State, October 12, 1944, Box 174, Harriman Papers; Harriman to Secretary of State, December 18, 1944, Box 175, Harriman Papers; Harriman to Elmer Davis, May 18, 1945, Box 179, Harriman Papers; Harriman to John W. Rumsey, June 16, 1945, Box 180, Harriman Papers; Harriman to Secretary of State, September 3 and November 21, 1945, FRUS, 1945, V: 880–1; 919–20.

94. For valuable exceptions to the general neglect of the wartime cultural programs, see Frank Ninkovich, *The Diplomacy of Ideas: US Foreign Policy and Cultural Relations, 1938–1950* (Cambridge, UK, 1981); Todd Bennett, "My 'Mission' to Moscow: Researching Soviet Propaganda in the Russian Archives," *SHAFR Newsletter*, Vol. 31, No. 4 (December 2000), 16–29, and Bennett, "Culture, Power, and *Mission to Moscow*: Film and Soviet-American Relations during World War II," *Journal of American History*, Vol. 88, No. 2 (September 2001), 489–518.

95. Kathleen to Mary, January 14, 1944 and December 24, 1943, Box 171, Harriman Papers, LC.

96. John F. Melby, "The Information Program in the Soviet Union," enclosed in Harriman to Secretary of State, October 12, 1944, Box 174, Harriman Papers, LC.

97. Kennan, paraphrase of cable to State Department, May 10, 1945, Box 179, Harriman Papers; Kennan, *Memoirs, 1925–1950*, 240–2. See also John R. Deane, *The Strange Alliance* (New York, 1947), 311.

98. Melby, "The Information Program in the Soviet Union," Box 174, Harriman Papers, LC.

99. "Memorandum of Conversations at London, May 2–May 5, 1944" and "Memorandum of Press Conference," May 4, 1944, Box 172, Harriman Papers, LC.

100. Harriman to Secretary of State, January 28, 1944, Box 171; "Interpretative Report on Developments in Soviet Policy Based on the Soviet Press for the

Period December 15, 1943 to January 28, 1944," Box 171; "Memorandum of Press Conference," May 4, 1944, Box 172; "Memorandum of Press Conference," October 14, 1944, Box 174, Harriman Papers, LC.

101. Draft of a telegram to FDR and Hull (not sent), August 25, 1944, Box 173, Harriman Papers, LC; Minutes, Secretary's Staff Committee, April 20, 1945, Box 178, Harriman Papers, LC; FRUS, 1945, V: 840. See also Harriman and Abel, *Special Envoy*, 519–20.

102. Harriman memorandum on conversations with FDR between October 21 and November 19, 1944 (Box 175); Harriman cables to Washington on December 28, 1944 (Box 176) and April 6, 1945 (Box 178), Harriman Papers, LC; Charles E. Bohlen, *Witness to History, 1929–1969* (New York, 1973), 127.

103. Kennan, "Russia – Seven Years Later," in *Memoirs 1925–1950*, 503, 516.

104. "Memorandum for the Ambassador" by "CEB," Box 170, Harriman Papers, LC.

105. Harriman to Secretary of State, August 25, 1944, FRUS, 1944, V: 986; "Present Relations Between the United States Military Mission, Moscow and the Soviet Military Authorities," Memorandum for the United States Joint Chiefs of Staff, 22 January 1945, Box 176, Harriman Papers. See also Deane, *Strange Alliance*, 307.

106. Frederick C. Barghoorn, *The Soviet Image of the United States: A Study in Distortion* (New York, 1950), 246, 121, 242, 248, 262.

107. Standley to Secretary of State, FRUS, 1943, III: 643–4.

108. Harriman to Molotov, November 12, 1943, Box 170; Molotov to Harriman, December 31, 1943, Box 171, Harriman Papers, LC.

109. Molotov to Harriman, March 25, 1944; Kathleen to Mary Harriman, June 14, 1944, Box 172, Harriman Papers, LC.

110. Memorandum of Staff Meeting, August 1, 1944, Box 173, Harriman Papers, LC.

111. Harriman to Secretary of State, August 25, 1944, FRUS, 1944, IV: 986; Harriman to Secretary of State, December 8, 1943, FRUS, 1943, III: 725; Harriman to A. Y. Vyshinskii, January 9, 1945, Box 176 and copy of Soviet Foreign Ministry note to British Embassy, 5 March 1945, Box 177, Harriman Papers.

112. Melby, "The Information Program in the Soviet Union," enclosed with Harriman dispatch, October 12, 1944, Box 174, Harriman Papers, LC.

113. Kennan, "Russia – Seven Years Later," in *Memoirs 1925–1950*, 528. For other references to the Great Wall of China see Joseph Phillips to Ed Barrett, October 15, 1944, Box 174, Harriman Papers, LC; Barghoorn, *The Soviet Image of the United States*, 69, 83.

114. Phillips' draft of a cable to the Secretary of State, enclosed in Phillips to Harriman, August 22, 1945, Box 182, Harriman Papers, LC.

115. Propaganda poster collection, Hoover Institution Archives; Kevin J. McKenna, *All the Views Fit to Print: Changing Images of the US in Pravda Political Cartoons, 1917–1991* (New York, 2001), 51–6; Wallace Carroll, Deputy Director, OWI, to Joseph Phillips, May 8, 1945, and Harriman to Secretary of State, June 6, 1945, Box 179; paraphrase of Embassy cable, July 11, 1945 (report on press from V-Day to July 1), Box 180, Harriman Papers, LC.

116. Summary of M. Slobodskoi, "The Hypnosis of Pearl-grey Trousers," *Krokodil*, No. 22, June 30, 1945, in Harriman Papers, Box 196.
117. Kennan, "Russia – Seven Years Later," *Memoirs 1925–1950*, 504; Deane, *The Strange Alliance*, 304–5.
118. George F. Kennan, "Trip to Novosibirsk and Stalinsk, June 1945," Box 181 Harriman Papers, LC. When Kennan published extracts from this report in *Sketches From a Life* (New York, 1989), 91–110, he changed the phrase "When a people places itself . . ." to the less judgmental "finds itself."
119. Harriman to Secretary of State, November 21, 1945, FRUS, 1945, V: 919–920; R. L. Buell memo to H. R. Luce, August 23, 1945, Box 23, Buell Papers, LC; C. L. Sulzberger, "Russia Lets Down Old Barriers," *New York Times Magazine*, November 14, 1943; W. M. Lawrence, "The Real Enigma Is the Russian Mind," *New York Times Magazine*, December 16, 1945.
120. "Communist Imperialism and America's Answer," n.d., c. 1954, Congressional Papers, Box D14, Gerald Ford Library; Reinhold Niebuhr, "The Long Ordeal of Co-existence," *New Republic*, March 30, 1959, 10–12. For further discussion of the relationship between the postwar disillusionment and Cold War antipathy, see Small, "How We Learned to Love the Russians," 470, 477.
121. "Innocent Abroad?" *Time*, August 26, 1946, p. 68.
122. Ralph W. Sockman, "A Minister in Moscow," *The Christian Century*, September 11, 1946, pp. 1089–91.
123. "How Can We Have Cultural Relations with Russia?" *The Christian Century*, March 5, 1947, p. 293.
124. Boris Shub, *The Choice* (New York, 1950), 49, 12, 189.
125. See John Foster Dulles, *War or Peace*, 5; Burnham, *The Coming Defeat of Communism*, 150; "American Aid to the Kremlin's Russian Enemies," ACLPR press release, c. May 1951, Box 5, Kelley Papers; R. Gordon Wasson, "Popular Fallacies About Russia," *US News & World Report*, March 16, 1951, 30; Edward W. Barrett, *Truth is Our Weapon* (New York, 1953), 276–7.

NOTES TO CHAPTER 5

1. "The Unwanted War [editorial]," Sherwood, "The Third World War," Kasenkina, "We Worship GOD Again," Higgins, "Women of Russia," *Collier's*, October 27, 1951.
2. Richard Townsend Davies to author, November 16, 1996; "The Reminiscences of Richard Townsend Davies," 13–6.
3. Kennan, *Memoirs 1950–1963* (Boston, 1972), 94–102; Kennan, "America and the Russian Future," *Foreign Affairs*, Vol. 29, No. 3 (April 1951), 351–70.
4. James Burnham, *The Struggle for the World* (New York, 1947); Wallace Carroll, *Persuade or Perish* (Boston, 1948); Burnham, *The Coming Defeat of Communism* (New York, 1950); John Foster Dulles, *War or Peace* (New York, 1950), Boris Shub, *The Choice* (New York, 1950), Eugene Lyons, *Our Secret Allies: The Peoples of Russia* (New York, 1953); Burnham, *Containment or Liberation?* (New York, 1953); William Henry Chamberlin, *Beyond Containment* (Chicago, 1953).

5. See Bennett Kovrig, *The Myth of Liberation: East-Central Europe in U.S. Diplomacy and Politics Since 1941* (Baltimore, 1973), 86–125; John Lewis Gaddis, *Strategies of Containment: A Critical Appraisal of Postwar American National Security Policy* (New York, 1982), esp. 128, 146, 155–6.

6. See Bennett Kovrig, *Of Walls and Bridges: The United States and Eastern Europe* (New York, 1991), esp. 39; Walter L. Hixson, *Parting the Curtain: Propaganda, Culture, and the Cold War, 1945–1961* (New York, 1997); Gregory Mitrovich, *Undermining the Kremlin: America's Strategy to Subvert the Soviet Bloc, 1947–1956* (Ithaca, 2000), and Scott Lucas, *Freedom's War: The American Crusade Against the Soviet Union* (New York, 1999).

7. *Foreign Relations of the United States [FRUS], 1945–1950: Emergence of the Intelligence Establishment* (Washington, 1996), 624–44, 653–5; Townsend Hoopes and Douglas Brinkley, *Driven Patriot: The Life and Times of James Forrestal* (New York, 1992), 311; Evan Thomas, *The Very Best Men: The Early Years of the CIA* (New York, 1995), 24–32.

8. "NSC 68: United States Objectives and Programs for National Security," April 7, 1950, in Ernest May, ed., *American Cold War Strategy: Interpreting NSC 68*, 29, 30.

9. Robert William Pirsein, *The Voice of America: A History of the International Broadcasting Activities of the United States Government* (New York, 1979), 201–27; Laura Ann Belmonte, "Defending a Way of Life: American Propaganda and the Cold War, 1945–1959," Ph.D. dissertation, University of Virginia, 1996, 40–2, 54, 56, 84.

10. "U.S. Raises 'Voice' in War of Ideas," *New York Times*, September 3, 1950; Edward W. Barrett, *Truth is Our Weapon* (New York, 1953), esp. 67–85.

11. Gene Sosin, *Sparks of Liberty: An Insider's Memoir of Radio Liberty* (University Park, PA, 1999), 17, xv.

12. For example, ORE 1/1, 6 January 1947, in Michael Warner, ed., *CIA Cold War Records: The CIA under Harry Truman* (Washington, DC, 1994), 102.

13. See, for example, *FRUS, 1951*, IV: 1215–6, 1230, 1259–60; CIA Special Estimate 13, September 24, 1951, in Warner, ed., *CIA Cold War Records: The CIA under Harry Truman*, 417; and SE-39, March 12, 1953, in Scott A. Koch, ed., *CIA Cold War Records: Selected Estimates on the Soviet Union* (Washington, DC, 1993), 7. See also Hixson, *Parting the Curtain*, 19, 93, 96.

14. Vojtech Mastny, *The Cold War and Soviet Insecurity: The Stalin Years* (New York, 1996), vii, 153, 164.

15. Elena Zubkova, *Russia After the War: Hopes, Illusions, and Disappointments, 1945–1957*, translated and edited by Hugh Ragsdale (Armonk, NY: M. E. Sharpe, 1998), esp. 23–32, 74; Yoram Gorlizki and Oleg Khlevniuk, *Cold Peace: Stalin and the Soviet Ruling Circle, 1945–1953* (New York, 2004), esp. 4, 12.

16. Ronald Grigor Suny, *The Soviet Experiment: Russia, the USSR, and the Successor States* (New York, 1998), 367, 374–5.

17. Belmonte, "Defending a Way of Life," 81–91; Review of 1949–52 decisions to reduce sales of *Amerika* from 50,000 to 25,000 and then 15,000, by the Central Committee of the Communist Party, Archive of the Foreign Policy of the Russian Federation (AVPRF), Fond 129, op. 39, papka 288, ll. 30–1.

18. Vera S. Dunham, *In Stalin's Time: Middleclass Values in Soviet Fiction* (Durham, NC, 1990); Jeffrey Brooks, *Thank You, Comrade Stalin! Soviet Public Culture from Revolution to Cold War* (Princeton, 2000).

19. Comments of Alan Kirk, Ambassador to Moscow, in Report of the Western European Ambassadors Conference, February 7, 1951, *FRUS, 1951*, IV: 153; Memorandum of Conversation with President Truman, by Kirk, February 4, 1952, *FRUS, 1952–1954*, VIII: 962–3.

20. See, for example, Richard T. Davies, "The View from Poland," in Thomas T. Hammond, ed., *Witnesses to the Origins of the Cold War* (Seattle, 1982), 249–77. See also George F. Kennan, "Morality and American Foreign Policy," *Foreign Affairs* (Winter 1985–86), 205–18.

21. Edward W. Barrett, *Truth is Our Weapon* (New York, 1953), 79.

22. Boris Shub to Sidney Hook, October 10, 1950, Box 154, Hook Papers, Hoover Institution Archives (HIA).

23. See, for example, Sosin, *Sparks of Liberty*, 27.

24. Frederick F. Travis, *George Kennan and the American-Russian Relationship 1865–1924* (Athens, Ohio, 1990); David Mayers, *George Kennan and the Dilemmas of US Foreign Policy* (New York, 1988), 19–20.

25. Kennan, *Memoirs 1925–1950* (Boston, 1967), 8–9; Robert T. Holt, *Radio Free Europe* (Minneapolis, 1958), 10; Mickelson, *America's Other Voice*, 14; tapes of Sig Mickelson interviews with Howland Sargeant, May 13, 1981, September 30, 1981, and May 11, 1982, Box 22, Mickelson Papers, HIA; *FRUS, 1945–1950: Emergence of the Intelligence Establishment*, esp. 670 and 721.

26. Kennan to Henry Suydam, February 28, 1952, Kennan to citizens of Norwalk, Ohio, March 15, 1952, Kennan to Vilhjalmur Stefanson, July 3, 1952, and Kennan to Gregoire Alexinsky, December 3, 1952,Box 29, Kennan Papers, Mudd Library; *Memoirs 1950–1963*, 151, 165; Kennan to Bernard Gufler, October 27, 1952, Kennan Papers, Mudd Library; Kennan to State Department, September 26, 1952, *FRUS, 1952–1954*, VIII: 1048–50; *Memoirs 1925–1950*, 240–5.

27. Frederick Reinhardt memorandum of January 17, 1951 and copy of George Kennan, "The Last Appeal of the Russian Liberals," *Century Magazine*, Vol. 35 (November 1887), 50–63, Box 11, George Kennan Papers, New York Public Library [NYPL].

28. On the bickering émigré's ties to Amcomlib see André Liebich, *From the Other Shore: Russian Social Democracy after 1921* (Cambridge, MA, 1997), esp. 294–309.

29. Sosin, *Sparks of Liberty*, 4–7, 23.

30. Kennan, "A Voice for the People of Russia," *Century*, Vol. XLVI (July 1893), 461–472; addresses of April 2, 1917 and September 1919 in Ray Stannard Baker and William E. Dodd, eds., *The Public Papers of Woodrow Wilson: War and Peace* [PPWW] (New York, 1927), I: 12–13, II: 6–7, 70, 85, 107, 193.

31. John Foster Dulles, *War or Peace*, 5; Burnham, *The Coming Defeat of Communism*, 150; "American Aid to the Kremlin's Russian Enemies," ACLPR press release, c. May 1951, Box 5, Kelley Papers; R. Gordon Wasson, "Popular Fallacies About Russia," *U.S. News & World Report*, March 16, 1951, 30; Barrett, *Truth is Our Weapon*, 276–7.

32. Boris Shub, *The Choice* (New York, 1950), 9, 202; Sosin, *Sparks of Liberty*, 17, 37; James Critchlow to author, August 17 and August 31, 1996. For reviews of *The Choice* see Albert Z. Carr, "Another Revolution for Russia," *Saturday Review*, November 25, 1950; Harry Schwartz, "The Achilles Heel of the Kremlin," *New York Times Book Review*, November 5, 1950; *The New Yorker*, November 25, 1950; *Commonweal*, November 3, 1950.

33. Phyllis Penn Kohler, ed., *Journey for Our Time: The Russian Journals of the Marquis de Custine* (Chicago, 1951), 26, 29, 33; Kennan to Philip Vaudrin of Oxford University Press, January 5, 1950, and Kennan to Phyllis Kohler, January 19, 1951, Box 29, Kennan Papers, Mudd Library. Kennan later made a similar criticism in *The Marquis de Custine and His Russia in 1839* (Princeton, 1971), 121–2.

34. Lyons, *Our Secret Allies*, 11, 65–7.

35. Lyons, *Our Secret Allies*, 253, 257–9, 274; Burnham, *The Coming Defeat of Communism*, 109, 118; Barrett, *Truth is Our Weapon*, 271–2; R. Gordon Wasson, "Popular Fallacies About Russia," *U.S. News & World Report*, March 16, 1951, 30–1; Sosin, *Sparks of Liberty*, 20.

36. Shub, *The Choice*, esp. 69–71, 127–8, 133–7, 160, 197–200; William Henry Chamberlin, "Russians Against Stalin," *Russian Review*, Vol. 11, No. 1 (January 1952), 18–22; Chamberlin, *Beyond Containment*, 305–316.

37. "Negotiations for an Effective Partnership: A Study of the Negotiations between the American Committee for Liberation from Bolshevism and Leaders of the Emigration from the USSR to Create a Central Emigre [sic] Organization for Anti-Bolshevik Activity," June 30, 1956, p. i , Box 5, Robert F. Kelley Papers, Georgetown University Library.

38. See Amir Weiner, "The Making of a Dominant Myth: The Second World War and the Construction of Political Identities within the Soviet Polity," *Russian Review*, Vol. 55, No. 4 (October 1996), 638–660; Vladislav Zubok and Constantine Pleshakov, *Inside the Kremlin's Cold War: From Stalin to Khrushchev* (Cambridge, MA, 1996), 2.

39. See, for example, Robert F. Byrnes, "Harvard, Columbia, and CIA: My Training in Russian Studies," in Byrnes, *A History of Russian and East European Studies in the United States* (Lanham, MD, 1994), 248; John Foster Dulles, *War or Peace*, 248, and Brien McMahon, "We Can Get Through the Iron Curtain," *New York Times Magazine*, June 24, 1951, p. 23.

40. Kennan, *American Diplomacy, 1900–1950* (Chicago, 1951); Walter L. Hixson, *George F. Kennan: Cold War Iconoclast* (New York, 1989), 118. In a letter to the editor of the *New York Times* on August 18, 1952, Kennan urged: "let us keep our morality to ourselves." Box 29, Kennan Papers, Mudd Library.

41. Kennan to Isaiah Berlin, April 26, 1950, Box 29, Kennan Papers, Mudd Library.

42. January 15, 1948 talk on "Old Muscovy" at the Grolier Club, New York, Box 17, Kennan Papers, Mudd Library.

43. January 15, 1948 talk on "Old Muscovy," Box 17, and "Russia and the United States," May 27, 1950, Box 2, Kennan Papers, Mudd Library. On Kennan's persistent interest in and ambivalent views of the Orthodox Church, see also "Christianity in Russia," a 20-page lecture at the First Presbyterian Church, Princeton, January 13, 1955, Box 19, Kennan Papers.

44. Anonymous memorandum by a leader of the Committee for the Promotion of Advanced Cultural Slavic Studies, October 23, 1950, Box 29, Kennan Papers, Mudd Library; Kennan remarks at a press conference, April 1, 1952, Records of the Policy Planning Staff, Box 48, RG 59, National Archives II.

45. Kennan to Right Reverend Ioann (Shakhovskoi), Orthodox Bishop of San Francisco, December 17, 1951, Box 29, Kennan Papers, Mudd Library.

46. Kennan to Matthews, July 15, 1952, and Kennan dispatches of June 13 and June 20, 1952, *FRUS, 1952–1954*, VIII: 1003, 1015, and 1021–34, esp. 1029.

47. Foglesong, *America's Secret War Against Bolshevism*, 44; Poole to Professor Quincey Wright, October 6, 1947, Box 1, Poole Papers; Poole, "What Kind of Peace Do You Want?" Town Hall, November 15, 1948, Box 11, Poole Papers; Poole, "Are We Meeting the World Challenge?" talk before the Economic Club in Detroit, December 3, 1951, Box 1, Poole Papers, State Historical Society of Wisconsin [SHSW], Madison; Poole remarks at a meeting on psychological warfare in Princeton, May 10, 1952," Box 218, Adolf Berle Papers, Franklin D. Roosevelt Library.

48. Burnham, *The Coming Defeat of Communism*, 113–23, 177–9, 143, 171. Burnham also discussed communism as a secular religion in *The Struggle for the World*, 119–21, and in *Containment or Liberation?*, 48.

49. Burnham, "Psychological Warfare or Else," an article written for (but not published by) *Reader's Digest* between October 1950 and July 1951, Box 2, Burnham Papers, Hoover Institution Archives [hereafter HIA]. Burnham also recommended the use of "phenomena appealing to religious awe, superstition, etc." in "The Strategy of the Politburo, and the Problem of American Counter-Strategy," Box 2, Burnham Papers. This may have been one of the many papers Burnham presented to his contacts in American intelligence organizations. On Burnham's connections to the CIA and the Office of Policy Coordination (OPC), see George H. Nash, *The Conservative Intellectual Movement in America Since 1945* (New York, 1976), 95–7, 372, and Michael Warner, "Origins of the Congress for Cultural Freedom, 1949–50," *Studies in Intelligence*, Vol. 38, No. 5 (1995), 89–98.

50. See, for example, President Eisenhower's comments at an NSC meeting on March 11, 1953, *FRUS, 1952–1954*, VIII: 1124; James Critchlow to author, August 17, 1996.

51. Barrett, *Truth is Our Weapon*, 98, 264; see also 15, 92–3, 162, 273, 276, 289. On the religious themes in American propaganda, see also Hixson, *Parting the Curtain*, 42, 64, 83, 93–4, and 122.

52. Leo Bogart, *Cool Words, Cold War: A New Look at USIA's Premises for Propaganda*, Revised Edition (Washington, DC, 1995), 63, 68, 89–90, 92; James Rorty, "Soviet Imperialism and Religion," June 13, 1951, Box 1, Sol Stein, "Stalin and the Ten Commandments," March 9, 1953, Box 3, and Bertram Wolfe, "Marxism and Religion in the Soviet Union," July 11, 1951, Box 1, Voice of America Papers, HIA. For additional examples, see the following scripts by Rorty: "The Communist War on Religions II," July 27, 1951, "Religious Resistance Back of the Iron Curtain," November 20, 1952, and "Tyrants Die, But Christ Lives," March 16, 1953.

53. "Statement of Mission, Operating Objectives, and Policy Guides," sent by Stevens to Division Heads of ACLPR, September 1, 1954, page 3, Box 5, Robert Kelley Papers.

54. Shub, *The Choice*, 188, 200. See also 98–9, 135, 177, 182, 187.

55. Sosin, *Sparks of Liberty*, 4–5.

56. Father Ioann Shakhovskoi Papers, Amherst Center for Russian Culture, Amherst, MA.

57. R. T. Davies to author, November 16, 1996.

58. Martin E. Marty, *Righteous Empire: The Protestant Experience in America* (New York, 1970), 244–57; Whitfield, *The Culture of the Cold War*, 77–100; William G. McLoughlin, *Revivals, Awakenings and Reform: An Essay on Religion and Social Change in America, 1607–1977* (Chicago, 1978).

59. *Saturday Evening Post*, December 10, 1949, 26–7; Walter Bedell Smith, *My Three Years in Moscow* (Philadelphia and New York, 1950), 261–5. Smith quoted without attribution from Kennan's paper, "Russia's International Position at the Close of the War with Germany," printed in Kennan, *Memoirs, 1925–1950*, 541–2. See Kennan to Wasson, December 7, 1949, Box 28, Kennan Papers.

60. John Foster Dulles, *War or Peace*, 2–3, 8, 15, 243, 250–9; Browne, *International Radio Broadcasting*, 101; Townsend Hoopes, *The Devil and John Foster Dulles* (Boston, 1973), esp. 65–6, 83–5, 115.

61. Lyons, *Our Secret Allies*, 374–6.

62. Nora Sayre, *Running Time: Films of the Cold War* (New York, 1982), 202; Stephen J. Whitfield, *The Culture of the Cold War* (Baltimore, 1991), 85; Tony Shaw, "Martyrs, Miracles, and Martians: Religion and Cold War Cinematic Propaganda in the 1950s," *Journal of Cold War Studies*, Vol. 4, No. 2 (Spring 2002), 3–22. The Policy Planning Staff of the State Department paid particular attention to the *Collier's* idea of placing a model of American life on an aircraft carrier that would tour the world. Pat Frank, "Main Street on a Flattop," *Collier's*, November 27, 1948; record of PPS meeting, December 7, 1948; PPS memo to Lovett, December 16, 1948; PPS Subject Files, RG 59, National Archives II.

63. Shub, *The Choice*, 12, 17, 22–7, 31–2; Sosin, *Sparks of Liberty*, 8. See also Mitrovich, *Undermining the Kremlin*, 78.

64. McMahon, "We *Can* Get Through the Iron Curtain," *New York Times Magazine*, June 24, 1951, pp. 1, 23–4, 26.

65. Memorandum of discussion at NSC meeting, March 11, 1953, and "The Chance for Peace" address, April 16, 1953, *FRUS, 1952–1954*, VIII: 1122–3, 1147–54. For further discussion of this theme, see Hixson, *Parting the Curtain*, esp. 43–5, 133–42, 167, 173–4, and 209.

66. See, for example, Kennan, "United States Objectives with Respect to Russia," August 18, 1948, PPS/38, in Nelson, ed., *The State Department Policy Planning Staff Papers 1947–1949*, II: 394, 374, 403–4; Burnham, *The Coming Defeat of Communism*, 33; *Containment or Liberation?*, 41; Jarmo Oikarinen, *The Middle East in the American Quest for World Order* (Helsinki, 1999), 40.

67. Kennan, "America and the Russian Future," *Foreign Affairs*, Vol. 29, No. 3 (April 1951), 352–5.

68. Kelley to Robert G. Hooker of the Division of Eastern European Affairs at the State Department, May 9, 1951, Box 5, Folder 1, Kelley Papers.

69. Lyons, *Our Secret Allies*, 257–60; Oleg Anisimov, "The Attitude of the Soviet People Toward the West," *Russian Review*, Vol. 13, No. 2 (April 1954), 87.

70. Belmonte, "Defending a Way of Life," 87–8; Alan M. Ball, *Imagining America: Influence and Images in Twentieth-Century Russia* (Lanham, MD, 2003), 184.

71. Poole, "What Kind of Peace Do You Want?" Town Hall, November 15, 1948, Box 11, Poole Papers; Poole, addresss to the American Hungarian Federation in New York, October 7, 1950, Box 1, Poole Papers.

72. Mickelson, *America's Other Voice*, 93; Lewis Galantiere, "Through the Russian Looking Glass: The Future in Retrospect," *Foreign Affairs*, Vol. 28, No. 1 (October 1949), 114–24.

73. Stevens, *Russian Assignment*, 12–3, 187, 169, 21, vii; see also 57 and 69.

74. Chamberlin to Kennan, June 1, 1950, and Kennan to Chamberlin, June 21, 1950, Box 29, Kennan Papers, Mudd Library. For an example of Russian emigré resentment of the common "Asiatic horde approach," see Anatole Shub's review of Chamberlin's *Beyond Containment* in *Russian Review*, Vol. 13, No. 2 (April 1954), 154.

75. "Russia and the Russians," lecture to the Commercial Club of Cincinnati, January 21, 1950, Box 18 Kennan Papers, Mudd Library; Kennan to Washington, May 1952, *FRUS, 1952–1954*, VIII: 976.

76. "Old Muscovy," lecture at the Grolier Club, New York, January 15, 1948, Box 17, Kennan Papers, Mudd Library.

77. Lecture 2 at Bad Nauheim, 1942, Box 16, Kennan Papers.

78. Wasson, "Popular Fallacies About Russia," *U.S. News & World Report*, March 16, 1951, 32–3; Wasson, "Russia and the Soviet Regime: A Second Look at Some Popular Beliefs," lecture to the Practicing Law Institute, New York, February 17, 1951, published in *Vital Speeches of the Day*, April 1, 1951, 357–60.

79. For examples of such comparisons, see DeWitt Poole, "The Bolshevik Revolution in Russia," p. 1, n.d., Box 11, Poole Papers, SHSW; Leslie Stevens, *Russian Assignment* (Boston, 1953), 31, 164. See also Critchlow, *Radio Hole-in-the-Head/Radio Liberty*, 44; and Sosin, *Sparks of Liberty*, 28.

80. Lyons, *Our Secret Allies*, 65, 57, 70.

81. Lyons, *Our Secret Allies*, 64–5; Nicolai N. Petro, *Crafting Democracy: How Novgorod Has Coped With Social Change* (Ithaca, 2004), Chapter 5; Shub, *The Choice*, 194. For a similar view, see Oleg Anisimov, *The Ultimate Weapon* (Chicago, 1953), 106–13.

82. Sosin, *Sparks of Liberty*, 10, 16; Radio Liberty brochure, n.d. (c. 1954), RFE/RL, Inc. Corporate Records, Box 75, HIA.

83. Kennan, "United States Objectives with Respect to Russia," August 18, 1948, PPS/38, in Nelson, ed., *The State Department Policy Planning Staff Papers 1947–1949*, II: 397–8.

84. Kennan, *Memoirs 1950–1963*, 96; Kennan to Waldemar J. Gallman, Deputy for Foreign Affairs, National War College, May 29, 1951, Box 29, Kennan Papers, Mudd Library, Princeton.

85. "U.S. Position with Respect to a Future Liberated Russia," January 16, 1951, Box 5, Kelley Papers. Kelley did not sign this paper, but the ideas presented are consistent with his later writing.
86. Memorandum enclosed in Kelley to Reginald T. Townsend, Director of Public Relations, AmComLib, August 29, 1955, Box 5, Kelley Papers; "Purpose of Radio Liberty," n.d, but apparently after Radio Liberation became Radio Liberty in 1959, Box 5, Kelley Papers.
87. "The Russian 'Solidarist Movement' (NTS) and its Program Announced in 'Look' Magazine of Oct. 26, 1948," Box 2, Burnham Papers, HIA; Sosin, *Sparks of Liberty*, 71. On the NTS (Natsional'no Trudovoi Soiuz or National Labor Alliance) and the Vlasovite organizations (KONR and SBONR), see Liebich, *From the Other Shore*, 291–5.
88. B. S. Kelsey, Memorandum to Mr. Gallman, 15 May 1951, enclosed with W. J. Gallman to Kennan, 17 May 1951; Kennan to Waldemar J. Gallman, Deputy for Foreign Affairs, National War College, May 29, 1951, Box 29, Kennan Papers, Mudd Library, Princeton.
89. PSB D-43 and NSC 158, quoted in Mitrovich, *Undermining the Kremlin*, 128–9, 134.
90. "Russia and the Russians," lecture to the Commercial Club of Cincinnati, January 21, 1950, Box 18, Kennan Papers.
91. Kennan, "America and the Russian Future," *Foreign Affairs*, Vol. 29, No. 3 (April 1951), 370.
92. Stenographic notes of "Princeton Session May 10, 1952," Box 218, Berle Papers. Participants in the Princeton meeting included Joseph Grew, Charles Bohlen, Allen Dulles, and C. D. Jackson.
93. May, ed., *American Cold War Strategy: Interpreting NSC 68*, 25, 36, 75, 80; Dulles, *War or Peace*; Richard H. Immerman, *John Foster Dulles: Piety, Pragmatism, and Power in U.S. Foreign Policy* (Wilmington, 1999), 27.
94. Burnham, *The Struggle for the World*, 24, 219; *Containment or Liberation?*, 208, 222, 41; *The Coming Defeat of Communism*, 1, 130n, 276–8.
95. Burnham, *The Struggle for the World*, 219–220; "The Strategy of the Politburo, and the Problem of American Counter-Strategy," n.d., c. late 1950, Box 2, James Burnham Papers, HIA.
96. Lyons, *Our Secret Allies*, 305–7, 356–8.
97. Chamberlin to Kennan, February 12, 1953, Box 29, Kennan Papers; Chamberlin, *Beyond Containment*, 299–300.
98. Kennan to Cincent Sheehan, June 15, 1951, Box 29, Kennan Papers, Mudd Library.
99. NSC 135 and CIA paper of May 15, 1952, quoted in Mitrovich, *Undermining the Kremlin*, 98, 102, 111; Kennan dispatches of June 13, June 20, and July 15, 1952, *FRUS, 1952–1954*, VIII: 1003, 1015, and 1021–1034.
100. Mitrovich, *Undermining the Kremlin*, 86–93; Bohlen to Kennan, November 9, 1951, Box 36, Charles Eustis Bohlen Papers, Library of Congress.
101. Mitrovich, *Undermining the Kremlin*, 103–8; John Foster Dulles, "A Policy of Boldness," *Life*, May 19, 1952; Lucas, *Freedom's War*, 163–6; Kenneth Osgood, *Total Cold War: Eisenhower's Secret Propaganda Battle at Home and Abroad* (Lawrence, KS, 2006).

102. Mitrovich, *Undermining the Kremlin*, 126–7; Bohlen testimony of February 24, 1953 and memorandum of March 10, 1953 in *FRUS, 1952–1954*, VIII: 53, 1108–10, 1146; Lucas, *Freedom's War*, 169–71.

103. Bohlen, *Witness to History*, 341–2; Suny, *The Soviet Experiment*, 387; Lucas, *Freedom's War*, 172. Andrea Graziosi, "The Great Strikes of 1953 in Soviet Labor Camps in the Accounts of Their Participants," *Cahiers du Monde Russe et Sovietique*, Vol. 33, No. 4 (1992), 419–46; Mitrovich, *Undermining the Kremlin*, 145.

104. Mitrovich, *Undermining the Kremlin*, 143–51.

105. Mitrovich, *Undermining the Kremlin*, 117; Richard Pipes, *Survival is Not Enough: Soviet Realities and America's Future* (New York, 1984), esp. 204–8, 274–9; Lucas, *Freedom's War*, 102; Stephen Vaughn, *Ronald Reagan in Hollywood: Movies and Politics* (New York, 1994), 199–208; Kevin J. Smant, "How Great the Triumph: James Burnham, Anticommunism, and the Conservative Movement," Ph.D. dissertation, University of Notre Dame, 1991, 1.

NOTES TO CHAPTER 6

1. J. C. Bennett, "A Condition for Coexistence," *Christianity and Crisis*, Vol. XVIII, No. 7, April 28, 1958, 53–4; David Lawrence to John C. Bennett, May 1, 1958; Bennett to Lawrence, May 21, 1958; Lawrence to Bennett, May 26, 1958; Bennett to Lawrence, June 3, 1958; Lawrence to Bennett, June 6, 1958; Bennett to Lawrence, June 9, 1958; Lawrence to Bennett, June 11, 1958; Bennett to Lawrence, July 1, 1958; Lawrence to Bennett, July 7, 1958, Box 22, David Lawrence Papers, Mudd Library, Princeton. For further discussion of Bennett's views, see: Mark Hulsether, *Building a Protestant Left:Christianity and Crisis Magazine, 1941–1993* (Knoxville, TN, 1999), esp. 88–90; Daniel Day Williams, "The Theology of John Coleman Bennett," in Edward LeRoy Long, Jr. and Robert T. Handy, ed., *Theology and Church in Times of Change* (Philadelphia, 1970), Chapter 11; and David H. Smith, *The Achievement of John C. Bennett* (New York, 1970).

2. "Thirteen Days," *The Dan Smoot Report*, Vol. 5, No. 40, October 5, 1959, 313–20, is one example of this thinking. For further illustrations, see below.

3. For a collection of Lawrence's writing, see *The Editorials of David Lawrence* 6 vols. (Washington, 1970). Bennett's many books included: *Christianity and Communism Today* (New York, 1960); *Nuclear Weapons and the Conflict of Conscience* (New York, 1962); and *U.S. Foreign Policy and Christian Ethics* (Philadelphia, 1977). On Bennett's more famous, but by the late 1950s less vigorous, colleague, see Paul Merkley, *Reinhold Niebuhr: A Political Account* (Montreal, 1975), Richard Wightman Fox, *Reinhold Niebuhr: A Biography* (Ithaca, 1996), and Leo P. Ribuffo, "Moral Judgments and the Cold War: Reflections on Reinhold Niebuhr, William Appleman Williams and John Lewis Gaddis," in Ellen Schrecker, ed., *Cold War Triumphalism* (New York, 2004).

4. For reviews of the extensive scholarly literature concerning the rise of détente, see Robert D. Schulzinger, ed., *A Companion to American Foreign Relations* (Malden, MA, 2003), Chapters 17, 19, and 23.

5. See, for example, Allen H. Kassof, "Scholarly Exchanges and the Collapse of Communism," *The Soviet and Post-Soviet Review*, Vol. 22, No. 3 (1995), 263–74, and Yale Richmond, *Cultural Exchange and the Cold War: Raising the Iron Curtain* (University Park, PA, 2003).

6. Memorandum of NSC discussion, January 27, 1955, *FRUS, 1955–1957, Volume XXIV: Soviet Union; Eastern Mediterranean*, 6; Memorandum of Eisenhower conference with Nixon, July 22, 1959, *FRUS, 1958–1960, Volume X, Part I* (Washington, 1993), 333.

7. JFK Diary quoted in Robert Dallek, *An Unfinished Life: John F. Kennedy, 1917–1963* (Boston, 2003), 51; JFK 1958 speech quoted in Arthur M. Schlesinger, Jr., *Robert Kennedy and His Times* (Boston, 1978), 417; Transcript of Interview Between President Kennedy and the Editor of *Izvestia* (Adzhubei), November 25, 1961, *FRUS 1961–1963, Vol. V, Soviet Union*: Document 134; JFK remark to Khrushchev at Vienna, quoted in Dallek, *An Unfinished Life*, 410.

8. Johnson endorsement of political offensive in 1955, cited in Eugene Lyons, *David Sarnoff: A Biography* (New York, 1966); Johnson speech on October 7, 1966, excerpted in Lyndon Baines Johnson, *The Vantage Point: Perspectives of the Presidency 1963–1969* (New York, 1971), 474; Johnson press conference, 27 September 1966, quoted in John Dumbrell, *President Lyndon Johnson and Soviet Communism* (New York, 2004), 182.

9. Memorandum of NSC discussion, January 27, 1955, *FRUS, 1955–1957, Volume XXIV*, 6; Memorandum of conversation between Nixon and A. I. Mikoyan, January 6, 1959, *FRUS, 1958–1960, Volume X, Part I*, 222–4; Memorandum of Nixon conference with Eisenhower, August 5, 1959, *FRUS, 1958–1960, Volume X, Part I*, 382; Nixon speech on July 28, 1960, in Richard M. Nixon, *Six Crises* (New York, 1962), 319, 455–7; Nixon address to Congress, June 1, 1972, *FRUS, 1969–1976, Vol. I: Foundations of Foreign Policy, 1969–1972* (Washington, 2003), 392–9.

10. Lucas, *Freedom's War*, 240; Richard H. Immerman, *John Foster Dulles: Piety, Pragmatism, and Power in U.S. Foreign Policy* (Wilmington, DE, 1999), 143.

11. NSC 5502/1, January 31, 1955, *FRUS, 1955–1957, Volume XXIV*, 16; Lucas, *Freedom's War*, 179, 211; Bohlen, *Witness to History*, 439–456; 1957 CIA report discussed in Erik Kulavig, *Dissent in the Years of Khrushchev: Nine Stories about Disobedient Russians* (New York, 2003), 158; NIE 11-4-60, December 1, 1960, *FRUS 1961–1963, Vol. V, Soviet Union*: Document 1; NIE 11-5-62, February 21, 1962, *FRUS 1961–1963, Vol. V, Soviet Union*: Document 160; NIE 11-9-62, May 2, 1962, *FRUS 1961–1963, Vol. V, Soviet Union*: Document 187.

12. Vladimir A. Kozlov, *Mass Uprisings in the USSR: Protest and Rebellion in the Post-Stalin Years* (Armonk, NY, 2002); Samuel H. Baron, *Bloody Saturday in the Soviet Union: Novocherkassk, 1962* (Stanford, 2001); Vladimir Bukovsky, *To Build a Castle – My Life as a Dissenter* (New York, 1979); Ludmilla Alexeyeva and Paul Goldberg, *The Thaw Generation: Coming of Age in the Post-Stalin Era* (Boston, 1990; paperback, Pittsburgh, 1993).

13. NIE 11–63, May 22, 1963, *FRUS 1961–1963, Vol. V, Soviet Union*: Document 326; CIA paper, "The USSR: Problems, Policies, and Prospects 1967–1968," January 9, 1968, *FRUS, 1964–1968, Vol. XIV*, Document 260; Robert Kennedy recollection of JFK's view of Thompson as "outstanding" in Schlesinger, *Robert Kennedy and His Times*, 433; Johnson, *Vantage Point*, 475 Thompson to State Department, January 24, 1961, *FRUS 1961–1963, Vol. V, Soviet Union*, Document 13; Thompson to State Department, February 1, 1961, *FRUS 1961–1963, Vol. V, Soviet Union*, Document 20; Thompson to State Department, January 11, 1968, *FRUS, 1964–1968, Vol. XIV*, Document 261. On JFK's frequent personal consultation of Thompson, see the Oral History Interviews with Llewellyn E. Thompson, March 25, 1964 and April 27, 1966, John F. Kennedy Presidential Library, Boston.

14. Lucas, *Freedom's War*, 218, 266, 213, 227; William Taubman, *Khrushchev: The Man and His Era* (New York, 2003), esp. 347.

15. Lucas, *Freedom's War*, 235, 269; Lyons, *David Sarnoff*, 328–30; Eugene Lyons, "The Soviet Regime and the Russian People," May 20, 1958, *Vital Speeches of the Day*, Vol. 24, No. 18, 556–60; Lyons, "Why the United States Should Stand Fast," February 16, 1959, *Vital Speeches of the Day*, Vol. 25, No. 11, 357–61; Lyons, "Is a New Revolution Brewing in the U.S.S.R.?" *Reader's Digest*, October 1965, 213–20; Frank R. Barnett to John Richardson, Jr., February 3, 1964, and Barnett memo to David Abshire, John Richardson, Leo Cherne, and others, 10 April 1964, Box 154 RFE/RL Corporate Records, HIA.

16. For the stimulating parallel comment that the "emerging stability in U.S.-Soviet relations *destabilized* alliances and societies," see Suri, *Power and Protest*, 43.

17. James Burnham, "The Third World War," *National Review*, Vol. 16, November 3, 1964, p. 952; William F. Buckley, Jr., "Inside Russia," *National Review*, Vol. 24, October 27, 1972, p. 1200.

18. "An American Policy," September 11, 1939, *The Editorials of David Lawrence* (6 vols., Washington, 1970), II: 216; "When Will Russia Become a 'Free' Nation?" October 29, 1943, Ibid., III: 157–8; "The Only Hope For Russia – And For Us," January 30, 1948, Ibid., IV: 231–2; "If Russia Would Only Return to God," *U.S. News & World Report*, Vol. 68, March 2, 1970, p. 82.

19. "Liberation – Not 'Appeasement,'" *The Editorials of David Lawrence*, IV: 351; "200,000,000 Slaves," *U.S. News & World Report*, February 18, 1955, p. 132; Lawrence to Liliana Munzi, July 17, 1959, Box 124, Lawrence Papers, Princeton; Lawrence, "Moscow Condemnation Widespread," Washington *Evening Star*, August 23, 1968; Lawrence, "People on Other Side Need Facts," Washington *Evening Star*, December 22, 1971; "Unrest in Russia: Reds' New Worry," *U.S. News & World Report*, Vol. XLII, No. 21, May 24, 1957, 27–9; "Revolt Coming in Russia?" *U.S. News & World Report*, June 21, 1965, 44–8; "Revolution Coming in Russia? A Yugoslav Says This," *U.S. News & World Report*, July 19, 1965, 72–3; "Discontent in Russia: Threat to the Kremlin?" *U.S. News & World Report*, December 28, 1970, 58–9; Goldwater to Lawrence, October 18/25, 1965, Box 53, Lawrence Papers.

20. Barry M. Goldwater, *The Conscience of a Conservative* (Washington, DC, 1990; first published in 1960), 98–116. L. Brent Bozell, a writer for *National Review*, helped Goldwater with the book. See Jonathan M. Schoenwald, *A Time for Choosing: The Rise of Modern American Conservatism* (New York, 2001), 126.

21. R. L. Duffus, "one Senator's Manifesto," *New York Times Book Review*, June 26, 1960, p. 14; Gerald W. Johnson, "Mutterings from Tombstone Territory," *New Republic*, May 23, 1960, p. 20; Patrick J. Buchanan, Introduction to *The Conscience of a Conservative* (1990), vii–xxi.

22. Barry M. Goldwater, *Why Not Victory? A Fresh Look at American Foreign Policy* (New York, 1962), 35, 150; 152; 161; Robert Alan Goldberg, *Barry Goldwater* (New Haven, 1995), 157; Schoenwald, *A Time for Choosing*, 3.

23. Walter Johnson in *Saturday Review*, July 7, 1962; Eric Goldman, "The World and Senator Goldwater," *New York Times Book Review*, April 29, 1962, p. 10; George F. Kennan, *On Dealing with the Communist World* (New York: Harper & Row, 1964), vii–20.

24. Barry Goldwater, *Where I Stand* (New York, 1964), 124–5, 10, 13; Kirk H. Porter and Donald Bruce Johnson, *National Party Platforms 1840–1964* (Urbana, IL, 1966), 676–9, 687; Walter Isaacson, *Kissinger: A Biography* (New York, 1992), 116.

25. James Reston, "San Francisco," *New York Times*, July 19, 1964; "The Truth Shall Make You Free," *Chicago Tribune* editorial, July 19, 1964.

26. "The Goldwater Nomination," *New York Times*, July 16, 1964; "Disaster at San Francisco," *New York Times*, July 19, 1964; Reston, "San Francisco," *New York Times*, July 19, 1964; William Martin, *With God on Our Side: The Rise of the Religious Right in America* (New York, 1996), 85.

27. Reagan address, October 27, 1964, in *A Time for Choosing: The Speeches of Ronald Reagan 1961–1982* (Chicago, 1983), 41–57; John A. Andrew, *The Other Side of the Sixties: Young Americans for Freedom and the Rise of Conservative Politics* (New Brunswick, NJ, 1997), 196–7; Martin, *With God on Our Side*, 87.

28. "In the Hands of the People," *Chicago Tribune*, July 17, 1964; Reagan address, October 27, 1964, in *A Time for Choosing*, 56; Jeremi Suri, *Power and Protest: Global Revolution and the Rise of Détente* (Cambridge, MA, 2003), 99–101.

29. "Platform for People, Not Robots," *Chicago Tribune*, July 13, 1964, p. 18.

30. Memorandum of conversation between Eisenhower and F. R. Kozlov, July 1, 1959, *FRUS, 1958–1960, Volume X, Part I*, 290–5; Stephen E. Ambrose, *Eisenhower: The President*, 262.

31. Memorandum of NSC discussion, January 27, 1955, *FRUS, 1955–1957, Volume XXIV*, 6; Memorandum of conversation between Eisenhower and F. R. Kozlov, July 1, 1959, *FRUS, 1958–1960, Volume X, Part 1*, 290–5; Memorandum of Discussion at NSC meeting, May 21, 1959 and Memorandum of Meeting Between President Eisenhower and His Special Assistant for National Security Affairs (Gray), July 13, 1959, *FRUS, 1958–1960, Volume X, Part 2: Eastern Europe; Finland; Greece; Turkey* (Washington, 1993), 25–7, 35–6. After Khrushchev denounced Stalin and loosened the Soviet grip on Eastern Europe, Foster Dulles shifted emphasis from ostracizing the "evil

men" in the Kremlin to inducing them "to shed their wicked ways." Memorandum of NSC meeting, June 28, 1956, *FRUS, 1955–1957, Volume XXIV*, 121.

32. Memorandum of Conversation between Nixon and Khrushchev, July 24, 1959, Nixon reports to Eisenhower from Moscow, July 26 and July 31, 1959, Memorandum of discussion at NSC meeting, August 6, 1959, *FRUS, 1958–1960, Volume X, Part 1*, 336–45, 372–3, 377–8, 386–7.

33. Memorandum of Nixon conference with Eisenhower, August 5, 1959, Memorandum of conversation between Khrushchev and Eisenhower, September 15, 1959, Memorandum of conference between Eisenhower and his diplomatic advisers, Memorandum of conversation between Khrushchev and Eisenhower at Camp David, September 27, 1959, in *FRUS, 1958–1960, Volume X, Part 1*, 381–4, 392–401, 454–7, 477. Taubman, *Khrushchev*, 405, 419, 426; Stephen E. Ambrose, *Eisenhower: The President* (New York, 1984), 542–3.

34. Cardinal Richard Cushing, quoted in "Not Everybody Favors Khrushchev's Visit," *U.S. News & World Report*, August 17, 1959, p. 65; Schoenwald, *A Time for Choosing*, 41–2; Gary John Tocchet, "September Thaw: Khrushchev's Visit to America, 1959," Ph.D dissertation, Stanford University, 1995, 154, 168; Richard M. Fried, *The Russians Are Coming! The Russians Are Coming! Pageantry and Patriotism in Cold War America* (New York, 1998), 142–5.

35. Report on the Khrushchev Visit, n.d., c. October 1959, *FRUS, 1958–1960, Volume X, Part 1*, 485–92; Tocchet, "September Thaw," 14, 263.

36. George Sherman, "Afterthoughts on Nixon and the Exhibition" (a report from Moscow), *New Republic*, September 21, 1959, pp. 6–7; Memorandum of conversation between Khrushchev and Ambassador Henry Cabot Lodge, September 21, 1959, *FRUS, 1958–1960, Volume X, Part 1*, 435–9; Strobe Talbott, ed., *Khrushchev Remembers: The Last Testament* (Boston, 1974), 376–415; Taubman, *Khrushchev*, 441.

37. Thompson to State Department, November 15, 1961 and February 21, 1962, *FRUS, 1961–1963, Vol. V*, Documents 128 and 158; Thompson to State Department, January 11, 1968, Document 261, *FRUS, 1964–1968, Vol. XIV*; Memorandum of discussion with Kohler at a State Department/JCS meeting, n.d., 1963, *FRUS, 1961–1963, Vol. V*, Document 289; Memorandum of conversation between Kohler and Johnson, November 18, 1965, Document 136, *FRUS, 1964–1968, Vol. XIV*; David Mayers, *The Ambassadors and America's Soviet Policy* (New York, 1995), 217–8.

38. Puddington, *Broadcasting Freedom*, 113–8; Lucas, *Freedom's War*, 229, 267; Lyons, "Is a New Revolution Brewing in the U.S.S.R.?" *Reader's Digest*, October 1965, p. 220.

39. Memorandum by Secretary of State Christian Herter, October 3, 1959, *FRUS, 1958–1960, Volume X, Part 2*, Document 20, p. 49; USIA paper sent to White House adviser Walt Rostow by Edward R. Murrow, May 8, 1961, *FRUS, 1961–1963, Vol. XXV: Foreign Relations, Organization of Foreign Policy, Information Policy; United Nations; Scientific Matters*, Document 122; A. M. Sperber, *Murrow: His Life and Times* (New York, 1986), 47, 58, 643, 677;

A. M. Schlesinger, Jr., *A Thousand Days: John F. Kennedy in the White House* (Boston, 1965), 900–2.

40. Richard Helms with William Hood, *A Look over My Shoulder: A Life in the Central Intelligence Agency* (New York, 2003), 368–73; Puddington, *Broadcasting Freedom*, 190–1, 195; Randall Bennett Woods, *Fulbright: A Biography* (Cambridge, 1995), 194–5, 643, 696–7; Pell quoted in Sosin, *Sparks of Liberty*, 136.

41. Sosin, *Sparks of Liberty*, 137–49; Puddington, *Broadcasting Freedom*, 204–5; "Muted Voice of America," *Time*, December 16, 1974, pp. 80, 85; Alan L. Heil, Jr., *Voice of America: A History* (New York, 2003), 159–61; Laurien Alexandre, *The Voice of America: From Détente to the Reagan Doctrine* (Norwood, NJ, 1988), 15–8.

42. Puddington, *Broadcasting Freedom*, 164; Howland H. Sargeant, remarks at a conference of the Advertising Council, March 6, 1962 and remarks at RFE symposium, "The War of Ideas," September 26, 1963, Box 40, RFE/RL Inc. Corporate Records, Hoover Institution Archives. See also Sosin, *Sparks of Liberty*, 105–6.

43. "Radio Liberty's Support of U.S. Strategic Objectives," n.d., c. 1967; James Critchlow, "Public Broadcasting to the Soviet Union – A Promoter of Safe Détente," May 1967, Box 166, RFE/RL Inc. Corporate Records, HIA.

44. Sosin, *Sparks of Liberty*, 69–71; Puddington, *Broadcasting Freedom*, 159–65; Critchlow, *Radio Hole-in-the-Head/Radio Liberty*, 93; Sargeant remarks at RFE symposium, "The War of Ideas," September 26, 1963, Box 40, RFE/RL Inc. Corporate Records, Hoover Institution Archives; Alexei Yurchak, *Everything Was Forever, Until It Was No More: The Last Soviet Generation* (Princeton, 2006), Chapter 5. On the compatibility and incompatibility of jazz and communism, see also S. Frederick Starr, *Red and Hot: The Fate of Jazz in the Soviet Union* (New York, 1985), esp. 262, 272.

45. Howland Sargeant talk on "Soviet Vulnerabilities to Western Ideas and Persuasions," summarized by John Dunning, March 2, 1966, Box 154, RFE/RL, Inc, Corporate Records; James Critchlow, "Public Broadcasting to the Soviet Union – A Promoter of Safe Détente," May 1967, p. 20, Box 166, RFE/RL Inc. Corporate Records, HIA; Sosin, *Sparks of Liberty*, 112–3.

46. Puddington, *Broadcasting Freedom*, 161; James Critchlow, *Radio Hole-in-the-Head/Radio Liberty: An Insider's Story of Cold War Broadcasting* (Washington, 1995), 100; RFE engineer Francis Sherwood to J. W. Fulbright, February 24, 1972, Box 128, Clifford Case Papers, Alexander Library, Rutgers University.

47. Kulavig, *Dissent in the Years of Khrushchev*, 34; Moshe Lewin, *The Gorbachev Phenomenon: A Historical Interpretation* (Berkeley, 1988).

48. G. Zhukov to V. V. Kuznetsov, 14 November 1960, Archive of the Foreign Policy of the Russian Federation (AVPRF), Op. 43, por., 24, papka 317, d. 170, ll. 14–9; Kulavig, *Dissent in the Years of Khrushchev*, 19, 24, 30; Puddington, *Broadcasting Freedom*, 216–8.

49. Fond 0129, op. 39, papka 288, d. 26 (Voprosy pressy), ll. 30–1, and op. 40, papka 297, d. 22 (Perepiska po raprostraneniiu zhurnala "SSSR" i "Amerika," 1956–1957), AVPRF; William S. B. Lacy to J. F. Dulles, July 25, 1958, *FRUS, 1958–1960, Vol. X*, Part 2, p. 13; Memorandum from Deputy

Director of USIA (Wilson) to Director (Rowan), June 1, 1964, Document 34; Kohler to Washington, January 26, 1966, Document 150, *FRUS, 1964–1968, Vol. XIV.*

50. Memorandum of Conversation between the Chinese Ambassador and William S. B. Lacy, June 24, 1958, *FRUS, 1958–1960, Vol. X*, Part 2, pp. 9–10; Memorandum of Discussion at NSC meeting, May 21, 1959, *FRUS, 1958–1960, Volume X, Part 2*, 26–7; J. D. Parks, *Culture, Conflict and Coexistence: American-Soviet Cultural Relations, 1917–1958* (Jefferson, NC, 1983), 149, 163–4; Tomas Tolvaisas, "U.S.A. on Display: American Commercial and Cultural Exhibitions in the Soviet Bloc Countries, 1961–1968," Ph.D. dissertation, Rutgers University, 2006.

51. Memorandum of Conversation between Khrushchev, Eisenhower, and others, September 26, 1959, *FRUS, 1958–1960, Volume X, Part 1*, 468–9; *Khrushchev Remembers: The Last Testament*, 364–7; State Department report, August 1959, and USIA paper, March 21, 1960, *FRUS, 1958–1960, Vol. X*, Part 2, 37–40, 55–9. For further discussion of the Moscow exhibition and Soviet responses, see Walter L. Hixson, *Parting the Curtain: Propaganda, Culture, and the Cold War, 1945–1961* (New York, 1997), Chapters 6–7, and Nigel Gould-Davies, "The Logic of Soviet Cultural Diplomacy," *Diplomatic History*, Vol. 27, No. 2 (April 2003), 193–214, esp. 210–2.

52. Johnson, *The Vantage Point*, 467; Memorandum from Deputy Director of USIA (Wilson) to Director (Rowan), June 1, 1964, Document 34, *FRUS, 1964–1968, Vol. XIV.* For other depictions of the exchanges as successful and "of paramount interest" to the US, see Kohler to Washington, January 8, 1964, Document 3, and Memorandum from Under Secretary of State Katzenbach to Johnson, May 29, 1968, Document 272, *FRUS, 1964–1968, Vol. XIV.*

53. Goldwater, *The Conscience of a Conservative*, 97–100; Richard T. Arndt, *The First Resort of Kings: American Cultural Diplomacy in the Twentieth Century* (Washington, D.C., 2005), x–xi; see also 483.

54. Memorandum from Rusk to Johnson, March 2, 1966, Document 153; Thompson to Washington, June 27, 1968, Document 275; and Memorandum from Under Secretary of State Katzenbach to Johnson, June 29, 1968, Document 276, *FRUS, 1964–1968, Vol. XIV*; Report by B. A. Borisov, President of the Presidium of the Trade-Industrial Chamber of the USSR, 27 November 1973, Fond 129, Op. 58, papka 246, d. 42, ll. 106–8, AVPRF.

55. Puddington, *Broadcasting Freedom*, 215.

56. *Khrushchev Remembers: The Last Testament*, 382–3, 404–6; Thompson to State Department, March 10, 1961, Document 42, *FRUS, 1961–1963, Vol. V*; Memorandum of Conversation between Khrushchev and Rusk, August 9, 1963, Document 346, *FRUS, 1961–1963, Vol. V*; Kennan to State Department, February 22, 1962, Document 161, *FRUS, 1961–1963, Vol. V.*

57. Rusk to Kennan (drafted by Nathaniel Davis), March 2, 1962, Document 164, *FRUS, 1961–1963, Vol. V.* On the efforts to broaden US influence in Eastern Europe, see: A. Paul Kubricht, "Politics and Foreign Policy: A Brief Look at the Kennedy Administration's Eastern European Diplomacy," *Diplomatic History*, Vol. 11, No. 1 (Winter 1987), 55–65; Frank

Costigliola, "Lyndon B. Johnson, Germany, and 'the end of the Cold War,'" in Warren I. Cohen and Nancy Bernkopf Tucker, eds., *Lyndon Johnson Confronts the World: American Foreign Policy 1963–1968* (Cambridge, UK, 1994), 173–210.

58. Summary of NSC meeting, October 1, 1963, Document 359, *FRUS, 1961–1963, Vol. V*; Memorandum from Brady to Murrow, September 26, 1963, Document 155, *FRUS, 1961–1963, Vol. XXV*. See also Highlights from Secretary of State's Policy Planning Meeting, March 26, 1963, Document 309, *FRUS, 1961–1963, Vol. V*.

59. Johnson, *The Vantage Point*, 472; Airgram from Embassy in Moscow, January 31, 1968, Document 265, *FRUS, 1964–1968, Vol. XIV*; President's meeting with GOP leadership, September 27, 1973, National Security Adviser Memoranda of Conversations, Box 2, Gerald Ford Library. For further discussion see Kovrig, *Of Walls and Bridges*, 248–9, and Dumbrell, *President Lyndon Johnson and Soviet Communism*, 41.

60. David Rockefeller, *Memoirs* (New York, 2002), 223–35; Marcus Gleisser, *The World of Cyrus Eaton* (Kent, Ohio, 2005). Another corporate leader who promoted détente was Donald Kendall of PepsiCo.

61. Johnson, *The Vantage Point*, 473; Bennett Kovrig, *Of Walls and Bridges: The United States and Eastern Europe* (New York, 1991), 248–9, 252; Dumbrell, *President Lyndon Johnson and Soviet Communism*, 17–8.

62. Nathaniel Davis, *A Long Walk to Church: A Contemporary History of Russian Orthodoxy* (Boulder, 1995, 38–9; Tatiana A. Chumachenko, *Church and State in Soviet Russia: Russian Orthodoxy from World War II to the Khrushchev Years* (Armonk, NY, 2002), 156; Walter Sawatsky, *Soviet Evangelicals Since World War II* (Scottdale, PA, 1981), 384; Steve Durasoff, *The Russian Protestants: Evangelicals in the Soviet Union, 1944–1964* (Madison, NJ, 1969), 247.

63. Sawatsky, *Soviet Evangelicals Since World War II*, 363; Davis, *A Long Walk to Church*, 36–43; Chumachenko, *Church and State in Soviet Russia*, 154; Gregory Freeze, ed., *Russia: A History* (New York, 1997), 364.

64. Chumachenko, *Church and State in Soviet Russia*, 192; Davis, *A Long Walk to Church*, 37–9; "What Sort of Détente?" *Commonweal*, Vol. 79, November 15, 1963, pp. 211–2.

65. Sawatsky, *Soviet Evangelicals*, 370, 384, 380, 11, 377.

66. Billy Graham, *Just As I Am: The Autobiography of Billy Graham* (San Francisco, 1997), 378–82; William Martin, *A Prophet with Honor: The Billy Graham Story* (New York, 1991), 257–8, 475.

67. Graham, *Just As I Am*, 378; David Edwin Harrell, Jr., *Oral Roberts: An American Life* (Bloomington, 1985), 258; "Reaching Russia by Radio," *Pentecostal Evangel*, February 1, 1959, p. 21; Paul and Ruth Demetrus, "Radio Reaches Russia!" *Pentecostal Evangel*, April 28, 1963, pp. 8–9; Steve Durasoff, *Pentecost Behind the Iron Curtain* (Plainfield, NJ, 1972), 56.

68. See, for example: Gunnar D. Kumlien, "Report from Russia," *Commonweal*, Vol. 67, November 15, 1957, pp. 172–3; "Religion in Russia," *Commonweal*, 18 March 1966, p. 685; T. Otto Nall, "The Hope for Religion in Russia," *The Christian Century*, March 4, 1959, pp. 261–2; Donald A. Lowrie, "Theological Atheism," *The Christian Century*, Vol. 78, January 25, 1961, pp. 109–11;

Donald A. Lowrie, "The Soviet Atheist's 'Sputnik,'" *The Christian Century*, Vol. 80, February 6, 1963, pp. 177–9; Michael Bourdeaux, "Transient Atheist Glory," *The Christian Century*, Vol. 85, February 21, 1968, p. 222; Paul Verghese, "The Flame of Faith Is Not Out in the U.S.S.R.," *The Christian Century*, Vol. 88, May 12, 1971, pp. 580–1.

69. Durasoff, *The Russian Protestants*, 227; Durasoff, *Pentecost Behind the Iron Curtain*, viii–ix; F. D. Nichols, "Poland and Russia," *Review and Herald*, July 23, 1959, pp. 7, 20; K. H. W., ""A Visit to the Soviet Union, *Review and Herald*, October 17, 1968, pp. 4–8; Theodore Carcich, "GC Vice-President Visits U.S.S.R. Believers," *Review and Herald*, July 25, 1974, p. 17.

70. Steve Durasoff, *The Russian Protestants: Evangelicals in the Soviet Union, 1944–1964* (Madison, NJ, 1969), 228–9; Iu. Senin, "Krestonosets 20 Veka," *Nauka I religiia*, No. 9, 1961, 40–43; "Ideologicheskie diversii i shpionazh pod prikritiem kresta," Kharkov, 1986, Hoover Institution Poster Collection, RU/SU 2321.1

71. See, for example, Leroy Brownlow, *Bible vs. Communism* (Fort Worth, 1961), a catechism, designed for use in Bible study classes, which stressed that the Bible and communism "are diametrically and unequivocally opposed to each other."

72. Martin E. Marty, *Modern American Religion, Volume 3: Under God, Indivisible* (Chicago, 1996), 367–75.

73. *Nuclear Weapons and the Conflict of Conscience*, 113–5. See also *Christianity and Communism Today*, 11–5.

74. Goldwater, *Why Not Victory?*, 149; Henry M. Jackson, "Does the Leopard Change His Spots?" *Vital Speeches of the Day*, Vol. XXXV, No. 4 (December 1, 1968), 98–100; Tom Mangold, *Cold Warrior: James Jesus Angleton: The CIA's Master Spy Hunter* (New York, 1991), 111–5.

75. Nitze to Theodore Sorensen, 9 October 1961, as quoted in Suri, *Power and Protest*, 19; Record of PPS meeting, February 8, 1961, Document 24, *FRUS, 1961–1963, Vol. V*.

76. Schlesinger memorandum to President Kennedy, April 5, 1961, quoted in Editorial Note, Document 54, *FRUS, 1961–1963, Vol. V*; Record of Meeting of the Policy Planning Council, June 23, 1961, Document 100, *FRUS, 1961–1963, Vol. V*.

77. James Critchlow, "The Moscow Trials," *Commonweal*, Vol. 87, 1 March 1968, p. 648.

78. "A Twisted Comparison," *Philadelphia Inquirer*, August 23, 1968; "Incredible Stupidity by McCarthy," *Philadelphia Inquirer*, August 26, 1968; David Lawrence, "Soviet Menace Proven No Myth," Washington *Evening Star*, August 22, 1968; Rusk statement at a news conference on August 22, 1968, *Department of State Bulletin*, Vol. LIX, No. 1524, September 9, 1968, p. 263; "Liberty Prostrate," *Chicago Tribune*, August 23, 1968; "Universal Moral Myopia," *The Christian Century*, Vol. LXXXV, No. 36, September 4, 1968, pp. 1095–6. See also William Pfaff's criticism of the "moral complacency" of those who felt Americans could not speak of Czechoslovakia because of US sins. "Czechoslovakia Invaded," *Commonweal*, Vol. 88, 6 September 1968, p. 581.

79. "Universal Moral Myopia," *The Christian Century*, Vol. LXXXV, No. 36, September 4, 1968, pp. 1095–6.

80. Patrick J. Buchanan, Introduction to Goldwater, *The Conscience of a Conservative* (1990), xv.


NOTES TO CHAPTER 7

1. Gerald R. Ford, *A Time to Heal* (New York, 1979), esp. 305; Henry Kissinger, *Years of Renewal* (New York, 1999), 652, 658; Ford interview, quoted in Amy Schapiro, *Millicent Fenwick: Her Way* (New Brunswick, NJ, 2003), 167, 175, 181.

2. Kenneth Cmiel, "The Emergence of Human Rights Politics in the United States," *Journal of American History*, Vol. 86, No. 3 (December 1999), 1231–50, and Cmiel, "The Recent History of Human Rights," *American Historical Review*, Vol. 109, No. 1 (February 2004), 117–35, esp. 130.

3. See Peter Berger's contribution to "Battered Pillars of the American System," *Fortune*, April 1975, 133–6; Kenneth E. Morris, *Jimmy Carter: American Moralist* (Athens, Georgia, 1996), esp. 205–9; Bruce J. Schulman, *The Seventies: The Great Shift in American Culture, Society, and Politics* (New York, 2001?). See also David Frum, *How We Got Here. The 70s: The Decade that Brought You Modern Life (For Better or Worse)* (New York, 2000), 4–5, xxiii–xxiv, 308.

4. Zbigniew Brzezinski, "America in a Hostile World," *Foreign Policy*, No. 23 (Summer 1976), 81–2, quoted in David Skidmore, *Reversing Course: Carter's Foreign Policy, Domestic Politics, and the Failure of Reform* (Nashville, 1996), 91; Kissinger comment on a speech he delivered in Memorandum of Conversation with Ford and the Shah of Iran, May 15, 1975, National Security Adviser Memcons, Box 11, Gerald R. Ford Library, Ann Arbor, Michigan; Goldwater speech, "Congressional Interference with Foreign Policy is Performing the Work of the Enemy," January 21, 1976, National Security Adviser Presidential Name File, Box 1, Ford Library; Daniel Patrick Moynihan, with Suzanne Weaver, *A Dangerous Place* (Boston, 1978), pp. 79, 279. Memorandum of Conversation between Moynihan and Ford on August 27, 1975, Ford Library, http://128.83.78.237/library/document/memcons/750827a.htm.

5. Alexander Solzhenitsyn, *Warning to the West* (New York, 1976), 10, 11–12, 26, 37, 23–4, 49, 46–7, 87; William Greider, "Solzhenitsyn Scolds U.S. For Détente," *Washington Post*, July 1, 1975, A1 and A7; Bernard Gwertzman, "Détente Scored by Solzhenitsyn," *New York Times*, July 1, 1975, p. 6; Robert G. Kaufman, *Henry M. Jackson: A Life in Politics* (Seattle, 2000), 292.

6. Meany introduction of Solzhenitsyn in *Warning to the West*, 3.

7. *Warning to the West*, 18–9.

8. Jeri Laber, *The Courage of Strangers: Coming of Age with the Human Rights Movement* (New York, 2002), 64–5; Michael Scammell, *Solzhenitsyn* (New York, 1984), 912, 870; comments on Solzhenitsyn's June 1978 address at Harvard University by Richard Pipes and William H. McNeill in Ronald Berman, ed., *Solzhenitsyn at Harvard* (Washington, D.C., 1980), 117, 123; Edward E. Ericson, Jr., *Solzhenitsyn and the Modern World* (Washington, DC,

1993), 80–5; D. M. Thomas, *Alexander Solzhenitsyn: A Century in His Life* (New York, 1998), 429–33, 450–1.

9. *Warning to the West*, 64–5; 23–4; Walter Stoessel to Washington, 23 July 1975, National Security Adviser, Presidential Country Files for Europe and Canada, Box 20, Ford Library; V. A. Kozlov, *Mass Uprisings in the USSR: Protest and Rebellion in the Post-Stalin Years* (Armonk, NY, 2002), 305; Gregory L. Freeze, "From Stalinism to Stagnation, 1953–1985," in Freeze, ed., *Russia: A History* (New York, 1997), esp. 374–6; Ronald Grigor Suny, *The Soviet Experiment* (New York, 1998), Chapter 19.

10. *Warning to the West*, 5; Ernest B. Furgurson, *Hard Right: The Rise of Jesse Helms* (New York, 1986), 16–19, 113–14; Gwertzman, "Détente Scored by Solzhenitsyn," *New York Times*, July 1, 1975, p. 6; Memorandum for Jack Marsh from Russ Rourke on telephone conversation with Helms, June 30, 1975, Marsh Files, Box 30, Ford Library.

11. Nixon remarks at news conference of February 25, 1974, attached to June 25, 1975 memo for Kissinger from Clift, Ford Library. A high-ranking State Department official (Kissinger?) made much the same point. *Time*, March 4, 1974, p. 32, quoted in Ericson, *Solzhenitsyn and the Modern World*, 76.

12. Outline of a Lincoln's Birthday message, originally prepared Feb. 12, 1974, retyped May 16, 1974, Box 15, Robert Goldwin Papers, Ford Library.

13. Ford speeches to House of Representatives, Feb. 11, 1952 and June 16, 1954, Box D14, Congressional Papers, Ford Library.

14. June 1, 1968 address at a dinner marking the fiftieth anniversary of Ukrainian independence and June 26, 1968 address at dedication ceremonies of the Center for Russian Jewry, New York City, Box 25, Series D, Congressional Papers, Ford Library; Congressional Research Service, "Analysis of the Philosophy and Voting Record of Representative Gerald R. Ford," October 25, 1973.

15. Remarks to be placed in the Congressional Record, June 25, 1973; Remarks at the Center for Strategic and International Studies, June 28, 1973, Box 35, Congressional Papers, Speeches File, Ford Library.

16. Memorandum of Conversation with Foreign Minister Andrei Gromyko, September 20, 1974, Box 1, Transition Materials, Ford Library.

17. Note by Ford quoted in Memorandum for Brent Scowcroft from Jerry H. Jones, March 25, 1975, White House Central Files (WHCF), IT 78–104, Box 13, Ford Library.

18. Memorandum of Conversation between Ford and Kissinger, April [no date], 1975, National Security Adviser Memcons, Box 10, Ford Library; Memorandum of Conversation between Ford and Kissinger, May 5, 1975, National Security Adviser Memcons, Box 11, Ford Library.

19. Max L. Friedersdorf, Assistant to the President, to Representative Margaret Heckler, May 31, 1975, WHCF, CO 158, Box 51, Ford Library.

20. Memorandum of Conversation between Ford, Kissinger, and Gromyko, September 20, 1974, Box 1, Transition Materials, Ford Library.

21. Memorandum for the President from Brent Scowcroft, Kissinger and Scowcroft Files, Box A1, Ford Library; Memorandum of Conversation at Vladivostok summit, November 24, 1974, National Security Adviser, Kissinger Reports, Box 1, Ford Library.

22. Memorandum of Conversation between Ford and Kissinger, April 25, 1975, National Security Adviser Memcons, Box 11, Ford Library; Memoranda of Conversations between Kissinger and Gromyko in Vienna, May 19 and May 20, 1975, National Security Adviser, Kissinger Reports, Box 1, Ford Library. For contrasting views, see John J. Maresca, *To Helsinki: The Conference on Security and Cooperation in Europe, 1973–1975* (Durham, NC, 1985, 1987), esp. xii, 120–1; Charles G. Stefan, "The Drafting of the Helsinki Final Act: A Personal View of the CSCE's Geneva Phase (September 1973 until July 1975), *SHAFR Newsletter*, Vol. 31, No. 2 (June 2000), 1–10; Jussi M. Hanhimaki, "'They Can Write It In Swahili': Kissinger, the Soviets, and the Helsinki Accords, 1973–1975," *Journal of Transatlantic Studies*, Vol. 1, No. 1 (2003), 37–58; and the report on a conference on the Helsinki process in September 2005: www.isn.ethz.ch/php/conferences/Previous Events/2005_CSCE_Report.pdf.

23. George S. Springsteen to Scowcroft, June 26, 1975, and Memorandum for Kissinger from Clift, June 26, 1975, National Security Adviser Presidential Name File, Box 3, Ford Library.

24. Ford, *A Time to Heal*, 298; Robert T. Hartmann, *Palace Politics: An Inside Account of the Ford Years* (New York, 1980), 337–9; Ron Nessen, *It Sure Looks Different from the Inside* (Chicago, 1978), 345.

25. "Solzhenitsyn's Politics," *Washington Post*, July 4, 1975; Joseph Kraft, "Solzhentisyn's Message," *Washington Post*, July 3, 1975; George F. Will, "Solzhentisyn and the President." *Washington Post*, July 11, 1975.

26. Steven D. Symms to Ford, July 10, 1975, WHCF, CO 158, Box 51, Ford Library; Cheney memorandum for Don Rumsfeld, July 8, 1975, Cheney Files, Box 10, Ford Library.

27. Wire service report, July 15, 1975; Memorandum for the President from Friedersdorf, July 12, 1975, Marsh Files, Box 30, Ford Library.

28. Reagan column, distributed by Copley News Service, July 18, 1975, Robert Hartmann Files, Box 175, Ford Library.

29. "Jerry, Don't Go," *Wall Street Journal*, July 23, 1975; Interview of the President by *New York Times* correspondents, July 23, 1975, Ron Nessen Papers, Box 51, Ford Library.

30. Meeting with Brezhnev at Helsinki, Ford noted bitterly that "Mr. Solzhenitsyn aligned himself with those who are very severe critics of the policy you and I believe in, détente." Memorandum of Conversation, July 30, 1975, National Security Adviser, Kissinger Reports, Box 1, Ford Library.

31. Scowcroft to Jack Marsh and Russ Rourk[e], December 4, 1975, National Security Adviser, Presidential Name File, Box 2, Ford Library.

32. Zbigniew Brzezinski, *Power and Principle: Memoirs of the National Security Adviser 1977–1981* (New York, revised edition, 1985), 156, 150, 474; Michael R. Beschloss and Strobe Talbott, *At the Highest Levels: The Inside Story of the End of the Cold War* (Boston, 1993), 103.

33. See the transcripts of Ford's interviews with New York Times and Newsweek correspondents on July 23 and 24, 1975, Box 51, Nessen Papers, Ford Library.

34. Two-part telegram from Stoessel to Kissinger, 24 July 1975, National Security Adviser, Presidential Country Files for Europe and Canada, Box 20, Ford Library.

35. "Statement by the President," White House press release, August 4, 1975, Box 176, Hartmann Papers, Ford Library; Paul Goldberg, *The Final Act: The Dramatic, Revealing Story of the Moscow Helsinki Watch Group* (New York, 1988), 59–64; William Korey, *The Promises We Keep: Human Rights, the Helsinki Process, and American Foreign Policy* (New York, 1993), 24–7; Amy Schapiro, *Millicent Fenwick: Her Way* (New Brunswick, NJ, 2003), 170–80.

36. Memorandum for Kissinger from Arthur Hartman, July 30, 1976, Bobbie Kilberg Papers, Box 4, Ford Library; Memorandum for Ford from Kissinger, September 30, 1976, National Security Adviser, Presidential Country Files for Europe and Canada, Box 19, Ford Library.

37. Schapiro, *Millicent Fenwick*, 180; Millicent Fenwick Papers, Boxes 20, 21, and 271, Alexander Library, Rutgers University, New Brunswick, New Jersey.

38. Memorandum for Dave Gergen from Stef Halper April 20, 1976, and Memorandum for Scowcroft from Gergen, September 10, 1976, Gergen Files, Box 8, Ford Library.

39. Jerry W. Sanders, *Peddlers of Crisis: The Committee on the Present Danger and the Politics of Containment* (Boston, 1983), 212.

40. Memorandum for Dick Cheney from Jim Reichley, June 24, 1976, Gergen Files, Box 5, Ford Library.

41. Ford, *A Time to Heal*, 398. Reagan broadcast, "Platforms C," taped September 1, 1976, in Kiron K. Skinner, Annelise Anderson, and Martin Anderson, eds., *Reagan's Path to Victory: The Shaping of Ronald Reagan's Vision: Selected Writings* (New York, 2004), 62–3.

42. Report on Harriman-Brezhnev meeting, September 20, 1976, in telegram from the Moscow Embassy to Washington, National Security Adviser Presidential Country Files for Europe and Canada, Box 21, Ford Library.

43. Joshua Muravchik, *The Uncertain Crusade: Jimmy Carter and the Dilemmas of Human Rights Policy* (Lanham, MD, 1986), 2–5; Robert A. Strong, *Working in the World: Jimmy Carter and the Making of American Foreign Policy* (Baton Rouge, 2000), 72–3.

44. Morris, *Jimmy Carter*, 4, 263; Leo Ribuffo, "Is Poland a Soviet Satellite? Gerald Ford, the Sonnenfeldt Doctrine and the Election of 1976," *Diplomatic History*, Vol. 14 (Summer 1990): 385–404; Muravchik, *The Uncertain Crusade*, 6; Rowland Evans and Robert Novak, "Carter and Solzhenitsyn," *Washington Post*, February 5, 1977, A13.

45. Jimmy Carter, *Keeping Faith: Memoirs of a President* (New York, 1982), 145; Joseph Kraft, "Crusader Carter And the Dissidents," *Washington Post*, February 24, 1977.

46. Joseph Kraft, "A Speech Is Just A Speech," *Washington Post*, January 23, 1977; "The Crusades for Human Rights," *Washington Post*, January 30, 1977, C6. See also "U.S. Visas and Helsinki," *Washington Post*, February 12, 1977, A14.

47. "The Soviets discover distrust," *Chicago Tribune*, March 16, 1977.

48. John Kelly Damico, "From Civil Rights to Human Rights: The Career of Patricia M. Derian," Ph.D. dissertation, Mississippi State University, 1999, 121–2, 126; Statement of Cyrus Vance at Helsinki Commission hearings, June 6, 1977, copy in Box 181, Millicent Fenwick Papers, Alexander Library, Rutgers University, New Brunswick, New Jersey.

49. Brzezinski, *Power and Principle*, 124, 149, 126.
50. Jimmy Carter, *Keeping Faith: Memoirs of a President* (New York, 1982), 21; see also 144, 154.
51. Presidential Review Memorandum/NSC-28, 7/7/77 revised draft, pages 29, 34, 73, Jimmy Carter Library, Atlanta.
52. PRM/NSC 28 (7/7/77), 4, 17, 19, 75, 72, 9, 13; Muravchik, *The Uncertain Crusade*, 16; Robert G. Kaufman, *Henry M. Jackson: A Life in Politics* (Seattle, 2000), 354; Carter, *Keeping Faith*, 143.
53. Carter, *Keeping Faith*, 142; Brzezinski, *Power and Principle*, 3, 557, 560. For different assessments of the depth and breadth of public interest in promotion of human rights abroad, see David Skidmore, *Reversing Course: Carter's Foreign Policy, Domestic Politics, and the Failure of Reform* (Nashville, 1996), 92–3, and PRM 28, 7/7/77, p. 82.
54. Muravchik, *The Uncertain Crusade*, 4; Kaufman, *Henry M. Jackson*, 58, 60, 285–6, 369. For a Russian dissident's view that the Chinese regime was more cruel and cynical, see Vladimir Bukovsky, *To Build a Castle – My Life as a Dissenter* (New York, 1979), 415–6.
55. Anatoly Dobrynin, *In Confidence: Moscow's Ambassador to America's Six Cold War Presidents* (New York, 1995), 338–9, 400–1.
56. Kiron K. Skinner, Annelise Anderson, and Martin Anderson, eds., *Reagan in His Own Hand: The Writings that Reveal His Revolutionary Vision for America* (New York, 2002), xv.
57. "Soviet Workers," taped May 25, 1977, *Reagan in His Own Hand*, 146–7.
58. Ibid., 147.
59. "Planned Economy," December 22, 1976, in *Reagan's Path to Victory*, 100.
60. "Human Rights III," taped January 9, 1978, *Reagan in His Own Hand*, 152–3; "Vietnam I," (February 1978), *Reagan's Path to Victory*, 390–1.
61. "Bukovsky," June 29, 1979, *Reagan, In His Own Hand*, 149–50.
62. Bukovsky, *To Build a Castle*, 56–7, 69–75, 324, 419, 52, 423–9, 277.
63. "Strategy II," May 4, 1977, *Reagan, In His Own Hand*, 111–13.
64. See *National Review*, July 21, 1978, reproduced in *Solzhenitsyn at Harvard*, 30–1; Reagan radio script, "Alex. Solzhenitsyn II," June 27, 1978, *Reagan's Path to Victory*, 326–8.
65. Carter, *Keeping Faith*, 144; handwritten note by Carter on draft of Presidential Directive 30, February 1978, Carter Library; PRM 28, p. 35, Carter Library.
66. Muravchik, *The Uncertain Crusade*, 14–16, 202; Jeri Laber, *The Courage of Strangers: Coming of Age with the Human Rights Movement* (New York, 2002), 80, 127; Damico, "From Civil Rights to Human Rights: The Career of Patricia M. Derian," 176, 189; Derian statement before the Subcommittee on International Organizations of the House Committee on Foreign Affairs, September 16, 1980, published by the State Department as *Human Rights in the U.S.S.R. and Eastern Europe*, Current Policy brochure No. 224; record of September 19, 1977 meeting between Derian and John Richardson, Box 18, Freedom House Archives, Mudd Library.
67. Laber, *The Courage of Strangers*, 71; Aryeh Neier, *Taking Liberties: Four Decades in the Struggle for Rights* (New York, 2003), 156.

68. Laber, *The Courage of Strangers*, 84, 88, 101, 98, 99.
69. Stephen S. Rosenfeld, "The 'Underside' of American Human Rights," *Washington Post*, March 25, 1977; Arch Puddington, *Broadcasting Freedom: The Cold War Triumph of Radio Free Europe and Radio Liberty* (Lexington, KY, 2000), 185–6; Paul Olkhovsky, "Mobilizing the Airwaves," Heritage Foundation report, November 13, 1981, copy in Fenwick Papers; Stephen S. Rosenfeld, "On the Beam," *Washington Post*, December 28, 1979.
70. Memorandum to Frank Shakespeare and Fred Iklé from Ken Adelman, July 22, 1980, Box 13, Iklé Papers, Hoover Institution Archives; Kenneth L. Adelman, "'Telling America's Story Abroad,'" *Washington Post*, July 6, 1980, D5.
71. Statement of Fred C. Iklé before the platform committee for the 1980 Republican convention, January 15, 1980, Box 11, Iklé Papers; Draft of a speech by Reagan on foreign information policy prepared by Allen Weinstein, enclosed in Weinstein to Fred Iklé, July 25, 1980, Iklé Papers. See also the foreign policy statement prepared by Richard Pipes, June 12, 1980, Box 14, Iklé Papers.
72. Andrei Sakharov, *Memoirs* (New York, 1990), 282, 563.
73. "Peace," address of August 18, 1980, *Reagan, In His Own Hand*, 480–6.
74. Muravchik, *The Uncertain Crusade*, 34; Carter, *Keeping Faith*, 147–9.
75. Morris, *Jimmy Carter*, 3–7; William H. Pemberton, *Exit with Honor: The Life and Presidency of Ronald Reagan* (Armonk, NY, 1997), 86–9.
76. Sakharov, *Memoirs*, 462–5.
77. Anatoly Dobrynin, *In Confidence: Moscow's Ambassador to America's Six Cold War Presidents* (New York, 1995), 378–92; Andropov to TsK KPSS, 18 February 1977 and Instructions to Dobrynin, enclosed in extract of protocol of Politburo meeting, 18 February 1977, *Soviet Archives*, posted by V. Bukovsky, http://psi.ece.jhu.edu/kaplan/IRUSS/BUK/GBARC/pdfs.
78. Andropov to TsK KPSS, 18 February 1977 and 29 March 1977, *Soviet Archives*, posted by V. Bukovsky.
79. Television commentary by Valentin Zorin, cited in Philip Caputo, "Carter is backing down – Kremlin," *Chicago Tribune*, March 21, 1977; "The Prophet Carter," *Washington Post*, March 20, 1977, C6.
80. "The President and Dr. Sakharov," *Chicago Tribune*, February 21, 1977; George F. Will, "Carter's 'Tougher' Soviet Standard," *Washington Post*, March 3, 1977, A23.
81. "The Prophet Carter," *Washington Post*, March 20, 1977, C6.
82. Dobrynin, *In Confidence*, 413, 460, 389.
83. Patricia Derian statement of September 16, 1980, published by the State Department as *Human Rights in the U.S.S.R. and Eastern Europe*; Laber, *The Courage of Strangers*, 123.
84. Martin Walker, *The Cold War: A History* (New York, 1996), 45; Peter G. Bourne, *Jimmy Carter: A Comprehensive Biography from Plains to Postpresidency* (New York, 1997), 390.
85. Korey, *The Promises We Keep*, xvii; Kovrig, *Of Walls and Bridges*, 174; Neier, *Taking Liberties*, 173.
86. David Skidmore, *Reversing Course: Carter's Foreign Policy, Domestic Politics, and the Failure of Reform* (Nashville, 1996), 90.

NOTES TO CHAPTER 8

1. Ronald Reagan (with Robert Lindsay), *An American Life* (New York, 1990), 715.
2. Stephen Vaughn, *Ronald Reagan in Hollywood: Movies and Politics* (New York, 1994), 199–200; Richard Pipes, *Vixi: Memoirs of a Non-Belonger* (New Haven, 2003), 165; Stephen Ambrose, *Eisenhower: The President* (New York, 1984), 542.
3. Peter Schweizer, *Victory: The Reagan Administration's Secret Strategy that Hastened the Collapse of the Soviet Union* (New York, 1994); Jay Winik, *On the Brink: The Dramatic, Behind-the-Scenes Saga of the Reagan Era and the Men and Women Who Won the Cold War* (New York, 1996); Peter Schweizer, *Reagan's War: The Epic Story of His Forty-Year Struggle and Final Triumph Over Communism* (New York, 2002).
4. Frances Fitzgerald, *Way Out There in the Blue: Reagan, Star Wars and the End of the Cold War* (New York, 2000), 17, 171, 175, 183, 268.
5. Fitzgerald, *Way Out There in the Blue*, 175; scripts for meetings with Suzanne Massie on February 29, 1984, March 6, 1985, and September 3, 1985, NSC Coordination Office papers, Reagan Library, Simi Valley, CA.
6. See, for example: Anthony Dolan to Donald Regan, January 14, 1985, WHORM Subject file FG 001; Pat Buchanan to Judith Mandel, November 9, 1985, WHORM Subject File, Box 74, Reagan Library.
7. Stephen Vaughn, *Ronald Reagan in Hollywood: Movies and Politics* (New York, 1994), 3, 8–15, 194; Edmund Morris, *Dutch: A Memoir of Ronald Reagan* (New York, 1999), 12, 17–18, 42, 63; Paul Kengor, *God and Ronald Reagan: A Spiritual Life* (New York, 2004), 9, 34, 15–16, 45–6, 22, 95.
8. Reagan, *An American Life*, 265, 544; Vaughn, *Ronald Reagan in Hollywood*, 150, 209–213, quoting *Hollywood Reporter*, June 6, 1951; Kengor, *God and Ronald Reagan*, 81, 226.
9. Vaughn, *Ronald Reagan in Hollywood*, 199–201, 236–7; Morris, *Dutch*, 303–321; William E. Pemberton, *Exit with Honor: The Life and Presidency of Ronald Reagan*, 49–51.
10. Vaughn, *Ronald Reagan in Hollywood*, 6. 9.
11. Caspar W. Weinberger, "Defense Spending is a Moral Issue," *Daughters of the American Revolution Magazine*, Vol. 121, No. 5 (May 1987), 314–7; George Shultz, *Turmoil and Triumph*, 717, 722; Robert Scheer, *With Enough Shovels: Reagan, Bush and Nuclear War* (New York, 1982), xi, 6; Fitzgerald, *Way Out There in the Blue*, 473; Caspar W. Weinberger, with Gretchen Roberts, *In the Arena: A Memoir of the 20th Century* (Washington, DC, 2001), xii–xiii, 261–2, 275, 282, 329.
12. Joseph E. Persico, *Casey: From the OSS to the CIA* (New York, 1990), xi, 19, 42–3, 217, 225, 356, 576.
13. Herbert E. Meyer, comments in Part 2 of PBS "American Experience" documentary, "Reagan" (WGBH Boston, 1998); Persico, *Casey*, 181, 185, 351, 361, 517, 227–8; Gates, *From the Shadows*, 218–9, 281.
14. Pipes, *Vixi*, 42, 56, 85, 115, 62, 183; Hedrick Smith, "Discordant Voices," *New York Times*, March 20, 1981; Pipes, *Survival is Not Enough: Soviet Realities and America's Future* (New York, 1984), 199–208, 278, 271.

15. Pipes, *Vixi*, 145, 175–6. Near the end of his NSC tenure, Clark belatedly tried to educate himself. Note from "klm" to "Jacque" on meeting between Clark and *New York Times* correspondent Hedrick Smith, May 31, 1983, William P. Clark Files, Box 91644, Reagan Library.

16. Raymond L. Garthoff, *The Great Transition: American-Soviet Relations and the End of the Cold War* (Washington, D.C., 1994), 23; Pipes, *Vixi*, 148; Robert McFarlane, *Special Trust* (New York, 1994), 183.

17. Gates, *From the Shadows*, 251, 319–321; George Crile, *Charlie Wilson's War* (New York, 2003); Schweizer, *Reagan's War*, 234; Steve Coll, *Ghost Wars: The Secret History of the CIA, Afghanistan, and bin Laden, from the Soviet Invasion to September 10, 2001* (New York, 2004), esp. 58, 97–8, 101–104, 127.

18. Schweizer, *Victory*; Schweizer, *Reagan's War*, esp. 241, 284; Kengor, *God and Ronald Reagan*, 175.

19. Handwritten notes of Cabinet Meeting, 1-27-81, Ken Khachigian Files, Reagan Library.

20. Pipes, *Vixi*, 202–3; Reagan to Franciszek Lachowicz, December 9, 1982, Ralph E. Weber and Ralph A. Weber, ed., *Dear Americans: Letters from the Desk of Ronald Reagan* (New York, 2003), 76–7.

21. Reagan, *An American Life*, 238, 273; Reagan to Brezhnev, April 24, 1981, in Weber, eds., *Dear Americans*, 17–18.

22. Pipes, *Vixi*, 178–180, 167, 172, 183–4. See also Gates, *From the Shadows*, 195.

23. Reagan to Jay Harris, April 26, 1982, Reagan to John Lindon, September 19, 1983, and Reagan to Meldrim Thomson, in Weber, eds., *Dear Americans*, 54, 125–9.

24. William E. Pemberton, *The Life and Presidency of Ronald Reagan* (Armonk, NY, 1997), 158; Coll, *Ghost Wars*, 98–9; Memorandum of Conversation, Reykjavik, Sunday, October 12, 1986, p. 20, Reagan Library.

25. Comment at press conference on January 29, 1981, quoted in Lou Cannon, *President Reagan: The Role of a Lifetime* (New York, 1991), 281–2; Address at Notre Dame, May 17, 1981, quoted in Kengor, *God and Ronald Reagan*, 201.

26. Statements by Max Kampelman at Plenary Sessions, CSCE, May 19 and November 13, 1981, and Millicent Fenwick et al to Ronald Reagan, April 23, 1982, Box 20, Fenwick Papers, Alexander Library, Rutgers University.

27. Alvin A. Snyder, *Warriors of Disinformation: American Propaganda, Soviet Lies, and the Winning of the Cold War* (New York, 1995), xiii, xv, 23–5, 184; Puddington, *Broadcasting Freedom*, 254–99; McFarlane, *Special Trust*, 221; Sosin, *Sparks of Liberty*, 176–81. Reagan quoted in Puddington, 263–4.

28. Text of Reagan conversation with Cronkite, March 3, 1981, William P. Clark Files, Reagan Library; Typed text of an insert, filed with draft of Reagan letter to Brezhnev, March 28, 1981, Matlock Files, Head of State Correspondence, Box 25, Reagan Library; Reagan, *An American Life*, 272; Kengor, *God and Ronald Reagan*, 199.

29. Pipes, *Vixi*, 194; Telegram from Secretary of State to American embassies, September 21, 1981, conveying Reagan message to Brezhnev, Matlock Files, Head of State Correspondence, Reagan Library.

30. Pipes, *Survival is Not Enough*, 274; Pipes, *Vixi*, 183.
31. Shultz, *Turmoil and Triumph*, 24, 6, 10–11, 897, 992, 266, 275–6; Persico, *Casey*, 158; Gates, *From the Shadows*, 278–80; NSDD 75, January 17, 1983, in McFarlane, *Special Trust*, 372–80. See also George P. Shultz, "New Realities and New Ways of Thinking," *Foreign Affairs* (Spring 1985), 705–21.
32. Henry R. Nau memo for NSC staff, November 25, 1981, WHORM Subject File, Box 71, Reagan Library.
33. Kengor, *God and Ronald Reagan*, 218–9, 238–40.
34. Robert P. Dugan, Jr., Director, National Association of Evangelicals, to speechwriter Tony Dolan, April 13, 1983, Box 19, Dolan Files, Reagan Library; William Martin, *With God on Our Side: The Rise of the Religious Right in America* (New York, 1996), 222–35.
35. Patrick Buchanan, "Secular City aghast at presidential piety," *Washington Times*, March 18, 1983, p. 3C; William F. Buckley, Jr., "So what did he say that upset critics," *Philadelphia Inquirer*, March 23, 1983; Edwin M. Yoder, Jr., "Presidential Preaching: Why Not?" *Washington Post*, March 19, 1983, A17; Arthur Schlesinger Jr., "Pretension in the Presidential Pulpit," *Wall Street Journal*, March 17, 1983; Charles Austin, "Religious Leaders Chide Reagan Talk," *New York Times*, March 15, 1983; William Safire, "President Reagan is paching," *Chicago Tribune*, March 18, 1983; Stanley Karnow, "'American Century' revisited," *Philadelphia Inquirer*, March 21, 1983; "As To Simple-Mindedness," *St. Louis Post-Dispatch*, March 10, 1983; Herblock cartoons in *Washington Post*, March 16, 20, and 22, 1983; Conrad cartoons in *Los Angeles Times*, March 14 and 20, 1983; Auth cartoon in *Philadelphia Inquirer*, March 10, 1983.
36. Reagan, *An American Life*, 570; Matlock, *Autopsy on an Empire*, 589; Morris, *Dutch*, 474; Kengor, *God and Ronald Reagan*, 235, 254–9, 261, 266–7. See also John Lewis Gaddis, *The Cold War: A New History* (New York: Penguin, 2005), 224–5.
37. John F. Burns, "Soviet Rebuts 'Focus of Evil' Speech," *New York Times*, March 18, 1983; Open Letter to Reagan from Patriarch Pimen, March 28, 1983, published as an advertisement in American newspapers.
38. "Ritorika Vremen 'Kholodnoi Voini,'" *Pravda*, March 10, 1983; John F. Burns, "Fight Reagan 'Crusade,' Soviet Aides Says," *New York Times*, June 15, 1983, A3; Mikhail Gorbachev, *Memoirs* (New York, 1995), 403, 406.
39. Reagan to Brezhnev, n.d. (July 1981), Weber, ed., *Dear Americans*, 20–1; Shultz, *Turmoil and Triumph*, 164–71.
40. Reagan, *An American Life*, 572–3, 597; Reagan to Andropov, July 11, 1983, Weber, eds., *Dear Americans*, 120.
41. Jack F. Matlock, Jr., *Autopsy on an Empire: The American Ambassador's Account of the Collapse of the Soviet Union* (New York, 1995), 670, 8, 15, 81, 739.
42. McFarlane to Clark, March 23, 1983, Clark Files, Reagan Library.
43. Shultz, *Turmoil and Triumph*, 24, 6, 10–11, 897, 992, 266, 275–6; Persico, *Casey*, 158; NSDD 75, January 17, 1983, in McFarlane, *Special Trust*, 372–80.
44. Interview of Arthur A. Hartman by William Miller, May 31, 1989, Association for Diplomatic Studies and Training Foreign Affairs Oral History

Project (quotation from page 27); "Strength, Consistency, and Constancy – The Basics for a Policy Toward the Soviet Union," address by Hartman on May 16, 1983, with critical analysis by Richard Pipes, enclosed in Pipes to Clark, May 23, 1983, Clark Files, Reagan Library.

45. Reagan, *An American Life*, 572, 589.

46. "Checklist of US-Soviet Issues: Status and Prospects, February 18, 1984, Matlock Files; Matlock agenda for Reagan meeting with Suzanne Massie, prepared February 29, 1984, Executive Secretariat, NSC, Country Files, Reagan Library; Matlock, *Reagan and Gorbachev*, 92–3, 97–8, 138–9, 175; English, *Russia and the Idea of the West*, 186–8.

47. Clark to Shultz, May 26, 1983, Clark files, Reagan Library; "Checklist of US-Soviet Issues: Status and Prospects," February 18, 1984, Matlock Files, US-USSR Relations, Reagan Library; Garthoff, *The Great Transition*, 42.

48. Handwritten comments on page 11 of speech draft, handwritten notes by a speechwriter, and Memorandum for Robert McFarlane and others by Anthony R. Dolan, "Soviet-American Relations Speech," January 11, 1984, WHORM Subject File, Box 74, Reagan Library; Matlock, *Reagan and Gorbachev*, 80–5.

49. Richard B. Wirthlin to James Baker et al, July 16, 1984, James Baker Files, Box 9, Reagan Library.

50. Reagan to John Koehler, July 9, 1981, quoted in Schweizer, *Reagan's War*, 173; Kengor, *God and Ronald Reagan*, 292; Handwritten insert by Reagan in March 5, 1983 draft of March 8, 1983 address, Box 8, Presidential Handwriting File: Presidential Speeches, Reagan Library; Reagan to Malcom Muggeridge, April 18, 1983, Ralph E. Weber and Ralph A. Weber, eds., *Dear Americans: Letters from the Desk of Ronald Reagan* (New York, 2003), 104.

51. Billy Graham, *Just As I Am: The Autobiography of Billy Graham* (San Francisco, 1997), 380–3, 499–511, 517–27; William Martin, *A Prophet with Honor: The Billy Graham Story* (New York, 1991), 495–524; Reagan to Graham, April 26, 1982 and Graham to Reagan, November 23, 1987, Presidential Handwriting File, Series II, Box 3 and Box 19, Reagan Library.

52. *Land of the Firebird: The Beauty of Old Russia* (Touchstone edition, New York, 1982), 13, 460.

53. Garthoff, *The Great Transition*, 145n; Script and Talking Points for Meeting with Mrs. Suzanne Massie on March 1, 1984, Executive Secretariat, NSC, Country Files, Reagan Library.

54. Morris, *Dutch*, 519; Reagan to Massie, February 15, 1984, Weber and Weber, eds., *Dear Americans*, 153; Talking points for a lunch with Massie on June 6, 1985, Coordination Office, NSC, Reagan Library.

55. Massie to Reagan, August 10, 1985, NSC Coordination Office files, Reagan Library; Matlock, *Reagan and Gorbachev*, 134.

56. Memoranda of Conversations at Geneva, November 19, 1985, 11:27 a.m., p. 3, 3:40 p.m., p. 6, 9:15 p.m., pp. 1 and 3, Reagan Library; Edmund Morris, *Dutch: A Memoir of Ronald Reagan* (New York, 1999), 519, 561, 569; Reagan to Elsa Sandstrom, November 25, 1985, and Reagan to Massie, February 10, 1986, in Weber and Weber, eds., *Dear Americans*, 236, 254.

57. Schweizer, *Reagan's War*, 249; Peggy Noonan, *What I Saw at the Revolution* (New York, 1990), 276; Memorandum of Conversation, Reykjavik, Sunday, October 12, 1986, pp. 1, 14, Matlock Series II, Reagan Library; George P. Shultz, *Turmoil and Triumph: My Years as Secretary of State* (New York, 1993), 983, 1006.

58. Memorandum of Conversation at Geneva, November 20, 1985, 10:15 a.m., Reagan Library; Memoranda of Conversation, Reykjavik, October 11, 1986, p. 2, October 12, 1986, p. 14, Matlock Series II, Reagan Library.

59. Shultz, *Turmoil and Triumph*, 586–7, 715, 887–93, 990, 1008, 1106–7.

60. Pat Buchanan memo to John Poindexter, February 6, 1986, WHORM Subject File, CO 165, Reagan Library; Donald Kimelman, "The Soviets are upbeat; the U.S. is downbeat," *Philadelphia Inquirer*, December 10, 1987; Benson cartoon in Arizona *Republic*, December 1987; George F. Will, "Reagan fixation on arms control has scrambled remaining policy," *Philadelphia Inquirer*, May 30, 1988.

61. AP dispatch, *San Jose Mercury*, May 25, 1988; Kengor, *God and Ronald Reagan*, 295–300; Matlock, *Reagan and Gorbachev*, 301; Speech draft, 5/16/88, for 5/30/88 speech at Danilov Monastery, SP 1263 561378, Ronald Reagan Library. See also Dolan's June 2 draft of Reagan remarks on returning to the US, Box 65, Dolan Files, Reagan Library.

62. Matlock, *Reagan and Gorbachev*, 302;

63. A. M. Rosenthal, "Formerly, The Evil Empire," *New York Times*, June 3, 1988; William Safire, "Doomed to Cooperate," *New York Times*, June 2, 1988; William F. Buckley, Jr., "A Russian Fairy Tale," *Washington Post*, June 7, 1988; Gerald M. Boyd, "Bush Says Rise in U.S. Arms Led to Soviet Reform," *New York Times*, June 29, 1988.

64. "Obituary for the Cold War," an interview with George Kennan in *New Perspectives Quarterly*, Summer 1988, reprinted in *Harper's Magazine*, November 1988, 17–19. Georgi Arbatov, one of the top Soviet experts on the United States, similarly remarked that "The United States needs the Soviet Union to satisfy the American psychological need for a villain. In this way, Americans can see themselves as a shining city on the hill." *Economist*, 6 June 1987, quoted in Snyder, *Warriors of Disinformation*, 166.

65. "Is the Cold War Over?" (summary of four *New York Times*/CBS News polls, November 1989–October 1990), *New York Times*, October 16, 1990; Frank R. Wolf (R-Va.), "We Must Use *Glasnost* to Win Freedom for Soviet Christians," *Christianity Today*, May 13, 1988, p. 12.

66. Kim A. Lawton, "Christianity in Russia: An Uncertain Birthday Party," *Christianity Today*, June 17, 1988, pp. 54–5; Terry Muck, "Still the Evil Empire?" *Christianity Today*, July 15, 1988, pp. 14–5.

67. Paul Boyer, *When Time Shall Be No More: Prophecy Belief in Modern American Culture* (Cambridge, MA, 1992), 172–9.

68. Graham, *Just As I Am*, 546–56; Edward E. Plowman, "Graham Joins Russian Church Festivities," *Christianity Today*, July 15, 1988, 49–51.

69. James Billington, "A Time of Danger, an Opening for Dialogue," *Washington Post*, November 23, 1983; Anatoly S. Chernyaev, *My Six Years with Gorbachev* (University Park, PA, 2000), 105.

70. Kengor, *God and Ronald Reagan*, 313–4.
71. Nathaniel Davis, *A Long Walk to the Church: A Contemporary History of Russian Orthodoxy* (Boulder, CO, 1995), 59–63; Gorbachev, *Memoirs*, 509, 453; Chernyaev, *My Six Years with Gorbachev*, 71–2.
72. Gerald M. Boyd, "Bush Says Rise in U.S. Arms Led to Soviet Reform," *New York Times*, June 29, 1988; Schweizer, *Reagan's War*, 244–5.
73. Chernyaev, *My Six Years with Gorbachev*, 76–85, 142; Garthoff, *The Great Transition*, esp. 773–7; Robert D. English, *Russia and the Idea of the West: Gorbachev, Intellectuals, and the End of the Cold War* (New York, 2000), esp. 169, 186, 174; Memoranda of conversations at Geneva, November 19, 1985, and at Reykjavik, October 12, 1986, Reagan Library; Philip Taubman, "Summit Talks End," *New York Times*, June 2, 1988.


NOTES TO CHAPTER 9

1. Martin Malia, *Russia Under Western Eyes: From the Bronze Horseman to the Lenin Mausoleum* (Cambridge, MA, 1999), 411–2; Jerry F. Hough, "The Failure of Party Formation and the Future of Russian Democracy," in Timothy Colton and Jerry Hough, eds., *Growing Pains: Russian Democracy and the Election of 1993* (Washington, D.C., 1998), 670; Anders Åslund, *How Russia Became a Market Economy* (Washington, D.C., 1995), 10, 312.
2. Timothy J. Colton and Michael McFaul, "America's Real Russian Allies," *Foreign Affairs*, Vol. 80, No. 6 (November/December 2001), 46–58; Michael McFaul, *Russia's Unfinished Revolution: Political Change From Gorbachev to Putin* (Ithaca, 2001).
3. Hough, "The Failure of Party Formation and the Future of Russian Democracy," 669.
4. Samuel Huntington, *The Clash of Civilizations and the Remaking of World Order* (New York, 1996), 20, 29, 142, 160–4, 270.
5. Richard Pipes, "Russia's Past, Russia's Future," *Commentary*, Vol. 101, No. 6 (June 1996), 30–8, esp. 32.
6. Janine R. Wedel, *Collision and Collusion: The Strange Case of Western Aid to Eastern Europe, 1989–1998* (New York: St. Martin's Press, 1998); Stephen F. Cohen, *Failed Crusade: America and the Tragedy of Post-Communist Russia* (New York: W. W. Norton, 2000); Peter Reddaway and Dmitri Glinski, *The Tragedy of Russia's Reforms: Market Bolshevism Against Democracy* (Washington, D.C., 2001).
7. Carol Bellamy, "The Peace Corps in the '90s: New Frontiers in the Former Soviet Republics," Princeton University lecture, February 6, 1995; Peace Corps *Congressional Budget Presentation* for Fiscal Year 2001, February 7, 2000; Patricia Wardley Hamilton, "An American Network for Russian Women, *New York Times*, January 22, 1995; Todd Foglesong, "Lost in Translation: The Lessons of Russian Judicial Reform," unpublished paper, January 12, 2002.
8. Transcript of Gorbachev press conference, *New York Times*, June 2, 1988, A8; Jonathan A. Becker, *Soviet and Russian Press Coverage of the United States: Press, Politics and Identity in Transition* (New York, 2002), 83–4, 123–30; Rose

Brady, *Kapitalizm: Russia's Struggle to Free Its Economy* (New Haven, 1999); George Cohon, *To Russia with Fries* (Toronto, 1997).

9. English, *Russia and the Idea of the West*.

10. George Bush and Brent Scowcroft, *A World Transformed* (New York, 1998), 12, 135, 43, 114, 13, 181; Michael R. Beschloss and Strobe Talbott, *At the Highest Levels: The Inside Story of the End of the Cold War* (Boston, 1993), 24, 123.

11. Bush and Scowcroft, *A World Transformed*, 5, xiii, 6, 46, 44, 63; Beschloss and Talbott, *At the Highest Levels*, 7–8, 24.

12. James A. Baker, *The Politics of Diplomacy: Revolution, War and Peace, 1989–1992* (New York, 1995), 43–5, 69–70.

13. Beschloss and Talbott, *At the Highest Levels*, 34, 73, 122, 168. Dan Quayle, *Standing Firm: A Vice-Presidential Memoir* (New York, 1994), esp. 163–75; Allan Bloom in "Responses to Fukuyama," *The National Interest* (Summer 1989), 19–20.

14. Beschloss and Talbott, *At the Highest Levels*, 5; Bush and Scowcroft, *A World Transformed*, 11–12.

15. Derek Chollet and James M. Goldgeier, "Once Burned, Twice Shy? The Pause of 1989," in W. C. Wohlforth, ed. *Cold War Endgame* (University Park, PA, 2003), 141–73; Bush and Scowcroft, *A World Transformed*, 20, 142; Beschloss and Talbott, *At the Highest Levels*, 166.

16. Baker, *The Politics of Diplomacy*, 69, 475, 528; Jack F. Matlock, Jr., *Autopsy on an Empire: The American Ambassador's Account of the Collapse of the Soviet Union* (New York, 1995), 182–3, 556–7; Beschloss and Talbott, *At the Highest Levels*, 20, 27.

17. Bush and Scowcroft, *A World Transformed*, 7.

18. Beschloss and Talbott, *At the Highest Levels*, 45, 50, 51, 73–5, 93, 166.

19. Beschloss and Talbott, *At the Highest Levels*, 22–3, 94, 167–8, 182, 319, 346.

20. Beschloss and Talbott, *At the Highest Levels*, 141, 237, 159, 167, 297, 351, 378, 412; Matlock, *Autopsy on an Empire*, 177–80, 538–9, 590–1.

21. National Security Directive 23, September 22, 1989, and National Security Directive 51, October 17, 1990, http://bushlibrary.tamu.edu/research/directives.html.)

22. Puddington, *Broadcasting Freedom*, 298–9; Sosin, *Sparks of Liberty*, xii–xiv, 217; Bush and Scowcroft, *A World Transformed*, 515; Beschloss and Talbott, *At the Highest Levels*, 416–8.

23. Beschloss and Talbott, *At the Highest Levels*, 41, 54, 179, 182, 203; Reddaway and Glinski, *The Tragedy of Russia's Reforms*, 200–25.

24. Beschloss and Talbott, *At the Highest Levels*, 422–33; Bush and Scowcroft, *A World Transformed*, 518–21; Puddington, *Broadcasting Freedom*, 306; Reddaway and Glinski, *The Tragedy of Russia's Reforms*, 167–72.

25. "Revolt of the powerful and privileged," *Chicago Tribune*, August 20, 1991; "Of Communism and history's dustbin," *Chicago Tribune*, August 23, 1991. See also Irwin Weil, "The USSR's creative democrats refused to be cowed," *Chicago Tribune*, August 23, 1991, p. 27.

26. Ronald Reagan, "Recognize the Free Republics," *Los Angeles Times*, August 29, 1991, B7; James H. Billington, *Russia Transformed: Breakthrough to Hope. Moscow, August 1991* (New York: Free Press, 1992), 4, 13, 104, 107, 122, 128,

134, 175. For Billington's later expressions of his religious interpretation, see "The Church in the World: Unexpected Joy," *Theology Today*, Vol. 52, No. 3 (October, 1995), 382–91; "The West's Stake in Russia's Future," *Orbis*, Vol. 41, No. 4 (Fall 1997), 545–53; and *Russia in Search of Itself* (Washington, D.C., 2004), esp. 42–5, 147.

27. Billington, "The West's Stake in Russia's Future," 552; see also *Russia in Search of Itself*, 147.

28. "Prayers and Bibles Welcomed in the Kremlin," *Christianity Today*, October 7, 1991, 42–3; Philip Yancey, "Praying with the KGB," *Christianity Today*, January 13, 1992, p. 19; "Moscow Opens Its Heart to the Gospel," *Christianity Today*, November 23, 1992, p. 50; "Help the Soviet People Meet the Real Jesus," advertisement in *Christianity Today*, September 16, 1991, p. 61.

29. Victoria Bonnell, Ann Cooper, and Gregory Freidin, *Russia at the Barricades: Eyewitness Accounts of the August 1991 Coup* (Armonk, NY, 1994), 13–14, 19; David Foglesong and Gordon M. Hahn, "Ten Myths About Russia: Understanding and Dealing with Russia's Complexity and Ambiguity," *Problems of Post-Communism*, Vol. 49, No. 6 (November/December 2002), 3–15.

30. "Populism vs. Tanks: Soviet Forces at Odds," *Los Angeles Times* editorial, August 21, 1991, B6; Madeleine Albright and Andrew Kohut, "The Yeltsin People," *Washington Post*, August 21, 1991.

31. Baker, *Politics of Diplomacy*, 523, 525, 531; "The Moscow Coup," *Washington Post*, August 20, 1991; "The People Defeat The Coup," August 22, 1991, and "What Is To Be Done?" August 23, 1991, *St. Louis Post-Dispatch*; Peter Gumbel and Gerald F. Seib, "Democratic Forces Roll Back Soviet Coup; A New Era May Dawn," *Wall Street Journal*, August 22, 1991. For additional depictions of an almost unanimous popular revolt, see Paul Greenberg, "Three Days that Shook the World: Courage had to come first," *Chicago Tribune*, August 23, 1991; Stephen Chapman, "Dying or not, communism still has Western fans," *Chicago Tribune*, August 29, 1991; and "The New Democratic Order," editorial, *Wall Street Journal*, August 22, 1991.

32. Don Wright cartoon, *Chicago Tribune*, June 2, 1988; Bob Rogers cartoon in *The Pittsburgh Press*, reprinted in *New York Times*, February 4, 1990.

33. Clarence Page, "Coups in the age of Big Macs and fax machines," *Chicago Tribune*, August 21, 1991.

34. Locher cartoon in *Chicago Tribune*, August 29, 1991, p. 26.

35. William Neikirk, "Gorbachev's fall is dispiriting for U.S. capitalists," *Chicago Tribune*, August 21, 1991, p. 23.

36. Author's interview with a Pentecostal group, June 1995.

37. See, for example, the op-ed piece by Ambassador to Russia Robert S. Strauss, "More U.S. Support for Russia," *New York Times*, November 15, 1992, and Jude Wanniski, "The Future of Russian Capitalism, *Foreign Affairs*, Vol. 71, No. 2 (Spring 1992), 17–25.

38. Bush and Scowcroft, *A World Transformed*, 540–4; Baker, *The Politics of Diplomacy*, 523, 535.

39. Bush and Scowcroft, *A World Transformed*, 48–52; Baker, *The Politics of Diplomacy*, 654; James M. Goldgeier and Michael McFaul, *Power and Purpose: U.S. Policy Toward Russia After the Cold War* (Washington, D.C., 2003), 37, 67–73.

40. "Cutting Torch," cartoon by Engelhardt in *St. Louis Post-Dispatch*, August 22, 1991; cartoon by Conrad, *Los Angeles Times*, August 22, 1991, B7; cartoon by Wright for the *Palm Beach Post*, reprinted in *Chicago Tribune*, August 27, 1991.

41. Leon Aron, *Yeltsin: A Revolutionary Life* (New York, 2000), Chapter 7.

42. Reddaway and Glinski, *The Tragedy of Russia's Reforms*, 241–8.

43. Yegor Gaidar, *Days of Defeat and Victory* (Seattle, 1999), 15–17, 68, 75, 57, 140; Reddaway and Glinski, *The Tragedy of Russia's Reforms*, 237–47.

44. Yeltsin speech on October 28, 1991, quoted in Reddaway and Glinski, *The Tragedy of Russia's Reforms*, 231.

45. Reddaway and Glinski, *The Tragedy of Russia's Reforms*, 234.

46. Reddaway and Glinski, *The Tragedy of Russia's Reforms*, 247, 340–3; Gaidar, *Days of Defeat and Victory*, 131; Goldgeier and McFaul, *Power and Purpose*, 82.

47. Reddaway and Glinski, *The Tragedy of Russia's Reforms*, 343; Jeffrey Sachs, "Home Alone 2," *New Republic*, December 21, 1992, pp. 23–5; Sachs, "Betrayal," *New Republic*, January 31, 1994, pp. 14–16.

48. Strobe Talbott, *The Russia Hand: A Memoir of Presidential Diplomacy* (New York, 2002), 31; Warren Christopher, *In the Stream of History: Shaping Foreign Policy for a New Era* (Stanford, 1998), 36.

49. Christopher, *In the Stream of History*, 17, 33, 269; Madeleine Albright, *Madam Secretary* (New York, 2003), xii; Bill Clinton, *My Life* (New York, 2004), 170.

50. See, for example, Deputy Secretary of State Strobe Talbott's speech, "America and Russia in a Changing World," October 29, 1996, State Department *Dispatch*, Vol. 7, No. 44, and Secretary of State Madeline Albright's address, "U.S. Strategy for Responding to Russia's Transformation," October 2, 1998, U.S. Department of State *Dispatch*, October 1998, p. 5.

51. Clinton, *My Life*, 506; Talbott, *The Russia Hand*, 47, 84, 246.

52. See, for example, Christopher, *In the Stream of History*: compare 47 and 101 with 37–8, 59, 94.

53. Talbott, *The Russia Hand*, 52, 41–2; Clinton, *My Life*, 505.

54. Talbott, *The Russia Hand*, 43, 56, 58.

55. Christopher, *In the Stream of History*, 36, 45; Talbott, *The Russia Hand*, 53, 150, Clinton, *My Life*, 503–5.

56. Clinton, *My Life*, 508.

57. Reddaway and Glinski, *The Tragedy of Russia's Reforms*, 400–29; Talbott, *The Russia Hand*, 86–90; Clinton, *My Life*, 549; Christopher, *In the Stream of History*, 97–8.

58. Professor Jeffrey Hahn, quoted in Peter Grier, "US Rethinks Russia Policy Following Yeltsin Victory," *Christian Science Monitor*, October 6, 1993; Michael Dobbs, "Far From a Victory for Yeltsin," *Washington Post*, October 6, 1993.

59. "Weekend War," *Washington Post* editorial, October 5, 1993, A18; Paul Greenberg, "In Yeltsin's Russia, parliament got armored tanks, but the people got a Lincoln," *Chicago Tribune*, October 8, 1993; Allen Weinstein, "The Work Ahead," *Washington Post*, October 5, 1993; "Surrender in Moscow"

and "Aftermath in Russia," *Christian Science Monitor* editorials, October 5 and 7, 1993.

60. "October Revolution," *St. Louis Post-Dispatch*, October 5, 1993 editorial.

61. Martin Malia, "Reinventing Peter the Great," *New York Times*, December 12, 1993.

62. See, for example, David F. Schmitz, *Thank God They're On Our Side: The United States and Right-Wing Dictatorships, 1921–1965* (Chapel Hill, 1999); David Ekbladh, "How to Build a Nation," *Wilson Quarterly*, Vol. 28, No. 1 (Winter 2004).

63. "Getting Over Chaos in Russia," *New York Times*, December 6, 1993.

64. See, for example, Christopher, *In the Stream of History*, 95–104.

65. Steven Erlanger, "Greater Russia's Champion," *New York Times*, December 13, 1993; Serge Schmemann, "Muscovite With Bravado," Celestine Bohlen, "Nationalist Move Far Out in Front in Voting," "Russia's Chastening Vote" (editorial), Thomas Friedman, "On the Russian Vote, Clinton Accentuates the Positive," all in *New York Times*, December 14, 1993.

66. A. M. Rosenthal, "To Russia in Constancy," *New York Times*, December 21, 1993; "A Safety Net for Russian Reform," *New York Times* editorial, December 22, 1993; Talbott, *The Russia Hand*, 76, 84, 106–7.

67. Reddaway and Glinski, *The Tragedy of Russia's Reforms*, 426–7; Dmitri Trenin and Aleksei V. Malashenko, *Russia's Restless Frontier: The Chechnya Factor in Post-Soviet Russia* (Washington, DC, 2004); Nabi Abdullaev, "Chechnya Tore Rights Movement Apart," *Moscow Times*, December 10, 2004.

68. Talbott, *The Russia Hand*, 185, 151, 195, 204.

69. Leonid Kishkovsky, "Russian Orthodoxy: Out of bondage, into the wilderness," *Christian Century*, October 6, 1993, p. 935.

70. Philip Yancey, "Praying with the KGB," *Christianity Today*, January 13, 1992, pp. 21, 25; Charles Colson, "Tyranny by Any Other Name," *Christianity Today*, January 13, 1992, p. 72; "CoMission: Teaching Teachers in Russia," *Christianity Today*, December 14, 1992, pp. 54–5.

71. "Russia Looks to Curb Missions," *Christian Century*, July 28-Aug 4, 1993, p. 736; "Will Growing Nationalism Stall Christian Outreach?" *Christianity Today*, Aug 12, 1996, p. 54; Beverly Nickles, "Restrictions on Religion Get Uneven Enforcement," *Christianity Today*, April 6, 1998, p. 20.

72. Beverly Nickles, "Training Shortfall May Imperil Growth," *Christianity Today*, April 7, 1997; Beverly Nickles, "Restrictions on Religion Get Uneven Enforcement," *Christianity Today*, April 6, 1998, p. 20; Mikhail M. Kulakov, "Seventh-day Adventists," in John Witte, Jr. and Michael Bourdeaux, eds., *Proselytism and Orthodoxy in Russia: The New War for Souls* (Maryknoll, NY, 1999), 151; *Adventist Review*, July 3, 2000, and November 23, 2000, p. 19.

73. "Iisus Khristos Loves You," *Newsweek*, January 4, 1993, p. 45; Elder Stephen McPherson, "Idaho Bearhugs Russia," *Newsletter of the Idaho Conference of Seventh-day Adventists*, Vol. 5, No. 1 (March 1994); Sharon Linzey and Iakov Krotov, "The Future of Religion and Religious Freedom in Russia," *Religion in Eastern Europe*, Vol. XXI, No. 5 (October 2001), p. 27; Author's interview, Moscow, June 1993.

74. "Russia looks to curb missions," *The Christian Century*, July 28-August 4, 1993, pp. 735–6; Metropolitan Kirill, "Gospel and Culture," in Witte and Bourdeaux, eds., *Proselytism and Orthodoxy in Russia*, 66–76.

75. See, for example, Leonid Kishkovsky (former president of the National Council of Churches), "Russian Orthodoxy: Out of bondage, into the wilderness," *Christianity Today*, October 6, 1993, pp. 934–5, and Irving Kristol in "Russia's Destiny," *Wall Street Journal*, February 11, 1994.

76. Philip Yancey, "Praying with the KGB," *Christianity Today*, January 13, 1992, pp. 22–3; Edward E. Roslof, "The myth of resurrection: Orthodox Church in postcommunist Russia," *The Christian Century*, March 17, 1993, 290–3.

77. Author's interview, June 1995.

78. "Russian Adventist Leader Confirms Worsening Climate for Religious Liberty," *Adventist Review*, June 11, 1998, p. 21; Stephen Chavez, "Unfinished Business," *Adventist Review*, February 12, 1998, 16–19.

79. "Teaching Christ at Moscow U.," *Christianity Today*, September 13, 1993, p. 86; Ivan I. Fahs, quoted in "Nyet to Religious Liberty," in *Christianity Today*, August 16, 1993, p. 44; Father Igor Talko, quoted in "U.S. missionaries in Russia contend with oversupply of faith offerings," AP dispatch in Lawrence, Kansas *Journal-World*, December 29, 1996, p. 10A; Metropolitan Kirill, "Gospel and Culture," in Witte and Bourdeaux, eds., *Proselytism and Orthodoxy in Russia*, 73; Besik Urigashvili, "Obyknovennye prikliucheniia amerikantsa v Saranske," *Izvestiia*, 19 April 1996. On the Soviet-style charges of missionary connections to the CIA, see also Nathaniel Davis, "Tribulations, Trials and Troubles for the Russian Orthodox Church," *Religion In Eastern Europe*, Vol. XX, No. 6 (December 2000), pp. 49–50.

80. "Russia looks to curb missions," *The Christian Century*, July 28-Aug 4, 1993, p. 735; Kim Lawton, "CoMission Agreement Canceled," *Christianity Today*, April 24, 1995; "Yeltsin vetoes bid to curb religion," *San Jose Mercury News*, July 23, 1997; "Yeltsin signs bill to restrict religions," *San Jose Mercury News*, September 27, 1997; William J. Kovatch, Jr., "All Religions Are Equal, But Some Are More Equal Than Others: Russia's 1997 Restrictive Law of Religious Practices," *Demokratizatsiya*, Vol. 6, No. 2 (Spring 1998), 416–25; John B. Dunlop, "Russia's 1997 Law Renews Religious Persecution," *Demokratizatsiya*, Vol. 7, No. 1 (Winter 1999), 28–41; ("Religion crackdown reported in Russia," *The Christian Century*, October 29, 1997, 970; Laurie Goodstein, "Russians Oust U.S. Missionary Under New Law," *New York Times*, April 18, 1998; "Jesuits contend with Russian law on religion," *The Christian Century*, May 19–26, 1999, pp. 561–2.

81. Metropolitan Kirill, "Gospel and Culture," in Witte and Bourdeaux, eds., *Proselytism and Orthodoxy in Russia*, 74; Kirill, quoted in Donald W. Shriver Jr. and Peggy L. Shriver, "Russian Orthodoxy in a time of upheaval," *The Christian Century*, April 5, 1995, p. 366; Beverly Nickles, "Will Growing Nationalism Stall Christian Outreach?" *Christianity Today*, August 12, 1996, p. 54; Alexei Podberezkin, deputy chairman of the foreign affairs committee of the Duma, quoted in Michael Wines, "Straining to See the Real Russia," *New York Times*, May 2, 1999.

82. Clinton, *My Life*, 654–5; J. L. Black, *Russia Faces NATO Expansion: Bearing Gifts or Bearing Arms?* (Lanham, MD, 2000), 31; Talbott, *The Russia Hand*, 141, 94; Albright, *Madam Secretary*, 252.

83. Talbott, *The Russia Hand*, 230; Black, *Russia Faces NATO Expansion*, 11, 17–20, 21, 40n, 95.

84. Black, *Russia Faces NATO Expansion*, 42; Eric Shiraev and Vladislav Zubok, *Anti-Americanism in Russia: From Stalin to Putin* (New York, 2000), 28, 91, 145–7; Serge Schmemann, "What Clinton Won't Find in Russia: Misty-Eyed Nostalgia for Jeans and Coca-Cola," *New York Times*, January 10, 1994; "The Measure of a Summit," *New York Times* editorial, May 7, 1995; Alessandra Stanley, "Stripped of Themes, Yeltsin Wraps Himself in Flag," *New York Times*, April 19, 1996. On post-Soviet Russian nationalism, see Vera Tolz, *Russia: Inventing the Nation* (London and New York, 2001), esp. 125–30, and Billington, *Russia in Search of Itself*. For an absurdist rendering of Russian resentment of American capitalist and Protestant influences, see Victor Pelevin, *The Life of Insects* (New York, 1998; first published in Moscow, 1994), esp. 4, 87, 176.

85. John Meroney, "Hollywood Knows What Voters Want," *Wall Street Journal*, August 13, 1997.

86. Michael Gordon, "Perry Says Caution is Vital to Russian Partnership," *New York Times*, March 15, 1994; William Safire, "And on Earth, Freedom," *New York Times*, December 25, 1995; Safire, "Yeltsin lets Russia slip away," *San Jose Mercury News*, February 9, 1996; Tom Toles cartoon for *Buffalo News*, December 24, 1995; Don Wright cartoon for *Palm Beach Post*, December 1995; Tom Toles cartoon, mycomicspage.com, September 3, 1998; Steve Benson cartoon for the *Arizona Republic*, September 21, 1998.

87. Timothy Egan, "Yeltsin Visits Seattle, a Good Market," *New York Times*, September 30, 1994; Richard W. Stevenson, "Foreign Capitalists Brush Risks Aside To Invest in Russia," *New York Times*, October 11, 1994; Joseph Kahn and Timothy O'Brien, "For Russia and Its US Bankers, Match Wasn't Made in Heaven," *New York Times*, October 18, 1998; John Varoli, "Russian Financial Woes Take a Toll in Cigarettes," *New York Times*, December 31, 1998; David Johnston, "Kazakh Mastermind or a New Ugly American?" *New York Times*, December 17, 2000.

88. Michael R. Gordon, "Yeltsin's Nominee, Besieged, Is Not Without Allies," *New York Times*, April 12, 1998, and Gordon, "With I.M.F. in Town, Yeltsin Pushes Economic Measures," *New York Times*, June 24, 1998.

89. See Wedel, *Collision and Collusion*, esp. 123, 137.

90. Philip Taubman, "A Gentler Breeze Is Blowing Through Moscow," *New York Times*, June 21, 1998; Vijai Maheshwari, "At Nightclubs in Moscow, a Taste for Quentin Tarantino," *New York Times*, July 6, 1998; Soros quoted in Alessandra Stanley, "2 Yeltsin Advisers Pushed More Deeply Into Shadows," *New York Times*, January 17, 1998.

91. Michael Specter, "Yeltsin the Improviser, Bathing in a New Limelight," *New York Times*, March 27, 1998. See also Specter's categorical statement that "the father of Russian democracy" had "become an autocrat" in "My Boris," *New York Times Magazine*, July 26, 1998, 24–7.

92. Robert D. Kaplan, "Sometimes, Autocracy Breeds Freedom," *New York Times*, June 28, 1998; "A Needed, but Risky Bailout," *New York Times*, July 22, 1998.

93. David E. Sanger, "I.M.F. Backs $17 Billion for Russia, but Delays First Payment," *New York Times*, July 21, 1998; Michael Wines, "Stock and Bond Prices Drop In Russia as Investors Bolt," *New York Times*, August 14, 1998; Celestine Bohlen, "Russia Acts to Fix Sinking Finances," *New York Times*, August 18, 1998; Nicholas Weinstock, "Who the Heck is Buck Wiley and Why is He Leaving? The American Expat Exodus," *New York Times Magazine*, December 27, 1998, 32–36.

94. Excerpts from Clinton news conference, *New York Times*, September 3, 1998; John M. Broder, "Clinton Tells Moscow Crowd That Future Won't Be Easy," and excerpts from Clinton's remarks, *New York Times*, September 2, 1998. Clinton reiterated his message two weeks later: "Clinton's Speech on World Economies," *New York Times*, September 15, 1998.

95. Martin Malia, "Russia's Retreat From the West," *New York Times*, September 3, 1998.

96. James A. Leach, "The New Russian Menace," *New York Times*, September 10, 1999; Eric Schmitt, "Republicans Step Up Attack On Clinton's Russia Policy," *New York Times*, September 15, 1999; John Lloyd, "Who Lost Russia?" *New York Times Magazine*, August 15, 1999, 34–41; Speaker's Advisory Group on Russia, *Russia's Road to Corruption: How the Clinton Administration Exported Government Instead of Free Enterprise and Failed the Russian People* (Washington, DC, September 2000), p. 175.

97. William Safire, "Welcome to Kremlingate," *New York Times*, September 9, 1999; Fareed Zakaria, "Lousy Advice Has Its Price," *Newsweek*, September 27, 1999, p. 40.

98. See, for example, Chrystia Freeland, *Sale of the Century: Russia's Wild Ride From Communism to Capitalism* (New York, 2000), esp. 8, 22, 171.

99. Zakaria, "Lousy Advice Has Its Price," *Newsweek*, September 27, 1999, p. 40; Matthew Brzezinski, *Casino Moscow: A Tale of Greed and Adventure on Capitalism's Wildest Frontier* (New York, 2001), 311, 186, 197.

100. Albright address, September 16, 1999, *U.S. Department of State Dispatch*, October 1999, 10–14; unnamed official quoted in "Romance versus realpolitik," *U.S. News and World Report*, February 14, 1994, p. 35.

101. Transcript of presidential campaign debate, *New York Times*, October 12, 2000.

102. Peter Finn, "Russian NGO Bill Moves Closer to Approval," *Washington Post*, December 22, 2005.

NOTES TO EPILOGUE

1. Transcript of debate between Bush and Gore, *New York Times*, October 12, 2000, esp. A22; George W. Bush, State of the Union Address to Congress, *New York Times*, January 30, 2002; George W. Bush, "Securing Freedom's Triumph," *New York Times*, September 11, 2002; "The National Security Strategy of the United States," full text in *New York Times*, September 20,

2002; Address by George W. Bush on November 6, 2003, as transcribed by FDCH e-Media, Inc.

2. Text of debate between Bush and Gore, *New York Times*, October 12, 2000; George W. Bush, "Securing Freedom's Triumph," *New York Times*, September 11, 2002; "The National Security Strategy of the United States," full text in *New York Times*, September 20, 2002; "Bush Says America Sees a 'Greater Hope,'" *New York Times*, April 18, 2002.

3. Jonathan Chait, "How Bush thinks: intuition over intellect," *Los Angeles Times*, August 5, 2005; Ivo H. Daalder and James M. Lindsay, *America Unbound: The Bush Revolution in Foreign Policy* (Washington, DC, 2003), 64; George W. Bush, "Securing Freedom's Triumph," *New York Times*, September 11, 2002; "The National Security Strategy of the United States," full text in *New York Times*, September 20, 2002; Serge Schmemann, "The Chechens Holy War: How Global Is It?" *New York Times*, October 27, 2002; Elisabeth Bumiller, "Bush Seeks New NATO at Summit Meeting," *New York Times*, November 19, 2002; Elisabeth Bumiller and Patrick E. Tyler, "Putin Questions U.S. Terror Allies," *New York Times*, November 23, 2002; Steven R. Weisman, "Powell Seeks to Reassure Russians on New Troops," *New York Times*, January 28, 2004; Nedra Pickler, "Bush Was Amazed by Red Square," *Moscow Times*, May 13, 2005.

4. William Safire, "Putin's Creeping Coup," *New York Times*, February 9, 2004 (endorsing the views of Republican Senator John McCain); Zbigniew Brzezinksi, "Moscow's Mussolini," *Wall Street Journal*, September 20, 2004.

5. Steven R. Weisman, "Powell Displays Tough U.S. Stance Toward Russians," *New York Times*, January 27, 2004.

6. Michael McFaul, "Veering From Reagan," *Washington Post*, June 18, 2004; "An Open Letter to the Heads of State and Government of the European Union and NATO," September 28, 2004, www.newamericancentury.org/russia-20040928.htm, accessed October 8, 2004; Transcript of September 30 debate, *New York Times*, October 1, 2004.

7. Andrew Jack, *Inside Putin's Russia: Can There Be Reform Without Democracy?* (New York, 2006), 206–15; Sabrina Tavernise and Timothy O'Brien, "Russian Tycoon Moves Into Politics and The Jail," *New York Times*, November 10, 2003; Catherine Belton, "The Oil Town That Won't Forget Yukos," *Moscow Times*, April 25, 2006; Catherine Belton, "Pichugin Gets 24 Years in Murders," *Moscow Times*, August 18, 2006.

8. Leon Aron, "Crime and Punishment for Capitalists," *New York Times*, October 30, 2003.

9. Rep. Tom Lantos, quoted in Kim Murphy, "Russian Tycoon Sentenced; System of Justice Indicted," *Los Angeles Times*, June 1, 2005.

10. Greg Walters, "Nevzlin Urges US to Pressure Russia," *Moscow Times*, July 15, 2005.

11. Transcript of September 30 debate, *New York Times*, October 1, 2004.

12. Nikolas K. Gvosdev and Dimitri Simes, "Rejecting Russia?" *The National Interest*, Issue 80 (Summer 2005), p. 6.

13. "Alexander Yakovlev," *Washington Post*, October 21, 2005.

14. Igor Baradachev and Sarah Lindemann-Komarova, "Trickle-Up Democracy," *Moscow Times*, July 20, 2006.
15. "An Open Letter to the Heads of State and Government of the European Union and NATO," September 28, 2004, www.newamericancentury.org/russia-20040928.htm, accessed October 8, 2004.
16. Steven R. Weisman, "Powell Displays Tough U.S. Stance Toward Russians," *New York Times*, January 27, 2004; Matthew Spence, "The Complexity of Success in Russia," in Thomas Carothers, ed., *Promoting the Rule of Law Abroad: In Search of Knowledge* (Washington, DC, 2006), 217–8, 241.
17. Peter Baker, "'Get Governing,' Bush Tells Iraqis," *Washington Post*, March 30, 2006; Stephen Boykewich and Oksana Yablokova, "Putin Says Russia Doesn't Need Any Lectures," *Moscow Times*, July 17, 2006.
18. Paul Richter, "Russia Policy Under Review," *Los Angeles Times*, December 12, 2004.
19. Mara D. Bellaby, "Rice Rebukes Russia Over NGO Bill," *Moscow Times*, December 8, 2005.
20. Stephen Boykewich, "Cheney Says Liberty at Risk in Russia," *Moscow Times*, May 5, 2006; Paul Richter and David Holley, "Cheney Has harsh Words for Moscow," *Los Angeles Times*, May 5, 2006.
21. David Holley and James Gerstenzang, "Bush Meets With Activists in Russia," *Los Angeles Times*, July 15, 2006; *RFE/RL Russian Political Weekly*, Vol. 6, No. 14, 7 August 2006.
22. John McCain, "A Crucial Choice for Ukraine," *Washington Post*, October 20, 2004.
23. George Will, "Putin blocks the 'march of freedom,'" *Trenton Times*, December 1, 2004.
24. Nicholas D. Kristof, "Let My People Go," *New York Times*, December 4, 2004.
25. Steven Lee Myers, "Letter From Europe: Why the Fever in Ukraine?" *New York Times*, December 22, 2004.
26. Mark Mazzetti, "NATO a Tough Sell at Home, Ukrainian Official Says," *Los Angeles Times*, October 24, 2005.
27. David Holley, "Ukraine Leader Faces Opposition on NATO Drive," *Los Angeles Times*, February 10, 2006; "Surrounding Russia," *Economist*, June 17, 2006.
28. Anders Aslund, "The Trick to Understanding Ukraine," *Moscow Times*, March 29, 2006; Judy Dempsey, "Putin Favorite Re-emerging in Ukraine," *New York Times*, July 19, 2006.
29. "Looking at Ukraine More Clearly," *New York Times*, January 20, 2006.
30. Anders Aslund and Michael McFaul, eds., *Revolution in Orange: The Origins of Ukraine's Democratic Breakthrough* (Washington, DC, 2006), 5; Michael McFaul, "Ukraine's Democracy Has a Lot of Life Yet," *National Post*, March 24, 2006.
31. For example: cartoon by Jeff Danziger, reprinted in *New York Times*, October 31, 1999; cartoon by Levine in *New York Review*, February 10, 2000; cartoon by Danziger, October 31, 2002, www.uclick.com; cartoons by Ben Sargent in *Austin American-Statesman*, November 3, 2003 and September

16, 2004; cartoons by Danziger, January 27, 2004 and July 19, 2004, www.danzigercartoons.com; cartoon by Bill DeOre in *Dallas Morning News*, October 4, 2004; cartoon by Scott Santis in *Birmingham News*, February 27, 2005.

32. Zbigniew Brzezinski, "Moscow's Mussolini," *Wall Street Journal*, September 20, 2004.

33. Nicholas Kristof, "The Poison Puzzle," *New York Times*, December 15, 2004.

34. "Mr. Putin's Counterrevolution," *Washington Post*, November 17, 2005; "Murder in Moscow," *Washington Post*, October 8, 2006; Jeff Danziger cartoon, October 8, 2006; Ann Telnaes cartoon, October 10, 2006; Tony Auth cartoon, October 12, 2006; Tom Toles cartoon, October 13, 2006; all cartoons from www.mycomicspage.com; Peter Baker and Susan Glasser, *Kremlin Rising: Vladimir Putin's Russia and the End of Revolution* (New York, 2005), 9.

35. See the political cartoons in the *Philadelphia Inquirer*, May 17 and May 25, 1903, reproduced in Foglesong, David S. and V. I. Zhuravleva, "Konstruirovanie obraza Rossii v amerikanskikh politicheskikh karikaturakh XX veka," in V. A. Koleneko, ed., *Rossiia i SShA na Stranitsakh Russkoi i Amerikanskoi Periodiki*. Moscow, 2007.

36. Baker and Glasser, *Kremlin Rising*, 12; 355; 370; 353; 129; 328; 5; 97; 374; 1; 221.

37. Steven Lee Myers, "Jailed Russian Tycoon Mourns Liberty's Losses," *New York Times*, March 30, 2004.

38. Steven Lee Myers, "Putin, Denouncing Prejudice, Meets With Victim of Bombing," *New York Times*, July 25, 2002; Steven Lee Myers, "As NATO Arrives on Its Border, Russia Grumbles," *New York Times*, April 3, 2004; "40 Protesters Seize a Kremlin Office," *Moscow Times*, December 15, 2004; Steven Lee Myers, "In Anti-Immigrant Mood, Russia Heeds Gadfly's Cry," *New York Times*, October 22, 2006.

39. Steven Lee Myers, "Norilsk Journal," *New York Times*, February 24, 2004; "Pretty pictures," *Economist*, March 4, 2006.

40. Igor Baradachev and Sarah Lindemann-Komarova, "Trickle-Up Democracy," *Moscow Times*, July 20, 2006.

41. "The Truth on Russia," *Washington Post*, October 2, 2004.

42. Nabi Abdullaev, "West Chided for Being Stuck in 1990s Mindset," *Moscow Times*, May 31, 2006; Council on Foreign Relations, *Russia's Wrong Direction: What the United States Can and Should Do* (New York, 2006).

43. Peter Baker, "Russian Relations Under Scrutiny," *Washington Post*, February 26, 2006, quoting Putin comment at a press conference in January 2006.

44. Valeria Korchagina, "Putin Looks to Preempt Criticism," *Moscow Times*, July 13, 2006; David Holley, "In Russia, a Debate Over Democracy," *Los Angeles Times*, July 13, 2006.

45. Peter Baker and Peter Finn, "In Russia, Putin, Bush Put On a Brave Face," *Washington Post*, July 16, 2006. Russia would develop democratic institutions, Putin added, but "we will do this by ourselves." James Gerstenzang and David Holley, "Bush, Putin Strain to Affirm Common Goals," *Los Angeles Times*, July 16, 2006.

46. Alexei Pankin, "Russians Remain Wary of Western Advice on Democracy," *Russia Profile*, Vol. 3, No. 4 (May 2006), 43.

47. "Chechnya in Moscow," *Washington Post*, October 25, 2002; "The Slaughter in Moscow," *New York Times*, October 28, 2002; "A Separate War," *New Republic*, December 2 and 9, 2002, p. 7.

48. "'American Gulag,'" *Washington Post*, May 26, 2005; Anne Applebaum, "Amnesty's Amnesia," *Washington Post*, June 8, 2005.

49. Steve Sack cartoon, June 2005; Pat Oliphant cartoon, June 6, 2005, www.uclick.com.

50. Stephen J. Hadley and Frances Fragos Townsend, "What We Saw in London," *New York Times*, July 23, 2005; Peter Beinart, "The Rehabilitation of the Cold-War Liberal," *New York Times Magazine*, April 30, 2006; Peter Beinart, *The Good Fight: Why Liberals – and Only Liberals – Can Win the War on Terror and Make America Great Again* (New York, 2006); Richard Holbrooke, "Authentically Liberal: How Democrats Can Defeat Terrorism and Win Elections," *Foreign Affairs*, Vol. 85, No. 4 (July/August 2006), 170–6.

51. Oksana Yablokova, "15 Years On, Coup Is a Dim Memory," *Moscow Times*, August 18, 2006.

# Bibliography

PRIMARY SOURCES

ARCHIVAL COLLECTIONS

Amherst, Massachusetts
  Amherst Center for Russian Culture
    Father Ioann Shakhovskoi Papers

Ann Arbor, Michigan
  Gerald R. Ford Library
    Richard Cheney Files
    Congressional Papers
    David Gergen Files
    Robert Goldwin Papers
    Robert Hartmann Files
    Kissinger and Scowcroft Files
    John Marsh Files
    National Security Adviser Files
      Kissinger Reports
      Presidential Country Files for Europe and Canada
      Presidential Name File
    Ron Nessen Papers
    Transition Materials
    White House Central Files

Atlanta, Georgia
  Jimmy Carter Library
    Presidential Directive 30
    Presidential Review Memoranda

Boston, Massachusetts
  John F. Kennedy Presidential Library
    Oral History Interviews with Llewellyn E. Thompson

Cambridge, Massachusetts
  Alice Stone Blackwell Papers, Schlesinger Library, Radcliffe
  College

College Park, Maryland
  National Archives II

RG 59: General Records of the Department of State
    Records of the Policy Planning Staff

Hyde Park, New York
  Franklin D. Roosevelt Library
    Adolf Berle Papers

Kliazma, Russia
  Julius F. Hecker Papers

Madison, New Jersey
  United Methodist Church Archives
  Administrative Files Series
    John L. Nuelsen Files
  Missionary Files Series
    George A. Simons Files
    Julius F. Hecker Files

Madison, Wisconsin
  State Historical Society of Wisconsin
    DeWitt Clinton Poole Papers
    Raymond Robins Papers
    William English Walling Papers

Moscow, Russia
  Archive of the Foreign Policy of the Russian Empire (AVPRI)
    Fond Kantseliariia MID
  Archive of the Foreign Policy of the Russian Federation (AVPRF)
    Fond 129/0129 Referentura po SShA

New Brunswick, New Jersey
  Alexander Library, Rutgers University
    Clifford Case Papers
    Millicent Fenwick Papers

New York City
  New York Public Library
    Isabel Hapgood Papers
    George Kennan Papers

Princeton, New Jersey
  Seeley G. Mudd Manuscript Library
    Arthur Bullard Papers
    Freedom House Archives
    George F. Kennan Papers
    David Lawrence Papers

Rochester, New York
  American Baptist-Samuel Colgate Historical Library
    Thomas S. Barbour Collection

Silver Spring, Maryland
  Seventh-day Adventist Archive
    E. G. White Estate
    General Conference Archives: RG 21, Secretariat

Simi Valley, California
  Ronald Reagan Library
    James Baker Files
    William P. Clark Files
    Anthony Dolan Files
    Ken Khachigian Files
    Jack Matlock Files
      Head of State Correspondence
    NSC Coordination Office Papers
    NSC Executive Secretariat, Country Files
    Presidential Handwriting File
    WHORM Subject Files

Springfield, Missouri
  Flower Pentecostal Heritage Center Archives
    Paul B. Peterson Files

Stanford, California
  Hoover Institution Archives
    James Burnham Papers
    Radio Free Europe/Radio Liberty, Inc. Corporate Records
    Sidney Hook Papers
    Fred Iklé Papers
    Sig Mickelson Papers
    Poster Collection: RU/SU series
    Voice of America Papers
    Felix Volkhovsky Collection

Valley Forge, Pennsylvania
  American Baptist Historical Society
    Official Correspondence, Board of International Ministries

Washington, D.C.
  Georgetown University Library
    Robert F. Kelley Papers
  Library of Congress
    Raymond Buell Papers
    Russell W. Davenport Papers
    Joseph Davies Papers
    William Dudley Foulke Papers
    Averell Harriman Papers
    George Kennan Papers
    Henry Luce Papers
    Laurence Steinhardt Papers
    Myron C. Taylor Papers

PUBLISHED DOCUMENTS

American Baptist Missionary Union, *Annual Reports*. Boston, 1888–1910.
*American Baptist Foreign Mission Society Report*. Boston, 1910–17.
Baker, Ray Stannard and William E. Dodd, eds. *The Public Papers of Woodrow Wilson: War and Peace*. 2 vols. New York, 1927.

Baptist World Alliance, Second Congress, June 19–25, 1911, *Record of Proceedings*. Philadelphia: Harper, 1911.

Bukovsky, V. *Soviet Archives. http://psi.ece.jhu.edu/kaplan/IRUSS/BUK/GBARC/ pdfs.*

Iakovlev, A. N., ed. *Rossiia i SShA: diplomaticheskie otnosheniia 1900–1917*. Moscow, 1999.

Koch, Scott A. ed. *CIA Cold War Records: Selected Estimates on the Soviet Union*. Washington, DC, 1993.

Link, Arthur S., et al, eds. *The Papers of Woodrow Wilson*. 69 vols. Princeton, 1966–93.

Nelson, Anna. ed. *The State Department Policy Planning Staff Papers 1947–9.*

Porter, Kirk H. compiler, *National Party Platforms*. New York, 1924.

Porter, Kirk H. and Donald Bruce Johnson, *National Party Platforms 1840–1964*. Urbana, IL, 1966.

Sevostianov, G. N. and J. Haslam, eds. *Sovetsko-Amerikanskie Otnosheniia: Gody Nepriznaniia 1918–1926*. Moscow, 2002.

Skinner, Kiron K., Annelise Anderson, and Martin Anderson, eds. *Reagan in His Own Hand: The Writings that Reveal His Revolutionary Vision for America*. New York: Simon and Schuster, 2002.

Skinner, Kiron K., Annelise Anderson, and Martin Anderson, eds. *Reagan's Path to Victory: The Shaping of Ronald Reagan's Vision: Selected Writings*. New York: Free Press, 2004.

U.S. Congress. Speaker's Advisory Group on Russia, *Russia's Road to Corruption: How the Clinton Administration Exported Government Instead of Free Enterprise and Failed the Russian People*. Washington: September, 2000.

U.S. Congress. *Congressional Record*, 1911, 1941–5.

U.S. Department of State. *Department of State Bulletin*.

U.S. Department of State. *Foreign Relations of the United States,1941, Vol. I: General. The Soviet Union*. Washington, 1958.

U.S. Department of State. *Foreign Relations of the United States, 1942, Vol. III. Europe*. Washington, 1961.

U.S. Department of State. *Foreign Relations of the United States, 1943, Vol. III.* Washington, 1963.

U.S. Department of State. *Foreign Relations of the United States, 1944, Vol. IV. Europe*. Washington, 1966.

U.S. Department of State. *Foreign Relations of the United States, 1945, Vol. V. Europe*. Washington, 1966.

U.S. Department of State. *Foreign Relations of the United States, 1952–1954*, Vol. VIII. Washington, 1988.

U.S. Department of State. *Foreign Relations of the United States, 1945–1950: Emergence of the Intelligence Establishment*. Washington, 1996.

U.S. Department of State. *Foreign Relations of the United States, 1955–1957, Volume XXIV: Soviet Union; Eastern Mediterranean*. Washington, 1990.

U.S. Department of State. *Foreign Relations of the United States, 1958–1960, Volume X, Part I*. Washington, 1993.

U.S. Department of State. *Foreign Relations of the United States, Volume X, Part 2: Eastern Europe; Finland; Greece; Turkey*. Washington, 1993.

U.S. Department of State. *Foreign Relations of the United States, 1961–1963, Vol. V, Soviet Union*. Washington, 1998.

U.S. Department of State. *Foreign Relations of the United States, 1961–1963, Vol. XXV: Foreign Relations, Organization of Foreign Policy, Information Policy; United Nations; Scientific Matters.* Washington, 2001.

U.S. Department of State. *Foreign Relations of the United States, 1964–1968, Vol. XIV, Soviet Union.* Washington, 2001.

U.S. Department of State. *Foreign Relations of the United States, 1969–1976, Vol. I: Foundations of Foreign Policy, 1969–1972.* Washington, 2003.

U.S. Department of State. *Human Rights in the U.S.S.R. and Eastern Europe.* Current Policy brochure No. 224. Washington: 1980.

U.S. Senate, *Brewing and Liquor Interests and German and Bolshevik Propaganda. Report and Hearings of the Subcommittee on the Judiciary.* Washington, DC, 1919.

Warner, Michael. ed. *CIA Cold War Records: The CIA under Harry Truman.* Washington, 1994.


LETTERS, DIARIES, MEMOIRS, AND CONTEMPORARY WRITINGS

Abbott, Lyman. *Reminiscences.* Boston, 1915.

Adams, Brooks. *America's Economic Supremacy.* New York, 1900.

Albright, Madeleine. *Madam Secretary.* New York, 2003.

Alexeyeva, Ludmilla and Paul Goldberg, *The Thaw Generation: Coming of Age in the Post-Stalin Era.* Boston, 1990; paperback, Pittsburgh, 1993.

Armstrong, William Jackson. *Siberia and the Nihilists: Why Kennan Went to Siberia.* Oakland, CA, 1890.

Anisimov, Oleg. "The Attitude of the Soviet People Toward the West," *Russian Review,* Vol. 13, No. 2 (April 1954), 79–90.

Anisimov, Oleg. *The Ultimate Weapon.* Chicago, 1953.

Baker, James A. *The Politics of Diplomacy: Revolution, War and Peace, 1989–1992.* New York: Putnam, 1995.

Barrett, Edward W. *Truth is Our Weapon.* New York, 1953.

Bennett. John C. *Christianity and Communism Today.* New York, 1960.

Bennett. John C. *Nuclear Weapons and the Conflict of Conscience.* New York: Charles Scribner's Sons, 1962.

Bennett. John C. and Harvey Seifert. *U.S. Foreign Policy and Christian Ethics.* Philadelphia: The Westminster Press, 1977.

Beinart, Peter. *The Good Fight: Why Liberals – and Only Liberals – Can Win the War on Terror and Make America Great Again.* New York: HarperCollins, 2006.

Berman, Ronald. ed. *Solzhenitsyn at Harvard.* Washington: The Ethics and Public Policy Center, 1980.

Beveridge, Albert J. *The Russian Advance.* New York, 1904.

Billington, James H. *Russia Transformed: Breakthrough to Hope. Moscow, August 1991.* New York: Free Press, 1992.

Billington, James H. "The Church in the World: Unexpected Joy," *Theology Today,* Vol. 52, No. 3 (October, 1995), 382–91.

Billington, James H. "The West's Stake in Russia's Future," *Orbis,* Vol. 41, No. 4 (Fall 1997), 545–53.

Bohlen, Charles E. *Witness to History 1929–1969.* New York: Norton, 1973.

Brackett, Charles, Billy Wilder, and Walter Reisch, screenplay of *Ninotchka*. New York, 1972.

Brzezinski, Zbigniew. *Power and Principle: Memoirs of the National Security Adviser 1977–1981*. New York: Farrar, Straus and Giroux, revised edition, 1985.

Brzezinski, Matthew. *Casino Moscow: A Tale of Greed and Adventure on Capitalism's Wildest Frontier*. New York, 2001.

Buel, J. W. *Russian Nihilism and Exile Life in Siberia: A Graphic and Chronological History of Russia's Bloody Nemesis, and a Description of Exile Life in All Its True But Horrifying Phases*. St. Louis: Historical Publishing Company, 1883, 1884.

Buel, J. W. *A Nemesis of Misgovernment: Republican, Monarchical, and Empirical Governments*. Philadelphia: Historical Publishing Company, 1899.

Bukovsky, Vladimir. *To Build a Castle – My Life as a Dissenter*. New York: Viking, 1979.

Bullard, Arthur. "The St. Petersburg Massacre and the Russian East Side," *The Independent*, Vol. 58, February 2, 1905, 252–6.

Bullitt, Orville H. ed. *For the President Personal and Secret: Correspondence Between Franklin D. Roosevelt and William C. Bullitt*. Boston, 1972.

Burnham, James. *The Struggle for the World*. New York, 1947. Burnham, *The Coming Defeat of Communism*. New York, 1950 Burnham, *Containment or Liberation?* New York, 1953.

Bush, George and Brent Scowcroft, *A World Transformed*. New York: Knopf, 1998.

Carroll, Wallace. *We're In This With Russia*. Boston, 1942.

Carroll, Wallace. *Persuade or Perish*. Boston, 1948.

Carter, Jimmy. *Keeping Faith: Memoirs of a President*. New York: Bantam, 1982.

Cater, Harold Dean, ed. *Henry Adams and His Friends: A Collection of His Unpublished Letters*. Boston, 1947.

Chamberlin, William H. *Soviet Russia*. Boston: Little, Brown, 1930.

Chamberlin, William H. "Missionaries of American Technique in Russia," *Asia*, Vol. 32 (July-August 1932), 422–7, 460.

Chamberlin, William H. "No," in "Can Stalin's Russia Go Democratic?" *American Mercury*, Vol. LVIII, No. 242 (February, 1944), 142–8.

Chamberlin, William H. "Russians Against Stalin," *Russian Review*, Vol. 11, No. 1 (January 1952), 18–22.

Chamberlin, William Henry. *Beyond Containment*. Chicago, 1953.

Chernyaev, Anatoly S. *My Six Years with Gorbachev*. University Park: Pennsylvania State University Press, 2000.

Child, Richard Washburn. *Potential Russia*. New York: Dutton, 1916.

Christopher, Warren. *In the Stream of History: Shaping Foreign Policy for a New Era*. Stanford: Stanford University Press, 1998.

Clinch, B. "The Russian State Church," *The American Catholic Quarterly Review*, Vol. XX, No. 79 (July, 1895), 449–59.

Clinton, *My Life*. New York, 2004.

Cohon, George. *To Russia with Fries*. Toronto, 1997.

Conradi, L. R. "A Visit to Russia," *Historical Sketches of the Foreign Missions of the Seventh-day Adventists*. Basel, 1886.

Cooper, Hugh L. "Russia," *Engineers and Engineering*, Vol. XLVIII, No. 4 (April 1931), 76–86.

Cooper, Wayne F. ed. *The Passion of Claude McKay*. New York, 1973.

Critchlow, James. *Radio Hole-in-the-Head/Radio Liberty: An Insider's Story of Cold War Broadcasting*. Washington: American University Press, 1995.

Culbert, David ed. *Mission to Moscow*. Madison: University of Wisconsin Press, 1980.

Davies, Joseph E. *Mission to Moscow*. New York, 1941.

Davies, Richard T. "The View from Poland," in Thomas T. Hammond, ed., *Witnesses to the Origins of the Cold War*. Seattle, 1982, 249–77.

Davies, Richard T. "The Reminiscences of Richard Townsend Davies." Unpublished manuscript.

De Marsh, E. J. "The Russia of Tomorrow," *Harper's Weekly*, January 1, 1916, p. 9.

Deane, John R. *The Strange Alliance*. New York, 1947.

Dobrynin, Anatoly. *In Confidence: Moscow's Ambassador to America's Six Cold War Presidents*. New York: Random House, 1995.

Dreiser, Theodore. *Dreiser Looks at Russia*. New York, 1928.

Dubinin, Iu. V. "Ternistyi Put' k Khel'sinki. 1975 g." *Novaia i noveishaia istoriia*, No. 4–5, 1994, 177–94.

Dulles, John Foster. *War or Peace*. New York, 1950.

Earle, J. C. "The Russo-Greek Church," *The American Catholic Quarterly Review*, Vol. XI, No. 43 (July 1886), 507–11.

Eddy, Sherwood. *Russia: A Warning and a Challenge*. New York, 1923.

Eddy, Sherwood. *The Challenge of Russia*. New York, 1931.

Eddy, Sherwood. *Russia Today: What Can We Learn From It?* New York, 1934.

Eddy, Sherwood. *Europe Today*. New York, 1937.

Eddy, Sherwood. *Eighty Adventurous Years: An Autobiography*. New York, 1955.

Edwards, Albert. [pseudonym for Arthur Bullard] "Rise of the Russian Proletariat," *The International Socialist Review*, July 1, 1907, 20–87.

Edwards, Albert. [Arthur Bullard] "The Russian Revolution," *The International Socialist Review*, September 1907, 155–203.

Edwards, Albert. [Arthur Bullard] "The Russian Revolution," *The International Socialist Review*, Vol. VIII, No. 4 (October 1907), pp. 193–203.

Edwards, Albert. [Arthur Bullard] "An Eye-witness's Story of the Russian Revolution," *Harper's Weekly*, February 24, 1906, 258–61.

Edwards, Albert. [Bullard] "Under the White Terror," *Collier's*, April 14, 1906, p. 13, and April 28, 1906, p. 25.

Filene, Peter G. ed. *American Views of Soviet Russia, 1917–1965*. Homewood, IL, 1968.

Ford, Alexander Hume. "America's Agricultural Regeneration of Russia," *Century*, Vol. LXI, No. 4 (August 1901), 501–7.

Ford, Gerald R. *A Time to Heal*. New York, 1979.

Ford, W. C. ed. *Letters of Henry Adams*. Boston, 1930.

Foulke, William Dudley. *Slav or Saxon: A Study of the Growth and Tendencies of Russian Civilization*. First edition, 1887; second edition, New York, 1899.

Foulke, *A Hoosier Autobiography*. New York, 1922.

Gaidar, Yegor. *Days of Defeat and Victory*. Seattle: University of Washington Press, 1999.

Galantiere, Lewis. "Through the Russian Looking Glass: The Future in Retrospect," *Foreign Affairs*, Vol. 28, No. 1 (October 1949), 114–24.

Gates, Robert. *From the Shadows: The Ultimate Insider's Story of Five Presidents and How They Won the Cold War*. New York: Simon & Schuster, 1996.

Gelb, Michael. ed. *An American Engineer in Stalin's Russia: The Memoirs of Zara Witkin, 1932–1934*. Berkeley: University of California Press, 1991.

Goldberg, Paul. *The Final Act: The Dramatic, Revealing Story of the Moscow Helsinki Watch Group*. New York: William Morrow, 1988.

Goldwater, Barry M. *The Conscience of a Conservative*. Washington, 1990; first published in 1960.

Goldwater, Barry M. *Why Not Victory? A Fresh Look at American Foreign Policy*. New York, 1962.

Goldwater, Barry. *Where I Stand*. New York, 1964.

Gorbachev, Mikhail. *Memoirs*. New York: Doubleday, 1995.

Graebner, Walter. *Round Trip to Russia*. New York, 1943.

Graham, Billy. *Just As I Am: The Autobiography of Billy Graham*. San Francisco: Harper, 1997.

Griffis, William Elliot. "The Russo-Greek Church and the World's Progress," *The Outlook*, 16 September 1905.

Grosvenor, Gilbert H. "Young Russia: The Land of Unlimited Possibilities," *National Geographic*, Vol. XXVI, No. 5 (November 1914).

Guild, Curtis. "Russia and Her Emperor," *Yale Review*, Vol. 4, No. 4 (July 1915), 712–22.

Hamlin, Cyrus. "The Dream of Russia," *Atlantic Monthly*, Vol. LVIII (December 1886), 771–82.

Hapgood, Isabel F. *Russian Rambles*. Boston, 1895.

Hapgood, Isabel F. "The Russian Church: Its Spiritual State and Possibilities," *The Outlook*, Vol. LIII (June 20, 1896), 1142–6; *The Nation*, Vol. 62, No. 1612 (May 21, 1896), p. 402.

Hapgood, Isabel F. "America's Share in the New Russian Reforms," *New York Times Magazine*, February 21, 1915, 15–6.

Hapgood, Norman. *The Changing Years: Reminiscences of Norman Hapgood*. New York, 1930.

Harcave, Sidney, ed. *The Memoirs of Count Witte*. Armonk: M.E. Sharpe, 1990.

Harriman, W. Averell and Elie Abel, *Special Envoy to Churchill and Stalin, 1941–1946*. New York: Random House, 1975.

Hartman, Arthur A. Interview by William Miller, May 31, 1989, Association for Diplomatic Studies and Training Foreign Affairs Oral History Project.

Hartmann, Robert T. *Palace Politics: An Inside Account of the Ford Years*. New York: McGraw-Hill, 1980.

Hecker, Julius F. *Russian Sociology: A Contribution to the History of Sociological Thought and Theory*. New York, 1915.

Hecker, Julius F. *Religion Under the Soviets*. New York, 1927.

Hecker, Julius F. *Religion and Communism: A Study of Religion and Atheism in Soviet Russia*. London, 1933.

Hellman, Lillian. *The North Star*. New York, 1943.

Helms, Richard, with William Hood, *A Look over My Shoulder: A Life in the Central Intelligence Agency*. New York: Random House, 2003.

Heymann, Hans. *We Can Do Business With Russia*. Chicago, 1945.

Holmes, John Haynes. *I Speak for Myself: The Autobiography of John Haynes Holmes*. New York, 1959.

Howe, M. A. DeWolfe. *George von Lengerke Meyer: His Life and Public Services*. New York, 1920.

Hubbard, James M. "Russia as a Civilizing Force in Asia," *The Atlantic Monthly*, Vol. LXXV (February 1895), 197–205.

Hulbert, Archer B. "The Better Side of Russian Rule in Asia," *The Independent*, November 1, 1900, 2632–4.

Johnson, Lyndon Baines. *The Vantage Point: Perspectives of the Presidency 1963–1969*. New York: Holt, Rinehart, Winston, 1971.

Johnson, William E. *The Liquor Problem in Russia*. Westerville, Ohio, 1915.

Johnston, Charles. "The New Russia," *Review of Reviews*, Vol. 51 (May 1915), 568–73.

Johnston, Eric A. "My Talk with Joseph Stalin," *Reader's Digest*, October 1944, 1–10.

Johnston, Eric. *America Unlimited*. New York, 1944.

Kennan, George. "Siberia – The Exiles' Abode," *Journal of the American Geographical Society of New York*, Vol. XIV (1882), 13–68.

Kennan, George. "The Last Appeal of the Russian Liberals," *Century*, XXXV (November 1887), 50–63.

Kennan, George. "Russian State Prisoners," *Century*, Vol. XXXV (March 1888), 765–6.

Kennan, George. "The Russian Police," *Century*, Vol. XXXVII, No. 6 (April 1889), 890–3.

Kennan, George. *Siberia and the Exile System* 2 vols., London, 1891.

Kennan, "A Voice for the People of Russia," *Century* (July 1893), 461–72.

Kennan, George. "A Russian Experiment in Self-Government," *Atlantic Monthly*, Vol. 80 (October 1897), 494–507.

Kennan, George. *Campaigning in Cuba*. New York, 1899.

Kennan, George. "Which is the Civilized Power?" *The Outlook*, 29 October 1904, 516–20.

Kennan, George. "Russian Despotism," *The Outlook*, Vol. 85, No. 13 (March 30, 1907), 754–5.

Kennan, George. "The Russian People: Repression and Oppression," *The Outlook*, 18 July 1914, 647–50.

Kennan, George. "The Russian Muzhik," *The Outlook*, Vol. 109, 24 March 1915, 680–3.

Kennan, George. "'Public Opinion' in an 'Oriental State,'" *The Outlook*, March 31, 1915, p. 768.

Kennan, George. *A Russian Comedy of Errors*. New York, 1915.

Kennan, George. "Can We Help Russia?" *The Outlook*, 22 May 1918, 141.

Kennan, George F. "America and the Russian Future," *Foreign Affairs*, Vol. 29, No. 3 (April 1951), 351–370.

Kennan, George F. *On Dealing with the Communist World*. New York: Harper & Row, 1964.

Kennan, George F. *Memoirs: 1925–1950*. Boston: Little, Brown, 1967.

Kennan, George F. *Memoirs 1950–1963*. New York: Pantheon, 1972.

Kennan, George F. *The Marquis de Custine and His Russia in 1839*. Princeton: Princeton University Press, 1971.

Kennan, George F. "Morality and American Foreign Policy," *Foreign Affairs* (Winter 1985–86), 205–18.

Kennan, George F. *Sketches From a Life*. New York: Pantheon, 1989.

Kerensky, Alexander. "Russia is Ripe for Freedom," *American Mercury*, Vol. LVII, No. 236 (August 1943), 158–65.

Kissinger, Henry. *Years of Renewal*. New York: Simon and Schuster, 1999.

Kohler, Phyllis Penn. ed. *Journey for Our Time: The Russian Journals of the Marquis de Custine*. Chicago, 1951.

Lawrence, David. *The Editorials of David Lawrence*, 6 vols. Washington: U.S. News and World Report, 1970.

Lesueur, Larry. *Twelve Months That Changed the World*. New York, 1943.

Levenson, J. C., ed. *The Letters of Henry Adams*, 6 vols., Cambridge, MA, 1982.

Lloyd, John. "Who Lost Russia?" *New York Times Magazine*, August 15, 1999, 34–41.

Lodge, Henry Cabot. "Some Impressions of Russia," *Scribner's Magazine*, Vol. XXXI (May 1902), 570–80.

Luce, Henry. "The American Century," reproduced in *Diplomatic History*, Vol. 23, No. 2 (Spring 1999), 159–71.

Lyons, Eugene. *Assignment in Utopia*. New York, 1937.

Lyons, Eugene. *Our Secret Allies: The Peoples of Russia*. New York, 1953.

McCormick, Anne O'Hare. *The Hammer and the Scythe: Communist Russia Enters the Second Decade*. New York, 1928.

McFarlane, Robert. *Special Trust*. New York: Cadell and Davies, 1994.

McRoberts, Samuel. "Russia's Future Needs for Capital," *The Annals of the American Academy of Political and Social Science*, Vol. LXVIII (November, 1916).

Morison, Elting E. ed. *The Letters of Theodore Roosevelt*, 4 vols., Cambridge, MA, 1951.

Moynihan, Daniel Patrick with Suzanne Weaver, *A Dangerous Place*. Boston, 1978.

Myers, Gustavus. "Our Millionaire Socialists," *Cosmopolitan*, October 1906, 596–605.

Neier, Aryeh. *Taking Liberties: Four Decades in the Struggle for Rights*. New York: Public Affairs, 2003.

Nessen, Ron. *It Sure Looks Different from the Inside*. Chicago: Playboy, 1978.

Nixon, Richard M. *Six Crises*. New York, 1962.

Noble, Edmund. "Island Democracy in the Caspian," *Atlantic Monthly*, Vol. LX (December 1887), 806–7.

Noble, Edmund. *The Russian Revolt*. London, 1885.

Noonan, Peggy. *What I Saw at the Revolution*. New York, 1990.

Pelevin, Victor. *The Life of Insects*. New York, 1998; first ed. Moscow, 1994.

Phillips, Wendell. *Speeches, Lectures, and Letters*. Boston, 1892.

Pipes, Richard. *Survival is Not Enough: Soviet Realities and America's Future*. New York: Simon and Schuster, 1984.

Pipes, Richard. "Russia's Past, Russia's Future," *Commentary*, Vol. 101, No. 6 (June 1996), 30–8.

Pipes, Richard. *Vixi: Memoirs of a Non-Belonger*. New Haven: Yale University Press, 2003.

Poole, Ernest. "St. Petersburg is Quiet!" *The Outlook*, 18 March 1905, 682–5.

Poole, Ernest. "Thou Shalt Not Think – In Russia," *The Outlook*, 8 April 1905, 881–2.

Poole, Ernest. "The Story of a Russian Workingman," *The Outlook*, 22 April 1905, 989–90.

Poole, Ernest. "The Peasant and the War," *The Outlook*, 27 May 1905, 220–1.

Poole, Ernest. "'Peasant Cattle': What the Cossacks Think of the Peasants," *Everybody's Magazine*, October 1905, 494–6.

Poole, Ernest. "Dounya," *The Independent*, October 26, 1905, 974–80.

Poole, Ernest. "The Night that Made Me a Revolutionist," *Everybody's Magazine*, November 1905, 637–9.

Poole, Ernest. *"The Dark People": Russia's Crisis*. New York, 1918.

Poole, Ernest. *The Bridge: My Own Story*. New York, 1940.

Pope, Arthur Upham. "Can Stalin's Russia Go Democratic?" *American Mercury*, Vol. LVIII, No. 242 (February, 1944), 135–42.

Quayle, Dan. *Standing Firm: A Vice-Presidential Memoir*. New York: Harper-Collins, 1994.

Reagan, Ronald. *A Time for Choosing: The Speeches of Ronald Reagan 1961–1982*. Chicago, 1983.

Reagan, Ronald (with Robert Lindsay). *An American Life*. New York: Simon and Schuster, 1990.

Reynolds, Elizabeth K. "Russian Art and the Police Force," *Harper's Weekly*, February 12, 1916, p. 158.

Reynolds, Elizabeth K. "America Realizing Russia," *Harper's Weekly*, May 6, 1916, p. 483.

Rockefeller, David. *Memoirs*. New York: Random House, 2002.

Ruchames, Louis, ed. *The Letters of William Lloyd Garrison*, 6 vols., Cambridge, MA, 1971–81.

Sakharov, Andrei. *Memoirs*. New York: Knopf, 1990.

Samuels, Ernest, ed. *The Education of Henry Adams*. Boston: Houghton Mifflin, 1973.

Scanlan, James P. ed. *Historical Letters*, by Peter Lavrov. Berkeley, 1967.

Scott, John. *Behind the Urals: An American Worker in Russia's City of Steel*. Bloomington: Indiana University Press, 1973; first ed., 1942.

Scott, Leroy. "The Travesty of Christ in Russia," *Everybody's Magazine*, Vol. XVII, No. VI (Christmas 1907), 800–9.

Shahan, Thomas J. "Roman Catholicism in Russia (1796–1825)," *American Catholic Quarterly Review*, Vol. XXX (1905), 533–51.

Sheehan, Marion Turner. ed. *The World at Home: Selections from the Writings of Anne O'Hare McCormick*. 1956; reprint, Freeport, NY, 1970.

Shub, Boris. *The Choice*. New York, 1950.

Shultz, George P. "New Realities and New Ways of Thinking," *Foreign Affairs* (Spring 1985), 705–21.

Shultz, George P. *Turmoil and Triumph*. New York: Charles Scribner's Sons, 1993.
Smith, Walter Bedell. *My Three Years in Moscow*. Philadelphia and New York, 1950.
Solzhenitsyn, Alexander. *Warning to the West*. New York: Farrar, Straus and Giroux, 1976.
Sosin, Gene. *Sparks of Liberty: An Insider's Memoir of Radio Liberty*. University Park: Pennsylvania State University Press, 1999.
Spargo, John. *Russia as an American Problem*. New York: Harper, 1920.
Standley, William H. and Arthur A. Ageton, *Admiral Ambassador to Russia*. Chicago, 1955.
Stevens, Leslie. *Russian Assignment*. Boston, 1953.
Strong, Anna Louise. *I Change Worlds: The Remaking of an American*. Seattle: Seal Press, 1979; first edn. 1935.
Talbott, Strobe. ed. *Khrushchev Remembers: The Last Testament*. Boston: Little, Brown, 1974.
Talbott, Strobe. *The Russia Hand: A Memoir of Presidential Diplomacy*. New York: Random House, 2002.
Tayler, Jeffrey. "Russia is Finished," *Atlantic Monthly*, May 2001.
Thompson, Dorothy. *The New Russia*. New York, 1928.
Thompson, Dorothy. *Christian Ethics and Western Civilization*. New York, 1940.
Twain, Mark. *A Connecticut Yankee in King Arthur's Court*. New York, 1971. First published 1889.
Twain, Mark. *The American Claimant*. Leipzig, 1892.
Velikanova, N. and R. Vittaker (Robert Whittaker), *L. N. Tolstoi I SshA*. Moscow: IMLI RAN, 2004.
Villard, Oswald Garrison. *Fighting Years: Memoirs of a Liberal Editor*. New York: Harcourt, Brace, 1939.
Wald, Lillian D. *The House on Henry Street*. New York, 1915.
Wald, Lillian D. *Windows on Henry Street*. Boston, 1934.
Walling, Anna Strunsky, ed. *William English Walling: A Symposium*. New York, 1938.
Walling, William English. "The Peasant's Revolution," *The Independent*, October 18, 1906, 906–7.
Walling, William English. "Will the Peasants Act?" *The Independent*, December 6, 1906, p. 1323.
Walling, William English. "How Is It With the Russian Revolution?" *The Outlook*, March 9, 1907.
Walling, William English. "The Real Russian People at Church," *The Independent*, Vol. 63, July 4, 1907, 27–8.
Walling, William English. "The Real Russian People," *The Independent*, September 26, 1907, p. 728.
Walling, William English. "An American View," *Free Russia*, April-June 1908, 4–6.
Walling, William English. "The Race War in the North," *The Independent*, September 3, 1908, pp. 529–534.
Walling, William English. *Russia's Message: The True World Import of the Revolution*. New York: Doubleday, 1908.

Walling, William English. "Nationalism and State Socialism," in *Publications of the American Sociological Society*, Vol. X: *War and Militarism in Their Sociological Aspects* (1915), 88–91.

Walling, William English. "The Great Illusions," *New Review*, June 1, 1915.

Walling, William English. *Russia's Message: The People Against the Czar*. New York, Knopf, 1917.

Walling, William English. *Sovietism: The ABC of Russian Bolshevism – According to the Bolshevists*. New York, 1920.

Wanniski, Jude. "The Future of Russian Capitalism, *Foreign Affairs*, Vol. 71, No. 2 (Spring 1992), 17–25.

Ward, Harry F. *In Place of Profit: Social Incentives in the Soviet Union*. New York: Charles Scribner's Sons, 1933.

Ward, Harry F. *The Soviet Spirit*. New York, 1944.

Washburn, Stanley. "America's Chance in Russia," *Harper's Weekly*, February 5, 1916.

Weber, Ralph E. and Ralph A. Weber, eds. *Dear Americans: Letters from the Desk of Ronald Reagan*. New York: Doubleday, 2003.

Weinberger, Caspar W. with Gretchen Roberts, *In the Arena: A Memoir of the 20$^{th}$ Century*. Washington: Regnery, 2001.

White, W. L. *Report on the Russians*. New York, 1945.

Williams, Albert Rhys. *The Soviets*. New York: Harcourt, Brace, 1937.

Wright, George Frederick. *Asiatic Russia*. New York, 1902.

Wright, George Frederick. "Russia's Civilizing Work in Asia," *The American Monthly Review of Reviews*, April 1904, 427–32.

NEWSPAPERS AND MAGAZINES

*Advent Review and Sabbath Herald*, 1906–77
*Adventist Review*, 1997–2002
*America*, 1941–5
*American Mercury*, 1941–5
*Atlanta Daily Constitution*, 1881, 1905–6
*Boston Evening Transcript*, 1890–4, 1911
*Catholic World*, 1940–5
*Christianity Today*, 1988–92
*Columbus Dispatch*, 1903–5
*Bradstreet's*, 1889–1904
*Chicago Tribune*, 1881–1991
*The Christian Advocate*, 1905–6, 1917
*The Christian Century*, 1930–68
*Christianity and Crisis*, 1941–5, 1958–60
*Christian Science Monitor*, 1941
*Columbus Dispatch*, 1881, 1905
*Commonweal*, 1937–45, 1958–70
*Fortune*, 1941–5
*Free Russia* (London), 1890–1914
*Free Russia* (New York), 1890–4

*Harper's Weekly*, 1877–1917
*Life*, 1890–1917, 1941–5, 1959–66
*Literary Digest*, 1893–1937
*Los Angeles Times*, 1911, 1941–5, 1953
Louisville *Courier Journal*, 1904–5
*The Missionary Review of the World*, 1903–18
*Moscow Times*, 1996–2006
*The Nation*, 1866, 1870, 1881–1945
*National Review*, 1964–72
*Nation's Business*, 1941–5
New Orleans *Daily Picayune*, 1881
*New Republic*, 1915–39, 1958–65
*New York Times*
*New York Tribune*, 1881, 1894, 1903–5
*New York World*, 1894, 1903–5, 1917–8
*Newsweek*, 1941–5, 1958–65
*The Outlook*, 1890–1920
*Pentecostal Evangel*, 1919–63
*Philadelphia Inquirer*, 1894, 1903–5, 1911–17, 1959–64, 1983–7
*Public Opinion*, 1887–1905
*Reader's Digest*, 1941–5, 1958–65
*Richmond Dispatch*, 1881
Salt Lake *Daily Tribune*, 1881, 1894
*San Jose Mercury*, 1988–9
*San Francisco Chronicle*, 1911
*Seattle Post-Intelligencer*, 1941
Springfield *Republican*, 1881
*The Watchman*, 1904–6
*The Weekly Evangel*, 1916–7
*Time*
*U.S. News & World Report*, 1951–72
*Vital Speeches of the Day*, 1940–70
*Wall Street Journal*
*Washington Post*, 1941, 1975–2006

## SECONDARY SOURCES

Abramson, Rudy. *Spanning the Century: The Life of W. Averell Harriman, 1891–1986*. New York, 1992.

Adas, Michael. *Dominance By Design: Technological Imperatives and America's Civilizing Mission*. Cambridge: Harvard University Press, 2006.

Adler, Les K. and Thomas G. Paterson, "Red Fascism: The Merger of Nazi Germany and Soviet Russia in the American Image of Totalitarianism, 1930s-1950s," *American Historical Review*, Vol. 70 (April 1970), 1046–64.

Alexander, Charles. "'Uncle Joe': Images of Stalin in the Period of the Highest Development of the Anti-Hitler Coalition" (in Russian), *Annual Studies of America/Amerikanskii Ezhegodnik 1989* (Moscow, 1990), 30–42.

Alexandre, Laurien. *The Voice of America: From Détente to the Reagan Doctrine.* Norwood, NJ, 1988.

Alexeev, Wassilij and Theofanis G. Stavrou, *The Great Revival: The Russian Church Under German Occupation.* Minneapolis, 1976.

Alpers, Benjamin L. *Dictators, Democracy, and American Public Culture: Envisioning the Totalitarian Enemy, 1920s–1950s.* Chapel Hill: University of North Carolina Press, 2003.

Ambrose, Stephen E. *Eisenhower: The President.* New York: Simon and Schuster, 1984.

Andrew, John A. *The Other Side of the Sixties: Young Americans for Freedom and the Rise of Conservative Politics.* New Brunswick, NJ, 1997.

Anschel, Eugene, ed., *The American Image of Russia, 1775–1917.* New York, 1974.

Arndt, Richard T. *The First Resort of Kings: American Cultural Diplomacy in the Twentieth Century.* Washington: Potomac Books, 2005.

Aron, Leon. *Yeltsin: A Revolutionary Life.* New York: St. Martin's Press, 2000.

Åslund, Anders. *How Russia Became a Market Economy.* Washington, D. C.: Brookings, 1995.

Åslund, Anders and Michael McFaul, eds. *Revolution in Orange: The Origins of Ukraine's Democratic Breakthrough.* Washington, DC: Carnegie Endowment, 2006.

Ayers, Edward L. *The Promise of the New South.* New York, 1992.

Axtell, James. *The Invasion Within: The Contest of Cultures in Colonial North America.* New York, 1985.

Babey, Anna M. *Americans in Russia 1776–1917: A Study of the American Travelers in Russia from the American Revolution to the Russian Revolution.* New York, 1938.

Bacino, Leo J. *Reconstructing Russia: U.S. Policy in Revolutionary Russia,1917–1922.* Kent, Ohio: Kent State University Press, 1999.

Bailes, Kendall. "The American Connection: Ideology and the Transfer of American Technology to the Soviet Union, 1917–1941," *Comparative Studies in Society and History,* Vol. 23, No. 3 (July 1981), 421–48.

Bailey, Thomas A. *America Faces Russia: Russian-American Relations From Early Times to Our Day.* Ithaca, 1950.

Baker, Peter and Susan Glasser. *Kremlin Rising: Vladimir Putin's Russia and the End of Revolution.* New York: Scribner, 2005.

Baldwin, Kate A. *Beyond the Color Line and the Iron Curtain: Reading Encounters Between Black and Red, 1922–1963.* Durham: Duke University Press, 2002.

Ball, Alan M. *Imagining America: Influence and Images in Twentieth-Century Russia.* Lanham, MD: Rowman and Littlefield, 2003.

Ball, Alan M. "The Roots of Golden America in Early Soviet Russia," in William B. Husband, ed., *The Human Tradition in Modern Russia.* Wilmington: Scholarly Resources, 2000, 51–64.

Barghoorn, Frederick C. *The Soviet Image of the United States: A Study in Distortion.* New York: Harcourt Brace, 1950.

Barnes, Harper. *Standing on a Volcano: The Life and Times of David Rowland Francis.* St. Louis: Missouri Historical Society Press, 2001.

Baron, Samuel H. *Bloody Saturday in the Soviet Union: Novocherkassk, 1962.* Stanford: Stanford University Press, 2001.

Bartlett, Irving H. *Wendell Phillips: Brahmin Radical.* Boston, 1961.

Bassin, Mark. "Turner, Solov'ev, and the 'Frontier Hypothesis': The Nationalist Signification of Open Spaces," *Journal of Modern History* 65 (September 1993): 473–511.

Baughman, James L. *Henry R. Luce and the Rise of the American News Media.* Boston, 1987.

Becker, Jonathan A. *Soviet and Russian Press Coverage of the United States: Press, Politics and Identity in Transition.* New York, 2002.

Belmonte, Laura Ann. "Defending a Way of Life: American Propaganda and the Cold War, 1945–1959," Ph.D. dissertation, University of Virginia, 1996.

Benjamin, Jules R. *The United States and the Origins of the Cuban Revolution: An Empire of Liberty in an Age of National Liberation.* Princeton: Princeton University Press, 1990.

Bennett, Todd. "My 'Mission' to Moscow: Researching Soviet Propaganda in the Russian Archives," *SHAFR Newsletter*, Vol. 31, No. 4 (December 2000), 16–29.

Bennett, Todd. "Culture, Power, and *Mission to Moscow*: Film and Soviet-American Relations during World War II," *Journal of American History*, Vol. 88, No. 2 (September 2001), 489–518.

Beschloss, Michael R. and Strobe Talbott. *At the Highest Levels: The Inside Story of the End of the Cold War.* Boston: Little, Brown, 1993.

Billington, James H. *Russia in Search of Itself.* Washington: Johns Hopkins University Press, 2004.

Black, J. L. *Russia Faces NATO Expansion: Bearing Gifts or Bearing Arms?* Lanham, MD: Rowman and Littlefield, 2000.

Boe, Jonathan Evers. *American Business: The Response to the Soviet Union, 1933–1947.* New York, 1987.

Bogart, Leo. *Cool Words, Cold War: A New Look at USIA's Premises for Propaganda, Revised Edition.* Washington: American University Press, 1995.

Bonnell, Victoria, Ann Cooper, and Gregory Freidin. *Russia at the Barricades: Eyewitness Accounts of the August 1991 Coup.* Armonk, NY: M. E. Sharpe, 1994.

Bourne, Peter G. *Jimmy Carter: A Comprehensive Biography from Plains to Postpresidency.* New York, 1997.

Boyer, Paul. *When Time Shall Be No More: Prophecy Belief in Modern American Culture.* Cambridge: Harvard University Press, 1992.

Boylan, James. *Revolutionary Lives: Anna Strunsky and William English Walling.* Amherst: University of Massachusetts Press, 1998.

Brady, Rose. *Kapitalizm: Russia's Struggle to Free Its Economy.* New Haven, 1999.

Brooks, Jeffrey. "Official Xenophobia and Popular Cosmopolitanism in Early Soviet Russia," *American Historical Review*, Vo. 97, No. 5 (December 1992), 1431–48.

Brooks, Jeffrey. *Thank You, Comrade Stalin! Soviet Public Culture from Revolution to Cold War.* Princeton: Princeton University Press, 2000.

Brown, Ira V. *Lyman Abbott: Christian Evolutionist.* Cambridge, MA, 1953.

Brown, James Seay, Jr. "Eugene Schuyler, Observer of Russia: His Years as a Diplomat in Russia, 1867–1875," Ph.D. dissertation, Vanderbilt University, 1971.

Budd, Louis J. "Twain, Howells, and the Boston Nihilists," *New England Quarterly*, Vol. XXXII, No. 3 (September 1959), 351–71.

Burns, James MacGregor. *Roosevelt: The Lion and the Fox*. New York, 1956.

Buzzanco, Robert. "Where's the Beef? Culture without Power in the Study of U.S. Foreign Relations," *Diplomatic History*, Vol. 24, No. 4 (Fall 2000), 623–32.

Byrnes, Robert F. *A History of Russian and East European Studies in the United States*. Lanham, MD, 1994.

Campbell, David. "Global Inscription: How Foreign Policy Constitutes the United States," *Alternatives*, Vol. XV (1990), 263–86.

Campbell, David. *Writing Security: United States Foreign Policy and the Politics of Identity*. Minneapolis, 1992.

Cannon, Lou. *President Reagan: The Role of a Lifetime*. New York: Simon and Schuster, 1991.

Carstensen, Fred V. *American Enterprise in Foreign Markets: Studies of Singer and International Harvester Company in Imperial Russia*. Chapel Hill: University of North Carolina Press, 1984.

Cassella-Blackburn, Michael. *The Donkey, the Carrot, and the Club: William C. Bullitt and Soviet-American Relations, 1917–1948*. Westport, CT, 2004.

Cassidy, Keith. "The American Left and the Problem of Leadership, 1900–1920," *South Atlantic Quarterly*, Vol. 82, No. 4 (1983), 386–97.

Caute, David. *The Dancer Defects: The Struggle for Cultural Supremacy During the Cold War*. New York, Oxford University Press, 2003.

Cheong, Yeong-Han. "No Ground to Stand On: The Diplomatic Biography of W. Averell Harriman," unpublished manuscript.

Christian, Reginald Frank. *Alexis Aladin: The Tragedy of Exile*. New York, 1999.

Chubaryan, A. O. ed. *Russkoe otkrytie Ameriki: Sbornik statei, posviashchennyi 70-letiiu akademika Nikolaia Nikolaevicha Bolkhovitinova*. Moscow: Rosspen, 2002.

Chumachenko, Tatiana A. *Church and State in Soviet Russia: Russian Orthodoxy from World War II to the Khrushchev Years*. Armonk, NY: M. E. Sharpe, 2002.

Claeys, Gregory. "Mass Culture and World Culture: On 'Americanisation' and the Politics of Cultural Protectionism," *Diogenes*, Vol. 136 (1986), 70–97.

Clark, Bruce. *An Empire's New Clothes: The End of Russia's Liberal Dream*. London, 1995.

Clifford, Deborah Pickman. *Mine Eyes Have Seen the Glory: A Biography of Julia Ward Howe*. Boston, 1979.

Clymer, Kenton J. *John Hay: The Gentleman as Diplomat*. Ann Arbor, 1975.

Cmiel, Kenneth. "The Emergence of Human Rights Politics in the United States," *Journal of American History*, Vol. 86, No. 3 (December 1999), 1231–50.

Cmiel, Kenneth. "The Recent History of Human Rights," *American Historical Review*, Vol. 109, No. 1 (February 2004), 117–35.

Cohen, Stephen F. *Failed Crusade: America and the Tragedy of Post-Communist Russia*. New York: W.W. Norton, 2000.

Coleman, Heather J. *Russian Baptists and Spiritual Revolution, 1905–1929.* Bloomington: Indiana University Press, 2005.

Coll, Steve. *Ghost Wars: The Secret History of the CIA, Afghanistan, and bin Laden, from the Soviet Invasion to September 10, 2001.* New York: Penguin, 2004.

Colton, Timothy, and Jerry Hough, eds., *Growing Pains: Russian Democracy and the Election of 1993.* Washington, 1998.

Colton Timothy J. and Michael McFaul, "America's Real Russian Allies," *Foreign Affairs,* Vol. 80, No. 6 (November/December 2001), 46–58.

Cortada, James W. *Two Nations Over Time: Spain and the United States, 1776–1917.* Westport, CT, 1978.

Costigliola, Frank. "Lyndon B. Johnson, Germany, and 'the end of the Cold War,'" in Warren I. Cohen and Nancy Bernkopf Tucker, eds., *Lyndon Johnson Confronts the World: American Foreign Policy 1963–1968* (Cambridge University Press, 1994), 173–210.

Costigliola, Frank. "'Mixed Up' and 'Contact': Culture and Emotion among the Allies in the Second World War," *International History Review,* Vol. 20, No. 4 (December 1998), 791–805.

Craig, Robert H. *Religion and Radical Politics: An Alternative Christian Tradition in the United States.* Philadelphia: Temple University Press, 1992.

Crile, George. *Charlie Wilson's War.* New York: Grove Press, 2003.

Crunden, Robert M. *Ministers of Reform: The Progressives' Achievement in American Civilization, 1889–1920.* New York, 1982.

Cuff, Robert. "Ernest Poole: Novelist as Propagandist, 1917–1918: A Note," *Canadian Review of American Studies,* Vol. 19 (Summer 1988), 183–94.

Curti, Merle. *American Philanthropy Abroad: A History.* New Brunswick, NJ, 1963.

Curtiss, John Shelton. *Church and State in Russia: The Last Years of the Empire, 1900–1917.* New York: Columbia University Press, 1940.

Daalder, Ivo H. and James M. Lindsay. *America Unbound: The Bush Revolution in Foreign Policy.* Washington, DC: Brookings, 2003.

Dallek, Robert. *An Unfinished Life: John F. Kennedy, 1917–1963.* Boston: Little, Brown, 2003.

Damico, John Kelly. "From Civil Rights to Human Rights: The Career of Patricia M. Derian," Ph.D. dissertation, Mississippi State University, 1999.

Daniloff, Nicholas. "George Kennan and the Challenge of Siberia," *Demokratizatsiya,* Vol. 7, No. 4 (Fall 1999), 601–12.

Davies, Robert Bruce. *Peacefully Working to Conquer the World: Singer Sewing Machines in Foreign Markets, 1854–1920.* New York, 1976.

Davis, Allen F. *Spearheads for Reform: The Social Settlements and the Progressive Movement, 1890–1914.* New Brunswick: Rutgers University Press, 1984.

Davis, Donald E. and Eugene P. Trani. *The First Cold War: The Legacy of Woodrow Wilson in U.S.-Soviet Relations.* Columbia: University of Missouri Press, 2002.

Davis, Kenneth S. *FDR: The War President 1940–1943.* New York, 2000.

Davis, Nathaniel. *A Long Walk to Church: A Contemporary History of Russian Orthodoxy.* Boulder: Westview Press, 1995.

Dekel-Chen, "Philanthropists, Commissars, and American Statesmanship Meet in Soviet Crimea, 1922–37," *Diplomatic History*, Vol. 27, No. 3 (June 2003), 353–76.

Dekel-Chen, Jonathan. *Farming the Red Land: Jewish Agricultural Colonization and Local Soviet Power, 1924–1941*. New Haven: Yale University Press, 2005.

Dennett, Tyler. *John Hay: From Poetry to Politics*. New York, 1963. First published, 1933.

Diamond, Sara. *Roads to Dominion: Right-Wing Movements and Political Power in the United States*. New York, 1995.

Dobbins, James et al. *America's Role in Nation-Building: From Germany to Iraq*. Santa Monica: RAND, 2003.

Drinnon, Richard. *Facing West: The Metaphysics of Indian Hating and Empire Building*. New York, 1980.

Duke, David Nelson. *In the Trenches with Jesus and Marx: Harry F. Ward and the Struggle for Social Justice*. Tuscaloosa: University of Alabama Press, 2003.

Dulles, Foster Rhea. *The Road to Teheran: The Story of Russia and America, 1781–1943*. Princeton, 1944.

Dumbrell, John. *President Lyndon Johnson and Soviet Communism*. Manchester: Manchester University Press, 2004.

Dunham, Vera S. *In Stalin's Time: Middleclass Values in Soviet Fiction*. Durham, NC: Duke University Press, 1990.

Dunlop, John B. "Russia's 1997 Law Renews Religious Persecution," *Demokratizatsiya*, Vol. 7, No. 1 (Winter 1999), 28–41.

Dunn, Dennis J. *Caught Between Roosevelt and Stalin: America's Ambassadors to Moscow*. Lexington: University Press of Kentucky, 1998.

Dunn, Dennis J. *The Catholic Church and Russia: Popes, Patriarchs, Tsars and Commissars*. Aldershot and Burlington: Ashgate, 2004.

Dunstan, John. "George A. Simons and the Khristianski Pobornik: A Neglected Source on St. Petersburg Methodism," *Methodist History*, Vol. 19, No. 1 (1980), 21–40.

Durasoff, Steve. *The Russian Protestants: Evangelicals in the Soviet Union, 1944–1964*. Madison, NJ: Fairleigh Dickinson University Press, 1969.

Durasoff, Steve. *Pentecost Behind the Iron Curtain*. Plainfield, NJ: Logos, 1972.

Ekbladh, David. "How to Build a Nation," *Wilson Quarterly*, Vol. 28, No. 1 (Winter 2004).

Engerman, David C. *Modernization From the Other Shore: American Intellectuals and the Romance of Russian Development*. Cambridge: Harvard University Press, 2003.

English, Robert D. *Russia and the Idea of the West: Gorbachev, Intellectuals, and the End of the Cold War*. New York: Columbia University Press, 2000.

Ericson, Edward E. Jr. *Solzhenitsyn and the Modern World*. Washington: Regnery Gateway, DC, 1993.

Farnsworth, Beatrice. *William C. Bullitt and the Soviet Union*. Bloomington, 1967.

Fehrenbach, Heide, and Uta G. Poiger, eds. *Transactions, Transgressions, Transformations: American Culture in Western Europe and Japan*. New York, 2000.

Furgurson, Ernest B. *Hard Right: The Rise of Jesse Helms*. New York, 1986.

Ferrell, Robert H. ed. *The American Secretaries of State and their Diplomacy, Vol. XI: Frank B. Kellogg and Henry L. Stimson.* New York, 1963.

Feuer, Lewis S. "American Travelers to the Soviet Union, 1917–32: The Formation of a Component of New Deal Ideology," *American Quarterly,* Vol. 14 (Summer 1962), 119–49.

Filene, Peter G. *Americans and the Soviet Experiment, 1917–1933.* Cambridge: Harvard University Press, 1967.

Fitzgerald, Frances. *Way Out There in the Blue: Reagan, Star Wars and the End of the Cold War.* New York: Simon and Schuster, 2000.

Fitzpatrick, Sheila. *The Commissariat of Enlightenment: Soviet Organization of Education and the Arts Under Lunacharsky, October 1917–1921.* Oxford University Press, 1970.

Foglesong, David S. *America's Secret War Against Bolshevism: U.S. Intervention in the Russian Civil War, 1917–1920.* Chapel Hill: University of North Carolina Press, 1995.

Foglesong, David S. "Redeeming Russia? American Missionaries and Tsarist Russia, 1886–1917," *Religion, State and Society,* Vol. 25, No. 4 (December 1997), 353–68.

Foglesong, David S. "Roots of 'Liberation': American Images of the Future of Russia in the Early Cold War, 1948–1953," *The International History Review,* Vol. XXI, No. 1 (March 1999), 57–79.

Foglesong, David, and Gordon M. Hahn. "Ten Myths About Russia: Understanding and Dealing with Russia's Complexity and Ambiguity," *Problems of Post-Communism,* Vol. 49, No. 6 (November/December 2002), 3–15.

Foglesong, David S. "Amerikanskie Nadezhdy na Preobrazovanie Rossii vo Vremia Vtoroi Mirovoi Voiny," *Novaia i Noveishaia Istoriia,* #1, January 2003, 80–105.

Foglesong, David S. and V. I. Zhuravleva. "Russkii 'Drugoi': Formirovanie Obraza Rossii v Soedinennykh Shtatakh Ameriki (1881–1917)," *Amerikanskii Ezhegodnik 2004.* Moscow: Nauka, 2006. Pp. 233–81.

Foglesong, David S. and V. I. Zhuravleva, "Konstruirovanie obraza Rossii v amerikanskikh politicheskikh karikaturakh XX veka," in V. A. Koleneko, *Rossiia I SShA na Stranitsakh Russkoi I Amerikanskoi Periodiki.* Moscow, 2007.

Foglesong, Todd. "Lost in Translation: The Lessons of Russian Judicial Reform," unpublished paper, January 12, 2002.

Fox, Richard Wightman. *Reinhold Niebuhr: A Biography.* Ithaca: Cornell University Press, 1996.

Freeland, Chrystia. *Sale of the Century: Russia's Wild Ride From Communism to Capitalism.* New York: Crown, 2000.

Freeze, Gregory, ed. *Russia: A History.* Oxford University Press, 1997.

Fried, Richard M. *The Russians Are Coming! The Russians Are Coming! Pageantry and Patriotism in Cold War America.* Oxford University Press, 1998.

Friedman, Thomas L. *The World is Flat: A Brief History of the Twenty-First Century.* New York: Farrar, Straus and Giroux, 2005.

Frum, David. *How We Got Here. The 70s: The Decade that Brought You Modern Life (For Better or Worse).* New York: Basic Books, 2000.

Fukuyama, Francis, ed. *Nation-Building: Beyond Afghanistan and Iraq*. Baltimore: Johns Hopkins University Press, 2006.

Gaddis, John Lewis. *Russia, the Soviet Union, and the United States: An Interpretive History*. New York: McGraw Hill, 1990 (Second Edition).

Gaddis, John Lewis. *Strategies of Containment: A Critical Appraisal of Postwar American National Security Policy*. Oxford University Press, 1982.

Gaddis, John Lewis. *The Cold War: A New History*. New York: Penguin, 2005.

Gardner, Lloyd C. *Economic Aspects of New Deal Diplomacy*. Madison, 1964.

Gardner, Lloyd. *Spheres of Influence: The Great Powers Partition Europe, from Munich to Yalta*. Chicago: Ivan Dee, 1993.

Garrison, Mark and Abbott Gleason, eds. *Shared Destiny: Fifty Years of Soviet-American Relations*. Boston, 1985.

Garthoff, Raymond L. *The Great Transition: American-Soviet Relations and the End of the Cold War*. Washington: Brookings, 1994.

Gati, Charles. *Failed Illusions: Moscow, Washington, Budapest, and the 1956 Hungarian Revolt*. Washington, D.C.: Woodrow Wilson Center Press, 2006.

Geyer, Dietrich. *Russian Imperialism: The Interaction of Domestic and Foreign Policy, 1860–1914*. New Haven: Yale University Press, 1987.

Giffin, Frederick C. "An American Railroad Man East of the Urals, 1918–1922," *Historian*, Vol. 60, No. 4 (Summer 1998), 813–30.

Glantz, Mary E. *FDR and the Soviet Union: The President's Battles over Foreign Policy*. Lawrence: University Press of Kansas, 2005.

Gleason, Abbott. "Republic of Humbug: The Russian Nativist Critique of the United States, 1830–1930," *American Quarterly*, Vol. 44 (March 1992), 1–23.

Gleason, Abbott. *Totalitarianism: The Inner History of the Cold War*. Oxford University Press, 1995.

Gleisser, Marcus. *The World of Cyrus Eaton*. Kent: Kent State University Press, 2005; first ed., 1965.

Goldberg, Robert Alan. *Barry Goldwater*. New Haven: Yale University Press, 1995.

Goldgeier, James M. and Michael McFaul. *Power and Purpose: U.S. Policy Toward Russia After the Cold War*. Washington, D.C.: Brookings, 2003.

Good, Jane E. "America and the Russian Revolutionary Movement, 1888–1905," *Russian Review*, Vol. 41, No. 3 (July 1982), 273–87.

Good, Jane E. "'I'd Rather Live in Siberia': V. G. Korolenko's Critique of America, 1893," *Historian*, Vol. XLIV, No. 2 (February 1982), 190–206.

Gould-Davies, Nigel. "The Logic of Soviet Cultural Diplomacy," *Diplomatic History*, Vol. 27, No. 2 (April 2003), 193–214.

Graziosi, Andrea. "The Great Strikes of 1953 in Soviet Labor Camps in the Accounts of Their Participants," *Cahiers du Monde Russe et Soviétique*, Vol. 33, No. 4 (1992), 419–46.

Grose, Peter. *Operation Rollback: America's Secret War Behind the Iron Curtain*. Boston: Houghton Mifflin, 2000.

Gorlizki, Yoram and Oleg Khlevniuk. *Cold Peace: Stalin and the Soviet Ruling Circle, 1945–1953*. Oxford University Press, 2004.

Grosul, V. Ia. "Rossiiskaia Politicheskaia Emigratsiia v SShA v XIX v.," *Novaia i noveishaia istoriia*, 1994 (2), 49–69.

Hanhimaki, Jussi M. "'They Can Write It In Swahili': Kissinger, the Soviets, and the Helsinki Accords, 1973–1975," *Journal of Transatlantic Studies*, Vol. 1, No. 1 (2003), 37–58.

Hanhimaki, Jussi. *The Flawed Architect: Henry Kissinger and American Foreign Policy*. Oxford University Press, 2004.

Harrell, David Edwin, Jr. *Oral Roberts: An American Life*. Bloomington: Indiana University Press, 1985.

Healy, Ann. "Tsarist Anti-Semitism and Russian-American Relations," *Slavic Review*, Vol. 42, No. 3 (Fall 1983), 408–25.

Healy, David. *US Expansionism: The Imperialist Urge in the 1890s*. Madison: University of Wisconsin Press, 1970.

Hecht, David. *Russian Radicals Look to America, 1825–1894*. Cambridge, MA, 1947.

Heil, Alan L. Jr. *Voice of America: A History*. New York: Columbia University Press, 2003.

Henning, Joseph M. *Outposts of Civilization: Race, Religion, and the Formative Years of American-Japanese Relations*. New York, 2000.

Herlihy, Patricia. *The Alcoholic Empire: Vodka and Politics in Late Imperial Russia*. New York, 2002.

Herzstein, Robert E. *Henry R. Luce: A Political Portrait of the Man Who Created the American Century*. New York, 1994.

Hixson, Walter. *George F. Kennan: Cold War Iconoclast*. New York: Columbia University Press, 1989.

Hixson, Walter L. *Parting the Curtain: Propaganda, Culture, and the Cold War, 1945–1961*. New York: St. Martin's Press, 1997.

Hofstadter, Richard. *The American Political Tradition and the Men Who Made It*. New York, 1948, 1973.

Hoganson, Kristin L. *Fighting for American Manhood: How Gender Politics Provoked the Spanish-American and Philippine-American Wars*. New Haven: Yale University Press, 1998.

Hollander, Paul. *Political Pilgrims: Travels of Western Intellectuals to the Soviet Union, China, and Cuba, 1928–1978*. New York, 1981.

Holt, Robert T. *Radio Free Europe*. Minneapolis, 1958.

Hoopes, Townsend. *The Devil and John Foster Dulles*. Boston: Little, Brown, 1973.

Hoopes, Townsend and Douglas Brinkley. *Driven Patriot: The Life and Times of James Forrestal*. New York, 1992.

Hoxie, Frederick. *A Final Promise: The Campaign to Assimilate the Indians, 1880–1920*. Cambridge University Press, 1989.

Hulsether, Mark. *Building a Protestant Left: Christianity and Crisis Magazine, 1941–1993*. Knoxville: University of Tennessee Press, 1999.

Hundley, H. S. "George Kennan and the Russian Empire: How America's Conscience Became an Enemy of Tsarism." Kennan Institute Occasional Paper. Washington: 2000.

Hunt, Michael H. "East Asia in Henry Luce's 'American Century,'" *Diplomatic History*, Vol. 23, No. 2 (Spring 1999), 321–53.

Hunt, Michael H. *Frontier Defense and the Open Door: Manchuria in Chinese-American Relations, 1895–1911*. New Haven: Yale University Press, 1973.

Huntington, Samuel P. *The Clash of Civilizations and the Remaking of World Order*. New York, 1996.

Husband, William B. *"Godless Communists": Atheism and Society in Soviet Russia, 1917–1932*. DeKalb, IL: Northern Illinois University Press, 2000.

Hutchison, William R. *Errand to the World: American Protestant Thought and Foreign Missions*. Chicago: University of Chicago Press, 1987.

Immerman, Richard H. *John Foster Dulles: Piety, Pragmatism, and Power in U.S. Foreign Policy*. Wilmington: Scholarly Resources, 1999.

Isaacson, Walter. *Kissinger: A Biography*. New York: Simon and Schuster, 1992.

Jack, Andrew. *Inside Putin's Russia: Can There Be Reform Without Democracy?* Oxford University Press, 2006.

Jacobs, Seth. "'Our System Demands the Supreme Being': The U.S. Religious Revival and the 'Diem Experiment,' 1954–55," *Diplomatic History*, Vol. 25, No. 4 (Fall 2001), 589–624.

Jacobson, Jon. *When the Soviet Union Entered World Politics*. Berkeley: University of California Press, 1994.

Jensen, Ronald J. "The Politics of Discrimination: America, Russia and the Jewish Question 1869–1872," *American Jewish History*, Vol. LXXV, No. 3 (March 1986), 280–95.

Jespersen, T. Christopher. *American Images of China, 1931–1949*. Stanford: Stanford University Press, 1996.

Kassof, Allen H. "Scholarly Exchanges and the Collapse of Communism," *The Soviet and Post-Soviet Review*, Vol. 22, No. 3 (1995), 263–74.

Kaufman, Robert G. *Henry M. Jackson: A Life in Politics*. Seattle: University of Washington Press, 2000.

Keefer, Truman Frederick. "The Literary Career and Literary Production of Ernest Poole, American Novelist." Ph.D. dissertation, Duke University, 1961.

Keefer, Truman Frederick. *Ernest Poole*. New York, 1966.

Kengor, Paul. *God and Ronald Reagan: A Spiritual Life*. New York: Regan Books, 2004.

Koppes, Clayton R. and Gregory D. Black. *Hollywood Goes to War: How Politics, Profits and Propaganda Shaped World War II Movies*. Berkeley: University of California Press, 1990.

Korelin, A. and S. Stepanov. *S. Iu. Vitte – Finansist, Politik, Diplomat*. Moscow, 1998.

Kovatch, William J. Jr. "All Religions Are Equal, But Some Are More Equal Than Others: Russia's 1997 Restrictive Law of Religious Practices," *Demokratizatsiya*, Vol. 6, No. 2 (Spring 1998), 416–25.

Kozlov, Vladimir A. *Mass Uprisings in the USSR: Protest and Rebellion in the Post-Stalin Years*. Armonk: M. E. Sharper, 2002.

Karpachev, M. D. and T. V. Logunova. "Amerikanskii Publitsist Dzhordzh Kennan o Revoliutsionnom dvizhenii v Rossii," *Istoriia SSSR*, 1988 (5), 189–99.

Kennedy, David M. "Culture Wars: The Sources and Uses of Enmity in American History," in Ragnhild Fiebig-von Hase and Ursula Lehmkuhl, eds. *Enemy Images in American History*. Providence, 1997, 339–56.

Keen, Sam. *Faces of the Enemy: Reflections of the Hostile Imagination*. San Francisco, 1986.

Kimball, Warren. *The Juggler: Franklin Roosevelt as Wartime Statesman*. Princeton: Princeton University Press, 1991.

Kimbrough, S. T. "The Living Church Conflict in the Russian Orthodox Church and the Involvement of the Methodist Episcopal Church," *Methodist History*, 40:2 (January 2002), 105–18.

Kirby, Dianne. "Anglican-Orthodox Relations and the Religious Rehabilitation of the Soviet Regime During the Second World War," *Revue d'Histoire Ecclésiastique*, Vol. 96 (2001), 101–22.

Kirby, Dianne, ed. *Religion and the Cold War*. Basingstoke: Palgrave, 2003.

Korey, William. *The Promises We Keep: Human Rights, the Helsinki Process, and American Foreign Policy*. New York, 1993.

Kotkin, Stephen. *Magnetic Mountain: Stalinism as a Civilization*. Berkeley: University of California Press, 1995.

Kovrig, Bennett. *The Myth of Liberation: East-Central Europe in U.S. Diplomacy and Politics Since 1941*. Baltimore, 1973.

Kovrig, Bennett. *Of Walls and Bridges: The United States and Eastern Europe*. New York, 1991.

Kozlov, V. A. *Mass Uprisings in the USSR: Protest and Rebellion in the Post-Stalin Years*. Armonk, NY: M. E. Sharpe, 2002.

Krebs, Ronald R. *Dueling Visions: U.S. Strategy toward Eastern Europe under Eisenhower*. College Station: Texas A & M University Press, 2001.

Kroes, Rob. "Americanization: What Are We Talking About?" in Kroes et al, eds. *Cultural Transmissions and Receptions: American Mass Culture in Europe*. Amsterdam: VU University Press, 1993.

Kubricht, A. Paul. "Politics and Foreign Policy: A Brief Look at the Kennedy Administration's Eastern European Diplomacy," *Diplomatic History*, Vol. 11, No. 1 (Winter 1987), 55–65.

Kulavig, Erik. *Dissent in the Years of Khrushchev: Nine Stories about Disobedient Russians*. New York: Palgrave, 2003.

Kurth, Peter. *American Cassandra: The Life of Dorothy Thompson*. Boston, 1990.

Laber, Jeri. *The Courage of Strangers: Coming of Age with the Human Rights Movement*. New York: Public Affairs, 2002.

LaFeber, Walter. *The American Search for Opportunity, 1865–1913, Vol. II in The Cambridge History of American Foreign Relations*. Cambridge University Press, 1993.

LaFeber, Walter. "The Turn of Russian-American Relations," in A. O. Chubaryan, ed. *Russkoe otkrytie Ameriki: Sbornik statei, posviashchennyi 70-letiiu akademika Nikolaia Nikolaevicha Bolkhovitinova*. Moscow: Rosspen, 2002, 280–91.

Lasch, Christopher. *The American Liberals and the Russian Revolution*. New York: Columbia University Press, 1962.

Laserson, Max M. *The American Impact on Russia, 1784–1917: Diplomatic and Ideological.* New York, 1950.

Legrain, Philippe. *Open World: The Truth About Globalization.* Chicago: Ivan Dee, 2004.

Levering, Ralph B. *American Opinion and the Russian Alliance, 1939–1945.* Chapel Hill: University of North Carolina Press, 1976.

Lewin, Moshe. *The Gorbachev Phenomenon: A Historical Interpretation.* Berkeley: University of California Press, 1988.

Libbey, James K. "The American-Russian Chamber of Commerce," *Diplomatic History*, Vol. 9, No. 3 (Summer 1985), 233–48.

Liebich, André. *From the Other Shore: Russian Social Democracy after 1921.* Cambridge: Harvard University Press, 1997.

Lincoln, W. Bruce. *The Great Reforms: Autocracy, Bureaucracy, and the Politics of Change in Imperial Russia.* DeKalb, IL, 1990.

Linderman, Gerald F. *The Mirror of War: American Society and the Spanish-American War.* Ann Arbor, 1974.

Lingeman, Richard. *Theodore Dreiser: An American Journey.* New York, 1993.

Logan, Rayford W. *The Betrayal of the Negro: From Rutherford B. Hayes to Woodrow Wilson.* New York, 1965; reprint, 1997.

Lourie, Richard. *Sakharov: A Biography.* Hanover: University Press of New England, 2002.

Lovell, Stephen. *Destination in Doubt: Russia Since 1989.* London: Zed, 2006.

Lucas, Scott. *Freedom's War: The American Crusade Against the Soviet Union.* New York: NYU Press, 1999.

Lyons, Eugene. *David Sarnoff: A Biography.* New York, 1966.

Elizabeth Kimball MacLean. *Joseph E. Davies: Envoy to the Soviets.* Westport, CT, 1992.

Maddux, Thomas R. "Red Fascism, Brown Bolshevism: The American Image of Totalitarianism in the 1930s," *Historian*, Vol. 40 (November 1977), 85–103.

Malia, Martin. *Russia Under Western Eyes: From the Bronze Horseman to the Lenin Mausoleum.* Cambridge, MA: Harvard University Press, 1999.

Mal'kova, I. K. "Istoriia i Politika SShA na Stranitsakh Russkikh Demokratich-eskikh Zhurnalov 'Delo' I 'Slovo'," *Amerikanskii Ezhegodnik*, 1971, 273–94.

Malone, Donald Carl. "A Methodist Venture in Bolshevik Russia," *Methodist History*, Vol. XVIII (July 1980), 239–61.

Malozemoff, Andrew. *Russian Far Eastern Policy 1881–1904.* Berkeley, 1958.

Mangold, Tom. *Cold Warrior: James Jesus Angleton: The CIA's Master Spy Hunter.* New York: Simon and Schuster, 1991.

Mann, Arthur. *Yankee Reformers in the Urban Age.* Cambridge, MA, 1954.

Marchio, James. "The Planning Coordination Group: Bureaucratic Casualty in the Cold War Campaign to Exploit Soviet-Bloc Vulnerabilities," *Journal of Cold War Studies*, Vol. 4, No. 4 (Fall 2002), 3–28.

Maresca, John J. *To Helsinki: The Conference on Security and Cooperation in Europe, 1973–1975.* Durham: Duke University Press, 1985.

Mark, Eduard. "October or Thermidor? Interpretations of Stalinism and the Perception of Soviet Foreign Policy in the United States, 1927–1947," *American Historical Review*, Vol. 94 (October 1989), 937–62.

Martin, William. *A Prophet with Honor: The Billy Graham Story*. New York: William Morrow, 1991.

Martin, William. *With God on Our Side: The Rise of the Religious Right in America*. New York: Broadway Books, 1996.

Massie, Suzanne. *Land of the Firebird: The Beauty of Old Russia*. New York: Touchstone, 1982.

May, Ernest, ed. *American Cold War Strategy: Interpreting NSC 68*. Boston: Bedford Books/St. Martin's Press, 1993.

Marty, Martin E. *Righteous Empire: The Protestant Experience in America*. New York: Dial Press, 1970.

Marty, Martin E. *Modern American Religion, Volume 3: Under God, Indivisible*. Chicago: University of Chicago Press, 1996.

Mastny, Vojtech. *The Cold War and Soviet Insecurity: The Stalin Years*. Oxford University Press, 1996.

Matlock, Jack F. Jr. *Autopsy on an Empire: The American Ambassador's Account of the Collapse of the Soviet Union*. New York: Random House, 1995.

May, Lary. "Making the American Consensus: The Narrative of Conversion and Subversion in World War II Films," in Lewis A. Erenberg and Susan E. Hirsch, ed. *The War in American Culture: Society and Consciousness During World War II*. Chicago, 1996, 71–104.

Mayers, David. *George Kennan and the Dilemmas of US Foreign Policy*. Oxford University Press, 1988.

Mayers, David. *The Ambassadors and America's Soviet Policy*. New York: Oxford University Press, 1995.

McFadden, David W. *Alternative Paths: Soviets and Americans, 1917–1920*. Oxford University Press, 1993.

McFadden, David and Claire Gorfinkel, *Constructive Spirit: Quakers in Revolutionary Russia*. Pasadena: Intentional Productions, 2004.

McFaul, Michael. *Russia's Unfinished Revolution: Political Change From Gorbachev to Putin*. Ithaca: Cornell University Press, 2001.

McKenna, Kevin J. *All the Views Fit to Print: Changing Images of the U.S. in Pravda Political Cartoons, 1917–1991*. New York: Peter Lang, 2001.

McLoughlin, William G. *Revivals, Awakenings, and Reform: An Essay on Religion and Social Change in America, 1607–1977*. Chicago, 1978.

McPherson, James. *The Abolitionist Legacy*. Princeton, 1975.

Mehr, Kahlile. "The 1903 Dedication of Russia for Missionary Work," *Journal of Mormon History*, Vol. 13 (1987), 111–21.

Melamed, E. I. *Dzhordzh Kennan protiv tsarizma*. Moscow, 1981.

Merkley, Paul. *Reinhold Niebuhr: A Political Account*. Montreal: McGill-Queen's University Press, 1975.

Mickelson, Sig. *America's Other Voice: The Story of Radio Free Europe and Radio Liberty*. New York: Praeger, 1983.

Miner, Steven Merritt. *Stalin's Holy War: Religion, Nationalism, and Alliance Politics, 1941–1945*. Chapel Hill: University of North Carolina Press, 2003.

Mitrovich, Gregory. *Undermining the Kremlin: America's Strategy to Subvert the Soviet Bloc, 1947–1956*. Ithaca: Cornell University Press, 2000.

Morray, J. P. *Project Kuzbas: American Workers in Siberia (1921–1926)*. New York, 1983.

Morris, Edmund. *Dutch: A Memoir of Ronald Reagan*. New York: Random House, 1999.

Morris, Kenneth E. *Jimmy Carter: American Moralist*. Athens, Georgia, 1996.

Mulder, John M. *Woodrow Wilson: The Years of Preparation*. Princeton: Princeton University Press, 1978.

Muravchik, Joshua. *The Uncertain Crusade: Jimmy Carter and the Dilemmas of Human Rights Policy*. Lanham, MD: Hamilton Press, 1986.

Nash, George H. *The Conservative Intellectual Movement in America Since 1945*. New York, 1976.

Ninkovich, Frank. *The Diplomacy of Ideas: U.S. Foreign Policy and Cultural Relations, 1938–1950*. Cambridge University Press, 1981.

Ninkovich, Frank. *The Wilsonian Century: U.S. Foreign Policy Since 1900*. Chicago, 1999.

Nordholt, Jan Willem Schulte. *Woodrow Wilson: A Life for World Peace*. Berkeley: University of California Press, 1991.

Nutt, Rick. *The Whole Gospel for the Whole World: Sherwood Eddy and the American Protestant Mission*. Macon: Mercer University Press, 1997.

Oikarinen, Jarmo. *The Middle East in the American Quest for World Order*. Helsinki, 1999.

O'Neill, William L. *The Last Romantic: A Life of Max Eastman*. Oxford University Press, 1978.

O'Neill, William L. *A Better World. The Great Schism: Stalinism and the American Intellectuals*. New York: Simon and Schuster, 1982.

Osgood, Kenneth A. "Hearts and Minds: The Unconventional Cold War," *Journal of Cold War Studies*, Vol. 4, No. 2, Spring 2002, 85–107.

Osgood, Kenneth. *Total Cold War: Eisenhower's Secret Propaganda Battle at Home and Abroad*. Lawrence: University Press of Kansas, 2006.

Parks, J. D. *Culture, Conflict and Coexistence: American-Soviet Cultural Relations, 1917–1958*. Jefferson, NC, 1983.

Patenaude, Bertrand M. *The Big Show in Bololand: The American Relief Expedition to Soviet Russia in the Famine of 1921*. Stanford: Stanford University Press, 2002.

Paterson, Thomas G. *Soviet-American Confrontation: Postwar Reconstruction and the Origins of the Cold War*. Baltimore, 1973.

Pells, Richard. *Radical Visions and American Dreams: Culture and Social Thought in the Depression Years*. Urbana: University of Illinois Press, 1998; first ed., 1973.

Pells, Richard. *Not Like Us: How Europeans have Loved, Hated, and Transformed American Culture Since World War II*. New York: Basic Books, 1997.

Pemberton, William H. *Exit with Honor: The Life and Presidency of Ronald Reagan*. Armonk, NY: M. E. Sharpe, 1997.

Pérez, Louis A. *The War of 1898: The United States and Cuba in History and Historiography*. Chapel Hill: University of North Carolina Press, 1998.

Peris, Daniel. *Storming the Heavens: The Soviet League of the Militant Godless*. Ithaca: Cornell University Press, 1998.

Peris, Daniel. "'God is Now on Our Side': The Religious Revival on Unoccupied Soviet Territory during World War II," *Kritika*, Vol. 1, No. 1 (Winter 2000), 97–118.

Perkins, Dexter. *Charles Evans Hughes and American Democratic Statesmanship.* Boston, 1956.

Persico, Joseph E. *Casey: From the OSS to the CIA.* New York: Penguin, 1990.

Petro, Nicolai N. *Crafting Democracy: How Novgorod Has Coped With Social Change.* Ithaca: Cornell University Press, 2004.

Pirsein, Robert William. *The Voice of America: A History of the International Broadcasting Activities of the United States Government.* New York, 1979.

Pittenger, Mark. "Science, Culture, and the New Socialist Intellectuals Before World War I," *American Studies*, Vol. 28, No. 1 (1987), 73–91.

Poe, Marshall. *The Russian Moment in World History.* Princeton: Princeton University Press, 2003.

Puddington, Arch. *Broadcasting Freedom: The Cold War Triumph of Radio Free Europe and Radio Liberty.* Lexington: University Press of Kentucky, 2000.

Queen, George S. *The United States and the Material Advance in Russia, 1881–1906.* New York, 1976.

Radzinsky, Edvard. *Alexander II: The Last Great Tsar.* New York: Free Press, 2005.

Raeff, Marc. "An American View of the Decembrist Revolt," *Journal of Modern History*, Vol. XXV, No. 3 (September 1953), 286–93.

Rand, Larry Anthony. "America Views Russian Serf Emancipation 1861," *Mid-America*, Vol. 50, No.1 (January 1968), 43–7.

Rassweiler, Anne D. *The Generation of Power: The History of Dneprostroi.* New York, 1988.

Rawnsley, Gary D. ed. *Cold-War Propaganda in the 1950s.* Basingstoke: Macmillan, 1999.

Reddaway, Peter and Dmitri Glinski. *The Tragedy of Russia's Reforms: Market Bolshevism Against Democracy.* Washington, D.C.: United States Institute of Peace Press, 2001.

Remnick, David. *Resurrection: The Struggle for a New Russia.* New York: Random House, 1997.

Ribuffo, Leo. "Is Poland a Soviet Satellite? Gerald Ford, the Sonnenfeldt Doctrine and the Election of 1976," *Diplomatic History*, Vol. 14 (Summer 1990): 385–404.

Ribuffo, Leo. "Religion and American Foreign Policy," *National Interest*, Issue 52, Summer 1998.

Ribuffo, Leo P. "Moral Judgments and the Cold War: Reflections on Reinhold Niebuhr, William Appleman Williams and John Lewis Gaddis," in Ellen Schrecker, ed., *Cold War Triumphalism.* New York, 2004.

Richman, John. *The United States and the Soviet Union: The Decision to Recognize.* Raleigh: Camberleigh and Hall, 1980.

Richmond, Yale. *Cultural Exchange and the Cold War: Raising the Iron Curtain.* University Park: Pennsylvania State University Press, 2003.

Robert, Dana L. "The Methodist Episcopal Church, South, Mission to Russians in Manchuria, 1920–1927," *Methodist History*, Vol. 26, No. 2 (January 1988), 67–83.

Rogger, Hans. "America in the Russian Mind – or Russian Discoveries of America," *Pacific Historical Review*, Vol. 47 (February 1978), 27–51.

Rogger, Hans. "*Amerikanizm* and the Economic Development of Russia," *Comparative Studies in Society and History*, Vol. 23, No. 3 (July 1981), 382–420.

Rogger, Hans. "America Enters the Twentieth Century: The View from Russia," in *Felder und Vorfelder Russischer Geschichte*, ed. Inge Auerbach, Andreas Hillgruber, and Gottfried Schramm. Freiburg, 1985, 160–77.

Rogin, Michael. *Ronald Reagan: The Movie*. Berkeley: University of California Press, 1987.

Roslof, Edward E. *Red Priests: Renovationism, Russian Orthodoxy, and Revolution, 1905–1946*. Bloomington: Indiana University Press, 2002.

Rossinow, Doug. "The Radicalization of the Social Gospel: Harry F. Ward and the Search for a New Social Order, 1898–1936," *Religion and American Culture*, Vol. 15, No. 1 (2005), 69–70.

Rotter, Andrew J. "Christians, Muslims, and Hindus: Religion and U.S.-South Asian Relations," *Diplomatic History*, Vol. 24, No. 4 (Fall 2000), 593–640.

Ruddy, T. Michael. *The Cautious Diplomat: Charles E. Bohlen and the Soviet Union, 1929–1969*. Kent, Ohio: Kent State University Press, 1986.

Ruotsila, Markku. *John Spargo and American Socialism*. New York: Palgrave, 2006.

Sakwa, Richard. *Putin: Russia's Choice*. London: Routledge, 2004.

Salzman, Neil V. *Reform and Revolution: The Life and Times of Raymond Robins*: Kent, OH: Kent State University Press, 1991.

Sanders, Jerry W. *Peddlers of Crisis: The Committee on the Present Danger and the Politics of Containment*. Boston: South End Press, 1983.

Saul, Norman. *Distant Friends: the United States and Russia, 1763–1867*. Lawrence: University Press of Kansas, 1991.

Saul, Norman. *War and Revolution: The United States and Russia, 1914–1921*. Lawrence: University Press of Kansas, 2001.

Saul, Norman E. *Friends or Foes? The United States and Russia, 1921–1941*. Lawrence: University Press of Kansas, 2006.

Sawatsky, Walter. *Soviet Evangelicals Since World War II*. Scottdale, PA: Herald Press, 1981.

Sayre, Nora. *Running Time: Films of the Cold War*. New York, 1982.

Scammell, Michael. *Solzhenitsyn*. New York: Norton, 1984.

Schaller, Michael. *The United States and China in the Twentieth Century*. Oxford University Press, 1990.

Schapiro, Amy. *Millicent Fenwick: Her Way*. New Brunswick, NJ: Rutgers University Press, 2003.

Scheer, Robert. *With Enough Shovels: Reagan, Bush and Nuclear War*. New York: Random House, 1982.

Schlesinger, A. M. Jr. *A Thousand Days: John F. Kennedy in the White House*. Boston: Houghton Mifflin, 1965.

Schlesinger, Arthur M. Jr. *Robert Kennedy and His Times*. Boston: Houghton Mifflin, 1978.

Schmidt, Hans. *The United States Occupation of Haiti, 1915–1934*. New Brunswick: Rutgers University Press, 1971

Schmitz, David F. *Thank God They're On Our Side: The United States and Right-Wing Dictatorships, 1921–1965*. Chapel Hill: University of North Carolina Press, 1999.

Schneider, Mark R. *Boston Confronts Jim Crow, 1890–1920*. Boston, 1997.

Schoenberg, Philip Ernest. "The American Reaction to the Kishinev Pogrom of 1903," *American Jewish Historical Quarterly*, Vol. LXIII, No. 3 (March 1974), 262–83.

Schoenwald, Jonathan M. *A Time for Choosing: The Rise of Modern American Conservatism*. New York, 2001.

Schulman, Bruce J. *The Seventies: The Great Shift in American Culture, Society, and Politics*. New York: Free Press, 2001.

Schulzinger, Robert D., ed. *A Companion to American Foreign Relations*. Malden, MA: Blackwell, 2003.

Schweizer, Peter. *Victory: The Reagan Administration's Secret Strategy that Hastened the Collapse of the Soviet Union*. New York, 1994.

Schweizer, Peter. *Reagan's War: The Epic Story of His Forty-Year Struggle and Final Triumph Over Communism*. New York: Doubleday, 2002.

Shankman, Arnold. "Brothers Across the Sea: Afro-Americans on the Persecution of Russian Jews, 1881–1917," *Jewish Social Studies*, Vol. XXXVII, No. 2 (Spring 1975), 114–21.

Shaw, Tony. "Martyrs, Miracles, and Martians: Religion and Cold War Cinematic Propaganda in the 1950s," *Journal of Cold War Studies*, Vol. 4, No. 2 (Spring 2002), 3–22.

Shiraev, Eric and Vladislav Zubok. *Anti-Americanism in Russia: From Stalin to Putin*. New York: Palgrave, 2000.

Simms, James Y., Jr. "Impact of Russian Famine, 1891–1892, Upon the United States," *Mid-America*, Vol. 60, No. 3 (October 1978), 171–84.

Sittser, Gerald. *A Cautious Patriotism: The American Churches and the Second World War*. Chapel Hill: University of North Carolina Press, 1997.

Skidmore, David. *Reversing Course: Carter's Foreign Policy, Domestic Politics, and the Failure of Reform*. Nashville, 1996.

Sherwin, Oscar. *Prophet of Liberty: The Life and Times of Wendell Phillips*. New York, 1958.

Sirgiovanni, George. *An Undercurrent of Suspicion: Anti-Communism in America During World War II*. New Brunswick: Transaction Publishers, 1990.

Small, Melvin. "How We Learned to Love the Russians: American Media and the Soviet Union During World War II," *Historian*, Vol. 36, No. 3 (May 1974), 455–78.

Smant, Kevin J. "How Great the Triumph: James Burnham, Anticommunism, and the Conservative Movement," Ph.D. dissertation, University of Notre Dame, 1991.

Smith, David H. *The Achievement of John C. Bennett*. New York: Herder and Herder, 1970.

Smith, Harold F. "Bread for the Russians: William C. Edgar and the Relief Campaign of 1892," *Minnesota History*, Vol. 42, No. 1 (Spring 1970), 54–62.

Smith, Shannon. "From Relief to Revolution: American Women and the Russian-American Relationship," *Diplomatic History*, Vol. 19, No. 4 (Fall 1995), 601–16.

Smith, Shannon Lee. "The Politics of Progress and the American-Russian Relationship, 1867–1917," Ph.D. dissertation, Cornell University, 1994.

Smith, Tony. *America's Mission: The United States and the Worldwide Struggle for Democracy in the Twentieth Century*. Princeton: Princeton University Press, 1994.

Snyder, Alvin A. *Warriors of Disinformation: American Propaganda, Soviet Lies, and the Winning of the Cold War*. New York: Arcade Publishing, 1995.

Spence, Matthew. "The Complexity of Success in Russia," in Thomas Carothers, ed., *Promoting the Rule of Law Abroad: In Search of Knowledge*, 217–49. Washington, DC: Carnegie, 2006.

Sperber, A. M. *Murrow: His Life and Times*. New York: Freundlich Books, 1986.

Spetter, Allan. "The United States, the Russian Jews and the Russian Famine of 1891–1892," *American Jewish Historical Quarterly*, Vol. LXIV, No. 3 (March 1975), 236–44.

Starr, S. Frederick. *Red and Hot: The Fate of Jazz in the Soviet Union*. New York: Oxford University Press, 1985.

Startt, James D. "American Film Propaganda in Revolutionary Russia," *Prologue*, Vol. 30, No. 3 (1998), 166–79.

Steele, Jonathan. *Eternal Russia: Yeltsin, Gorbachev, and the Mirage of Democracy*. Cambridge, MA, 1995.

Stefan, Charles G. "The Drafting of the Helsinki Final Act: A Personal View of the CSCE's Geneva Phase (September 1973 until July 1975)," *SHAFR Newsletter*, Vol. 31, No. 2 (June 2000), 1–10.

Stephanson, Anders. *Kennan and the Art of Foreign Policy*. Cambridge: Harvard University Press, 1989.

Strong, Robert A. *Working in the World: Jimmy Carter and the Making of American Foreign Policy*. Baton Rouge, 2000.

Strong, Tracy B. and Helene Keyssar. *Right in Her Soul: The Life of Anna Louise Strong*. New York: Random House, 1983.

Stuart, Jack Meyer. "William English Walling: A Study in Politics and Ideas." Ph.D. dissertation, Columbia University, 1968.

Stults, Taylor. "George Kennan: Russian Specialist of the 1890s," *Russian Review*, Vol. 29, No. 3 (July 1970), 275–85.

Stults, Taylor. "Imperial Russia Through American Eyes, 1894–1904: A Study in Public Opinion," Ph.D. dissertation, University of Missouri, Columbia, 1970.

Suny, Ronald Grigor. *The Soviet Experiment: Russia, the USSR, and the Successor States*. New York: Oxford University Press, 1998.

Suri, Jeremi. *Power and Protest: Global Revolution and the Rise of Détente*. Cambridge: Harvard University Press, 2003.

Sutton, Antony C. *Western Technology and Soviet Economic Development, 1917 to 1930*. Stanford: Hoover Institution Press, 1968.

Taubman, William. *Khrushchev: The Man and His Era*. New York: Norton, 2003.

Thomas, D. M. *Alexander Solzhenitsyn: A Century in His Life*. New York: St. Martin's Press, 1998.

Thomas, Evan. *The Very Best Men: The Early Years of the CIA*. New York, 1995.

Thompson, Arthur W. and Robert A. Hart. *The Uncertain Crusade: America and the Russian Revolution of 1905*. Amherst: University of Massachusetts Press, 1970.

Thompson, John A. *Reformers and War: American Progressive Publicists and the First World War*. Cambridge University Press, 1987.

Tocchet, Gary John. "September Thaw: Khrushchev's Visit to America, 1959," Ph.D dissertation, Stanford University, 1995.

Tolvaisas, Tomas. "U.S.A. on Display: American Commercial and Cultural Exhibitions in the Soviet Bloc Countries, 1961–1968," Ph.D. dissertation, Rutgers University, 2006.

Tolz, Vera. *Russia: Inventing the Nation*. London: Arnold, 2001.

Travis, Frederick F. "The Kennan-Russel Anti-Tsarist Propaganda Campaign Among Russian Prisoners of War in Japan," *Russian Review*, Vol. 40, No. 3 (July 1981), 263–77.

Travis, Frederick F. *George Kennan and the American-Russian Relationship, 1865–1924*. Athens: Ohio University Press, 1990.

Treadgold, "Russian Expansion in the Light of Turner's Study of the American Frontier," *Agricultural History* 26:4 (October 1952), 147–52.

Treadgold, Donald W. *The Great Siberian Migration: Government and Peasant in Resettlement from Emancipation to the First World War*. Princeton: Princeton University Press, 1957.

Trenin, Dmitri and Aleksei V. Malashenko. *Russia's Restless Frontier: The Chechnya Factor in Post-Soviet Russia*. Washington: Carnegie, 2004.

Uldricks, Teddy J. "Russia and Europe: Diplomacy, Revolution, and Economic Development in the 1920s," *International History Review*, Vol. 1, No. 1 (January 1979), 55–83.

Varg, Paul A. *Missionaries, Chinese, and Diplomats: The American Protestant Missionary Movement in China, 1890–1952*. Princeton, 1958.

Vaughn, Stephen. *Ronald Reagan in Hollywood: Movies and Politics*. Cambridge University Press, 1994.

Violette, Aurele J. "William Dudley Foulke and Russia," *Indiana Magazine of History*, Vol. LXXXII, No. 1 (March 1986), 69–96.

Von Laue, T. H. "Imperial Russia at the Turn of the Century: The Cultural Slope and the Revolution from without," *Comparative Studies in Society and History*, Vol. 3, No. 4 (July 1961), 353–67.

Wagnleitner, Reinhold. *Coca-Colonization and the Cold War: The Cultural Mission of the United States in Austria after the Second World War*. Chapel Hill: University of North Carolina Press, 1994.

Walker, Martin. *The Cold War: A History*. New York, 1996.

Ward, Geoffrey. *A First-Class Temperament: The Emergence of Franklin Roosevelt*. New York, 1989.

Wardin, Albert. "Pentecostal Beginnings among Russians in Finland and Northern Russia, 1911–1921," *Fides et Historia*, Vol. XXVI, No. 2 (Summer 1994), 50–61.

Warner, Michael. "Origins of the Congress for Cultural Freedom, 1949–50," *Studies in Intelligence*, Vol. 38, No. 5 (1995), 89–98.

Warren, Frank A. *Liberals and Communism: The "Red Decade" Revisited.* New York: Columbia University Press, 1993; first edn., 1966.

Watson, James L., ed. *Golden Arches East: McDonald's in East Asia.* Stanford, 1997.

Wedel, Janine R. *Collision and Collusion: The Strange Case of Western Aid to Eastern Europe, 1989–1998.* New York: St. Martin's Press, 1998.

Weiner, Amir. "The Making of a Dominant Myth: The Second World War and the Construction of Political Identities within the Soviet Polity," *Russian Review*, Vol. 55, No. 4 (October 1996), 638–60.

Weiner, Amir. *Making Sense of War: The Second World War and the Fate of the Bolshevik Revolution.* Princeton: Princeton University Press, 2001.

Weissman, Benjamin M. *Herbert Hoover and Famine Relief to Soviet Russia: 1921–1923.* Stanford: Hoover Institution Press, 1974.

Whitfield, Stephen. *The Culture of the Cold War.* Baltimore: Johns Hopkins University Press, 1991.

Wieczynski, Joseph L. *The Russian Frontier: The Impact of Borderlands upon the Course of Early Russian History.* Charlottesville, 1976.

Williams, Daniel Day. "The Theology of John Coleman Bennett," in Edward LeRoy Long, Jr. and Robert T. Handy, eds. *Theology and Church in Times of Change.* Philadelphia: The Westminster Press, 1970, 239–64.

Williams, William Appleman. *American-Russian Relations 1781–1947.* New York, 1952.

Williams, William Appleman. "Brooks Adams and American Expansion," in Thomas J. McCormick and Walter LaFeber, eds. *Behind the Throne: Servants of Power to Imperial Presidents.* Madison: University of Wisconsin Press, 1993, 21–34.

Williams, William Appleman. *The Roots of the Modern American Empire.* New York, 1969.

Wilson, Francesca. *Muscovy: Russia Through Foreign Eyes, 1553–1900.* London, 1970.

Wilson, Joan Hoff. *Ideology and Economics: U.S. Relations with the Soviet Union, 1918–1933.* Columbia: University of Missouri Press, 1974.

Winik, Jay. *On the Brink: The Dramatic, Behind-the-Scenes Saga of the Reagan Era and the Men and Women Who Won the Cold War.* New York, 1996.

Witte, John Jr. and Michael Bourdeaux, eds. *Proselytism and Orthodoxy in Russia: The New War for Souls.* Maryknoll, NY: Orbis, 1999.

Wohlforth, W. C., ed. *Cold War Endgame.* University Park: Pennsylvania State University Press, 2003.

Wolf, Martin. *Why Globalization Works.* New Haven: Yale University Press, 2004.

Wolper, Gregg. "The Origins of Public Diplomacy: Woodrow Wilson, George Creel, and the Committee on Public Information," Ph.D. dissertation, University of Chicago, 1991.

Woods, Randall Bennett. *Fulbright: A Biography.* Cambridge University Press, 1995.

Woodward, C. Vann. *The Strange Career of Jim Crow.* Third edition, New York, 1974.

Wreszin, Michael. *Oswald Garrison Villard: Pacifist at War.* Bloomington: Indiana University Press, 1965.

Yurchak, Alexei. *Everything Was Forever, Until It Was No More: The Last Soviet Generation.* Princeton: Princeton University Press, 2006.

Zabriskie, Edward H. *American-Russian Rivalry in the Far East: A Study in Diplomacy and Power Politics.* Philadelphia, 1946.

Zipser, Arthur and Pearl Zipser, *Fire and Grace: The Life of Rose Pastor Stokes.* Athens, GA: University of Georgia Press, 1989.

Zubkova, Elena. *Russia After the War: Hopes, Illusions, and Disappointments, 1945–1957.* Translated and edited by Hugh Ragsdale. Armonk, NY: M. E. Sharpe, 1998.

Zubok, Vladislav, and Constantine Pleshakov. *Inside the Kremlin's Cold War: From Stalin to Khrushchev.* Cambridge: Harvard University Press, 1996.

# Index